Lecture Notes in Computer Science 13439

Yo-Sub Han · György Vaszil (Eds.)

Descriptional Complexity of Formal Systems

24th IFIP WG 1.02 International Conference, DCFS 2022
Debrecen, Hungary, August 29–31, 2022
Proceedings

Springer

Editors
Yo-Sub Han
Yonsei University
Seoul, Korea (Republic of)

György Vaszil
University of Debrecen
Debrecen, Hungary

ISSN 0302-9743 ISSN 1611-3349 (electronic)
Lecture Notes in Computer Science
ISBN 978-3-031-13256-8 ISBN 978-3-031-13257-5 (eBook)
https://doi.org/10.1007/978-3-031-13257-5

This Springer imprint is published by the registered company Springer Nature Switzerland AG
The registered company address is: Gewerbestrasse 11, 6330 Cham, Switzerland

Preface

This volume contains the papers presented at the 24th International Conference on Descriptional Complexity of Formal Systems (DCFS 2022) which was held at the University of Debrecen, Hungary, during August 29–31, 2022. It was jointly organized by the Working Group 1.02 on Descriptional Complexity of the International Federation for Information Processing (IFIP) and by the Department of Computer Science at the Faculty of Informatics of the University of Debrecen.

The DCFS conference series is an international venue for the dissemination of new results related to all aspects of descriptional complexity including, but not limited to, the following:

- Automata, grammars, languages, and other formal systems; various modes of operations and complexity measures
- Succinctness of description of objects, state-explosion-like phenomena
- Circuit complexity of Boolean functions and related measures
- Size complexity of formal systems
- Structural complexity of formal systems
- Trade-offs between computational models and modes of operation
- Applications of formal systems (e.g., in software and hardware testing, in dialogue systems, in systems modeling or in modeling natural languages) and their complexity constraints
- Cooperating formal systems
- Size or structural complexity of formal systems for modeling natural languages
- Complexity aspects related to the combinatorics of words
- Descriptional complexity in resource-bounded or structure-bounded environments
- Structural complexity as related to descriptional complexity
- Frontiers between decidability and undecidability
- Universality and reversibility
- Nature-motivated (bio-inspired) architectures and unconventional models of computing
- Blum static (Kolmogorov/Chaitin) complexity, algorithmic information

DCFS became an IFIP working conference in 2016, continuing the former Workshop on Descriptional Complexity of Formal Systems, which was a merger in 2002 of two other workshops: Formal Descriptions and Software Reliability (FDSR) and Descriptional Complexity of Automata, Grammars and Related Structures (DCAGRS). DCAGRS was previously held in Magdeburg (1999), London (2000), and Vienna (2001). FDSR was previously held in Paderborn (1998), Boca Raton (1999), and San Jose (2000). Since 2002, DCFS has been successively held in London, Ontario, Canada (2002), Budapest, Hungary (2003), London, Ontario, Canada (2004), Como, Italy (2005), Las Cruces, New Mexico, USA (2006), Nový Smokovec, High Tatras, Slovakia (2007), Charlottetown, Prince Edward Island, Canada (2008), Magdeburg,

Germany (2009), Saskatoon, Canada (2010), Giessen, Germany (2011), Braga, Portugal (2012), London, Ontario, Canada (2013), Turku, Finland (2014), Waterloo, Ontario, Canada (2015), Bucharest, Romania (2016), Milan, Italy (2017), Halifax, Nova Scotia, Canada (2018), and Košice, Slovakia (2019). The next DCFS conferences were planned to be held in Vienna, Austria (2020), and in Seoul, South Korea (2021), but both of these events were canceled as in-person meetings due to the COVID-19 pandemic. The accepted papers appeared only in the conference proceedings.

This year 17 papers were submitted by authors from 14 different countries. The number of submissions was less than usual, probably due to the current problems in the world and to the desirable and aspired return to an in-person conference. On the other hand, these submissions were of extraordinary quality. Therefore, after the review of each paper by three referees, the Program Committee were able to accept 14 papers out of the 17 submissions.

The program also included four invited talks by

- Mikołaj Bojańczyk, University of Warsaw, Poland,
- Stefano Crespi Reghizzi, Polytechnic University of Milan, Italy,
- Szabolcs Iván, University of Szeged, Hungary,
- Galina Jirásková, Slovak Academy of Sciences, Košice, Slovakia.

We thank all invited speakers, contributing authors, Program Committee members, and external referees for their valuable contributions towards the realization of DCFS 2022.

We are also grateful to the editorial staff at Springer for their guidance and help during the process of publishing this volume, and for supporting the event through publication in the LNCS series.

Partial financial support for the conference was provided by the Department of Computer Science and by the Faculty of Informatics of the University of Debrecen.

Finally, we would like to thank the members of the organizing committee who worked hard to make this edition successful and all participants who, either in-person or virtually, contributed to the success of the conference.

We are looking forward to DCFS 2023 in Potsdam, Germany.

June 2022

Yo-Sub Han
György Vaszil

Organization

Steering Committee

Cezar Câmpeanu	University of Prince Edward Island, Canada
Erzsébet Csuhaj-Varjú	Eötvös Loránd University, Hungary
Stavros Konstantinidis	Saint Mary's University, Canada
Martin Kutrib (Chair)	Justus Liebig University Giessen, Germany
Giovanni Pighizzini	University of Milan, Italy
Rogério Reis	University of Porto, Portugal
Kai Salomaa	Queen's University, Canada

Program Committee

Henning Bordihn	University of Potsdam, Germany
Johanna Björklund	University of Umeå, Sweden
Cezar Câmpeanu	University of Prince Edward Island, Canada
Erzsébet Csuhaj-Varjú	Eötvös Loránd University, Hungary
Szilárd Zsolt Fazekas	Akita University, Japan
Pawel Gawrychowski	University of Wrocław, Poland
Dora Giammarresi	Tor Vergata University of Rome, Italy
Yo-Sub Han (Co-chair)	Yonsei University, South Korea
Géza Horváth	University of Debrecen, Hungary
Galina Jirásková	Slovak Academy of Sciences, Košice, Slovakia
Stavros Konstantinidis	Saint Mary's University, Canada
Martin Kutrib	Justus Liebig University Giessen, Germany
Ian McQuillan	University of Saskatchewan, Canada
Alexander Okhotin	St. Petersburg State University, Russia
Andrei Păun	University of Bucharest, Romania
Giovanni Pighizzini	University of Milan, Italy
Narad Rampersad	University of Winnipeg, Canada
Rogério Reis	University of Porto, Portugal
Michel Rigo	University of Liège, Belgium
Kai Salomaa	Queen's University, Canada
György Vaszil (Co-chair)	University of Debrecen, Hungary
Matthias Wendlandt	Justus Liebig University Giessen, Germany
Lynette van Zijl	Stellenbosch University, South Africa

Additional Reviewers

Sabine Broda
Jürgen Dassow
Jozef Jirásek
Andreas Malcher
Nelma Moreira
Timothy Ng
Luca Prigioniero
Marek Szykuła
Bianca Truthe

Organizing Committee

Bence Hegedűs	University of Debrecen, Hungary
Géza Horváth	University of Debrecen, Hungary
Arnold Pintér	University of Debrecen, Hungary
György Vaszil	University of Debrecen, Hungary

Abstracts of Invited Talks

Polyregular Functions

Mikołaj Bojańczyk

Institute of Informatics, University of Warsaw, Poland
bojan@mimuw.edu.pl

Transducers are like automata, but instead of accepting/rejecting they produce an output, such as a string or a tree. This talk is about a class of string-to-string functions, called the polyregular functions, which can be seen as a candidate for the notion of regular string-to-string transducers of polynomial growth. The class has many equivalent characterisations, including monadic second-order logic, two-way automata, an imperative programming language with for loops, and functional programming languages.

On Scattered Context-free Order Types (Extended Abstract)

Szabolcs Iván[1]

Department of Informatics, University of Szeged, Hungary
szabivan@inf.u-szeged.hu

1 Introduction

When the alphabet Σ of a language $L \subseteq \Sigma^*$ is linearly ordered, the language itself can be seen as a linearly ordered set, by the lexicographic ordering $<$ in which $xay < xbz$ if $a < b$ and $x < xy$ if $y \in \Sigma^+$. As an example, with $\Sigma = \{a, b\}$ and $a < b$, the order types of the languages a^*, $a^* + b^*$ and b^*a^* are ω, $\omega + \omega$ and ω^2, respectively, with ω denoting the order type of the natural numbers. (For the last one, consider the chain $\varepsilon < a < aa < \ldots < b < ba < baa < \ldots < bb < \ldots$)

Clearly, we can encode any such Σ by a constant-length homomorphism into $\{a, b\}^*$ preserving the order type of the language (e.g. for $\Sigma = \{a, b, c, d\}$ we can use $\{aa, ab, ba, bb\}$ as the image of the letters) so generally it suffices to consider the binary alphabet when we are interested only in the order types. An order type is called *regular* (*context-free*, resp.) if it is the order type of some regular (context-free, resp.) language. Since the set Σ^* of all Σ-words is countable as well, the order type of any language is countable; on the other hand, since every countable order type can be embedded into the order type η of the rationals and $L = \{aa, bb\}^*ab$ has the order type η (since it is a dense ordering without least and greatest elements), every countable order type arises as the order type of some language.

An operational characterization of the regular order types was given in [11]. It was shown in [2] that an ordinal is regular if and only if it is less than ω^ω.

The central topic of the presentation, the study of context-free order types was initiated in [1]. From the model checking aspect of interactive programs, studying *scattered* order types might have its actual usage: an order type is scattered if it does not have a dense subordering. Hausdorff assigned a (countable) ordinal to the (countable) scattered orderings (see e.g. [13]), called its *rank*. In our results, we use a slightly modified definition of the original rank as follows: finite order types have rank 0 and if an order type is a finite sum of ζ-sums of scattered order types each having a rank less then α, then its order type is at most α. Formally we can define for each ordinal α a class H_α of (scattered, countable) order types as H_0 consisting of the finite order types and H_α being the smallest class containing each order type of the form $\sum_{j \in \{1,\ldots,n\}} \sum_{i \in \mathbb{Z}} o_{j,i}$ with

[1] Support of the ITM NKFIA TKP2021 grant is acknowledged.

each $o_{j,i}$ being a member of some H_β with $\beta<\alpha$. Then the *rank* of a (scattered countable) order type o is the least ordinal α with $o \in H_\alpha$. Due to Hausdorff's theorem, every scattered order type has a rank. As examples, ω, ζ, ω^k and ω^ω have ranks 1, 1, k and ω respectively, for the latter one we can write e.g. $\omega^\omega = 1+\omega+\omega^2+\omega^3+\ldots$ which is an ω-sum of order types having a finite rank.

2 Selected Results

It is known [3] that an ordinal is regular if and only if it is less than ω^ω and it is context-free if and only if it is less than ω^{ω^ω}. Also, the rank of any scattered regular (context-free, resp.) order type is less than ω (ω^ω, resp.) [7, 11]. The other reason why it is interesting to study scattered context-free orderings is that it is decidable whether a context-free grammar G generates a scattered language [5] while it is undecidable whether it generates a dense one [6]. For the general case, it is even undecidable whether the order type of a context-free language is η [6]. However, for scattered context-free order types we do have some positive results: it is known [10] that the order type of a well-ordered language generated by a prefix grammar (i.e. in which each nonterminal generates a prefix-free language) is computable, thus the isomorphism problem of context-free ordinals is decidable if the ordinals in question are given as the lexicograpic ordering of *prefix* grammars. Also, the isomorphism problem of regular orderings is decidable as well [4, 14]. It is unknown whether the isomorphism problem of scattered context-free orderings is decidable – a partial result in this direction is that if the rank of such an ordering is at most one (that is, the order type is a finite sum of the terms ω, $-\omega$ and 1), then the order type is effectively computable from a context-free grammar generating the language [8, 9]. Moreover, it is also decidable whether a context-free grammar generates a scattered language of rank at most one. It is a very plausible scenario though that the isomorphism problem of scattered context-free orderings is undecidable in general – the rank 1 is quite low compared to the upper bound ω^ω of the rank of these orderings, and there is no known structural characterization of scattered context-free orderings. Clearly, among the well-orderings, exactly the ordinals smaller than ω^{ω^ω} are context-free but for scattered orderings the main obstacle is the lack of a finite "normal form" – as every ω-indexed sum of the terms ω and $-\omega$ is scattered of rank two, there are already uncountably many scattered orderings of rank two and thus only a really small fraction of them can possibly be context-free. So it makes sense to study language classes lying strictly between the regular and the context-free languages. One candidate can be that of the deterministic context-free languages: for these it is known that their order types are exactly the (general) context-free order types [7].

Another candidate for the next step is the class of the *one-counter languages*: these are the ones that can be recognized by a pushdown automaton having only one stack symbol. In [12], a family of well-ordered languages $L_n \subseteq \{a,b,c\}^*$ was given for each integer $n \geq 0$ so that the order type of L_n is $\omega^{\omega\times n}$ (thus its rank is $\omega \times n$) and Kuske formulated two conjectures: i) the order type of well-ordered one-counter languages is strictly less than ω^{ω^2} and more generally, ii) the rank of scattered one-counter languages is strictly less than ω^2. Of course the second conjecture implies the first.

In the main part of the presentation we aim to prove this second conjecture.

References

1. Bloom, S.L., Ésik, Z.: Regular and algebraic words and ordinals. In: Mossakowski, T., Montanari, U., Haveraaen, M. (eds.) Algebra and Coalgebra in Computer Science, vol. 4624, pp. 1–15. Springer, Berlin, Heidelberg (2007). 10.1007/978-3-540-73859-6_1
2. Bloom, S.L., Choffrut, C.: Long words: the theory of concatenation and omega-power. Theor. Comput. Sci. **259**(1), 533–548 (2001)
3. Bloom, S.L., Ésik, Z.: Algebraic ordinals. Fundam. Inform. **99**(4), 383–407 (2010)
4. Bloom, S.L., Ésik, Z.: The equational theory of regular words. Inform. Comput. **197**(1), 55–89 (2005)
5. Ésik, Z.: Scattered context-free linear orderings. In: Mauri, G., Leporati, A. (eds.) Developments in Language Theory, vol. 6795, pp. 216–227. Springer, Berlin, Heidelberg (2011). 10.1007/978-3-642-22321-1_19
6. Ésik, Z.: An undecidable property of context-free linear orders. Inform. Process. Lett. **111** (3), 107–109 (2011)
7. Ésik, Z., Iván, S.: Hausdorff rank of scattered context-free linear orders. In: Fernández-Baca, D. (eds.) LATIN 2012: Theoretical Informatics, vol. 7256, pp. 291–302. Springer, Berlin, Heidelberg (2012). 10.1007/978-3-642-29344-3_25
8. Gelle, K., Iván, S.: On the order type of scattered context-free orderings. In: The Tenth International Symposium on Games, Automata, Logics, and Formal Verification, 2–3 September 2019, pp. 169–182 (2019)
9. Gelle, K., Iván, S.: The order type of scattered context-free orderings of rank one is computable. In: Alexander, C., et al. (eds.) SOFSEM 2020: Theory and Practice of Computer Science - 46th International Conference on Current Trends in Theory and Practice of Informatics, SOFSEM 2020, Limassol, Cyprus, 20–24 January 2020, Proceedings of Lecture Notes in Computer Science, vol. 12011, pp. 273–284. Springer, Cham (2020). 10.1007/978-3-030-38919-2_23
10. Gelle, K., Iván, S.: The ordinal generated by an ordinal grammar is computable. Theor. Comput. Sci. **793**, 1–13 (2019)
11. Heilbrunner, S.: An algorithm for the solution of fixed-point equations for infinite words. RAIRO – Theor. Inform. Appl. **14**(2), 131–141 (1980)
12. Kuske, D.: Logical aspects of the lexicographic order on 1-counter languages. In: Chatterjee, K., Sgall, J. (eds.) Mathematical Foundations of Computer Science 2013 - 38th International Symposium, MFCS 2013, Klosterneuburg, Austria, 26–30 August 2013. Proceedings, vol. 8087 of Lecture Notes in Computer Science, vol. 8087, pp. 619–630. Springer, Berlin, Heidelberg (2013). 10.1007/978-3-642-40313-2_55
13. Rosenstein, J.G.: Linear orderings. Pure Appl. Math. (1982)
14. Thomas, W.: On frontiers of regular trees. ITA **20**(4), 371–381 (1986)

Operations on Unambiguous Finite Automata (Extended Abstract)

Galina Jirásková[1]

Mathematical Institute, Slovak Academy of Sciences, Grešákova 6, 040 01, Košice, Slovakia
jiraskov@saske.sk

Abstract. We investigate the complexity of basic regular operations on languages represented by unambiguous finite automata. We get tight upper bounds for intersection (mn), left and right quotients ($2^m - 1$), positive closure $\left(\frac{3}{4} \cdot 2^n - 1\right)$, star $\left(\frac{3}{4} \cdot 2^n\right)$, shuffle ($2^{mn} - 1$), and concatenation $\left(\frac{3}{4} \cdot 2^{m+n} - 1\right)$. To describe witnesses, we use a binary alphabet for intersection and left and right quotients, a ternary alphabet for positive closure and star, a five-letter alphabet for shuffle, and a seven-letter alphabet for concatenation. We also discuss some partial results for complementation (between $2^{\log\log\log n}$ and $\sqrt{n+1} \cdot 2^{n/2}$) and union (between $mn+m+n$ and $m+n \cdot \sqrt{m+1} \cdot 2^{m/2}$ where $m \leq n$).

1 Introduction

A nondeterministic finite automaton (with multiple initial states, NFA) is *unambiguous* (UFA) if it admits at most one accepting computation on every input string. Ambiguity in finite automata was first considered by Schmidt [15] in his unpublished thesis, where he developed a lower bound method for the size of unambiguous automata based on the rank of certain matrices. He also obtained a lower bound of $2^{\Omega(\sqrt{n})}$ on the conversion of unambiguous finite automata into deterministic finite automata (DFAs).

Leung [10] improved the UFA-to-DFA trade-off to the tight upper bound 2^n. He described, for every n, a binary n-state UFA with a unique initial state whose equivalent DFA requires 2^n states. A similar binary example with multiple initial states was given by Leiss [8], and a ternary one was presented already by Lupanov [11]; notice that the reverse of Lupanov's witness for NFA-to-DFA conversion is deterministic. Using an elaborated Schmidt's lower bound method, Leung [11] described, for every n, an n-state NFA, in fact, a DFA with multiple initial states, whose equivalent UFA requires $2^n - 1$ states.

Stearns and Hunt [17] showed that it can be tested in polynomial time whether or not a given nondeterministic finite automaton is unambiguous. They also provided polynomial-time algorithms for the equivalence and containment problems for unambiguous finite automata.

[1] Research supported by VEGA grant 2/0132/19.

Hromkovič et al. [4] further elaborated a lower bound method for UFAs. Using communication complexity they showed that so-called exact cover of all 1's with monochromatic sub-matrices in a communication matrix of a language provides a lower bound on the size of any UFA for this language, and they simplified some proofs presented in [15, 17].

Okhotin [13] examined unambiguous automata over a one-letter alphabet. He proved that the UFA-to-DFA trade-off in the unary case is given by a function in $e^{\Theta(\sqrt[3]{n(\ln n)^2})}$, while the NFA-to-UFA trade-off is $e^{\sqrt{n \ln n}(1+o(1))}$. He also obtained the tight upper bound $(n-1)^2+1$ for star, an upper bound mn, tight if m, n are relatively prime, for concatenation, and a lower bound $n^{2-\varepsilon}$ for complementation of unary unambiguous automata.

Here we discuss the results on the complexity of basic regular operations on languages represented by unambiguous finite automata over an arbitrary alphabet obtained by Jirásek, Jirásková, and Šebej [6]. To get upper bounds, we provide a construction of a UFA recognizing the language resulting from an operation. In the case of intersection, the corresponding product automaton is unambiguous. In all the remaining cases, we first describe a nondeterministic automaton for the resulting language, and then count the number of its reachable non-empty sets. Such a number provides an upper bound on the size of an equivalent partial deterministic, so unambiguous, subset automaton.

To get lower bounds, we first restate the lower bound method from [10, 15]. To any NFA N, we assign a matrix M_N whose rows are indexed by sets that are reachable in N and columns by sets that are co-reachable in N, and whose entry (S, T) includes 0 if S and T are disjoint and it includes 1 otherwise. The rank of such a matrix provides a lower bound on the number of states in any unambiguous automaton recognizing the language $L(N)$. Then, using the known fact that the rank of the matrix is $2^n - 1$ if its rows and columns are indexed by all the non-empty subsets of a set of size n and its entries are as described above, we get an observation that the number of reachable sets in any NFA provides a lower bound on the size of any equivalent UFA if all the non-empty sets are co-reachable in the given NFA.

We use this observation to get lower bounds for quotients, positive closure, shuffle, and concatenation. We describe witness languages in such a way that in an NFA for the resulting language, all the non-empty sets are co-reachable, and the number of reachable sets is as large as possible. In the case of our intersection witnesses, the matrix corresponding to the resulting product automaton is an identity matrix of size mn, while in the case of star, we must inspect carefully the rank of the corresponding matrix.

An upper bound on the complexity of complementation of a language represented by a UFA is given by the number of reachable set in a given UFA, as well as by the number of its co-reachable sets. We show that the minimum of these two numbers is at most $2^{0.79n + \log n}$. This upper bound can be further decreased to $\sqrt{n+1} \cdot 2^{n/2}$ as shown by Indzhev and Kiefer [5]. A superpolynomial lower bound on the complexity of complementation on unambiguous automata has been recently obtained by Raskin [14].

2 Preliminaries

We assume that the reader is familiar with basic notions in formal languages and automata theory. For details and all the unexplained notions, the reader may refer to [3, 16].

A *nondeterministic finite automaton* (NFA) is a 5-tuple $N = (Q, \Sigma, \Delta, I, F)$, where Q is a finite nonempty set of states, Σ is a finite nonempty set of input symbols called the input alphabet, $\Delta \subseteq Q \times \Sigma \times Q$ is the transition relation, $I \subseteq Q$ is the set of initial states, and $F \subseteq Q$ is the set of final states. Each element (p, a, q) of Δ is called a *transition* of N. A *computation* of N on an input string $a_1 a_2 \cdots a_n$ is a sequence of transitions $(q_0, a_1, q_1)(q_1, a_2, q_2) \cdots (q_{n-1}, a_n, q_n) \in \Delta^*$. The computation is *accepting* if $q_0 \in I$ and $q_n \in F$; in such a case we say that the string $a_1 a_2 \cdots a_n$ is accepted by N. The *language accepted by* the NFA N is the set of strings $L(N) = \{w \in \Sigma^* \mid w \text{ is accepted by } N\}$.

An NFA $N = (Q, \Sigma, \Delta, I, F)$ is *unambiguous* (UFA) if it has at most one accepting computation on every input string, and it is *(partial) deterministic* (DFA) if $|I| = 1$ and for each state p in Q and each symbol a in Σ, there is at most one state q in Q such that (p, a, q) is a transition of N. It follows immediately from the definition that every (partial) deterministic automaton is unambiguous.

The transition relation Δ may be viewed as a function $\cdot : Q \times \Sigma \to 2^Q$, and it can be extended to the domain $2^Q \times \Sigma^*$ in the natural way. We denote this extended function by $\cdot$ as well. Then $L(N) = \{w \in \Sigma^* \mid I \cdot w \cap F \neq \emptyset\}$.

Every NFA $N = (Q, \Sigma, \cdot, I, F)$ can be converted to an equivalent deterministic automaton $\mathcal{D}(N) = (2^Q, \Sigma, \cdot, I, \{S \in 2^Q \mid S \cap F \neq \emptyset\})$, called the *subset automaton* of N [16]. Removing the empty set from the subset automaton results in an equivalent partial deterministic, so unambiguous, automaton. This gives the following observation.

Proposition 1. *Every language accepted by an n-state* NFA *is recognized by a* UFA *of at most $2^n - 1$ states.* □

A subset S of the state set Q of an NFA $N = (Q, \Sigma, \cdot, I, F)$ is *reachable* if $S = I \cdot w$ for some string w, and it is *co-reachable* if it is reachable in the reverse of N obtained from N be reversing all its transitions and by swapping the roles of its initial and final states. Using these notions we get the following characterization of unambiguous automata.

Proposition 2. *A nondeterministic finite automaton is unambiguous if and only if $|S \cap T| \leq 1$ for each reachable set S and each co-reachable set T.* □

If the reverse of an NFA is deterministic, then each co-reachable set in N is of size one,which gives the next observation.

Proposition 3. *An nondeterministic finite automaton is unambiguous if its reverse is (partial) deterministic.* □

Now we restate the lower bound method from [10, 15].

Proposition 4 (Lower bound method for UFAs). *Let N be an NFA. Let M be the matrix with rows (columns) indexed by reachable (co-reachable) sets of N, in which the entry (S,T) includes 0 if S and T are disjoint, and 1 otherwise. Then every UFA recognizing $L(N)$ has at least $rank(M)$ states.*

Proof. Let A be a minimal n-state unambiguous automaton recognizing $L(N)$. Consider a matrix M'_A whose rows are indexed by the states of A, and columns are indexed by strings generating the co-reachable sets in N. The entry (q,w) of M'_A is 1 if w^R is accepted by A from the state q, and it is 0 otherwise. Since A is unambiguous, for every column in M'_A there is at most one row that contains a 1. It follows that the row of M_N indexed by a set S is a sum of the rows of M'_A corresponding to the states in S. Thus every row of M_N is a linear combination of rows in M'_A, and therefore $rank(M_N) \leq rank(M'_A) \leq n$. □

Let M_n be a matrix with rows and columns indexed by all the non-empty subsets of a set of size n, and such that the entry (S,T) is 0 if S and T are disjoint, and it is 1 otherwise. Then $rank(M_n) = 2^n - 1$ [9, Lemma 3]. This gives the following corollary.

Proposition 5. *If every non-empty set is co-reachable in a nondeterministic finite automaton, then the number of its reachable sets provides a lower bound on the number of states in any equivalent unambiguous automaton.* □

3 Results

Let us start with the trade-offs between deterministic, nondeterministic, and unambiguous finite automata. Every unambiguous automaton of n states can be simulated by a DFA of at most 2^n states obtained by the subset construction. To get tightness, consider an NFA from from Fig. 1. Since its reverse is deterministic, this NFA is unambiguous. As shown by Leung [10, Theorem 1], every equivalent DFA has at least 2^n states.

Every NFA of n states can be simulated by a partial deterministic, so unambiguous, subset automaton of at most 2^n-1 states. To get tightness of this upper bound, consider the binary NFA from Fig. 2, a witness for complementation on NFAs from [7, Theorem 5]. Every non-empty set is reachable in this NFA, and since the reverse of this

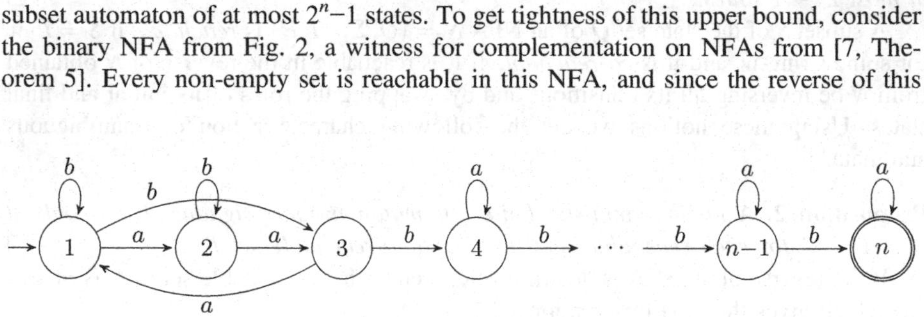

Fig. 1. A binary UFA-to-DFA witness meeting the upper bound 2^n [10].

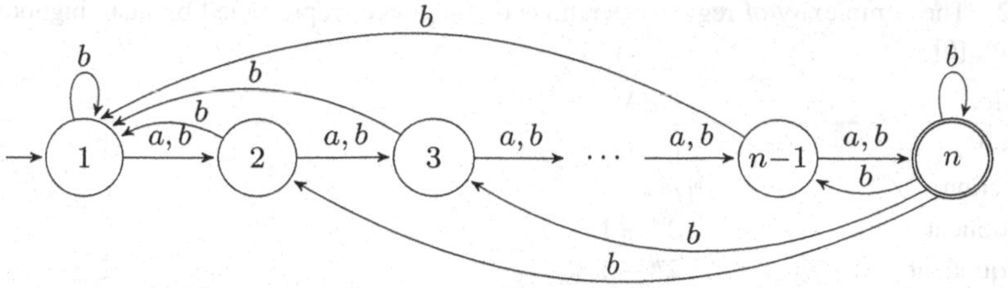

Fig. 2. A binary NFA-to-UFA witness meeting the upper bound 2^n-1.

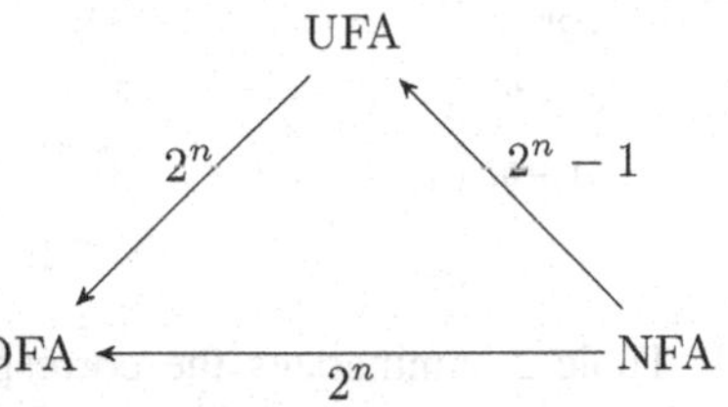

Fig. 3. The trade-offs between deterministic, nondeterministic, and unambiguous finite automata.

NFA is, in fact, the same NFA, every non-empty set is co-reachable as well. Hence every equivalent UFA has at least 2^n-1 states. Moreover, every equivalent DFA has at least 2^n states, since the empty set is reachable in the NFA from Fig. 2. The trade-offs between these three models of automata are shown in Fig. 3.

Now we continue with operational complexity on languages represented by unambiguous finite automata. Table 1 shows the known results on the complexity of basic regular operations on languages represented by deterministic and nondetermin-

Table 1. The complexity of regular operations on languages represented by deterministic and nondeterministic finite automata [2, 7, 12, 18].

Operation	DFA	$\|\Sigma\|$	NFA	$\|\Sigma\|$
Reversal	2^n	2	n	2
Intersection	mn	2	mn	2
Left quotient	2^m-1	2	$m+1$	2
Right quotient	m	1	m	1
Shuffle	?		mn	2
Concatenation	$m\cdot 2^n-2^{n-1}$	2	$m+n$	2
Positive closure	$\frac{3}{4}\cdot 2^n-1$	2	n	1
Star	$\frac{3}{4}\cdot 2^n$	2	$n+1$	1
Complementation	n	1	2^n	2
Union	mn	2	$m+n$	2

Table 2. The complexity of regular operations on languages represented by unambiguous finite automata [6].

Operation	UFA	$\|\Sigma\|$
Reversal	n	1
Intersection	mn	2
Left quotient	$2^m - 1$	2
Right quotient	$2^m - 1$	2
Shuffle	$2^{mn} - 1$	5
Concatenation	$\frac{3}{4} \cdot 2^{m+n} - 1$	7
Positive closure	$\frac{3}{4} \cdot 2^n - 1$	3
Star	$\frac{3}{4} \cdot 2^n$	3
Complementation	$\leq 2^{0.8n}$	–
Union ($m \leq n$)	$mn+m+n \leq \cdot \leq m+n \cdot 2^{0.8m}$	4

istic finite automata, while Table 2 summarizes the corresponding results for unambiguous automata from Jirásek Jr., Jirásková, Šebej [6]. Both tables also display the size of alphabet used to describe witness languages. Let us discuss the results for UFAs in more detail.

Reversal. Since the reverse of an unambiguous automaton is unambiguous, the upper bound is n for the reversal operation. This upper bound is met by a one-string unary language a^{n-1} recognized by an n-state partial deterministic, so unambiguous, automaton. Its reversal is the same language which cannot be accepted by any nondeterministic automaton with less than n states.

Intersection. Notice that the product automaton for intersection of two unambiguous automata is unambiguous. This gives an upper bound mn for the intersection operation. The binary languages $\{w \in \{a,b\} \mid |w|_a = m-1\}$ and $\{w \in \{a,b\} \mid |w|_b = n-1\}$ meet this upper bound since in the corresponding product automaton each singleton set is reachable and co-reachable, and therefore the corresponding matrix is the identity matrix of size mn.

Left and Right Quotient. The left (right) quotient of a given language is recognized by a nondeterministic automaton obtained from an automaton for the given language by changing the set of initial (final) states. Applying the subset construction to the resulting automaton and omitting the empty set results in an incomplete deterministic, so also unambiguous, automaton for the language resulting from the quotient operation. This gives the upper bound $2^m - 1$ in both cases. To get witness for left quotient, consider the partial deterministic, so unambiguous, automaton from Fig. 4 and its left quotient by the language a^* recognized by a one-state unambiguous automaton. In the corresponding nondeterministic automaton for the left quotient, each non-empty set is reachable and co-reachable; notice that a shifts every subset cyclically by one, and b eliminates the state m. A similar idea works for the right quotient of the language recognized by the automaton from Fig. 4 by the empty string. Let us recall that the

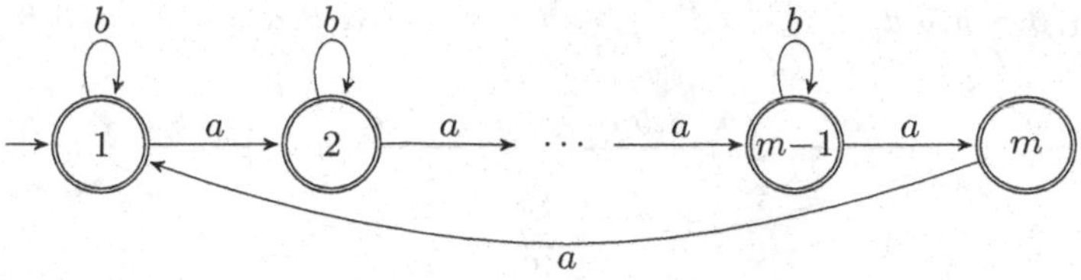

Fig. 4. A binary witness for left quotient (by a*) meeting the upper bound $2^m - 1$.

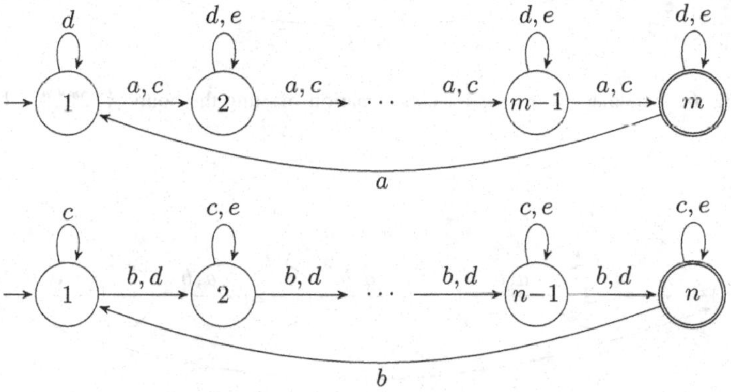

Fig. 5. Quinary witnesses for shuffle meeting the upper bound $2^{mn} - 1$.

upper bound on the complexity of right quotient on DFAs and NFA is just n since changing the set of final states in any DFA or NFA results in a DFA or NFA, respectively. However, changing the set of final states in an unambiguous automaton may not be unambiguous.

Shuffle. The shuffle of two languages represented by UFAs of m and n states is recognized by an mn-state NFA. This gives an upper bound $2^{mn} - 1$ for the shuffle operation on unambiguous automata. To describe witnesses, we use a five-letter alphabet and consider the languages recognized by partial deterministic, so unambiguous, automata shown in Fig. 5; cf.[1]. In the corresponding shuffle automaton, each non-empty set is reachable and co-reachable.

Concatenation. An automaton for the concatenation of two languages can be constructed from the corresponding unambiguous automata by adding the ε-transition from every final state of the first automaton to the initial state of the second automaton. In the resulting automaton, at least 2^{m+n-2} set of states are unreachable – those including a fixed final state of the first automaton and not including the initial state of the second automaton. After excluding the empty set, we get an upper bound $\frac{3}{4} \cdot 2^{m+n} - 1$ for the concatenation operation. For tightness, we consider the languages recognized by unambiguous automata shown in Fig. 6 defined over the seven-letter alphabet

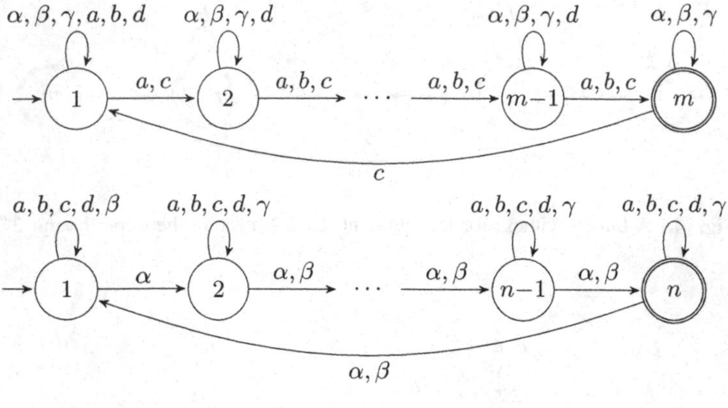

Fig. 6. Septenary witnesses for concatenation meeting the bound $\frac{3}{4} \cdot 2^{m+n} - 1$.

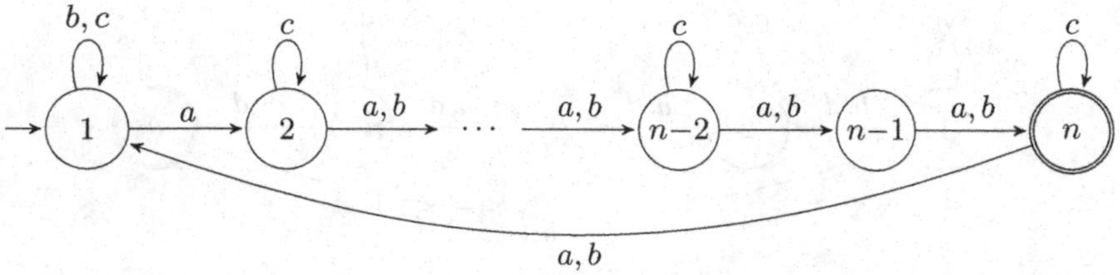

Fig. 7. A ternary witness for positive closure meeting the upper bound $\frac{3}{4} \cdot 2^n - 1$.

$\{a, b, c, d, \alpha, \beta, \gamma\}$; notice that the reverse of the first automaton as well as the second automaton are deterministic. In the corresponding automaton for concatenation of these two languages, each non-empty set is co-reachable, while $\frac{3}{4} \cdot 2^{m+n} - 1$ non-empty sets are reachable.

Positive Closure. To get an automaton for the positive closure of a regular language represented by an unambiguous automaton, we only need to add the ε-transition from every final state of this automaton to its initial state. In the resulting automaton, each set of states that contains a fixed final state and does not contain the initial state is unreachable which, after excluding the empty set, gives the upper bound $\frac{3}{4} \cdot 2^n - 1$. For tightness, we consider the binary witness DFA for star from [18], and we add a loop on a new symbol c in each state, except for the state $n - 1$ to get a ternary partial deterministic, so unambiguous, automaton shown in Fig. 7. The third symbol guarantees the co-reachability of every non-empty subset in the corresponding NFA for positive closure, while by strings over $\{a, b\}$ we get the reachability of $\frac{3}{4} \cdot 2^n - 1$ non-empty sets.

Star. In the case of the star operation, we need to add a new initial (and final) state in the construction from the previous paragraph which increases the upper bound by one.

The witness is the same as for the positive closure, but now we have to inspect carefully the binary matrix corresponding to the automaton for its star since now we cannot have the case when all non-empty sets are co-reachable.

Complementation. The complementation operation looks to be really challenging on unambiguous automata. A lower bound of $\Omega(n^{2-\varepsilon})$ has been obtained by Okhotin [13], while a superpolynomial lower bound has been recently provided by Raskin [14]. Although we are not able to improve these lower bounds, we can decrease the trivial upper bound 2^n to $2^{0.79n+\log n}$. The idea of the proof is to observe that given an n-state unambiguous automaton, the complement of its language is recognized by an unambiguous automaton of $\min\{|\mathcal{R}|, |\mathcal{C}|\}$ states, where $\mathcal{R}$ and $\mathcal{C}$ are the families of reachable and co-reachable sets in a given UFA, respectively. If the maximum of sizes of reachable sets is k, then

$$|\mathcal{R}| \leq \binom{n}{1} + \binom{n}{2} + \cdots + \binom{n}{k}$$

$$|\mathcal{C}| \leq (k+1) \cdot 2^{n-k}$$

since every co-reachable set may have just one state from a fixed reachable set of size k. If $k \geq n/2$, then $|\mathcal{C}|$ is small enough. Otherwise, $|\mathcal{R}|$ is upper bounded by an increasing function $r(k) = n \cdot \left(\frac{en}{k}\right)^k$ and $|\mathcal{C}|$ is upper bounded by a decreasing function function $c(k) = n \cdot 2^{n-k}$, and we show that $\min\{r(k), c(k)\}$ is at most $2^{0.79n+\log n}$. Recently, Indzhev and Kiefer [5] decreased this upper bound to $\sqrt{n+1} \cdot 2^{n/2}$ by showing that the size of a UFA for the complemented language recognized by an n-state unambiguous automaton is upper bounded by the minimum of the number of cliques and co-cliques (independent sets) of a graph with n vertices, and then by showing that in every such graph the product of the number of its cliques with the number of its cocliques is bounded by $(n+1) \cdot 2^n$.

Union. First, notice that the standard NFA for union is unambiguous if two languages represented by unambiguous automata are disjoint. Without loss of generality, we may assume that $m \leq n$. Since $K \cup L = K \cup (L \cap K^c)$, and the languages K and $L \cap K^c$ are disjoint, we get an upper bound $m + n \cdot 2^{0.79m+\log m}$ for union on unambiguous automata. Taking into account the result from [5], this upper bound can be decreased to $m + n \cdot \sqrt{m+1} \cdot 2^{m/2}$. To get a lower bound of $mn + m + n$, we consider the quaternary partial deterministic, so unambiguous, automata with all states final such that in the first automaton, the symbol a performs a cyclic permutation, while b maps each state, except for the initial one, to itself, and c, d perform the identity. In the second automaton, the symbols a and b perform the identity, while c and d play the same role as a and b in the first automaton. Then, in the NFA for their union, all the non-empty sets are co-reachable, while $mn + m + n$ sets of size one and two are reachable.

4 Open Problems

In this section we state some problems that remain open in the research of the complexity of regular operations on languages represented by unambiguous automata. The problem of finding the exact complexity of complementation seems to be the most challenging.

Open Problem 1. *What is the exact complexity of complementation for unambiguous automata?*

Even some better lower or upper bounds for the complementation operation would be of interest; recall that the known lower bound is $2^{\log\log\log n}$ [14], while the best known upper bound is $\sqrt{n+1} \cdot 2^{n/2}$ [5]. We used the results for complementation to get an upper bound for union. Nevertheless, the gap between lower and upper bound is large in the case of union.

Open Problem 2. *What is the complexity of union for unambiguous automata?*

Our strategy for finding a witness for positive closure was to take the binary witness for the star operation on DFAs, and then define the transition on one more symbol to guarantee the co-reachability of all non-empty subsets in an NFA for positive closure. Perhaps, a new, completely different, witness could be described over a binary alphabet. A similar question arises in the case of the star operation.

Open Problem 3. *What is the complexity of positive closure or star for unambiguous automata in the binary case?*

In the case of shuffle and concatenation, our witnesses are defined over a five-letter and seven-letter alphabet, respectively. Our aim was to have proofs as simple as possible in [6], and we did not consider the possibility of decreasing the size of input alphabet.

Open Problem 4. *Can unambiguous witnesses for shuffle or concatenation be described over a smaller alphabet?*

The research on the complexity of operations for unambiguous automata [6] was really interesting, funny, and exciting for all three of us, and we believe that trying to solve the open problems stated above could be interesting, funny, and exciting as well.

Acknowledgment

I would like to thank my son Jozef and my student Juraj for our Mondays' seminars while working on the topic. I really miss them a lot.

References

1. Câmpeanu, C., Salomaa, K., Yu, S.: Tight lower bound for the state complexity of shuffle of regular languages. J. Autom. Lang. Comb. **7**(3), 303–310 (2002)
2. Holzer, M., Kutrib, M.: Nondeterministic descriptional complexity of regular languages. Int. J. Found. Comput. Sci. **14**(6), 1087–1102 (2003). 10.1142/S0129054103002199

3. Hopcroft, J.E., Ullman, J.D.: Introduction to Automata Theory, Languages and Computation. Addison-Wesley (1979)
4. Hromkovič, J., Seibert, S., Karhumäki, J., Klauck, H., Schnitger, G.: Communication complexity method for measuring nondeterminism in finite automata. Inf. Comput. **172**(2), 202–217 (2002). 10.1006/inco.2001.3069
5. Indzhev, E., Kiefer, S.: On complementing unambiguous automata and graphs with many cliques and Cocliques. Inf. Process. Lett. **177** (2022). 10.1016/j.ipl.2022.106270. To apper
6. Jirásek Jr, J., Jirásková, G., Šebej, J.: Operations on unambiguous finite automata. Int. J. Found. Comput. Sci. **29**(5), 861–876 (2018). 10.1142/S012905411842008X
7. Jirásková, G.: State complexity of some operations on binary regular languages. Theor. Comput. Sci. **330**(2), 287–298 (2005). 10.1016/j.tcs.2004.04.011
8. Leiss, E.L.: Succint representation of regular languages by Boolean automata. Theor. Comput. Sci. **13**, 323–330 (1981). 10.1016/S0304-3975(81)80005-9
9. Leung, H.: Separating exponentially ambiguous finite automata from polynomially ambiguous finite automata. SIAM J. Comput. **27**(4), 1073–1082 (1998). 10.1137/S0097539793252092
10. Leung, H.: Descriptional complexity of NFA of different ambiguity. Int. J. Found. Comput. Sci. 16(5), 975–984 (2005). 10.1142/S0129054105003418
11. Lupanov, O.B.: Uber den vergleich zweier typen endlicher quellen. Probleme der Kybernetik **6**, 328–335 (1966)
12. Maslov, A.N.: Estimates of the number of states of finite automata. Soviet Math. Doklady **11**, 1373–1375 (1970)
13. Okhotin, A.: Unambiguous finite automata over a unary alphabet. Inf. Comput. **212**, 15–36 (2012), 10.1016/j.ic.2012.01.003
14. Raskin, M.A.: A superpolynomial lower bound for the size of non-deterministic complement of an unambiguous automaton. In: Chatzigiannakis, I., Kaklamanis, C., Marx, D., Sannella, D. (eds.) ICALP 2018. LIPICS, vol. 107, pp. 138:1–138:11. Schloss Dagstuhl - Leibniz-Zentrum für Informatik (2018). 10.4230/LIPIcs.ICALP.2018.138
15. Schmidt, E.M.: Succinctness of description of context-free, regular, and finite languages. Ph. D. thesis. Cornell University (1978)
16. Sipser, M.: Introduction to the theory of computation. Cengage Learn. (2013)
17. Stearns, R.E., Hunt, H.B.: On the equivalence and containment problems for unambiguous regular expressions, regular grammars and finite automata. SIAM J. Comput. **14**(3), 598–611 (1985). 10.1137/0214044
18. Yu, S., Zhuang, Q., Salomaa, K.: The state complexities of some basic operations on regular languages. Theor. Comput. Sci. **125**(2), 315–328 (1994). 10.1016/0304-3975(92)00011-F

Contents

The Alphabetic Complexity in Homomorphic Definitions of Word, Tree and Picture Languages

Stefano Crespi Reghizzi(✉)

DEIB and CNR - IEIIT, Politecnico di Milano, Milan, Italy
stefano.crespireghizzi@polimi.it

Abstract. The Medvedev's Theorem (MT) characterizes a regular language as the projection of a local, i.e., a strictly-locally-testable language of order $k = 2$ (2-slt), over an alphabet larger than the terminal one by a factor depending on the state complexity of the finite automaton (FA). MT was later generalized to other language domains that instead of words contain trees or rectangular pictures, namely the regular tree languages and the tiling-system recognizable (TS-rec) languages. For trees and pictures the notion of local testability based on the occurrence of digram (2-factors) in a word, is changed into a suitable neighborhood of size 2, resp. a tree of height one, or a two-by-two tile, to be generically called 2-grams- A more recent MT extension goes in the direction of enlarging the neighborhood using as generators the languages, characterized by the k-grams, $k > 2$, and called k-slt; of course the k-gram types are different for words, trees and pictures. For all three domains a remarkably similar Extended Medvedev's Theorem (EMT) holds: a word/tree/picture language R over a terminal alphabet Σ is regular/regular/TS-rec if there exists a k-slt language L over an alphabet Λ of size double of Σ, and a letter-to-letter homomorphism from Σ to Λ such that R is the image of L; the value of k is in $\mathcal{O}(\lg(n))$, n being the state set size of an automaton recognizing the word/tree language R (the tiling system alphabet size for pictures). The alphabetic ratio $|\Lambda|/|\Sigma|$ of EMT is thus two, against the value n of MT. For some languages the value two of the ratio is the minimal possible. We present a new simplified proof of EMT for words and hints to the similar proofs for trees and for pictures. The central idea, say for words, is to sample a run of the FA so that the states traversed every k transition steps are evidenced; then each state is encoded by means of a comma-free binary code-word of length k; such an encoding is known to be a $2k$-slt language. For trees the same idea requires to lay the code-word bits over the root-to-leaf tree paths. For pictures 2D comma-free codes are needed. The possibility of further generalizations of EMT is raised at the end.

1 Introduction

Of the several approaches available to define formal language families, the homomorphic characterization of interest here essentially says that a language belongs to a certain family, if, and only if, it is the homomorphic image of a language belonging to a simpler sub-family. Since it would be difficult to be more precise without fixing a language family, we start with a classic case: Medvedev's theorem [15, 18] (MT) for regular word languages. The theorem says that a language R over a terminal alphabet Σ is regular if,

Published by Springer Nature Switzerland AG 2022
Y.-S. Han and G. Vaszil (Eds.): DCFS 2022, LNCS 13439, pp. 1–14, 2022.
https://doi.org/10.1007/978-3-031-13257-5_1

and only if, there exists a *local* language L over another alphabet Λ and a letter-to-letter homomorphism $\vartheta : \Sigma^* \to \Lambda^*$ such that $R = \vartheta(L)$. Therefore each word $x \in R$ is the image $\vartheta(y)$ of a word y in Λ, also called a pre-image of x.

We recall that a local language is a *strictly locally testable* [14] (slt) language of testability order $k = 2$, in short a 2-slt language; the k-slt families form a strict hierarchy with respect to inclusion. The notion of local testability is the pivot of all the developments reported here, also for tree languages and for picture languages. For an slt language the validity of a word can be decided by a series of local tests: by moving on the word a sliding window of width k and collecting the window contents, i.e., the k-factors present in the word, and then by checking that they are included in a given set called a *test set*, where also the prefixes and suffixes are specified as such.

For the other two families, the k-factors, become respectively certain finite pieces of trees and of pictures, that we may call k-grams (k-tiles for pictures).

The local alphabet in the proof [18] of MT is $\Lambda = \Sigma \times Q$, where Q is the state set of a finite-state automaton (FA) recognizing language R. We prefer to say that the *alphabetic ratio* $\frac{|\Lambda|}{|\Sigma|}$ of MT is $|Q|$, to evidence how the local alphabet size depends on the state complexity of the language.

It is known that homomorphic characterizations *à la* Medvedev exist also for languages comprising entities more complex than words, when a suitable definition of locality and strict local testability is possible. This is the case of the *regular tree languages* (e.g. in [3,9]) and of the picture languages defined by the *tiling systems* [10,11] (TS-rec), for brevity simply called tree languages and picture languages.

The question addressed in a series of studies concerns the reduction of the alphabetic ratio that can be achieved in a Medvedev's theorem if the local language is replaced by a k-slt language, where $k \geq 2$. The series started with a result [5] for regular word languages, further developed in [6], then similar results where obtained for the regular tree languages [7], and lastly for the picture languages defined by the tiling systems [4]. In all such cases a similar *Extended Medvedev's Theorem* (EMT) with alphabetic ratio 2 was proved.

The EMT instance for words says that a word language is regular if, and only if, it is the image of a k-slt language of alphabetic ratio 2. Moreover the value of k is in $\mathcal{O}(\lg(|Q|))$ where Q is the state set of a finite-state automaton (FA) recognizing the language. The value two is the minimal possible for some regular languages, no matter how large a k is taken. Such an EMT is a new property that carries over from regular word languages to tree languages and to picture languages.

Since it would be too long to cover the word, tree and picture cases at the same level of detail, we concentrate on the basic case of words for which we provide a new simpler proof. The other two cases cannot be discussed here and their specific aspects are intuitively presented in a later section.

EMT for Words. It may be surprising at first that the EMT property holds for three very different language domains, but a deep justification comes from the common approach used in all the three proofs. We explain it, referring to the regular word languages over an alphabet Σ. The chief aspects present in the proof are:

(1) The focus in the MT proof [18] on the recognizing runs performed by an FA, represented as state-labeled paths over the local alphabet $\Lambda = \Sigma \times Q$. The projection on Σ are the recognized words.

(2) The encoding of the states on the run by means of *comma-free* code-words [2,12]. Actually not all the states are encoded but only those that occur $k-1$ transition steps apart from each other. This means that the states are taken with a fixed *sampling rate* $k \geq 2$. The value of k determines the code-word length, hence the code dictionary numerosity that must suffice to encode the states.
(3) The self-synchronization property of comma-free codes permits to decode such an encoded run using a $2k$-slt machine, which is the same as saying that the successful encoded runs belong to an slt language of order $2k$. The known results on the numerosity of binary comma-free codes of length k permit to prove that k is in $\mathcal{O}(\lg(|Q|))$.

We raise a technical point that has to do with the words (and also with trees and pictures) which are (i) smaller than k or (ii) of a size that is not multiple of k. Case (i) is easily dismissed as in the classic theory of k-slt word languages, by stipulating that any words shorter than k belonging to the language are simply united to the language defined by the k-slt test. On the other hand, in case (ii) a language may comprise an infinite number of words that cannot be encoded (as in item (2) above) with a uniform comma-free code $X \subset \{0,1\}^k$ since X just contains code-words of fixed-length k. The solution we adopt here transforms the language into a *padded* version by appending to every word not in $(\Sigma^k)^+$ up to $k-1$ new symbols ($) so that all words have the required length for encoding. EMT is proved initially for the padded language, obtaining the k-slt test set. The test set is then pruned from the $'s and adjusted to construct the final test set.

Paper Organization. Section 2 contains the basic definitions for word languages and for comma-free codes, and some preliminary properties. Section 3 contains a result on the minimal alphabetic ratio, the proof of EMT for the regular word languages, and a complete example. Section 4 briefly describes the cases of tree languages and picture languages by comparing them with the case of words. The Conclusion Sect. 5 indicates a possible generalization.

2 Basic Definitions and Properties

2.1 Regular and Strictly Locally Testable Word Languages

For brevity, we omit the classical definitions for language and automata theory and just list our notations. The empty word is denoted ε. The Greek upper-case letters $\Gamma, \Delta, \Theta, \Lambda$ and Σ denote finite terminal alphabets.

The i-th letter of a word x is $x(i)$, $1 \leq i \leq |x|$, i.e., $x = x(1)x(2)\ldots x(|x|)$. The character # is not present in the alphabets, and is used as word *delimiter* to mark the start and end of a word, but it is not counted as true input symbol. A *homomorphism* $\xi : \Lambda^* \to \Sigma^*$ is *letter-to-letter* if for every $b \in \Lambda$, $\xi(b)$ is in Σ; we only use letter-to-letter homomorphisms.

A *finite automaton* (FA) $\mathcal{A}$ is defined by a 5-tuple $(\Sigma, Q, \to, I, F)$ where Q is the set of states, $\to$ is the state-transition relation (or graph) $\to \subseteq Q \times \Sigma \times Q$; I and F are resp. the nonempty subsets of Q comprising the initial and final states. If $(q, a, q') \in \to$, we write $q \xrightarrow{a} q'$. The transitive closure of $\rightarrow$ is defined as usual, e.g., we also write $q \xrightarrow{x} q'$ with $x \in \Sigma^+$ with obvious meaning. If $q \in I$ and $q' \in F$, then the word x is *recognized* by $\mathcal{A}$.

Strictly Locally Testable Languages. There are different yet asymptotically equivalent definitions of the family of strictly locally testable (*slt*) languages [14]; the following definition is based on delimited words. Notice also that in the definition and throughout the paper we disregard for simplicity a finite number of short words that may be present in the language. The next notation is useful: given an alphabet Λ and for all $k \geq 2$, let $\Lambda_{\#}^k = \#\Lambda^{k-1} \cup \Lambda^k \cup \Lambda^{k-1}\#$. Thus the set $\Lambda_{\#}^k$ includes all the words of length k over Λ and all the words of length $k-1$ bordered on the left or on the right by $\#$. For all words x, $|x| \geq k$, let $F_k(x) \subseteq \Lambda_{\#}^k$ be the *set of factors of length k* (*k-factors*) present in $\#x\#$. The definition of F_k is extended to languages as usual.

Definition 1 (Strict local testability). *A language $L \subseteq \Gamma^*$ is k-strictly locally testable (k-slt), if there exist a set $M_k \subseteq \Gamma_{\#}^k$ such that, for every word $x \in \Gamma^*$, x is in L if, and only if, $F_k(x) \subseteq M_k$. Then, we write $L = L(M_k)$, and we call M_k the* test set *of L. A language is slt if it is k-slt for some value k, which is called the testability order. A forbidden factor of M_k is a word in $\Gamma_{\#}^k - M_k$.*

The order $k = 2$ yields the family of *local* languages. The k-slt languages form an infinite hierarchy under inclusion, ordered by k.

2.2 Comma-Free Codes

A finite set or *dictionary* $X \subset \Delta^+$ is a *code* [2] if every word in Δ^+ has at most one factorization (i.e., decoding) in words of X, also known as *code-words*. We assume that Δ is the binary alphabet $\{0, 1\}$. We use a code X to represent a finite alphabet Γ by means of a one-to-one homomorphism, denoted by $[\![\ ]\!]_X : \Gamma^* \rightarrow \Delta^*$, called *encoding*, such that $[\![\alpha]\!]_X \in X$ for every $\alpha \in \Gamma$.

The family of codes we use is named comma-free [2,12] because the code-words in a text are not separated by a reserved character (the "comma"). Let $k \geq 1$. A code dictionary $X \subset \Delta^k$ is *comma-free* [12], if, intuitively, no code-word overlaps the concatenation of two code-words, more precisely:

$$X^2 \cap \Delta^+ X \Delta^+ = \emptyset \text{ i.e., } \forall t, u, v, w \in \Delta^* \text{ if } tu, uv, vw \in X \text{ then } \begin{cases} u = w = \varepsilon \vee \\ t = v = \varepsilon \end{cases} . \tag{1}$$

An example of comma-free code dictionary is $X = \{0010, 0011, 1110\}$.

Numerosity of Comma-Free Code Dictionaries

Proposition 1. *For every $m \geq 2$, there exist $k \geq 2$ and a comma-free code $X \subset \Delta^k$ such that $|X| \geq m$, with $k \in O(\lg m)$.*

Proof. Assume without loss of generality that m is a power of 2, i.e., $m = 2^h$ for some $h \geq 1$. Let k be any prime number between $2h$ and $4h$, which always exists by Bertrand-Chebyshev theorem; hence, k is in $O(\lg m)$. From [8] (as a special case of Theorem 2 pag. 267) it is known that for every prime integer $k > 1$ there is a comma-free code of length k with $\frac{2^k-2}{k}$ code-words, whence the following inequality: $\frac{2^k-2}{k} \geq \frac{2^{2h}-2}{2h} \geq \frac{2^{2h-1}}{2h}$. Then, this value is at least as large as m if $\frac{2^{2h-1}}{2h} \geq 2^h$, i.e., if $2^{h-1} \geq 2h$ which is true for every $h \geq 2$. □

Comma-Free Codes and slt Languages. To prepare for later proofs, we state a fundamental relation between comma-free codes and slt languages. Given an alphabet Λ and a comma-free dictionary X that encodes the symbols of Λ, let $L \subseteq \Lambda^*$ be a local language. Then the encoding of L, i.e., the language $[\![L]\!]_X \subseteq (\Delta^k)^*$ is slt. Such result is known and derives from early studies on local parsability [13,17].

Theorem 1 (preservation of slt by encoding). *Let $L \subseteq \Gamma^+$ be the 2-slt language $L(M_2)$ defined by a test set $M_2 \subseteq \Gamma^2_{\#}$. The encoding of L by means of a comma-free code X of length k, i.e., the language $[\![L]\!]_X \subseteq (\Delta^k)^*$, is a $2k$-slt language.*

In the special case when $L = \Gamma\,\Gamma^+$ the encoding XX^+ is the $(2k)$-slt language defined by the set $F_{2k}(XX^+)$ of the factors of length $2k$ of $\#X\,X^+\#$.

3 The Extended Medvedev's Theorem for Words

Theorem 2 (Medvedev's Theor. for words (see e.g. [18])). *A language $R \subseteq \Sigma^*$ is regular if, and only if, there exist a local language $L \subseteq \Lambda^*$ and a letter-to-letter homomorphism $\vartheta : \Lambda^* \to \Sigma^*$ such that $R = \vartheta(L)$. If R is recognized by an FA with state set Q the alphabet is $\Lambda = \Sigma \times Q$.*

Thus, each element of Λ can be written as $\xrightarrow{a} q$, intuitively meaning that from some state an a labeled arc goes to state q. We call *alphabetic ratio* the quotient $\frac{|\Lambda|}{|\Sigma|}$. Thus the alphabetic ratio of the MT statement is $|Q|$. A natural question is whether, by relaxing the condition that language L is local and permitting it to be k-slt with $k > 2$, the alphabetic ratio of such an extended Medvedev's statement may be reduced and how much. First, we prove with a simple witness that in general, no matter how large k, the alphabetic ratio cannot be smaller than two.

Theorem 3 (minimality of alphabetic ratio two *[5]***).** *For every alphabet Σ, there exists a regular language $R \subseteq \Sigma^+$ such that for every $k \geq 2$, R is not the homomorphic image of a k-slt language $L \subseteq \Lambda$, with $|\Lambda| = (2 \cdot |\Sigma| - 1)$.*

Proof. Let $R = \bigcup_{a \in \Sigma} (aa)^*$. By contradiction, assume that there exist $k \geq 2$ and a local alphabet Λ of cardinality $2|\Sigma| - 1$, a mapping $\pi : \Lambda \to \Sigma$ and a k-slt language $L \subseteq \Lambda^+$ such that $\pi(L) = R$. Since $|\Lambda| = 2 \cdot |\Sigma| - 1$, there exists at least one element of Σ, say, a, such that there is only one symbol $b \in \Lambda$ with $\pi(b) = a$. Since $a^{2k} \in R$, there exists $x \in L$ such that $\pi(x) = a^{2k}$. By definition of π and of Λ, $x = b^{2k}$. Consider the word $xb = b^{2k+1}$. Clearly, $\pi(xb) = a^{2k+1}$, which is not in R, since all words in R have even length. Hence, $xb \notin L$. But the k-factors of $\#x\#$ coincide with the k-factors of $\#xb\#$ therefore xb is in L, a contradiction. □

In other words, some regular languages cannot be generated as images of an slt language, if the alphabetic ratio is too small. The remaining question whether an alphabetic ratio of two is sufficient was positively settled in [5].[1] The proof presented here is simpler than the original one and is based on the use of comma-free codes (as already in [6] where local functions are used instead of homomrphisms), combined with a convenient padding technique, already in [4] for picture languages.

Sampled Runs. Referring to Theorem 2, given $k \geq 2$, reorganize each computation as follows. Starting in the initial state, group together every k consecutive steps, until the computation ends in a final state or $h < k$ residual steps are left before the end; in the second case, group together all the h steps. Such a representation is called a *run with sampling rate k* schematized as:

$$\overset{y_1}{\rightarrow} q_{i_1} \overset{y_2}{\rightarrow} q_{i_2} \dots \overset{y_{n-1}}{\rightarrow} q_{i_{n-1}} \overset{z}{\rightarrow} q_{i_n}, y_i \in \Sigma^k, z \in \Sigma^h, (1 \leq h \leq k), q \in Q, q_{i_n} \in F.$$

Now, interpret each symbol such as $\overset{y_2}{\rightarrow} q_{i_2}$ in the run as an element of a finite set called *sampling alphabet*, $\Lambda_k = \Sigma^k \times Q \cup \Sigma^h \times F \ (1 \leq h \leq k)$ where $F \subseteq Q$ are the final states. Thus, a sampled run is a word over Λ_k. To illustrate, consider for the FA in Example 1 the sampled run recognizing a^5b: $\overset{aaaa}{\rightarrow} q_0 \cdot \overset{ab}{\rightarrow} q_2$

From Theorem 2 the following is obvious: (i) the projection on alphabet Σ of a sampled run is exactly the word recognized by the corresponding run of FA $\mathcal{A}$; and (ii) the language of sampled runs is local.

Padding to a Multiple of the Sampling Rate. To prove EMT we will encode the states visible in the sampled run, using binary comma-free code-words of length k. In Example 1 see at item 3. the encoding of the states by code-words of length 4. Thus the concatenation of the code-words $[\![q_1]\!]\,[\![q_0]\!]$ is a an 8 bit string, against an input word $aaaaab$ of length just 6, too short to assign one bit per input character when encoding the states visible in the run. Since it would be complicated to use code-words of variable length, we prefer to stretch the last symbol of a sampled run, in the example $\overset{ab}{\rightarrow} q_2$. We append to it as many symbols \$ (assumed not in Σ) as needed to obtain a length equal to the sampling rate. We call *padded* such modified sampled runs and from now on we only deal with them. In our case the padded sampled run is $\overset{aaaa}{\rightarrow} q_0 \quad \overset{ab\$\$}{\rightarrow} q_2$.

Definition 2 (sampled runs). *The* sampling alphabet *(with padding) is* $\Lambda_{k\$} \subseteq \Sigma^k \times Q \cup \left(\Sigma^h \cdot \$^{k-h}\right) \times F$ *where* $1 \leq h < k$. *A sampled run is*

$$\overset{y_1}{\rightarrow} q_{i_1} \overset{y_2}{\rightarrow} q_{i_2} \dots \overset{y_{n-1}}{\rightarrow} q_{i_{n-1}} \overset{z}{\rightarrow} q_{i_n} \text{ where } \begin{cases} q_0 \overset{y_1}{\rightarrow} q_{i_1}, \\ y_i \in \Sigma^k, z \in \Sigma^h \cdot \$^{k-h}, \\ \textit{all } q \in Q \textit{ and } q_{i_n} \in F. \end{cases} \tag{2}$$

The following proposition is immediate.

[1] A similar construction in [19] (proof of Theorem 5.2) is used to logically characterize regular languages; it may provide an alternative proof that the alphabetic ratio of EMT is two, though with the $k \in \mathcal{O}(|Q|)$ bound.

Proposition 2 (language of sampled runs). *Let $R \subseteq \Sigma^*$ be the language recognized by an FA $\mathcal{A}$. Let $k \geq 2$ be the sampling rate and $\Lambda_{k\$}$ the sampling alphabet with padding. A word x is in R if, and only if, $\mathcal{A}$ has a sampled run $y \in {\Lambda_{k\$}}^+$ such that the projection of y on Σ is equal to x. The language of sampled runs $L \subseteq (\Lambda_{k\$})^+$ is local.*

Merged Comma-Free Code-Words. It is convenient to introduce a binary operator that merges two words of identical length into one of the same length on the Cartesian product of the alphabets. Define the operator $\otimes : \Delta^+ \times \Sigma^+ \to (\Delta \times \Sigma)^+$ for any two words $y \in \Sigma^+, u \in \Delta^+$, with $|y| = |u|$, as: $y \otimes u = (y(1), u(1),) \ldots (y(|y|, u(|y|)))$. E.g., if $y = aabb$ and $u = 0101$ then $y \otimes u = (a, 0)(a, 1)(b, 0)(b, 1)$. The operator can be extended in the usual way to a pair of languages. We also need the projections, resp. denoted by $[\,]_\Sigma$ and $[\,]_\Delta$ onto the alphabets Σ and Δ i.e., $[u \otimes y]_\Sigma = y$, $[u \otimes y]_\Delta = u$.

Proposition 3 (merged comma-free code). *If $X \subset \Delta^k$ is a comma-free code of length k, then every subset $Z \subseteq \Sigma^k \otimes X$ is also a comma-free code of length k.*

Proof. We prove that Z satisfies the definition of comma-free code in Sect. 2.2, Eq. (1). Let $t, u, v, w \in (\Sigma \times \Delta)^*$ be such that $tu, uv, vw \in Z$. By definition of Z, $[tu]_\Delta$, $[uv]_\Delta$, $[vw]_\Delta \in X$, with $[u]_\Delta = [w]_\Delta = \varepsilon$ or $[t]_\Delta = [v]_\Delta = \varepsilon$ since X is a comma-free code; by definition of $\otimes$, it must be that also $u = w = \varepsilon$ or $t = v = \varepsilon$. □

The EMT for words (Theorem 8 of [5]) is now straightforward to prove.

Theorem 4 (Extended Medvedev's theorem for words). *For any regular language $R \subseteq \Sigma^*$, there exist an slt language $L \subseteq \Lambda^*$, where Λ is an alphabet of size $|\Lambda| = 2|\Sigma|$, and a letter-to letter homomorphism $\vartheta : \Lambda^* \to \Sigma^*$, such that $R = \vartheta(L)$.*
If R is recognized by an FA with $|Q|$ states, the language L is k-slt with k in $\mathcal{O}(\lg(|Q|))$.

Proof. Let $R = L(\mathcal{A})$ where $\mathcal{A} = (\Sigma, Q, \to, q_0, F)$. Let $k \in \mathcal{O}(\lg|Q|)$ be a value such that by Proposition 1 there is a comma-free dictionary X with $|X| = |Q|$. With reference to Definition 2, let $L \subseteq \Lambda^+_{k\$}$ be the 2-slt language of the sampled (padded) runs of $\mathcal{A}$. Define the comma-free code $Z = \Lambda_{k\$} \otimes X$, and apply this encoding to L, obtaining the language $[\![L]\!]_Z$. Notice that it exclusively contains (padded) words of length multiple of k. The language $[\![L]\!]_Z$ is $2k$-slt by Theorem 1. Denote with M_{2k} the test set such that $[\![L]\!]_Z = L(M_{2k})$.
The next transformation of M_{2k} eliminates or modifies the $2k$-factors containing one or more \$'s in order to clean $[\![L]\!]_Z$ from the padding symbols.

(1) Remove from set M_{2k} any $2k$-factor that contains as substring $(\$, \beta)(\$, \gamma)$ or $(\$, \beta)\#$, $\beta, \gamma \in \{0, 1\}$.
(2) At last, replace any occurrence of $(\$, \beta)$ with $\#$ (dropping the bit β).

Let M'_{2k} be the resulting set. Clearly, $L(M'_{2k}) \subseteq L(M_{2k})$. Since it is obvious that $[L(M'_{2k})]_\Sigma \subseteq R$, it remains to prove $[L(M'_{2k})]_\Sigma \supseteq R$.

By contradiction, assume that a sampled run α of $\mathcal{A}$ is such that $[\![\alpha]\!]_Z$ is not in $L(M'_{2k})$.

Let x be the projection of α on Σ. If $|x|$ is a multiple of k, all the $2k$-factors of $[\![\alpha]\!]_Z$ are free from \$ symbols, therefore they are all preserved in M'_{2k} since they are untouched by the steps 1. and 2. above. If $|x|$ is not a multiple of k, α terminates with a symbol of $\Lambda_{k\$}$ having the form $\overset{u(\$)^{k-h}}{\longrightarrow} q$ with $q \in F$ and $u \in \Sigma^h$, $1 \leq h < k$. For brevity we discuss the case $\alpha = \ldots \overset{y}{\rightarrow} q' \overset{c(\$)^{k-1}}{\longrightarrow} q$ where $y = a_1 a_2 \ldots a_k \in \Sigma^k$ and $c \in \Sigma$. The encoded run $[\![\alpha]\!]_Z$ has therefore the form $\ldots a_1\beta_1\, a_2\beta_2 \ldots a_k\beta_k\;\; c\gamma_1\, \$\gamma_2\, \ldots\, \$\gamma_{k-1}$ where each Greek letter stands for a bit. The $2k$-factor $a_2\beta_3 \ldots a_k\beta_k\;\; c\gamma_1\, \$\gamma_2$ occurs in $[\![\alpha]\!]_Z$, it is in M_{2k} and after step (2) above becomes $a_2\beta_3 \ldots a_k\beta_k\;\; c\gamma_1\, \# \in M'_{2k}$. Since all dollar-less $2k$-factors are untouched, $[\![\alpha]\!]_Z \in L(M'_{2k})$. □

Example 1. The example illustrates the constructions used in the proof of EMT applied to a case simple enough to fit in the paper.

1. Finite automaton: 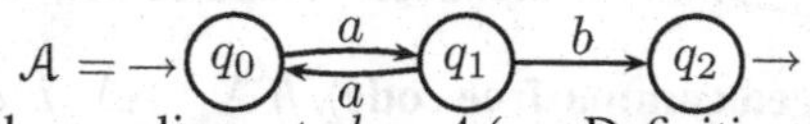 $R = a(aa)^*b$

2. Sampled padded runs with sampling rate $k = 4$ (see Definition 2)
   - Alphabet $\Lambda_{4\$} = \left\{ \overset{aaaa}{\rightarrow} q_0,\ \overset{aaab}{\rightarrow} q_2,\ \overset{ab\$\$}{\rightarrow} q_2 \right\}$ and two sampled runs:

word	*sampled run*
a^5b	$\overset{aaaa}{\rightarrow} q_0 \cdot \overset{ab\$\$}{\rightarrow} q_2$
$a^{11}b$	$\overset{aaaa}{\rightarrow} q_0 \cdot \overset{aaaa}{\rightarrow} q_0 \cdot \overset{ab\$\$}{\rightarrow} q_2$

(3)

   - The language L of sampled runs is local (Proposition 2) and defined by the test set:

$$M_2 = \left\{ \begin{array}{l} \# \overset{aaaa}{\rightarrow} q_0,\ \# \overset{aaab}{\rightarrow} q_2,\ \# \overset{ab\$\$}{\rightarrow} q_2, \\ \overset{aaaa}{\rightarrow} q_0 \overset{aaaa}{\rightarrow} q_0,\ \overset{aaaa}{\rightarrow} q_0 \overset{aaab}{\rightarrow} q_2,\ \overset{aaaa}{\rightarrow} q_0 \overset{ab\$\$}{\rightarrow} q_2, \\ \overset{aaab}{\rightarrow} q_2 \#,\ \overset{ab\$\$}{\rightarrow} q_2 \# \end{array} \right\}$$

3. Comma-free dictionary X and encoding of FA states:

$[\![q_0]\!]_X$	$[\![q_1]\!]_X$	$[\![q_2]\!]_X$
0001	0011	0111

4. The merged comma-free dictionary $Z = \Lambda^4_{4\$} \otimes X$ of Proposition 3 is:

$aaaa \otimes [\![q_0]\!]_X$	$aaab \otimes [\![q_2]\!]_X$	$ab\$\$ \otimes [\![q_2]\!]_X$
$a0 \cdot a0 \cdot a0 \cdot 1a$	$a0 \cdot a1 \cdot 1a \cdot b1$	$a0 \cdot b1 \cdot \$1 \cdot \$1$

5. Apply the encoding $[\![\ldots]\!]_Z : (\Lambda_{4\$})^+ \rightarrow Z^+$ to the sampled runs, obtaining the language $[\![L]\!]_Z$, which is 8-slt by Theorem 1. It is defined by a test set M_8 that contains the 8-factors occurring in the runs at line (3):

$$\#\ a0\ a0\ a0\ a1\ \ a0\ a0\ a0\ a1\ \ a0\ a1\ a1\ b1\ \#$$
$$\#\ a0\ a0\ a0\ a1\ \ a0\ b1\ \$1\ \$1\ \ \#$$

6. To obtain the final test set M'_8, transform the set M_8 as follows:
   - The 8-factors $a0\ a0\ a0\ a1\ \ a0\ b1\ \$1\ \$1$ and $a0\ a0\ a1\ \ a0\ b1\ \$1\ \$1\ \#$ contain two \$ and are canceled.
   - The 8-factor $a1\ \ a0\ a0\ a0\ a1\ \ a0\ b1\ \$1$ is replaced by $a1\ \ a0\ a0\ a0\ a1\ \ a0\ b1\ \#$.

The test set is $M'_8 = \left\{ \begin{array}{l} \#\ a0\ a0\ a0\ a1\ \ a0\ a0\ a0,\ \ a0\ a0\ a0\ a1\ \ a0\ a0\ a0\ a1, \\ a0\ a0\ a1\ \ a0\ a0\ a0\ a1\ \ a0,\ a0\ a1\ \ a0\ a0\ a0\ a1\ \ a0\ a1, \\ a1\ \ a0\ a0\ a0\ a1\ \ a0\ a1\ a1,\ a0\ a0\ a0\ a1\ \ a0\ a1\ a1\ b1, \\ a0\ a0\ a1\ \ a0\ a1\ a1\ b1\ \#,\ \ \#\ a0\ a0\ a0\ a1\ \ a0\ b1\ \# \end{array} \right\}.$

7. The projection of language $L(M'_8)$ on Σ is $R - \{ab,\ aaab\}$.

Notice that this language admits a more economical *ad hoc* EMT statement with alphabetic ratio $\frac{3}{2}$, represented by the projection on $\{a, b\}$ of the 2-slt language $a(a'\, a)^*b$.

4 The Extended Medvedev's Theorem for Trees and Pictures

For comparability sake, the same presentation scheme is used in both cases: (i) the definition of the language family, (ii) the notion of k-gram, (iii) the Medvedev's theorem, (iv) the extended Medvedev's theorem.

4.1 Tree Languages

The ranked tree languages are recognized by nondeterministic root-to-leaves *tree automata* [3,9] (TA), assumed to be familiar to the reader. Given a tree with internal nodes labeled over the ranked alphabet Σ, and leaves labeled over $\Sigma_0 \subset \Sigma$, the machine starts in an initial state in the root, then it computes in one step the states of the sibling nodes. Then recursively it does the same for each sibling subtree, until the computation reaches a leaf. The state must be a final one in all leaves for the tree to be recognized. Thus the effect of the computation run is to label each node with a state from the state set Q.

The analogy with the runs of an FA on words is manifest; the difference is that an FA run traverses a linear graph whereas a TA run traverses a tree graph along all the root-to-leaf paths. The result is a *state-labeled* tree, isomorphic to the original one, where nodes are labeled over the alphabet $\Sigma \times Q$.

The notion of k-gram, $k \geq 2$, requires some preliminary concepts. A *tree domain* D is a finite, non empty, prefix-closed subset of $\mathbb{N}^*_{>0}$ satisfying the following condition: if $xi \in D$ for $x \in \mathbb{N}^*_{>0}$ and $i \in \mathbb{N}_{>0}$, then $xj \in D$ for all j with $1 \leq j \leq i$. A *tree* t over a finite alphabet Σ is a mapping $t : dom_t \to \Sigma$, where dom_t is a tree domain. A node of t is an element x of dom_t. The *root* of t is the node ε. The *successors* of a node x are all the nodes of the form xi, with $xi \in dom_t, i \in \mathbb{N}_{>0}$. The *yield* or frontier of a tree is the word of leaf labels read from left to right. A *path* is a sequence of nodes $x_1 \dots x_m$, such that x_{i+1} is a successor of x_i. The *label of a path* $x_1 \dots x_m$ is the word $t(x_1) \cdots t(x_m)$, i.e., the concatenation of the labels of nodes $x_1, \dots, x_m$.

Given a node $x \in dom_t$, the portion of the tree rooted at x is denoted as $t_{|x}$ and called the *subtree* of t at node x, i.e., $t_{|x}$ is the subset of nodes of dom_t having the form xy, $y \in \mathbb{N}^*_{>0}$. A subtree $t_{|x}$ is not formally a tree but it can be made into a tree t' by removing the prefix x from every node of $t_{|x}$, by positing $t'(y) = t_{|x}(xy)$ for all $y \in \mathbb{N}^*_{>0}$; in this case, the subtree is said to be *normalized.*

Tree Languages Defined by Local Tests

Definition 3 (k-gram). *Let $k \geq 2$, let $t \in \mathcal{T}_\Delta$ and x a node of t. The* k-gram[2] *of t at node $x \in dom_t$ is the subset of nodes of the normalized subtree $t_{|x}$ at downwards*

[2] The meaning of digram is a sequence of 2 letters or symbols; or also of patterns such as the colors in a flag. For non-textual languages the term k-gram is preferable to k-factor. Other terms are in use, e.g., our definition of k-gram corresponds to the $(k-1)$-type of [16].

distance less than k from x. When $x = \varepsilon$ *(i.e., the root of t) the k-gram is called a* root *k-gram. The set of k-grams of t is denoted by* $\langle\langle t \rangle\rangle_h$.

Note: the yield of a k-gram, unlike the one of a tree, may include symbols in $\Sigma - \Sigma_0$.

Definition 4 (strictly locally testable tree language). *Let* $k \geq 2$. *A language* $T \subseteq \mathcal{T}_\Sigma$ *is* k-strictly locally testable *(k-slt) if there exist two sets* Γ_k *and* Θ_k *of k-grams, called the* test sets, *with* $\Theta_k \subseteq \Gamma_k$, *such that the membership of a tree in T can be decided just by considering its k-grams, namely, for all* $t \in \mathcal{T}_\Sigma$: $t \in T$ *if, and only if,* $\langle\langle t \rangle\rangle_k \subseteq \Gamma_k$ *and the root k-gram of t is in* Θ_k. *Then we write* $T = T(\Gamma_k, \Theta_k)$. *The value k is called the* order *of T. A language is* strictly locally testable *(slt) if it is k-slt for some* $k \geq 2$; *if* $k = 2$ *it is also called* local.

Two examples of local language are: the state-labeled trees, denoted by $\widehat{T(\mathcal{M})}$, of a language $T(M) \subseteq \mathcal{T}_\Sigma$, and the syntax trees of a context-free grammar.

Medvedev's Theorem and Its Extension The next well-known proposition (e.g., in [9], Sect. 2.8) is a Medvedev-like characterization of tree languages.

Theorem 5 (MT for trees). *A tree language* $T \subseteq \mathcal{T}_\Sigma$ *is regular if, and only if, there exists a ranked alphabet* Λ, *a local (i.e. 2-slt) tree language* $T' \subseteq \mathcal{T}_\Lambda$ *and a projection* $\eta : \Lambda \to \Sigma$ *such that* $T = \eta(T')$. *Moreover, if a tree automaton recognizing T has the state set Q, then the* alphabetic ratio *is* $\frac{|\Lambda|}{|\Sigma|} \leq |Q|$.

The proof of the theorem is based on the observation that the set of all state-labeled trees of a TA $\mathcal{M}$ is a local tree language, since a transition of $\mathcal{M}$ operates on the neighborhood of a node consisting of its children.

The EMT (Theorem 4) for words and the minimality of the alphabetic ratio 2 (Theorem 3) have been recently proved for tree languages [7]; the mimality result simply comes from the fact that a word is also a linear tree. therefore the same witness holds in both cases.

Theorem 6 (EMT for trees (theorem 1 of [7])). *For every ranked alphabet* Σ, *there exist a ranked alphabet* Λ, *with alphabetic ratio* $\frac{|\Lambda|}{|\Sigma|} \leq 2$, *and a projection* $\eta : \mathcal{T}_\Lambda \to \mathcal{T}_\Sigma$, *such that for every regular tree language* $T \subseteq \mathcal{T}_\Sigma$ *there exist* $k \geq 2$ *and a* $2k$*-slt tree language* $\widetilde{T} \subseteq \mathcal{T}_\Lambda$ *such that* $T = \eta(\widetilde{T})$.

To explain the proof of EMT for trees, we look at a state-labeled tree, and we consider each root-to-leaf path. On each path we encode, with binary comma-free code-words of length k, the states that are located at nodes at distance $0, k, 2k, \ldots$ from the root. Notice that, for any internal node at a distance multiple of k from the root, the same code-word is placed on all the downward paths originating from it. Paths too short to contain a whole code-word, will contain just a prefix. Having placed the binary code-words on the path, we cancel all state labels that where present in the state-labeled tree. The result is a tree isomorphic to the state-labeled one, aptly called an *encoding* tree. As said, its node labels are over the alphabet $\Sigma \times \{0, 1\}$. Analogously with Theorem 1 about the preservation of the slt property by encoding, it is possible to prove that the language of encoded trees is $2k$-slt, and its projection on Σ coincides with language T.

4.2 Picture Languages

The case of TS-rec pictures sets itself apart from the cases of words and trees since the primary definition of the tiling-system recognizable picture languages is not based on an automaton (or on a regular expression) but on Medvedev's theorem.

Assuming some familiarity with the subject, we list a few essential definitions (see [10,11]). A picture p is a rectangular array with $|p|_{row}$ rows and $|p|_{col}$ columns, each cell containing a symbol (or pixel) from an alphabet Σ. The set of all pictures of size m, n is $\Sigma^{m,n}$ and the set of all pictures is Σ^{++}. A picture contained in another one is a subpicture. A (square) picture in $\Sigma^{k,k}$, $k \geq 2$, is called *k-tile* and simply *tile* if $k = 2$: k-tiles play the role of k-factors for words and k-grams for trees. The *bordered* version $\widehat{p}$ of p is the picture of size $(|p|_{row} + 2, |p|_{col+2}$ that surrounds p with a rectangular frame containing the reserved symbol $\#$.

Definition 5 (strictly locally testable picture languages). *A picture language, $L \subseteq (\Sigma \cup \{\#\})^{++}$ is k-*strictly-locally testable *(k-slt) if there is a set $T_k \subseteq (\Sigma \cup \{\#\})^{k,k}$ of k-tiles, called the* test set *such that $p \in L$ if, and only if, the k-tiles occurring in $\widehat{p}$ as subpictures are included in T_k. Then we write $L = L(T_k)$. A pictures language is slt if it is k-slt for some k.*

The k-slt, $k \geq 2$, family is an infinite strict hierarchy, for every non-unary alphabet.

As said, the definition of TS-rec is an MT statement.

Theorem 7 (MT for pictures). *A picture language $R \subseteq \Sigma^{++}$ is* tiling-system recognizable *(TS-rec) if it is the* projection *of a 2-slt (i.e., local) language $L \subseteq \Lambda^{++}$, i.e., defined by a test set $T_2 \subseteq (\Sigma \cup \{\#\})^{2,2}$. In formula, $R = \pi(L(T_2))$ where $\pi : \Lambda \to \Sigma$. The quadruple $(\Sigma, \Lambda, T_2, \pi)$ is called a* tiling system.

Tradeoff Between Alphabet Cardinality and Tile Size. The definition of tiling system has been extended towards the *k-tiling system*. It uses a set $T_k \subseteq \Gamma^{k,k}$ of k-tiles, $k \geq 2$ instead of 2-tiles. The *alphabetic ratio* of a k-tiling system is the quotient $\frac{|\Gamma|}{|\Sigma|}$.

Theorem 8. *Given a k-slt language $L \subseteq \Sigma^{++}$ defined as $L = L(T_k)$ where $T_k \subseteq (\Sigma \cup \{\#\})^{k,k}$, there exists an alphabet Γ, a local language $L' \subseteq \Gamma^{++}$ and a projection $\pi : \Gamma \to \Sigma$ s.t. $L = \pi(L')$. Hence the family of k-TS recognizable languages coincides with TS-rec.*

The proof in [10] has the alphabet size $|\Gamma| = |\Sigma| \cdot |T_k|$.

Extended Medvedev's Theorem. The EMT (Theorem 4) for words and the minimality of the alphabetic ratio 2 (Theorem 3) have been recently proved for TS-rec pictures [4]; the minimality simply follows from the fact that a word is also a one-row picture.

Theorem 9 (EMT for pictures). *For any $R \subseteq \Sigma^{++}$ in TS-rec there exist $k \geq 2$ and a $2k$-tiling system with alphabetic ratio 2, recognizing R. Moreover, if n is the size of the local alphabet of a tiling system recognizing R then the value of k is $\mathcal{O}(\lg(n))$.*

The proof follows the one for words in Sect. 3 with some important differences.

1. If the number of rows or columns is not multiple of k, the picture has to be *padded* (as we did for words in Sect. 3) on the east and south sides with \$ symbols, so that the padded picture can be tessellated with k-tiles, that fit in a mesh of a $k \times k$ grid.
2. A comma-free picture (i.e., 2D) code is, intuitively, a set of k-tiles (code-pictures) such that, for any picture tessellated with such tiles, none of the $k \times k$ subpictures at positions misaligned with respect to the grid, can be a code-picture. The slt properties of such 2D codes and for code-words are similar.
The property of code-words that XX^+ is $2k$-slt (special case of Theorem 1) becomes: let $X \subseteq \Lambda^{k,k}$ be a comma-free code, then the language X^{++} is $2k$-slt.
Instead of Theorem 1, the statement is: let $T \subseteq \Gamma^{2,2}$ be a set of tiles defining the local language $L(T)$ and let $X \subseteq \Delta^{k,k}$ be a comma-free 2D code with numerosity $|X| = |\Gamma|$. The encoding $[\![L(T)]\!]_X$ is a $2k$-slt language.
Although a general formula for the numerosity of 2D comma-free codes is lacking, in [1] a useful lower bound for a family of codes that cannot overlap is given; the non-overlapping condition is stronger than the comma-free one.
3. The major difference is that for pictures we cannot rely on an automaton analogous to FA for words and TA for trees.

Therefore the technique in Sect. 3 of sampled computations labeled with the states traversed has to be replaced by another approach. The *frame* $f(p)$ of a picture $p \in \Gamma^{k,k}$ is the square ring composed by the four sides (n_p, e_p, s_p, w_p) each one being a word of length k; each corner is shared by two words. A bordered picture of size $(2k, 2k)$ tessellated with four k-tiles each one with its frame, is shown.

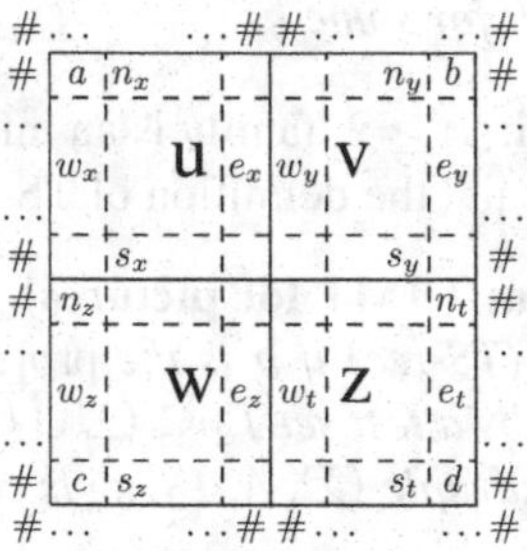

4. A comma-free code-picture encodes each frame, i.e., a quadruple (n_p, e_p, s_p, w_p); code-pictures are schematized by u, v, w, z in the figure. The frame contains $4k$ symbols of Γ and can be encoded by a code-picture in X, which contains k^2 bits, since for k large enough, the numerosity of the family of non-overlapping 2D codes [1] suffices to encode all possible frames.
5. In each pixel the original terminal symbol from Σ is accompanied by a bit of the code-picture, so that the alphabetic ratio is $\frac{|\Sigma|\cdot|\{0,1\}|}{|\Sigma|} = 2$.
6. The language of encoded pictures is $2k$-slt, hence language R is $2k$-TS recognizable with alphabetic ratio 2. The proof is more combinatorial than for words.

5 Conclusion

For words, trees and pictures we have evidenced the similarity between the statements and proofs of the Extended Medvedev's Theorem. At closer reflection, we may attribute such similarity to the fact that in all cases a recognizing computation sweeps over a discrete structure, a directed graph whose nodes are labeled with terminal symbols and states. The graph is respectively a total order, a tree order, and an acyclic graph with square meshes. The computation never returns to an already visited node. The sampling technique with sampling rate k clusters the computation into k-grams. Such k-grams are then taken as symbols of a new alphabet and the correct adjacencies between k-grams are specified by a 2-slt language. Then the encoding of each k-gram symbol by means of a binary comma-free code transforms the 2-slt language into a $2k$-slt language over the doubled alphabet $\Sigma \times \{0, 1\}$.

An open question is whether the EMT property holds for other language domains beyond the three considered, as for instance the directed-acyclic-graph automata that from time to time have been proposed in the literature.

Acknowledgment. The present simpler proof of EMT for words has been worked out jointly with P. San Pietro and incorporates an original idea of A. Restivo about padding.

References

1. Anselmo, M., Giammarresi, D., Madonia, M.: Non-expandable non-overlapping sets of pictures. Theor. Comput. Sci. **657**, 127–136 (2017)
2. Berstel, J., Perrin, D., Reutenauer, C.: Codes and Automata. Encyclopedia of Mathematics and its Applications, vol. 129. CUP (2009)
3. Comon, H., et al.: Tree automata techniques and applications (2007). http://www.grappa.univ-lille3.fr/tata
4. Crespi Reghizzi, S., Restivo, A., San Pietro, P.: Reducing local alphabet size in recognizable picture languages. In: Moreira, N., Reis, R. (eds.) DLT 2021. LNCS, vol. 12811, pp. 103–116. Springer, Cham (2021). https://doi.org/10.1007/978-3-030-81508-0_9
5. Crespi-Reghizzi, S., San Pietro, P.: From regular to strictly locally testable languages. Int. J. Found. Comput. Sci. **23**(8), 1711–1728 (2012)
6. Crespi Reghizzi, S., San Pietro, P.: Regular languages as local functions with small alphabets. In: Ćirić, M., Droste, M., Pin, J.É. (eds.) CAI 2019. LNCS, vol. 11545, pp. 124–137. Springer, Cham (2019). https://doi.org/10.1007/978-3-030-21363-3_11
7. Crespi Reghizzi, S., San Pietro, P.: Homomorphic characterization of tree languages based on comma-free encoding. In: Leporati, A., Martín-Vide, C., Shapira, D., Zandron, C. (eds.) LATA 2021. LNCS, vol. 12638, pp. 241–254. Springer, Cham (2021). https://doi.org/10.1007/978-3-030-68195-1_19
8. Eastman, W.L.: On the construction of comma-free codes. IEEE Trans. Inf. Theory **11**(2), 263–267 (1965)
9. Gecseg, F., Steinby, M.: Tree Automata. arXiv (2015)
10. Giammarresi, D., Restivo, A.: Recognizable picture languages. Int. J. Pattern Recogn. Artif. Intell. **6**(2–3), 241–256 (1992)
11. Giammarresi, D., Restivo, A.: Two-dimensional languages. In: Rozenberg, G., Salomaa, A. (eds.) Handbook of Formal Languages, pp. 215–267. Springer, Heidelberg (1997). https://doi.org/10.1007/978-3-642-59126-6_4
12. Golomb, S.W., Gordon, B., Welch, L.: Comma-free codes. Can. J. Math. **10**, 202–209 (1958)
13. Hashiguchi, K., Honda, N.: Properties of code events and homomorphisms over regular events. J. Comput. Syst. Sci. **12**(3), 352–367 (1976)
14. McNaughton, R., Papert, S.: Counter-Free Automata. MIT Press, Cambridge (1971)
15. Medvedev, Y.T.: On the class of events representable in a finite automaton. In: Moore, E.F. (ed.) Sequential Machines - Selected Papers, pp. 215–227. Addison-Wesley (1964). Originally Published in Russian in Avtomaty, pp. 385–401 (1956)
16. Place, T., Segoufin, L.: A decidable characterization of locally testable tree languages. Log. Methods Comput. Sci. **7**(4) (2011)

17. Restivo, A.: On a question of McNaughton and Papert. Inf. Control **25**(1), 93–101 (1974)
18. Eilenberg, S.: Automata, Languages, and Machines, vol. A. Academic Press (1974)
19. Thomas, W.: Classifying regular events in symbolic logic. J. Comput. Syst. Sci. **25**(3), 360–376 (1982)

Ranking Binary Unlabelled Necklaces in Polynomial Time

Duncan Adamson(✉)

Reykjavik University, Reykjavik, Iceland
duncana@ru.is

Abstract. Unlabelled Necklaces are an equivalence class of cyclic words under both the rotation (cyclic shift) and the relabelling operations. The relabelling of a word is a bijective mapping from the alphabet to itself. The main result of the paper is the first polynomial-time algorithm for ranking unlabelled necklaces of a binary alphabet. The time-complexity of the algorithm is $O(n^6 \log^2 n)$, where n is the length of the considered necklaces. The key part of the algorithm is to compute the rank of any word with respect to the set of unlabelled necklaces by finding three other ranks: the rank over all necklaces, the rank over symmetric unlabelled necklaces, and the rank over necklaces with an enclosing labelling. The last two concepts are introduced in this paper.

1 Introduction

For classes of words under lexicographic (or dictionary) order, a unique integer can be assigned to every word corresponding to the number of words smaller than it. Such an integer is called the *rank* of a word. The *ranking* problem asks to compute the rank of a given word. Ranking has been studied for various objects including partitions [13], permutations [9,10], combinations [12], etc.

The ranking problem is straightforward for the set of all words over a finite alphabet (assuming the standard lexicographic order), however this ceases to be the case once additional symmetry is introduced. One such example is combinatorial necklaces [6]. A *necklace*, also known as a *cyclic word*, is an equivalence class of all words under the cyclic rotation operation, also known as a cyclic shift. Necklaces are classical combinatorial objects and they remain an object of study in other contexts such as total search problems [4] or circular splicing systems [3]. The first class of cyclic words to be ranked were *Lyndon words* - fixed length aperiodic cyclic words - by Kociumaka et al. [7] who provided an $O(n^3)$ time algorithm, where n is the length of the word. An algorithm for ranking necklaces - fixed length cyclic words - was given by Kopparty et al. [8], without tight bounds on the complexity. A quadratic algorithm for ranking necklaces was provided by Sawada et al. [11]. More recently algorithms have been presented for ranking multidimensional necklaces [1] and bracelets [2].

Our Results. This paper presents the first polynomial time algorithm for ranking *binary unlabelled necklaces*. Informally, binary unlabelled necklaces can be

Published by Springer Nature Switzerland AG 2022
Y.-S. Han and G. Vaszil (Eds.): DCFS 2022, LNCS 13439, pp. 15–29, 2022.
https://doi.org/10.1007/978-3-031-13257-5_2

though of as necklaces over a binary alphabet with the additional symmetry over the *relabelling* operation, a bijection from the set of symbols to itself. Considered in terms of binary values, the words 0001 and 1110 are equivalent under the relabelling operation, however 1010 and 1100 are not. We provide an $O(n^6 \log^2 n)$ time algorithm for ranking an unlabelled binary necklace within the set of unlabelled binary necklaces of length n.

2 Preliminaries

Let Σ be a finite alphabet. For the remainder of this work we assume Σ to be $\{0, 1\}$ where $0 < 1$. We denote by Σ^* the set of all words over Σ and by Σ^n the set of all words of length n. The notation $\bar{w}$ is used to clearly denote that the variable $\bar{w}$ is a word. The length of a word $\bar{w} \in \Sigma^*$ is denoted by $|\bar{w}|$. We use $\bar{w}_i$, for any $i \in \{1, \ldots, |\bar{w}|\}$ to denote the ith symbol of $\bar{w}$. Given two words $\bar{w}, \bar{u} \in \Sigma^*$, the *concatenation operation* is denoted by $\bar{w} : \bar{u}$, returning the word of length $|\bar{w}| + |\bar{u}|$ where $(\bar{w} : \bar{u})_i$ equals either $\bar{w}_i$, if $i \leq |\bar{w}|$ or $\bar{u}_{i-|\bar{w}|}$ if $i > |\bar{w}|$. The tth power of a word $\bar{w}$, denoted by $\bar{w}^t$, equals $\bar{w}$ repeated t times.

Let $[n]$ be the ordered sequence of integers from 1 to n inclusive and let $[i, j]$ be the ordered sequence of integers from i to j inclusive. Given two words $\bar{u}, \bar{v} \in \Sigma^*$, $\bar{u} = \bar{v}$ if and only if $|\bar{u}| = |\bar{v}|$ and $\bar{u}_i = \bar{v}_i$ for every $i \in [|\bar{u}|]$. A word $\bar{u}$ is *lexicographically smaller* than $\bar{v}$ if there exists an $i \in [|\bar{u}|]$ such that $\bar{u}_1\bar{u}_2 \ldots \bar{u}_{i-1} = \bar{v}_1\bar{v}_2 \ldots \bar{v}_{i-1}$ and $\bar{u}_i < \bar{v}_i$. Given two words $\bar{v}, \bar{w} \in \Sigma^*$ where $|\bar{v}| \neq |\bar{w}|$, $\bar{v}$ is smaller than $\bar{w}$ if $\bar{v}^{|\bar{w}|} < \bar{w}^{|\bar{v}|}$ or $\bar{v}^{|\bar{w}|} = \bar{w}^{|\bar{v}|}$ and $|\bar{v}| < |\bar{w}|$. For a given set of words $\mathbf{S}$, the *rank* of $\bar{v}$ with respect to $\mathbf{S}$ is the number of words in $\mathbf{S}$ that are smaller than $\bar{v}$.

The *subword* of a cyclic word $\bar{w} \in \Sigma^n$ denoted $\bar{w}_{[i,j]}$ is the word $\bar{u}$ of length $n + j - i + 1 \bmod n$ such that $\bar{u}_a = \bar{w}_{i+a \bmod n}$, i.e. the word such that the ath symbol of $\bar{u}$ corresponds to the symbol at position $i + a \bmod n$ of $\bar{w}$. The value of the tth symbol of $\bar{w}_{[i,j]}$ is the value of the symbol at position $i + t - 1$ of $\bar{w}$. By this definition, given $\bar{u} = \bar{w}_{[i,j]}$, the value of $\bar{u}_t$ is the $i + t - 1^{th}$ symbol of $\bar{w}$ and the length of $\bar{u}$ is $|\bar{u}| = j - i + 1$. The notation $\bar{u} \sqsubseteq \bar{w}$ denotes that $\bar{u}$ is a subword of $\bar{w}$. Further, $\bar{u} \sqsubseteq_i \bar{w}$ denotes that $\bar{u}$ is a subword of $\bar{w}$ of length i.

The *rotation* of a word $\bar{w} \in \Sigma^n$ by $r \in [0, n-1]$ returns the word $\bar{w}_{[r+1,n]} : \bar{w}_{[1,r]}$, and is denoted by $\langle \bar{w} \rangle_r$, i.e. $\langle \bar{w}_1\bar{w}_2 \ldots \bar{w}_n \rangle_r = \bar{w}_{r+1} \ldots \bar{w}_n\bar{w}_1 \ldots \bar{w}_r$. Under the rotation operation, the word $\bar{u}$ is equivalent to the word $\bar{v}$ if $\bar{v} = \langle \bar{u} \rangle_r$ for some r. A word $\bar{w}$ is *periodic* if there is a subword $\bar{u} \sqsubseteq \bar{w}$ and integer $t \geq 2$ such that $\bar{u}^t = \bar{w}$. Equivalently, word $\bar{w}$ is *periodic* if there exists some rotation $0 < r < |\bar{w}|$ where $\bar{w} = \langle \bar{w} \rangle_r$. A word is *aperiodic* if it is not periodic. The *period* of a word $\bar{w}$ is the aperiodic word $\bar{u}$ such that $\bar{w} = \bar{u}^t$.

A *necklace* is an equivalence class of words under the rotation operation. The notation $\tilde{\mathbf{w}}$ is used to denote that the variable $\tilde{\mathbf{w}}$ is a necklace. Given a necklace $\tilde{\mathbf{w}}$, the *canonical representation* of $\tilde{\mathbf{w}}$ is the lexicographically smallest element of the set of words in the equivalence class $\tilde{\mathbf{w}}$. The canonical representation of $\tilde{\mathbf{w}}$ is denoted by $\langle \tilde{\mathbf{w}} \rangle$, and the rth shift of the canonical representation is denoted by $\langle \tilde{\mathbf{w}} \rangle_r$. Given a word $\bar{w}$, $\langle \bar{w} \rangle$ denotes the canonical representation of the necklace containing $\bar{w}$, i.e. the canonical representation of the necklace $\tilde{\mathbf{u}}$ where $\bar{w} \in \tilde{\mathbf{u}}$. The set of necklaces of length n over an alphabet of size q is denoted by $\mathcal{N}_q^n$. Let $\bar{w} \in \mathcal{N}_q^n$ denote that the word $\bar{w}$ is the canonical representation of some necklace $\tilde{\mathbf{w}} \in \mathcal{N}_q^n$. An aperiodic necklace, known as a *Lyndon word*, is a necklace representing the equivalence class of some aperiodic word. Note that if a word is aperiodic, then every rotation of the word is also aperiodic. The set of Lyndon words of length n over an alphabet of size q is denoted by $\mathcal{L}_q^n$.

As both necklaces and Lyndon words are classical objects, there are many fundamental results regarding each objects. The first results for these objects were equations determining the number of necklaces or Lyndon words of a given length. The number of (1D) necklaces is given by the equation $|\mathcal{N}_q^n| = \frac{1}{n}\sum_{d|n} \phi\left(\frac{n}{d}\right) q^d$ where $\phi(n)$ is Euler's totient function [6]. Similarly the number of Lyndon words is given with the equation $|\mathcal{L}_q^n| = \sum_{d|n} \mu\left(\frac{n}{d}\right) |\mathcal{N}_q^d|$, where $\mu(x)$ is the Möbius function [6]. The *rank* of a word $\bar{w}$ in the set of necklaces $\mathcal{N}_q^n$ is the number of necklaces with a canonical representation smaller than $\bar{w}$.

2.1 Unlabelled Necklaces

An *unlabelled necklace* is a generalisation of the set of necklaces. At a high level, two words $\bar{v}, \bar{u} \in \Sigma^n$ belong to the same unlabelled necklace class $\tilde{\mathbf{w}}$ if there exists some labelling function $\psi(x) : \Sigma \mapsto \Sigma$ and rotation $r \in [n]$ such that $(\langle\bar{v}\rangle_r)_i = \psi(\bar{u}_i)$ for every $i \in [n]$. More formally, let $\psi(x)$ be a bijection from Σ into Σ, i.e. a function taking as input some symbol in Σ and returning a symbol in Σ such that $\{\psi(x) | \forall x \in \Sigma\} = \Sigma$. For notation $\psi(\bar{w})$ is used to denote the word constructed by applying $\psi(x)$ to every symbol in $\bar{w}$ in order, formally $\psi(\bar{w}) = \psi(\bar{w}_1)\psi(\bar{w}_2)\ldots\psi(\bar{w}_n)$. Similarly, the notation $\psi(\tilde{\mathbf{w}})$ is used to denote the necklace class constructed by applying $\psi(w)$ to every word $\bar{w} \in \tilde{\mathbf{w}}$. Further, let $\Psi(\Sigma)$ be the set of all such functions. The unlabelled necklace $\tilde{\mathbf{w}}$ with a canonical representation $\bar{w}$ contains every word $\bar{v} \in \Sigma^n$ where $\psi(\langle\bar{v}\rangle_r) = \bar{w}$ for some $\psi(x) \in \Psi(\Sigma)$ and $r \in [n]$. As in the labelled case, the canonical representation of an unlabelled necklace $\tilde{\mathbf{w}}$, denoted $\langle\tilde{\mathbf{w}}\rangle$, is the lexicographically smallest word in the equivalence class. The set of unlabelled q-arry necklaces of length n is denoted $\hat{\mathcal{N}}_q^n$, and the set of q-arry Lyndon words of length n $\hat{\mathcal{L}}_q^n$.

In this paper we study *binary unlabelled necklaces*, in other words unlabelled necklaces restricted to a binary alphabet. In this case $\Sigma = \{0, 1\}$ and $\Psi(\Sigma)$ contains the identity function $I(x)$, where $I(x) = x$, and the swapping function $S(x)$ where $S(x) = \begin{cases} 0 & x = 1 \\ 1 & x = 0 \end{cases}$. Gilbert and Riordan [5] provide the following equations for computing the sizes of $\hat{\mathcal{N}}_2^n$ and $\hat{\mathcal{L}}_2^n$:

$$|\hat{\mathcal{N}}_2^n| = \sum_{\text{odd } d|n} \phi(d) 2^{n/d}$$

$$|\hat{\mathcal{L}}_2^n| = \sum_{\text{odd } d|n} \mu(d) 2^{n/d}$$

In this paper we introduce two subclasses of unlabelled necklaces, the class of *symmetric unlabelled necklaces* and the class of *enclosing unlabelled necklaces* for some given word $\bar{w}$. Observe that a binary unlabelled necklace $\tilde{\mathbf{w}}$ may correspond to either one or two (labelled) necklaces. Informally, a symmetric unlabelled necklaces is such an unlabelled necklaces that corresponds to only a single necklace. An enclosing unlabelled necklace relative to a word $\bar{w}$ is a non-symteric unlabelled necklace corresponding to a pair of necklaces $\tilde{\mathbf{v}}$ and $\tilde{\mathbf{u}}$ such that $\tilde{\mathbf{v}} < \bar{w} < \tilde{\mathbf{u}}$. Any Lyndon word that is a symmetric unlabelled necklace is a *symmetric unlabelled Lyndon word*, and any unlabelled Lyndon word that encloses a word $\bar{w}$ is an *enclosing unlabelled Lyndon word* of $\bar{w}$.

Definition 1 (Symmetric Necklaces). *A binary necklace* $\tilde{\mathbf{w}}$ *is* symmetric *if and only if* $\tilde{\mathbf{w}} = S(\tilde{\mathbf{w}})$.

Definition 2 (Enclosing Unlabelled Necklaces). *An unlabelled necklace* $\tilde{\mathbf{u}}$ encloses *a word* $\bar{w}$ *if* $\langle \tilde{\mathbf{u}} \rangle < \bar{w} < \langle S(\tilde{\mathbf{u}}) \rangle$. *An unlabelled necklace* $\tilde{\mathbf{u}}$ *is an* enclosing unlabelled necklace *of* $\bar{w}$ *if* $\tilde{\mathbf{u}}$ *encloses* $\bar{w}$.

2.2 Bounding Subwords

One important tool that is used in the ranking of unlabelled necklaces are *bounding subwords*, introduced in [2]. Informally, bounding subwords of length $l \leq n$ provide a means to partition Σ^l into $n+2$ sets based on the subwords of some $\bar{w} \in \Sigma^n$ of length l. Given two subwords $\bar{v}, \bar{u} \sqsubseteq_l \bar{w}$ such that $\bar{v} < \bar{u}$ the set $S(\bar{v}, \bar{u})$ contains all words in Σ^l that are between the value of $\bar{v}$ and $\bar{u}$, formally $S(\bar{v}, \bar{u}) = \{\bar{x} \in \Sigma^l | \bar{v} \leq \bar{x} < \bar{u}\}$. In this paper we are only interested in sets between pairs $\bar{v}, \bar{u} \sqsubseteq_l \bar{w}$ where there exists no $\bar{s} \sqsubseteq_l \bar{w}$ such that $\bar{v} < \bar{s} < \bar{u}$. As such, we define a subword of $\bar{w}$ as *bounding* some word $\bar{v}$ if it is the lexicographically largest subword of $\bar{w}$ that is smaller than $\bar{v}$.

Definition 3 (Bounding Subwords). *Let* $\bar{w}, \bar{v} \in \Sigma^*$ *where* $|\bar{w}| \leq |\bar{v}|$. *The word* $\bar{w}$ *is* bounded *(resp. strictly bounded) by* $\bar{s} \sqsubseteq_{|\bar{w}|} \bar{v}$ *if* $\bar{s} \leq \bar{w}$ *(resp.* $\bar{s} < \bar{w}$*) and there is no* $\bar{u} \sqsubseteq_{|\bar{w}|} \bar{v}$ *such that* $\bar{s} < \bar{u} \leq \bar{w}$.

Proposition 1 ([2]). *Let* $\bar{v} \in \Sigma^n$. *The array* $WX[\bar{s} \sqsubseteq \bar{v}, x \in \Sigma]$, *such that* $WX[\bar{s}, x]$ *strictly bounds* $\bar{w} : x$ *for every* $\bar{w}$ *strictly bounded by* $\bar{s}$, *can be computed in* $O(k \cdot n^3 \cdot \log(n))$ *time where* $|\Sigma| = k$.

For the remainder of this paper, we can assume that the array WX has been precomputed for every $\bar{s} \sqsubseteq \bar{v}, x \in \Sigma$. Note that in our case $k = 2$, therefore the process of computing WX requires only $O(n^3 \cdot \log(n))$ time.

3 Ranking

In this section we present our ranking algorithm. For the remainder of this section, we assume that we are ranking the word $\bar{w}$ that is the canonical representation of the binary unlabelled necklace $\tilde{\mathbf{w}}$. We first provide an overview of the main idea behind our ranking algorithm.

Theorem 1. *Let $RankAN(\bar{w}, m)$ be the rank of the word $\bar{w} \in \Sigma^n$ within the set of non-symmetric unlabelled necklaces of length n that do not enclose $\bar{w}$, let $RankSN(\bar{w}, m)$ be the rank of $\bar{w}$ within the set of symmetric necklaces of length m and let $RankEN(\bar{w}, m)$ be the rank of $\bar{w}$ within the set of necklaces of length m that enclose $\bar{w}$. The rank of any necklace $\tilde{\mathbf{w}}$ represented by the word $\bar{w}$ within the set of binary unlabelled necklaces of length m is given by $RankAN(\bar{w}, m) + RankSN(\bar{w}, m) + RankEN(\bar{w}, m)$. Further the rank can be found in $O(n^6 \log^2 n)$ time for any $m \leq n$.*

Proof. Observe that every unlabelled necklace must be one of the above classes. Therefore the rank of $\bar{w}$ within the set of all binary unlabelled necklaces of length m is given by $RankAN(\bar{w}, m) + RankSN(\bar{w}, m) + RankEN(\bar{w}, m)$. Lemma 1 shows that the rank of $\bar{w}$ within the set of non-symmetric unlabelled necklaces of length m that do not enclose $\bar{w}$ can be found in $O(n^6 \log^2(n))$ time. Theorem 2 shows that the rank of $\bar{w}$ within the set of symmetric necklaces can be found in $O(n^6 \log^2 n)$ time. Theorem 3 shows that the rank of $\bar{w}$ within the set of necklaces enclosing $\bar{w}$ can be found in $O(n^6 \log n)$ time.

Lemma 1. *Let $RankAN(\bar{w}, m)$ be the rank of $\bar{w}$ within the set of non-symmetric unlabelled necklaces of length m that do not enclose $\bar{w}$, and let $RankN(\bar{w}, m)$ be the rank of $\bar{w}$ within the set of all necklaces of length m. Then $RankAN(\bar{w}, m) = (RankN(\bar{w}, m) - RankSN(\bar{w}, m) - RankEN(\bar{w}, m))/2$. Further, this rank can be found in $O(n^6 \log^2 n)$ time for any $m \leq n$.*

Proof. Note that any asymmetric unlabelled necklace appears exactly twice in the set of necklaces smaller than $\bar{w}$. Further, any enclosing or symmetric necklace appears exactly once in the same set. Therefore $RankAN(\bar{w}, m) = \frac{RankN(\bar{w}, m) - RankSN(\bar{w}, m) - RankEN(\bar{w}, m)}{2}$. As the value of $RankN(\bar{w}, m)$ can be found in $O(n^2)$ time using the algorithm due to Sawada and Williams [11], the value of $RankSN(\bar{w}, m)$ found in $O(n^6 \log^2 n)$ time from Theorem 2, and the of $RankEN(\bar{w}, m)$ found in $O(n^6 \log n)$ time from Theorem 3, the total time complexity is $O(n^6 \log^2 n)$.

4 Symmetric Necklaces

In this section we show how to rank a word $\bar{w}$ within the set of symmetric necklaces of length m. Before presenting our computational tools, we first introduce the key theoretical results that form the basis for our ranking approach. The key observation is that any symmetric necklace $\tilde{\mathbf{v}}$ must have a period of length $2 \cdot r$ where r is the smallest rotation such that $\langle \tilde{\mathbf{v}} \rangle_r = S(\langle \tilde{\mathbf{v}} \rangle)$. This is formally proven in Proposition 2, and restated in Observation 1 in terms of Lyndon words.

Proposition 2. *A necklace* $\tilde{\mathbf{w}}$ *represented by the word* $\bar{w} \in \Sigma^n$ *is symmetric if and only if there exists some* $r \in [n]$ *s.t.* $\bar{w}_i = S(\bar{w}_{i+r \bmod n})$ *for every* $i \in [n]$. *Further, the period of* $\bar{w}$ *equals* $2 \cdot r$ *where* $r \in [n]$ *is the smallest rotation such that* $\langle \bar{w} \rangle_r = S(\bar{w})$.

Proof. As $\tilde{\mathbf{w}}$ is symmetric, $S(\bar{w})$ must belong to the necklace class $\tilde{\mathbf{w}}$. Therefore, there must be some rotation r such that $\langle \bar{w} \rangle_r = S(\bar{w})$. We now claim that $r \leq \frac{n}{2}$. Assume for the sake of contradiction that $r > \frac{n}{2}$. Then $\bar{w}_i = S(\bar{w}_{i+r \bmod n}) = \bar{w}_{i+2r \bmod n} = \ldots = \bar{w}_{i+2 \cdot k \cdot r \bmod n} = S(\bar{w}_{i+(2 \cdot k+1)r \bmod n})$. As $r > \frac{n}{2}$ this sequence must imply that either $\bar{w}_i = S(\bar{w}_i)$, an obvious contradiction, or that there exists some smaller value $p = GCD(n, r) \leq \frac{n}{2}$ such that $\bar{w}_i = S(\bar{w}_{i+p \bmod n})$. Further, $\bar{w}$ must have a period of at most $2 \cdot r$.

Assume now that r is the smallest rotation such that $\langle \bar{w} \rangle_r = S(\bar{w})$ and for the sake of contradiction further assume that the period of $\bar{w}$ is $p < r$. Then, as $\bar{w}_i = \bar{w}_{i+p \bmod n}$ for every $i \in [n]$, $\bar{w}_{i+r \bmod n} = \bar{w}_{i+r-p \bmod n}$, hence $\bar{w}_i = S(\bar{w}_{i+r-p \bmod n})$, contradicting the initial assumption. The period can not be equal to the value of r as by definition $\bar{w}_i = S(\bar{w}_{i+r \bmod n})$. Assume now that the period p of $\bar{w}$ is between r and $2 \cdot r$. As $\bar{w}_i = \bar{w}_{i+c \cdot p+2k \cdot r \bmod n}$ for every $c, k \in \mathbb{N}$ and $i \in [n]$. Further both r and p must be less than $\frac{n}{2}$. Therefore $\bar{w}_i = \bar{w}_{i+((n/p)-1)p+2 \cdot r \bmod n} = i + 2 \cdot r - p \bmod n$ and hence $\bar{w}$ is periodic in $2 \cdot r - p$. As $p > r, 2 \cdot r - p < r$, however as no such period can exist, this leads to a contradiction. Therefore, $2 \cdot r$ is the smallest period of $\bar{w}$. ∎

Lemma 2. *Let* $\mathbf{RA}(\bar{w}, m, S, r)$ *contain the set of words belonging to an symmetric necklace smaller than* $\bar{w}$ *such that* $\bar{v}_i = S(\bar{v}_{i+r \bmod m})$ *for every* $\bar{v} \in \mathbf{RA}(\bar{w}, m, S, r)$. *Further let* $\mathbf{RB}(\bar{w}, m, S, r) \subseteq \mathbf{RA}(\bar{w}, m, S, r)$ *contain the set of words belonging to an symmetric Lyndon word smaller than* $\bar{w}$ *such that* r *is the smallest value for which* $\bar{v}_i = S(\bar{v}_{i+r \bmod m})$ *for every* $\bar{v} \in \mathbf{RB}(\bar{w}, m, S, r)$. *The size of* $\mathbf{RB}(\bar{w}, m, S, r)$ *is given by:*

$$|\mathbf{RB}(\bar{w}, m, S, r)| = \sum_{p|r} \mu\left(\frac{m}{p}\right) |\mathbf{RA}(\bar{w}, m, S, p)|$$

Proof. Observe that every word in $\mathbf{RA}(\bar{w}, m, S, r)$ must have a unique period which is a factor of $2 \cdot r$. Therefore, the size of $\mathbf{RA}(\bar{w}, m, S, r)$ can be expressed as $\sum_{d|r} |\mathbf{RB}(\bar{w}, m, S, r)|$. Applying the Möbius inversion formula to this equation gives $|\mathbf{RB}(\bar{w}, m, S, r)| = \sum_{p|r} \mu\left(\frac{m}{p}\right) |\mathbf{RA}(\bar{w}, m, S, p)|$. ∎

Observation 1. *Observe that any symmetric Lyndon word* $\tilde{\mathbf{v}}$ *must have length* $2 \cdot r$, *where* r *is the smallest rotation such that* $\langle \bar{v} \rangle_r = S(\langle \bar{v} \rangle)$.

Lemma 3. *Let* $RankSL(\bar{w}, 2 \cdot r)$ *be the rank of* $\bar{w}$ *within the set of symmetric Lyndon words of length* $2 \cdot r$. *The value of* $RankSL(\bar{w}, r)$ *is given by* $\frac{|\mathbf{RB}(\bar{w}, 2 \cdot r, S, r)|}{2 \cdot r}$.

Proof. Observe that any symmetric Lyndon word has exactly $2 \cdot r$ unique translations. Further, as any word in $\mathbf{RB}(\bar{w}, 2 \cdot r, S, r)$ must correspond to an aperiodic word, following Observation 1, the size of $\mathbf{RB}(\bar{w}, 2 \cdot r, S, r)$ can be used to find $RankSL(\bar{w}, 2r)$ by dividing the cardinality of $\mathbf{RB}(\bar{w}, 2 \cdot r, S, r)$ by $2 \cdot r$.

Lemma 4. *Let $RankSN(\bar{w}, m, r)$ be the rank of $\bar{w}$ within the set of symmetric necklaces of length m such that for each such necklace $\tilde{\mathbf{v}}$, r is the smallest rotation such that $\langle \tilde{\mathbf{v}} \rangle_r = S(\langle \tilde{\mathbf{v}} \rangle)$. The value of $RankSN(\bar{w}, m, r)$ is given by $\sum_{d|2r} RankSL(\bar{w}, d)$.*

Proof. Following the same arguments as in Lemma 2, observe that every necklace counted by $RankSN(\bar{w}, m, r)$ must have a period that is a factor of $2 \cdot r$. Therefore, the value of $RankSN(\bar{w}, m, r)$ is given by $\sum_{d|2r} RankSL(\bar{w}, d)$.

Lemma 5. *Let $RankSN(\bar{w}, m)$ be the rank of $\bar{w}$ within the set of symmetric necklaces of length m and let $RankSN(\bar{w}, m, r)$ be the rank of $\bar{w}$ within the set of symmetric necklaces of length m such that for each such necklace $\tilde{\mathbf{v}}$, r is the smallest rotation such that $\langle \tilde{\mathbf{v}} \rangle_r = S(\langle \tilde{\mathbf{v}} \rangle)$. The value of $RankSN(\bar{w}, m)$ is given by $\sum_{r|(m/2)} RankSN(\bar{w}, m, r)$.*

Proof. Observe that every necklace counted by $RankSN(\bar{w}, m)$ must have a unique translation that is the minimal translation under which it is symmetric. Further this translation must be a factor of $\frac{m}{2}$. Therefore $RankSN(\bar{w}, m) = \sum_{r|(m/2)} RankSN(\bar{w}, m, r)$.

Following Lemmas 2, 3, 4, and 5 the main challenge in computing $RankSN(\bar{w}, m)$ is computing the size of $\mathbf{RA}(\bar{w}, m, S, r)$. In order to do so, $\mathbf{RA}(\bar{w}, m, S, r)$ is partitioned into two sets, $\alpha(\bar{w}, r, j)$ and $\beta(\bar{w}, r, j)$ where $j \in [r]$. Let $\bar{v}$ be some arbitrary word in the set $\mathbf{RA}(\bar{w}, m, S, r)$. The set $\alpha(\bar{w}, r, j)$ contains the word $\bar{v}$ if j is the smallest rotation under which $\langle \bar{v} \rangle_j \leq \bar{w}$. The set $\beta(\bar{w}, r, j)$ contains $\bar{v}$ if j is the smallest rotation under which $\langle \bar{v} \rangle_j \leq \bar{w}$ and $\langle \bar{v} \rangle_t > \bar{w}$ for every $t \in [r+1, 2 \cdot r]$. Note that by this definition, $\beta(\bar{w}, r, j) \subseteq \alpha(\bar{w}, r, j)$.

Observation 2. *Given any word $\bar{v} \in \mathbf{RA}(\bar{w}, m, S, r)$ such that $\bar{v} \notin \alpha(\bar{w}, r, j)$ for any $j \in [r]$, there exists some $j' \in [r]$ for which $\langle \bar{v} \rangle_r \in \beta(\bar{w}, r, j')$.*

Proof. As $\bar{v} \in \mathbf{RA}(\bar{w}, m, S, r)$, there must be some rotation t such that $\langle \bar{v} \rangle_t < \bar{w}$. As $\bar{v} \notin \alpha(\bar{w}, r, j)$, t must be greater than r. Therefore, $\langle \bar{v} \rangle_r$ must belong to $\beta(\bar{w}, r, t - r)$ confirming the observation.

Observation 3. *For any $\bar{v} \in \beta(\bar{w}, r, j)$, $\langle \bar{v} \rangle_r \notin \alpha(\bar{w}, r, j')$ for any $j' \in [r]$.*

Proof. As $\bar{v} \in \beta(\bar{w}, r, j)$, for any rotation $t > r, \langle \bar{v} \rangle_t > \bar{w}$. Therefore $\langle \bar{v} \rangle_t \notin \alpha(\bar{w}, r, j')$ for any $j' \in [r]$.

Combining Observations 2 and 3, the size of $\mathbf{RA}(\bar{w}, m, S, r)$ can be given in terms of the sets $\alpha(\bar{w}, r, j)$ and $\beta(\bar{w}, r, j)$ as $\sum_{j \in [r]} |\alpha(\bar{w}, r, j)| + |\beta(\bar{w}, r, j)|$. The remainder of this section is laid out as follows. We first provide a high level overview of how to compute the size of $\alpha(\bar{w}, r, j)$. Then we provide a high level overview on computing the size of $\beta(\bar{w}, r, j)$. Finally, we state Theorem 2, summarising the main contribution of this section and showing that $RankSN(\bar{w}, m)$ can be computed in at most $O(n^6 \log^2 n)$ time.

Computing the size of $\alpha(\bar{w}, r, j)$. We begin with a formal definition of $\alpha(\bar{w}, r, j)$. Let $\alpha(\bar{w}, r, j) \subseteq \mathbf{RA}(\bar{w}, m, S, r)$ be the subset of words in $\mathbf{RA}(\bar{w}, m, S, r)$ such that for every word $\bar{v} \in \alpha(\bar{w}, r, j)$, j is the smallest rotation for which $\langle \bar{v} \rangle_j \leq \bar{w}$. Note that if j is the smallest rotation such that $\langle \bar{v} \rangle_j \leq \bar{w}$, the first j symbols of $\bar{v}$ must be such that for every $j' \in [j-1], \bar{v}_{[j', 2r]} > \bar{w}$. Let $\mathbf{A}(\bar{w}, p, \bar{B}, i, j, r) \subseteq \alpha(\bar{w}, r, j)$ be the set of words of length $2 \cdot r$ such that every word $\bar{v} \in \mathbf{A}(\bar{w}, p, \bar{B}, i, j, r)$:

1. $\langle \bar{v} \rangle_s > \bar{w}$ for every $s \in [j-1]$.
2. $\langle \bar{v} \rangle_j < \bar{w}$.
3. $\bar{v}_{[1,r]} = S(\bar{v}_{[r+1, 2 \cdot r]})$.
4. The subword $\bar{v}_{[r+1, r+i]}$ is strictly bound by $\bar{B} \sqsubseteq_i \bar{w}$.
5. The subword $\bar{v}_{[i-p, i]} = \bar{w}_{[1,p]}$.

Rather than computing the size of $\mathbf{A}(\bar{w}, p, \bar{B}, i, j, r)$ directly, we are instead interested in the number of unique suffixes of length $r - i$ of the words in $\mathbf{A}(\bar{w}, p, \bar{B}, i, j, r)$. Note that as every word in $\mathbf{A}(\bar{w}, p, \bar{B}, i, j, r)$ belongs to a symmetric necklace, the number of possible suffixes on length $r - i$ of words in $\mathbf{A}(\bar{w}, p, \bar{B}, i, j, r)$ equals the number of unique subwords of words in $\mathbf{A}(\bar{w}, p, \bar{B}, i, j, r)$ between position $i + 1$ and r. Let $SA(\bar{w}, p, \bar{B}, i, j, r)$ be a function returning the number of unique suffixes of length $r - i$ of the words within $\mathbf{A}(\bar{w}, p, \bar{B}, i, j, r)$. The value of $SA(\bar{w}, p, \bar{B}, i, j, r)$ is computed in a dynamic manner relaying on a key structural proposition regarding $\mathbf{A}(\mathbf{A}(\bar{w}, p, \bar{B}, i, j, r))$.

Proposition 3. *Given $\bar{v} \in \mathbf{A}(\bar{w}, p, \bar{B}, i, j, r)$, such that $\bar{v}_{[i-s, i+1]} \geq \bar{w}_{[1,s]}$ for every $s \in [i]$, $\bar{v}$ also belongs to $\mathbf{A}(\bar{w}, p', WX[\bar{B}, \bar{v}_{i+1}], i+1, j, r)$ where $p' = p + 1$ if $\bar{v}_{i+1} = \bar{w}_{p+1}$ and 0 otherwise.*

Proof. By definition, if $\bar{v} \in \mathbf{A}(\bar{w}, p, \bar{B}, i, j, r)$ then there must exists some $p' \in [i+1]$, and $\bar{B} \sqsubseteq_i \bar{w}$ such that $\bar{v} \in \mathbf{A}(\bar{w}, p', \bar{B}', i, j, r)$. From Proposition 1, the value of $\bar{B}' = WX[\bar{B}, S(\bar{v}_{i+1})]$. Further $\bar{v}_{i+1} \geq \bar{w}_{p+1}$ as otherwise $\bar{v}_{[i-p, i+1]} < \bar{w}_{[1,p+1]}$, contradicting the original assumption. If $\bar{v}_{i+1} = \bar{w}_{p+1}$ then $p' = p + 1$ by definition. Otherwise $p' = 0$ as $\bar{v}_{[i-s, i+1]} > \bar{w}_{[1,s+1]}$.

Corollary 1. *Let $\bar{v}, \bar{u} \in \mathbf{A}(\bar{w}, p, \bar{B}, i, j, r)$ be a pair of words and let $\bar{v}' = \bar{u}_{[1,i]} : \bar{v}_{[i+1,r]} : S(\bar{v}_{[1,i]} : \bar{u}_{[i+1,r]})$. Then $\bar{v}' \in \mathbf{A}(\bar{w}, p', WX[\bar{B}, \bar{v}_{i+1}], i+1, j, r)$ if and only if $\bar{v} \in \mathbf{A}(\bar{w}, p', WX[\bar{B}, \bar{v}_{i+1}], i+1, j, r)$.*

Proposition 3 and Corollary 1 provide the basis for computing the value of $SA(\bar{w}, p, \bar{B}, i, j, r)$. This is done by considering 4 cases based on the value of i relative to the values of j and r which we will sketch bellow. The key observation behind this partition is that the value of the symbol at position $i+1$ is restricted differently depending on the values of i, j, r and p.

If $i < j$, then $\bar{v}_{i+1}$ must be greater than or equal to $\bar{w}_{p+1}$ for every $v \in \mathbf{A}(\bar{w}, p, \bar{B}, i, j, r)$, to avoid a contradiction caused by there being a rotation smaller than j for which $\bar{v}$ is smaller than $\bar{w}$. This gives two cases. If $\bar{w}_p = 1$ then the only possible value of $\bar{v}_{i+1}$ is 1 and therefore the value of $SA(\bar{w}, p, \bar{B}, i, j, r)$ is equal to the value $SA(\bar{w}, p+1, WX[\bar{B}, 0], i+1, j, r)$. Alternatively, if $\bar{w}_{p+1} = 0$, then $\bar{v}_{i+1}$ can be either 0 or 1. The number of suffixes of length $r-i$ of words in $\mathbf{A}(\bar{w}, p, \bar{B}, i, j, r)$ where the symbol at position $i+1$ is 0 equals the value of $SA(\bar{w}, p+1, WX[\bar{B}, 1], i+1, j, r)$. The number of suffixes of length $r-i$ of words in $\mathbf{A}(\bar{w}, p, \bar{B}, i, j, r)$ where the symbol at position $i+1$ is 1 equals the value of $SA(\bar{w}, 0, WX[\bar{B}, 0], i+1, j, r)$. Therefore, if $i < j$ and $\bar{w}_{p+1} = 0$, the value of $SA(\bar{w}, p, \bar{B}, i, j, r)$ is $SA(\bar{w}, p+1, WX[\bar{B}, 1], i+1, j, r) + SA(\bar{w}, 0, WX[\bar{B}, 0], i+1, j, r)$.

If $i = j$ then the value of $\bar{v}_{i+1}$ depends on the value of p for every $\bar{v} \in \mathbf{A}(\bar{w}, p, \bar{B}, i, j, r)$. In order for j to be the smallest rotation for which $\bar{v}$ is smaller than $\bar{w}$, the value of p must be 0, as otherwise the rotation by $j - p$ would be a smaller rotation for which $\bar{v}$ is smaller than $\bar{w}$. Hence, if $p > 0$, $\mathbf{A}(\bar{w}, p, \bar{B}, i, j, r) = \emptyset$ and by extension $SA(\bar{w}, p, \bar{B}, i, j, r) = 0$. If $p = 0$ and $i = j$, then the value of $\bar{v}_{i+1}$ must be 0, as otherwise the rotation by r leads to a word that is greater than $\bar{w}$. Therefore, when $p = 0$ and $i = r$, the value of $SA(\bar{w}, p, \bar{B}, i, j, r)$ is exactly equal to the value $SA(\bar{w}, 1, WX[\bar{B}, 1], i+1, j, r)$ of length $r-i-1$.

If $j < i < r$ and $p < i - j$, then the rotation of $\bar{v} \in \mathbf{A}(\bar{w}, p, \bar{B}, i, j, r)$ by j leads to a word smaller than $\bar{w}$ regardless of the value of $\bar{v}_{i+1}$, and hence $SA(\bar{w}, p, \bar{B}, i, j, r) = 2^{r-i}$, corresponding to the set of all possible words of length $i - r$ over the binary alphabet. If $j < i < r$ and $p = i - j$, then the symbol at position $i+1$ must be less than or equal to $\bar{w}_{p+1}$, therefore the value of $SA(\bar{w}, p, \bar{B}, i, j, r)$ of length $r - i$ is determined by the value of $\bar{w}_{p+1}$. If $\bar{w}_{p+1} = 0$ then the value of $\bar{v}_{i+1}$ must be 0 to avoid a contradiction, and hence the value of $SA(\bar{w}, p, \bar{B}, i, j, r)$ equals the value of $SA(\bar{w}, p+1, WX[\bar{B}, 1], i+1, j, r)$. Otherwise, if $\bar{w}_{p+1} = 1$ then the value of $\bar{v}_{i+1}$ can be either 0 or 1. Any word in $\mathbf{A}(\bar{w}, p, \bar{B}, i, j, r)$ where the symbol at position $i+1$ is 0 will be smaller than $\bar{w}$ after being rotated by j regardless of the value of the symbols at position $i+2$ to r. Therefore, the number of suffixes of length $r - i$ of words in $\mathbf{A}(\bar{w}, p, \bar{B}, i, j, r)$ where the symbol at position $i+1$ is 0 is 2^{r-i-2}. Further, the number of suffixes of length $r - i$ of words in $\mathbf{A}(\bar{w}, p, \bar{B}, i, j, r)$ where the symbol at position $i+1$ is 1 is equal to the value of $SA(\bar{w}, p+1, WX[\bar{B}, 0], i+1, j, r)$.

Finally, if $i = r$ then the number of unique zero length suffixes of words in $\mathbf{A}(\bar{w}, p, \bar{B}, i, j, r)$ is determined by the value of p and $\bar{B}$. If $p < i - j$, then for every $\bar{v} \in \mathbf{A}(\bar{w}, p, \bar{B}, i, j, r)$, the rotation of $\bar{v}$ by j is less than $\bar{w}$ regardless of the value of $\bar{B}$. Therefore the number of possible suffixes of length 0 of words in $\mathbf{A}(\bar{w}, p, \bar{B}, i, j, r)$ is 1, representing the empty word. On the other hand, if

$p = i - j$, then the number of possible suffixes of length 0 can be determined by the value of $\bar{B}$. Note that the rotation of any word in $\mathbf{A}(\bar{w}, p, \bar{B}, i, j, r)$ by j is less than $\bar{w}$ if and only if $\bar{w}_{[1,p]} : \bar{B} < \bar{w}_{[1,p+r]}$. Therefore the value of $SA(\bar{w}, p, \bar{B}, i, j, r)$ is either 1, if $\bar{w}_{[1,p]} : \bar{B} < \bar{w}_{[1,p+r]}$, or 0 otherwise.

Lemma 6. *The value of $SA(\bar{w}, p, \bar{B}, i, j, r)$ can be computed in $O(n^3)$ time.*

Proof (Sketch). Following the outline given above, the value of $SA(\bar{w}, p, \bar{B}, i, j, r)$ is computed in a dynamic manner, starting with $i = r$ as a base case, and progressing in descending value of i. For each value of i, the value of $SA(\bar{w}, p, \bar{B}, i, j, r)$ is computed for every $\bar{B} \sqsubseteq_i \bar{w}$, and $p \in [1, i]$ if $i \leq j$, or $p = i - j$ if $i > j$. For $i = r$, the value of $SA(\bar{w}, i - j, \bar{B}, i, j, r)$ can be computed in $O(n)$ time for every $\bar{B} \sqsubseteq_i \bar{w}$. For $i < r$ the value of $SA(\bar{w}, p, \bar{B}, i, j, r)$ can be computed in $O(1)$ time provided the value of $SA(\bar{w}, p', \bar{B}', i+1, j, r)$ has been precomputed for every $p' \in \{p+1, 0\}$ and $\bar{B}' \sqsubseteq_{i+1} \bar{w}$. As there are only n values of $\bar{B} \sqsubseteq_r \bar{w}$ to consider in the base case, and at most $O(n^3)$ total possible value of $i, p \in [r], \bar{B} \sqsubseteq_i \bar{w}$, the total complexity of this process is $O(n^3)$.

Lemma 7. *The size of $\alpha(\bar{w}, j, r)$ can be computed in $O(n^4)$ time.*

Proof. From Lemma 6, the value of $SA(\bar{w}, p, \bar{B}, i, j, r)$ can be computed in $O(n^3)$ time for any value of $i, p \in [n]$ and $\bar{B} \sqsubseteq_i \bar{w}$. Note that $SA(\bar{w}, 0, \emptyset, 0, j, r)$ allows us to count the number of words $\bar{v} \in \alpha(\bar{w}, j, r)$ where $\bar{v}_{[r+1,r+i]} \not\sqsubseteq \bar{w}$ for every $i \in [r]$, or equivalently, where $S(\bar{v}_{[1,i]}) \not\sqsubseteq \bar{w}$. To compute the remaining words, let $\bar{u} \sqsubseteq_{i-1} \bar{w}$ and let $x \in \{0, 1\}$ be a symbol such that $\bar{u} : x \not\sqsubseteq \bar{w}$. Further let $\bar{B} \sqsubseteq_i \bar{w}$ be the subword of $\bar{w}$ strictly bounding $\bar{u} : x$ and let p be the length of the longest suffix of $S(\bar{u} : x)$ that is a prefix of $\bar{w}$, i.e. the largest value such that $S(\bar{u} : x)_{[i-p:i]} = \bar{w}_{[1,p]}$. Observe that $S(\bar{u} : x)_{[1,p]}$ is the prefix of some word $\bar{v} \in \alpha(\bar{w}, j, r)$ if and only if one of the following holds:

- if $i < r$ then $(\bar{u} : x)_{[i-s,i]} > \bar{w}_{[1,s]}$ for every $s \in [p+1, i]$.
- if $i = r$ then $p = 0$.
- if $i > r$ then $p = i - r$.

As each condition can be checked in at most $O(n)$ time, and there are at most $O(n^2)$ subwords of $\bar{w}$, it is possible to check for every such subword if it is a prefix of some word in $\mathbf{A}(\bar{w}, p, \bar{B}, i, j, r)$ in $O(n^3)$ time. Following Corollary 1, the number of suffixes of each word in $\mathbf{A}(\bar{w}, p, \bar{B}, i, j, r)$ is equal to the value of $SA(\bar{w}, p, \bar{B}, i, j, r)$. By precomputing $SA(\bar{w}, p, \bar{B}, i, j, r)$, the number of words in $\alpha(\bar{w}, j, r)$ with $\bar{u} : x$ as a prefix can be computed in $O(1)$ time. Therefore the total complexity of computing the size of $\alpha(\bar{w}, j, r)$ is $O(n^3)$.

Computing the Size of $\beta(\bar{w}, r, j)$. We start by subdividing $\beta(\bar{w}, r, j)$ into the subsets $\mathbf{B}(\bar{w}, p_f, p_b, \bar{B}_f, \bar{B}_b, i, j, r)$. Let $\mathbf{B}(\bar{w}, p_f, p_b, \bar{B}_f, \bar{B}_b, i, j, r) \subseteq \beta(\bar{w}, r, j)$ be the subset of $\beta(\bar{w}, r, j)$ containing every word $\bar{v} \in \beta(\bar{w}, r, j)$ where $\bar{v}$ satisfies:

1. $\bar{v}_{[1,r]} = S(\bar{v}_{[r+1,2 \cdot r]})$.
2. The first i symbols of $\bar{v}$ are strictly bound by $\bar{B}_f \sqsubseteq_i \bar{w}$ ($\bar{B}_f$ standing for bounding the front).

3. The subword $\bar{v}_{[r+1,r+i]}$ is strictly bound by $\bar{B}_b \sqsubseteq_i \bar{w}$ ($\bar{B}_b$ standing for bounding the back).
4. The subword $\bar{v}_{[i-p_f,i]} = \bar{w}_{[p_f]}$ (p_f standing for the front prefix).
5. the subword $\bar{v}_{[r+i-p_b,r+i]} = \bar{w}_{[p_b]}$ (p_b standing for the back prefix).

Proposition 4. *Given $\bar{v} \in \mathbf{B}(\bar{w}, p_f, p_b, \bar{B}_f, \bar{B}_b, i, j, r)$, where $\bar{v}_{[i-s,i+1]} \geq \bar{w}_{[1,s]}$ for every $s \in [i]$, $\bar{v}$ also belongs to $\mathbf{B}(\bar{w}, p'_f, p'_b, XW[\bar{B}_f, \bar{v}_{i+1}], XW[\bar{B}_b, S(\bar{v}_{i+1})], i, j, r)$ where $p'_f = p_f + 1$ if $\bar{v}_{i+1} = w_{p_f+1}$ or 0 otherwise, and $p'_b = p_b + 1$ if $S(\bar{v}_{i+1}) = \bar{w}_{p_b+1}$, and 0 otherwise.*

Proof. Following the same arguments as Proposition 3, observe that $\bar{v}_{[1,i+1]}$ is bound by $XW[\bar{B}_f, \bar{v}_{i+1}]$ and $S(\bar{v}_{[1,i+1]})$ is bound by $XW[\bar{B}_b, S(\bar{v}_{i+1})]$. Similarly, the value of p'_f is $p_f + 1$ if and only if $\bar{v}_{i+1} = \bar{w}_{p_f+1}$, and must be 0 otherwise. Further the value of p'_b is $p_b + 1$ if and only if $S(\bar{v}_{i+1}) = \bar{w}_{p_b+1}$, and 0 otherwise.

Corollary 2. *Let $\bar{v}, \bar{u} \in \mathbf{B}(\bar{w}, p_f, p_b, \bar{B}_f, \bar{B}_b, i, j, r)$ be a pair of words and let $\bar{v}' = \bar{u}_{[1,i]} : \bar{v}_{[i+1,r]} : S(\bar{v}_{[1,i]} : \bar{u}_{[i+1,r]})$. Then $\bar{v}' \in \mathbf{B}(\bar{w}, p'_f, p'_b, \bar{B}_f{}', \bar{B}_b{}', i, j, r)$ if and only if $\bar{v} \in \mathbf{B}(\bar{w}, p'_f, p'_b, \bar{B}_f{}', \bar{B}_b{}', i, j, r)$.*

Proposition 4 and Corollary 2 are used in an analogous manner the Proposition 3. As before, the goal is not to directly compute the size of $\mathbf{B}(\bar{w}, p_f, p_b, \bar{B}_f, \bar{B}_b, i, j, r)$, but rather to compute the number of suffixes of length $r-i$ of the words therein. To that end, let $SB(\bar{w}, p_f, p_b, \bar{B}_f, \bar{B}_b, i, j, r)$ be the number of unique suffixes of length $r - i$ of words in $\mathbf{B}(\bar{w}, p_f, p_b, \bar{B}_f, \bar{B}_b, i, j, r)$. Note that the number of suffixes of length $r - i$ of words in $\mathbf{B}(\bar{w}, p_f, p_b, \bar{B}_f, \bar{B}_b, i, j, r)$ equals the number of unique subwords between positions $i + 1$ and r of the words $\mathbf{B}(\bar{w}, p_f, p_b, \bar{B}_f, \bar{B}_b, i, j, r)$. Additionally, note that following Corollary 2, the size of $\mathbf{B}(\bar{w}, p_f, p_b, \bar{B}_f, \bar{B}_b, i, j, r)$ can be computed by taking the product of the number of unique prefixes of words in $\mathbf{B}(\bar{w}, p_f, p_b, \bar{B}_f, \bar{B}_b, i, j, r)$, and the number of unique suffixes of words in $\mathbf{B}(\bar{w}, p_f, p_b, \bar{B}_f, \bar{B}_b, i, j, r)$. The process of computing the number of such suffixes is divided into four cases based on the values of i, j and r.

When $i < j$, for every word $\bar{v} \in \mathbf{B}(\bar{w}, p_f, p_b, \bar{B}_f, \bar{B}_b, i, j, r)$, v_{i+1} must be greater than or equal to $\bar{w}_{p_f+1}$ to avoid there being a rotation less than j for which $\bar{v}$ is less than $\bar{w}$. Further, the value of the relabelling of $\bar{v}_{i+1}$ must be greater than or equal to $\bar{w}_{p_b+1}$ to avoid any rotation in $[r + 1, 2 \cdot r]$ being less than $\bar{w}$. Therefore, the symbol at position $i + 1$ can be 0 if and only if $\bar{w}_{p_f+1} = 0$, and can be 1 if and only if $\bar{w}_{p_b+1} = 0$. The number of suffixes of length $r - i$ of words in $\mathbf{B}(\bar{w}, p_f, p_b, \bar{B}_f, \bar{B}_b, i, j, r)$ where the symbol at position $i + 1$ is 0 is equal to the value of $SB(\bar{w}, p'_f, p'_b, XW[\bar{B}_f, 0], XW[\bar{B}_b, 1], i, j, r)$, and the number of suffixes where the symbol at position $i + 1$ is 1 is equal to the value of $SB(\bar{w}, p'_f, p'_b, XW[\bar{B}_f, 1], XW[\bar{B}_b, 0], i, j, r)$.

When $i = j$, then the value of $SB(\bar{w}, p_f, p_b, \bar{B}_f, \bar{B}_b, i, j, r)$ depends primarily on the value of p_f. If $p_f > 0$, then as $\langle v \rangle_j < \bar{w}$ for every $v \in \mathbf{B}(\bar{w}, p_f, p_b, \bar{B}_f, \bar{B}_b, i, j, r)$, $\langle v \rangle_{j-p_f} < \bar{w}$, contradicting the assumption that j is the smallest rotation for which $\bar{v}$ is smaller than $\bar{w}$. Hence, if $p_f > 0$, then the set $\mathbf{B}(\bar{w}, p_f, p_b, \bar{B_f}, \bar{B_b}, i, j, r)$ must be empty and by extension have no suffixes of length $r-i$. If $p_f = 0$ then as $\bar{w}_1 = 0$, the symbol $\bar{v}_{i+1}$ must be 0 for every $\bar{v} \in \mathbf{B}(\bar{w}, p_f, p_b, \bar{B_f}, \bar{B_b}, i, j, r)$. Therefore, the value of $SB(\bar{w}, p_f, p_b, \bar{B_f}, \bar{B_b}, i, j, r)$ is exactly equal to the value of $SB(\bar{w}, 1, p_b',, XW[\bar{B_f}, 0], WX[\bar{B_b}, 1], i+1, j, r)$ of length $r-i-1$.

To count the number of suffixes of length $r-i$ when $i > j$, an auxiliary, technical set $\mathbf{Y}(\bar{w}, i, p_b, \bar{B_f})$ is introduced. Informally, $\mathbf{Y}(\bar{w}, i, p_b, \bar{B_f})$ contains the set of words of length i such that every pair of words $\bar{u} \in \mathbf{Y}(\bar{w}, r-i, p_b, \bar{B_f})$ and $\bar{v} \in \mathbf{B}(\bar{w}, p_f, p_b, \bar{B_f}, \bar{B_b}, r-i, j, r)$, every suffix of the word $S(\bar{v}_{[1,r-i]} : u) : \bar{B_f}$ of length at least r is greater than the prefix of $\bar{w}$ of the same length. In other words, $\mathbf{Y}(\bar{w}, i, p_b, \bar{B_f})$ contains the set of words that can be appended to prefixes of $\mathbf{B}(\bar{w}, p_f, p_b, \bar{B_f}, \bar{B_b}, r-i, j, r)$ while maintaining the condition that any rotation by more than r results in a word strictly greater than $\bar{w}$. Treating the method of counting $\mathbf{Y}(\bar{w}, i, p_b, \bar{B_f})$ as a black box, the number of suffixes of length $i-r$ in $\mathbf{B}(\bar{w}, p_f, p_b, \bar{B_f}, \bar{B_b}, i, j, r)$ when $p_f < i-j$ is exactly the size of $\mathbf{Y}(\bar{w}, i, p_b, \bar{B_f})$. If $p_f = i-j$, then the observe that every word $\bar{v} \in \mathbf{B}(\bar{w}, p_f, p_b, \bar{B_f}, \bar{B_b}, i, j, r)$ must satisfy the conditions that $\bar{v}_{i+1} \leq \bar{w}_{p_f+1}$ and $S(\bar{v}_{i+1}) \geq \bar{w}_{p_b+1}$. If $\bar{w}_{p_f+1} = 1$ and $\bar{w}_{p_b+1} = 1$ then $\bar{v}_{i+1}$ must be 0, giving a total of $|\mathbf{Y}(\bar{w}, r-i-1, p_b+1, WX[\bar{B_f}, 0])|$ suffixes of length $r-i$. If $\bar{w}_{p_f+1} = 1$ and $\bar{w}_{p_b+1} = 0$ then there are $|\mathbf{Y}(\bar{w}, r-i-1, 0, WX[\bar{B_f}, 0])|$ suffixes of length $r-i$ where the first symbol is 0, and the number of $r-i$ length suffixes where the first symbol equals 1 is equal to the value of $SB(\bar{w}, p_f+1, p_b+1, WX[\bar{B_f}, 1], WX[\bar{B_b}, 0], i+1, j, r)$. If $\bar{w}_{p_f+1} = 0$ then $\bar{v}_{i+1}$ must be 0, and hence the value of $SB(\bar{w}, p_f, p_b, \bar{B_f}, \bar{B_b}, i, j, r)$ is $SB(\bar{w}, p_f+1, p_b', WX[\bar{B_f}, 0], WX[\bar{B_b}, 1], i+1, j, r)$.

When $i = r$, the number of zero length suffixes of $\mathbf{B}(\bar{w}, p_f, p_b, \bar{B_f}, \bar{B_b}, i, j, r)$ is either 0, if $\bar{w}_{[1,p_f]} : \bar{B_f} \geq \bar{w}_{[1,p_f+r]}$, or 1 otherwise.

Lemma 8. *The size of $\beta(\bar{w}, j, r)$ can be computed in $O(n^5)$ time.*

Proof (Sketch). The size of $\beta(\bar{w}, j, r)$ is computed in an analogous manner to the size of $\alpha(\bar{w}, j, t)$ as shown in Lemma 7. This is done by computing the size value of $SB(\bar{w}, p_f, p_b, \bar{B_f}, \bar{B_b}, i, j, r)$ using the layout given above.

The value of $SB(\bar{w}, p_f, p_b, \bar{B_f}, \bar{B_b}, i, j, r)$ can be computed in $O(n)$ time if $i = r$, and $O(1)$ time if $i < r$ and the size of $SB(\bar{w}, p_f', p_b', \bar{B_f}', \bar{B_b}', i+1, j, r)$ has been precomputed for every $p_f' \in \{0, p_f+1\}, p_b \in \{0, p_b+1\}$ and $\bar{B_b}', \bar{B_f}' \sqsubseteq_i \bar{w}$. As there are at most $O(n^4)$ possible values of $p_f, p_b \in [r]$ and $\bar{B_b}, \bar{B_f} \sqsubseteq_r \bar{w}$, the value of $SB(\bar{w}, p_f, p_b, \bar{B_f}, \bar{B_b}, r, j, r)$ can be computed for every $p_f, p_b \in [r]$ and $\bar{B_b}, \bar{B_f} \sqsubseteq_r \bar{w}$ in $O(n^5)$ time. Similarly, as there are at most $O(n^5)$ possible values of $i \in [r], p_f, p_b \in [i]$ and $\bar{B_b}, \bar{B_f} \sqsubseteq_i \bar{w}$, the value of $SB(\bar{w}, p_f, p_b, \bar{B_f}, \bar{B_b}, i, j, r)$ can be computed in $O(n^5)$ time for every value of $i \in [r], p_f, p_b \in [i]$ and $\bar{B_b}, \bar{B_f} \sqsubseteq_i \bar{w}$.

Note that the set $\mathbf{B}(\bar{w}, p_f, p_b, \bar{B_f}, \bar{B_b}, i, j, r)$ does not include the words in $\beta(\bar{w}, r, j)$ with a prefix that is a subword of $\bar{w}$. The number of such words can be computed in a brute force manner by finding the length of the longest prefix that is a subword of $\bar{w}$, and determining the number of possible suffixes. The number of such suffixes are counted in using $SB(\bar{w}, p_f, p_b, \bar{B_f}, \bar{B_b}, i, j, r)$ in a manner analogous to the way $SA(\bar{w}, p, i, j, r)$ is used in Lemma 7, to count the number of words in $\alpha(\bar{w}, j, r)$ with a prefix that is a subword of $\bar{w}$.

Theorem 2. *The value of $RankSN(\bar{w}, m)$ can be computed in $O(n^6 \log^2 n)$ time for any $m \leq n$.*

Proof. Following Lemmas 2, 3, and 4, the value of $RankSN(\bar{w}, m, r)$ is:

$$RankSN(\bar{w}, m, r) = \sum_{d|r} \left(\frac{1}{2 \cdot r} \sum_{p|d} \mu\left(\frac{d}{p}\right) |\mathbf{RA}(\bar{w}, m, S, p)| \right)$$

From Observations 3 and 2 , the size of $\mathbf{RA}(\bar{w}, m, S, r)$ equals $\sum_{j \in [m]} |\alpha(\bar{w}, r, j)| + |\beta(\bar{w}, r, j)|$. Following Lemma 7, the size of $\alpha(\bar{w}, r, j)$ can be computed in $O(n^3)$ time. Following Lemma 8, the size of $\beta(\bar{w}, r, j)$ can be computed in $O(n^5)$ time. As there are at most $O(n)$ values of j, the total time complexity for determining the size of $\mathbf{RA}(\bar{w}, m, S, r)$ is $O(n^6)$. As there are at most $O(\log n)$ possible divisors of r, the size of $\mathbf{RA}(\bar{w}, m, S, p)$ needs to be evaluated at most $O(\log n)$ times, giving a total time complexity of $O(n^6 \log n)$. The value of $RankSN(\bar{w}, m, r)$ can then be computed in at most $O(\log^2 n)$ time once the size of $\mathbf{RA}(\bar{w}, m, S, p)$ has been precomputed for every factor p of r. Finally, following Lemma 5, the value of $RankSN(\bar{w}, m)$ can be computed from the value of $RankSN(\bar{w}, m, r)$ for at most $O(\log n)$ values of r. Therefore the total time complexity of computing $RankSN(\bar{w}, m)$ is $O(n^6 \log^2 n)$.

5 Enclosing Necklaces

This section shows how to rank a word $\bar{w}$ within the set of binary unlabelled necklaces enclosing $\bar{w}$. Note that the rank of $\bar{w}$ within this set is equivalent to the number of binary unlabelled necklaces enclosing $\bar{w}$. As with the ranking approach to symmetric necklaces, we start with the key theoretical results that inform our approach.

Lemma 9. *Let $RankEN(\bar{w}, m)$ be the rank of $\bar{w}$ within the set of necklaces of length m that enclose $\bar{w}$ and let $RankEL(\bar{w}, m)$ be the rank of $\bar{w}$ within the set of Lyndon words of length m that enclose $\bar{w}$. $RankEN(\bar{w}, m) = \sum_{d|m} RankEL(\bar{w}, d)$.*

Proof. Observe that every necklace counted by $RankEN(\bar{w}, m)$ must have a unique period that is a factor of m, hence $RankEN(\bar{w}, m) = \sum_{d|m} RankEL(\bar{w}, d)$.

Lemma 10. *Let $\mathbf{EL}(\bar{w}, m)$ be the set of words of length m belonging to a Lyndon word that encloses $\bar{w}$. $RankEL(\bar{w}, m) = \frac{|\mathbf{EL}(\bar{w}, m))}{m}$.*

Proof. Following the same arguments as in Lemma 3, every aperiodic necklace counted by $RankEL(\bar{w}, m)$ must have exactly m words in $\mathbf{EL}(\bar{w}, m)$ representing it. Therefore $RankEL(\bar{w}, m) = \frac{|\mathbf{EL}(\bar{w}, m))}{m}$.

Lemma 11. *Let* $\mathbf{EL}(\bar{w}, m)$ *be the set of words of length* m *belonging to a Lyndon word that encloses* $\bar{w}$ *and let* $\mathbf{EN}(\bar{w}, m)$ *be the set of words of length* m *belonging to a necklace that encloses* $\bar{w}$*. The size of* $\mathbf{EL}(\bar{w}, m)$ *equals* $\sum_{d|m} \mu\left(\frac{m}{d}\right) |\mathbf{EN}(\bar{w}, d)|$.

Proof. Following the same arguments as in Lemma 9, the size of $\mathbf{EN}(\bar{w}, m)$ can be expressed in terms of the size of $\mathbf{EL}(\bar{w}, d)$ for every factor d of m as $|\mathbf{EN}(\bar{w}, m)| = \sum_{d|m} |\mathbf{EL}(\bar{w}, d)|$. Applying the Möbius inversion formula to this equation gives $|\mathbf{EL}(\bar{w}, m)| = \sum_{d|m} \mu\left(\frac{m}{d}\right) |\mathbf{EN}(\bar{w}, d)|$.

As in the Symmetric case, we partition the set of necklaces into a series of subsets for ease of computation. Let $\gamma(\bar{w}, m, r)$ denote the set of words belonging to a necklace which encloses $\bar{w}$ such that r is the smallest rotation for which $\bar{v} \in \gamma(\bar{w}, m, r)$ is smaller than $\bar{w}$, i.e. the smallest value where $\langle \bar{v} \rangle_r < \bar{w}$. We further introduce the set $\mathbf{C}(\bar{w}, i, r, \bar{B}_f, \bar{B}_b, p_f, p_b) \subseteq \gamma(\bar{w}, m, r)$ as the set of words where every $\bar{v} \in \mathbf{C}(\bar{w}, i, r, \bar{B}_f, \bar{B}_b, p_f, p_b)$ satisfies the following conditions:

1. $\langle \bar{v} \rangle_s > \bar{w}$ for every $s \in [r-1]$.
2. $\langle S(\bar{v}) \rangle_s > \bar{w}$ for every $s \in [m]$.
3. $\langle \bar{v} \rangle_r < \bar{w}$.
4. $\bar{v}_{[1,i]}$ is bound by $\bar{B}_f \sqsubseteq_i \bar{w}$.
5. $S(\bar{v}_{[1,i]})$ is bound by $\bar{B}_b \sqsubseteq_i \bar{w}$.
6. p_f is the length of the longest suffix of $\bar{v}_{[1,i]}$ that is a prefix of $\bar{w}$, i.e. the largest value such that $\bar{v}_{[i-p_f,i]} = \bar{w}_{[1,p_f]}$.
7. p_b is the length of the longest suffix of $S(\bar{v}_{[1,i]})$ that is a prefix $\bar{w}$, i.e. the largest value such that $S(\bar{v}_{[i-p_b,i]}) = \bar{w}_{[1,p_b]}$.

Note that Conditions 1, 2, and 3 are the necessary conditions for $\bar{v}$ to be in $\gamma(\bar{w}, m, r)$. As before, we break our dynamic programming based approach into several sub cases based on the value of i relative to r. As in the symmetric case, we relay upon a technical proposition.

Proposition 5. *Given* $\bar{v} \in \mathbf{C}(\bar{w}, i, r, \bar{B}_f, \bar{B}_b, p_f, p_b)$*,* $\bar{v}$ *also belongs to* $\mathbf{C}(\bar{w}, i+1, r, WX[\bar{B}_f, \bar{v}_{i+1}], WX[\bar{B}_b, \bar{v}_{i+1}], p'_f, p'_b)$

Corollary 3. *Given a pair of words* $\bar{v}, \bar{u} \in \mathbf{C}(\bar{w}, i, r, \bar{B}_f, \bar{B}_b, p_f, p_b)$ *let* $\bar{v}' = \bar{v}_{[1,i]} : \bar{u}_{[i+1,m]}$*. Then* $\bar{v}' \in \mathbf{C}(\bar{w}, i+1, r, \bar{B}_f{}', \bar{B}_b{}', p'_f, p'_b)$ *if and only if* $\bar{v} \in \mathbf{C}(\bar{w}, i+1, r, \bar{B}_f{}', \bar{B}_b{}', p'_f, p'_b)$.

Theorem 3. *Let* $RankEN(\bar{w}, m)$ *be the rank of* $\bar{w}$ *within the set of necklaces of length* m *which enclose* $\bar{w} \in \Sigma^n$*. The value of* $RankEN(\bar{w}, n)$ *can be computed in* $O(n^6 \log n)$ *time for any* $m \le n$.

Proof (Sketch). The high level idea is to compute the size of $\mathbf{C}(\bar{w}, i, r, \bar{B}_f, \bar{B}_b, p_f, p_b)$ in a dynamic manner analogous to the computation of the size of $\mathbf{A}(\bar{w}, p, \bar{B}, i, j, r)$. Starting with $i = m$ as the base case and progressing in descending value of i, the size of $\mathbf{C}(\bar{w}, i, r, \bar{B}_f, \bar{B}_b, p_f, p_b)$ is computed for every

$\bar{B}_f, \bar{B}_b \sqsubseteq_i \bar{w}, p_f, p_b \in [i]$. By showing that the size of $\mathbf{C}(\bar{w}, i, r, \bar{B}_f, \bar{B}_b, p_f, p_b)$ can be computed in $O(1)$ time for any $i < m$, and $O(n)$ time when $i = m$, the size of $\mathbf{C}(\bar{w}, i, r, \bar{B}_f, \bar{B}_b, p_f, p_b)$ for every $i, j \in [m], \bar{B}_f, \bar{B}_b \sqsubseteq_i \bar{w}$, and $p_f, p_b \in [i]$ is computed in $O(n^6)$ time. The additional complexity is due to number of lengths that need to be computed following Lemmas 9, 10 and 11.

References

1. Adamson, D., Deligkas, A., Gusev, V.V., Potapov, I.: Combinatorial algorithms for multidimensional necklaces. arXiv preprint https://arxiv.org/abs/2108.01990 (2021)
2. Adamson, D., Deligkas, A., Gusev, V.V., Potapov, I.: Ranking bracelets in polynomial time. In: 32nd Annual Symposium on Combinatorial Pattern Matching (CPM 2021). Leibniz International Proceedings in Informatics (LIPIcs), vol. 191, pp. 4:1–4:17 (2021)
3. De Felice, C., Zaccagnino, R., Zizza, R.: Unavoidable sets and circular splicing languages. Theor. Comput. Sci. **658**, 148–158 (2017). Formal languages and automata: models, methods and application. In: Honour of the 70th birthday of Antonio Restivo
4. Filos-Ratsikas, A., Goldberg, P.W.: The complexity of splitting necklaces and bisecting ham sandwiches. In: Charikar, M., Cohen, E. (eds.) Proceedings of the 51st Annual ACM SIGACT Symposium on Theory of Computing, STOC 2019, Phoenix, AZ, USA, 23–26 June 2019, pp. 638–649. ACM (2019)
5. Gilbert, E.N., Riordan, J.: Symmetry types of periodic sequences. Ill. J. Math. **5**(4), 657–665 (1961)
6. Graham, R.L., Knuth, D.E., Patashnik, O.: Concrete Mathematics: A Foundation for Computer Science. Addison-Wesley (1994)
7. Kociumaka, T., Radoszewski, J., Rytter, W.: Computing k-th Lyndon word and decoding lexicographically minimal de Bruijn sequence. In: Kulikov, A.S., Kuznetsov, S.O., Pevzner, P. (eds.) CPM 2014. LNCS, vol. 8486, pp. 202–211. Springer, Cham (2014). https://doi.org/10.1007/978-3-319-07566-2_21
8. Kopparty, S., Kumar, M., Saks, M.: Efficient indexing of necklaces and irreducible polynomials over finite fields. Theory Comput. **12**(1), 1–27 (2016)
9. Mareš, M., Straka, M.: Linear-time ranking of permutations. In: Arge, L., Hoffmann, M., Welzl, E. (eds.) ESA 2007. LNCS, vol. 4698, pp. 187–193. Springer, Heidelberg (2007). https://doi.org/10.1007/978-3-540-75520-3_18
10. Myrvold, W., Ruskey, F.: Ranking and unranking permutations in linear time. Inf. Process. Lett. **79**(6), 281–284 (2001)
11. Sawada, J., Williams, A.: Practical algorithms to rank necklaces, Lyndon words, and de Bruijn sequences. J. Discret. Algorithms **43**, 95–110 (2017)
12. Shimizu, T., Fukunaga, T., Nagamochi, H.: Unranking of small combinations from large sets. J. Discret. Algorithms **29**, 8–20 (2014)
13. Williamson, S.G.: Ranking algorithms for lists of partitions. SIAM J. Comput. **5**(4), 602–617 (1976)

On the Power of Recursive Word-Functions Without Concatenation

Jérôme Durand-Lose(✉)

Univ. Orléans, INSA Centre Val de Loire, LIFO, EA 4022, 45067 Orléans, France
jerome.durand-lose@univ-orleans.fr

Abstract. Primitive recursion can be defined on words instead of natural numbers. Up to usual encoding, primitive recursive functions coincide. Working with words allows to address words directly and not through some integer encoding (of exponential size). Considering alphabets with at least two symbols allows to relate simply and naturally to complexity theory. Indeed, the polynomial-time complexity class (as well as **NP** and exponential time) corresponds to delayed and dynamical evaluation with a polynomial bound on the size of the trace of the computation as a direct acyclic graph.

Primitive recursion in the absence of concatenation (or successor for numbers) is investigated. Since only suffixes of an input can be output, computation is very limited; e.g. pairing and unary encoding are impossible. Yet non-trivial relations and languages can be decided. Some algebraic ($\mathtt{a}^n\mathtt{b}^n$, palindromes) and non-algebraic ($\mathtt{a}^n\mathtt{b}^n\mathtt{c}^n$) languages are decidable. It is also possible to check arithmetical constrains like $\mathtt{a}^n\mathtt{b}^m\mathtt{c}^{P(n,m)}$ with P polynomial with positive coefficients in two (or more) variables. Every regular language is decidable if recursion can be defined on multiple functions at once.

Keywords: Primitive recursion · Recursion on words · String recursion · Word-Functions

1 Introduction

Primitive recursion and general recursion (or μ-recursion) are well-known and addressed in every textbook on computability. They are based on Peano's axiomatisation of natural numbers and form a neat definition of *computable* functions over numbers. They have been studied for a century and are the topic of innumerable articles. Nowadays, computability is not anymore considered to be just about numbers but to be about any kind of information that can be represented and manipulated through textual/symbolic representations. In recent decades, the term *recursive* has been shifting to be replaced by *computable* [10] to reflect the preeminence of the computer age and to stress on operational models rather than conceptual definitions.

The present paper advocates an alternative definition of primitive recursion grounded on sequences of symbols, i.e. words, instead of numbers. Although the

Published by Springer Nature Switzerland AG 2022
Y.-S. Han and G. Vaszil (Eds.): DCFS 2022, LNCS 13439, pp. 30–42, 2022.
https://doi.org/10.1007/978-3-031-13257-5_3

definition is natural with more than one *successor*, it has not been much studied. Or rather it has been proved that all the *main properties* coincide, so that there is little interest in a less refined design.

We feel otherwise for at least two epistemological reasons. The first one is that many articles addressing recursion on words first provide an encoding of words as numbers then work on numbers. It certainly proves that words can be represented as numbers and worked upon this way (at the cost of complexity). Shouldn't it be the other way round? Numbers are represented by words and all our basic arithmetical algorithms (e.g. multiplication) are taught for decimal representation and implemented with binary-based representations. The second reason is meeting colleagues not keen on proving by induction, and instead, they introduce some numerical measure (e.g. depth of a formula) and then make a (numerical) recursion. When dealing with words, we should use induction to manipulate them (and numbers and recursion when we need counting)[1].

There are also more practical reasons for word recursion: connections to complexity theory with a natural measure of evaluations and to language theory. The first point is to note that the time complexity naturally corresponds to the size of trace of the evaluations when nothing is reevaluated (dynamic programming) and evaluated only if needed (delayed evaluation).

The connection with language theory is developed in the paper by considering recursion without concatenation/successor (preventing encoding between numbers and words as well as pairing). It already exhibits the ability to decide some non-algebraic languages and do some arithmetic checking. In the rest of the introduction, we present a brief state of the art on recursion on words, then, the complexity connection, some results on language decision without concatenation, and finally, the outline of the paper.

In the literature, the topic is referred to as *recursion on string*, *recursion on word*, *recursive word/string-functions* or *recursion on representation*. The last denomination often means a representation of natural numbers by words enumerated in shortlex/military order (length then alphabetically) leading to a non-trivial successor word-function. The literature is rather ancient (for computer science) with a peak in the 1960's. Most of the literature deal with hierarchies and, like almost everything in the field in those days, is number-centric. We concentrate on overviews and more recent and accessible papers (and in English).

The transcription by B. Kapron of notes on a course of S. Cook in Berkeley in 1967 [5] contains the m-adic notation of numbers (digits does not include 0) and relations on weak classes (including polynomial time functions, **FP**, from [4]). This paper does not exactly use word-functions: it has primitives $\{n \mapsto 10n+i\}_{0\leq i\leq 9}$ emulating concatenation on words together with number ordering.

In [6], the authors provide a survey on counterparts on words of classical results for primitive number recursion (Ackermann function, limited recursion, Grzegorczyk and loop hierarchies). They prove that everything coincides.

[1] We restrain from coining the *primitive induction* term to avoid any misunderstanding with close fields of research.

There exists research on infinite alphabet (not the case here) like [11]. Up to some encoding with numbers, it corresponds to computation over finite sequences of numbers encoded by numbers.

Variations on base functions and operators exist in mentioned papers (e.g. limited recursion for Grzegorczyk hierarchy) as well as others. A restriction to unitary word-functions is considered in [1,3,9]. To mention a more recent work, the nowhere defined function is added to primitive recursive word-functions in [7].

As expected, as soon as a class is powerful enough to provide functions to encode and decode from one setting to another, the hierarchies correspond with the number setting. This is a motivation to investigate restrained classes. As far as we know, recursion without concatenation was not investigated.

Comparing to primitive recursion on numbers, the successor function is replaced by left concatenation for every symbol and the recursion operator has to consider every possible first symbol. Various examples of word-functions are provided, some have no counterpart in the number setting like reverting a word or testing whether a word is a palindrome. An encoding of tuples of words on any alphabet as a word in a 2-symbol alphabet is provided; thus multiple recursion is not adding any power to primitive recursion and the number of symbols does not change the hierarchies and complexity classes when there are at least two symbols.

The numbers in Peanos's axiomatisation are identified with words of a 1-symbol alphabet, and so are the functions. Proving that primitive recursive functions on integers coincide is quite straightforward with the following encoding. Let $\Sigma = \{\mathsf{a}_1, \mathsf{a}_2, \cdots, \mathsf{a}_r\}$ be the alphabet, the *r-adic* encoding function of words into natural numbers: $\langle\varepsilon\rangle = 0$ and $\mathsf{a}_k \cdot w$, $\langle \mathsf{a}_k \cdot w\rangle = k + r \cdot \langle w\rangle$. This encoding is onto and corresponds to the ranking number (starting from 0) of the reverse of w in the shortlex order[2]. For example $\langle \mathsf{a}_{i+1} \cdot w\rangle = \langle \mathsf{a}_i \cdot w\rangle + 1$ and $\langle \mathsf{a}_j\mathsf{a}_{i+1} \cdot w\rangle = \langle \mathsf{a}_j\mathsf{a}_i \cdot w\rangle + r$.

The natural evaluation scheme of primitive recursion functions is not very efficient (especially for numbers in unary notations), so a different scheme is used to show the proximity with the Turing machine model. The *delayed dynamic evaluation scheme* of word-functions is when the functions are called by name (not value) and only the needed expressions are evaluated (delayed) and all the evaluation results are stored so that nothing is re-evaluated (dynamic programming). An evaluation is represented by a direct acyclic graph (DAG) whose nodes are calls to function evaluations. Each node is labelled with the call: expressions of the function and of the arguments and its value (if computed). The *DAG-complexity* of an evaluation of a function is the number of nodes in the DAG. The size of the input is defined by the sum of the lengths of the input words. Given the expression of the initial function, the out-degrees of the nodes are bounded by present arities; the number of edges is thus linearly bounded in the number of nodes. Nodes are atomic operations, the length of any value is

[2] The usual definition is on the reversed word, but we define it in coherence with the restriction to left concatenation.

bounded by the input size and the DAG depth. The whole description of the labelled DAG is bounded by a polynomial in the size of its complexity.

The class of polynomial-time functions (from classical complexity theory) corresponds to the class of word-functions such that the DAG-complexity of any evaluation is bounded by a polynomial in the input size. One way, given the expression of the function, it is possible to generate an algorithm that, for any input, builds the DAG and outputs the result in polynomial time. The other way, consider a Turing machine implantation of any polynomial-time algorithm together with a polynomial that bounds its execution time. It is possible to evaluate the entry size and then the polynomial, to get the result in unary and then to do a recursion on the TM simulation. The DAG-complexity is linear in the polynomial value that bounds the iteration time of the Turing machine. Although we are using unary representation, it is still polynomial in the size of the input.

This proof can be adapted to **NP** (with polynomial-size certificates) and to exponential time. Please note that there also exists syntactic characterisation of **FP** in the number setting [2].

The paper focuses on primitive recursion without concatenation. Recursion can be used to chop off initial symbols and only suffix of the input can be output preventing the existence of any pairing or encoding function. As functions, they look rather bland; but, as language deciders (as pre-images of the empty word) they prove quite rich. Some algebraic ($\mathtt{a}^n\mathtt{b}^n$, palindromes) and non-algebraic ($\mathtt{a}^n\mathtt{b}^n\mathtt{c}^n$) languages are decidable. It is also possible to check arithmetical constrains like $\mathtt{a}^n\mathtt{b}^m\mathtt{c}^{P(n,m)}$ with P polynomial with positive coefficients in two (or more) variables. As a side results, this provides non-trivial examples of unary languages.

Multiple recursion allows to define various functions in one recursion. Usually, this operator is synthesised from single recursion using some pairing function, but no such function is available without concatenation. If multiple recursion is available, any regular language can be decided. Basically, each function corresponds to a state of a finite deterministic automaton.

A rough companion python3 library was developed to manipulate primitive recursive word-functions and check our constructions. It is available at https://www.univ-orleans.fr/lifo/Members/Jerome.Durand-Lose/Recherche/Companion/2022_DCFS.tgz.

Section 2 collects all the definitions while Sect. 3 provides the expression of various usual functions. Section 4 investigates the concatenation-less primitive recursion functions as language deciders. Section 5 shows that adding multiple recursion to the concatenation-less primitive recursion functions allows to decide all the recursive languages. Concluding remarks and perspectives are gathered in Sect. 6.

2 Definitions

An *alphabet*, Σ, is a non-empty finite set: $\{\mathtt{a}_1, \mathtt{a}_2, \cdots, \mathtt{a}_r\}$ where r is its *size*. Unless otherwise specified, its size is least 2; The set of *words* are defined by the free monoid Σ^*. Let $\cdot$ denote the concatenation operator and ε denote the empty word. Teletype fonts are used to denote symbols from Σ and math fonts to denote words. To ease notation, the concatenation symbol is often omitted, e.g. $\mathtt{aaa}$ stands for $\mathtt{a} \cdot \mathtt{a} \cdot \mathtt{a}$.

For any number k, a *k-ary (word-)function* is a function from $(\Sigma^*)^k$ to Σ^*. The *projection* of the ith component of a tuple of size n ($1 \leq i \leq n$) is denoted π_n^i. The *identity function* is denoted id ($=\pi_1^1$). The *constant ε function* is denoted $\widehat{\varepsilon}$ (formally there is one of arity 1, others are generated with compositions and projections). For any symbol $\mathtt{a}$, the 1-ary *left concatenation* function associated with $\mathtt{a}$, is defined by: ${}_{\mathtt{a}}\cdot(w) = \mathtt{a} \cdot w = \mathtt{a}w$. The notation $\vec{x}$ denotes a vector of arguments. Sans serif fonts are used to denote functions (in lower case) and operators (capitalised).

Numbers correspond to a 1-symbol alphabet (0 corresponds to ε). The successor of n is denoted $S(n)$ (the only available left concatenation).

Composition Operator. Let j, k be positive numbers. Let g be a k-ary function and $(h_i)_{1 \leq i \leq k}$ be j-ary functions. The j-ary function $f = \mathsf{Comp}(g, (h_i)_{1 \leq i \leq k})$ is uniquely defined by:

$$f(\vec{x}) = g\left(h_1(\vec{x}), \cdots, h_k(\vec{x})\right)$$

where $\vec{x}$ represents j arguments.

(Single) Recursion Operator on Σ. Let k be a positive number. Let g be a k-ary function and, for each $\mathtt{a}$ of Σ, $h_{\mathtt{a}}$ be a k+2-ary function. The k+1-ary function $f = \mathsf{Rec}(g, (h_{\mathtt{a}})_{\mathtt{a} \in \Sigma})$ is uniquely defined by:

$$f(\varepsilon, \vec{y}) = g(\vec{y}) \quad \text{and}$$
$$\forall \mathtt{a} \in \Sigma, f(\mathtt{a} \cdot w, \vec{y}) = h_{\mathtt{a}}(w, f(w, \vec{y}), \vec{y})$$

where $\vec{y}$ represents k arguments and w is any word in Σ^*.

To increase readability, vertical displays of function vectors are often used for composition and recursion.

The set of *primitive recursive functions* is the smallest set of functions containing the empty-word function, left concatenation for every symbol, all the projections, and closed for the composition and the recursion operators.

From functions, *relations* are defined as the pre-image of the ε. A unary relation represents a subset of Σ^*, i.e., a *language*.

3 First Constructions

In the spirit of the next section, concatenations are avoided as much as possible. Expressions are provided for an alphabet of size 3 (or 2 when the expression is large). The generalisation to larger alphabets is straightforward.

A *test* is a function that returns ε if and only if the condition is satisfied. It is a membership test for languages and relations.

3.1 Word Manipulations

By composition, it is possible to get any function concatenating a fixed word on the left, e.g. ${}_{\mathsf{a}_1\mathsf{a}_2\mathsf{a}_3}\cdot = \mathbf{Comp}({}_{\mathsf{a}_1}\cdot, (\mathbf{Comp}({}_{\mathsf{a}_2}\cdot, ({}_{\mathsf{a}_3}\cdot))))$. By composing with constant empty-word function, it is possible to get any constant function, e.g. $\widehat{\mathsf{a}_1\mathsf{a}_2\mathsf{a}_3} = \mathbf{Comp}({}_{\mathsf{a}_1}\cdot, (\mathbf{Comp}({}_{\mathsf{a}_2}\cdot, (\mathbf{Comp}({}_{\mathsf{a}_3}\cdot, (\widehat{\varepsilon}))))))$.

Basic operations on words are straightforward. The 2-ary concatenation operator can be generated from composition and recursion:

$$\cdot = \mathbf{Rec}\left(\mathsf{id}, \left(\mathbf{Comp}\left({}_{\mathsf{a}_1}\cdot, (\pi_3^2)\right), \mathbf{Comp}\left({}_{\mathsf{a}_2}\cdot, (\pi_3^2)\right), \mathbf{Comp}\left({}_{\mathsf{a}_3}\cdot, (\pi_3^2)\right)\right)\right).$$

Right concatenation functions can be generated as in:

$$\cdot_{\mathsf{a}_1} = \mathbf{Rec}\left(\widehat{\mathsf{a}_1}, \left(\mathbf{Comp}\left({}_{\mathsf{a}_1}\cdot, (\pi_2^2)\right), \mathbf{Comp}\left({}_{\mathsf{a}_2}\cdot, (\pi_2^2)\right), \mathbf{Comp}\left({}_{\mathsf{a}_3}\cdot, (\pi_2^2)\right)\right)\right).$$

It is possible to manipulate a word as a stack/list with functions to extract the first symbol and the rest of a word:

$$\mathsf{head} = \mathbf{Rec}(\widehat{\varepsilon}, (\widehat{\mathsf{a}_1}, \widehat{\mathsf{a}_2}, \widehat{\mathsf{a}_3})) \quad \text{and} \quad \mathsf{tail} = \mathbf{Rec}(\widehat{\varepsilon}, (\pi_2^1, \pi_2^1, \pi_2^1))$$

Please note that for head, the first symbol is *consumed* by the recursion so that it has to be generated again using a concatenation. This phenomenon makes more involving if not prevent the expression of functions without concatenation. In the following, we avoid constant functions (to avoid concatenation), so that needed constants have to be provided as arguments.

The following functions act depending on the presence of a_1 at the beginning of the first argument. The first function returns the rest of the first argument if present, the second argument otherwise. The second function returns its argument with leading a_1 removed (if any).

$$\begin{aligned} \mathsf{suppress}_{\mathsf{a}_1}^{\mathsf{else}} &= \mathbf{Rec}\left(\mathsf{id}, (\pi_3^1, \pi_3^3, \pi_3^3)\right), \\ \mathsf{suppress}_{\mathsf{a}_1?} &= \mathbf{Comp}(\mathsf{suppress}_{\mathsf{a}_1}^{\mathsf{else}}, (\mathsf{id}, \mathsf{id})). \end{aligned}$$

The usual test for equality over numbers does not yield a test for equality but a test to decide whether one word is the reverse of the other. This is because computation in the recursion is done after the recursive call. This is invisible with numbers since in unary notation all words are palindrome.

$$\mathsf{test}_{\mathsf{reverse}} = \mathbf{Comp}\left(\begin{array}{c|c} \mathbf{Rec}\left(\begin{array}{c|l} \pi_1^2 & \begin{array}{l} \mathbf{Comp}\left(\mathbf{Rec}\left(\begin{array}{c|c} \mathsf{id} & \begin{array}{c}\pi_3^1\\ \pi_3^3\end{array}\end{array}\right) \,\middle|\, \begin{array}{c}\pi_4^2\\ \pi_4^4\end{array}\right) \\ \mathbf{Comp}\left(\mathbf{Rec}\left(\begin{array}{c|c} \mathsf{id} & \begin{array}{c}\pi_3^3\\ \pi_3^1\end{array}\end{array}\right) \,\middle|\, \begin{array}{c}\pi_4^2\\ \pi_4^4\end{array}\right) \end{array} \end{array}\right) & \begin{array}{c}\pi_2^1\\ \pi_2^2\\ \pi_2^1\end{array} \end{array}\right).$$

This can be used to test if a word is a palindrome:

$$\mathsf{test}_{\mathsf{palindrome}} = \mathbf{Comp}\left(\begin{array}{c|c} \mathsf{test}_{\mathsf{reverse}} & \begin{array}{c}\mathsf{id}\\ \mathsf{id}\end{array}\end{array}\right).$$

It is possible to reverse a word and then test for equality:

$$\mathsf{reverse} = \mathbf{Rec}\left(\widehat{\varepsilon} \;\middle|\; \begin{array}{l} \mathbf{Comp}\left(\mathbf{Rec}\left(\widehat{\mathsf{a}_1} \;\middle|\; \begin{array}{l}\mathbf{Comp}\left(\mathsf{a}_1 \cdot \middle| \pi_2^2\right) \\ \mathbf{Comp}\left(\mathsf{a}_2 \cdot \middle| \pi_2^2\right)\end{array}\right) \middle| \pi_2^2\right) \\ \mathbf{Comp}\left(\mathbf{Rec}\left(\widehat{\mathsf{a}_2} \;\middle|\; \begin{array}{l}\mathbf{Comp}\left(\mathsf{a}_1 \cdot \middle| \pi_2^2\right) \\ \mathbf{Comp}\left(\mathsf{a}_2 \cdot \middle| \pi_2^2\right)\end{array}\right) \middle| \pi_2^2\right) \end{array}\right),$$

$$\mathsf{test_{equality}} = \mathbf{Comp}\left(\mathsf{test_{reverse}} \;\middle|\; \begin{array}{l} \pi_2^1 \\ \mathbf{Comp}\left(\mathsf{reverse} \middle| \pi_2^2\right) \end{array}\right).$$

3.2 Logical Functions

Each of these if functions works like a ternary operator with a condition/test on the first argument returning the second argument if the test succeeds, otherwise the third argument. A test succeeds if it evaluates to the empty word. The most basic function just tests whether the first argument is the empty word ($\mathsf{if}_\varepsilon(\varepsilon, y, z) = y$, and $\forall x \neq \varepsilon, \mathsf{if}_\varepsilon(x, y, z) = z$). It is defined by:

$$\mathsf{if}_\varepsilon = \mathbf{Rec}\left(\pi_2^1, (\pi_4^4, \pi_4^4)\right).$$

Conjunction and disjunction operators are defined as 2-ary functions:

$$\mathsf{and}_\varepsilon = \mathbf{Comp}\left(\mathsf{if}_\varepsilon, (\pi_2^1, \pi_2^2, \pi_2^1)\right) \quad \text{and} \quad \mathsf{or}_\varepsilon = \mathbf{Comp}\left(\mathsf{if}_\varepsilon, (\pi_2^1, \widehat{\varepsilon}, \pi_2^2)\right).$$

If a non-ε constant is provided, the negation function can be defined by $\mathbf{Comp}\left(\mathsf{if}_\varepsilon, (\pi_2^1, \pi_2^2, \widehat{\varepsilon})\right)$. This function has arity 2 (for the constant).

The following functions use the conditions: to start with a_1, to belong to the regular language a_1^*, and to the language a_1^+:

$$\begin{aligned} \mathsf{if}_{\mathsf{a}_1\Sigma^*} &= \mathbf{Rec}\left(\pi_2^2, (\pi_4^3, \pi_4^4, \pi_4^4)\right), \\ \mathsf{if}_{\mathsf{a}_1^*} &= \mathbf{Rec}\left(\pi_2^1, (\pi_4^2, \pi_4^4, \pi_4^4)\right), \text{and} \\ \mathsf{if}_{\mathsf{a}_1^+} &= \mathbf{Rec}\left(\pi_2^2, \left(\mathbf{Comp}\left(\mathsf{if}_{\mathsf{a}_1^*}, (\pi_4^1, \pi_4^3, \pi_4^4)\right), \pi_4^4, \pi_4^4\right)\right). \end{aligned}$$

3.3 Encoding and Pairing

Any word on any finite alphabet can be encoded on 2-symbol alphabet by:

$$\begin{aligned} \varepsilon &\mapsto \mathsf{a}_1\mathsf{a}_1, \text{and} \\ \mathsf{a}_{i_1} \cdot \mathsf{a}_{i_2} \cdot \cdots \cdot \mathsf{a}_{i_k} &\mapsto \mathsf{a}_1\mathsf{a}_2^{i_1}\mathsf{a}_1\mathsf{a}_2^{i_2}\mathsf{a}_1 \cdots \mathsf{a}_2^{i_k}\mathsf{a}_1. \end{aligned}$$

This function is primitive recursive like its decoding function as constructed below. The special value for ε has to be taken into account both in coding and decoding. The encoding is constructed by concatenating all $\mathsf{a}_1\mathsf{a}_2^i$ to a final a_1.

$$\mathsf{encode} = \mathbf{Comp}\left(\mathsf{if}_\varepsilon \left| \begin{array}{l} \mathsf{id} \\ \widehat{\mathsf{a}_1\mathsf{a}_2} \\ \mathbf{Rec}\left(\widehat{\mathsf{a}_1} \left| \begin{array}{l} \mathbf{Comp}\left(_{\mathsf{a}_1\mathsf{a}_2} \cdot \middle| \pi_2^2\right) \\ \mathbf{Comp}\left(_{\mathsf{a}_1\mathsf{a}_2^2} \cdot \middle| \pi_2^2\right) \\ \mathbf{Comp}\left(_{\mathsf{a}_1\mathsf{a}_2^3} \cdot \middle| \pi_2^2\right) \end{array}\right.\right) \end{array}\right.\right).$$

For decoding, a new $\mathsf{a}_{|\Sigma|}$ to be rotated is concatenated on the left for each a_1 but the first. For each a_2 the function $\mathsf{rot}_{\mathsf{first}}$ rotates the first symbol of its argument.

$$\begin{array}{r} \varepsilon \mapsto \varepsilon \\ \mathsf{a}_k \cdot w \mapsto \mathsf{a}_{k \bmod \mathsf{r}+1} \cdot w \end{array} \qquad \text{and } \mathsf{rot}_{\mathsf{first}} = \mathbf{Rec}\left(\widehat{\varepsilon} \left| \begin{array}{l} \mathbf{Comp}\left(\mathsf{a}_2 \cdot \middle| \pi_2^1\right) \\ \mathbf{Comp}\left(\mathsf{a}_3 \cdot \middle| \pi_2^1\right) \\ \mathbf{Comp}\left(\mathsf{a}_1 \cdot \middle| \pi_2^1\right) \end{array}\right.\right).$$

$$\mathsf{decode} = \mathbf{Comp}\left(\mathsf{if}_\varepsilon \left| \begin{array}{l} \mathbf{Comp}\left(\mathsf{tail} \middle| \mathsf{tail}\right) \\ \widehat{\varepsilon} \\ \mathbf{Comp}\left(\mathbf{Rec}\left(\widehat{\varepsilon} \left| \begin{array}{l} \mathbf{Comp}\left(_{\mathsf{a}_3} \cdot \middle| \pi_2^2\right) \\ \mathbf{Comp}\left(\mathsf{rot}_{\mathsf{first}} \middle| \pi_2^2\right) \\ \widehat{\varepsilon} \end{array}\right.\right) \middle| \mathsf{tail}\right) \end{array}\right.\right).$$

The special value for ε allows a simple pairing by concatenation.

$$\mathsf{pair} = \mathbf{Comp}\left(\cdot \left| \begin{array}{l} \mathbf{Comp}\left(\mathsf{encode} \middle| \pi_2^1\right) \\ \mathbf{Comp}\left(\mathsf{encode} \middle| \pi_2^2\right) \end{array}\right.\right).$$

To recover the first and second values of the pair, the middle $\mathsf{a}_1\mathsf{a}_1$ should be found while potential leading or ending $\mathsf{a}_1\mathsf{a}_1$ encoding ε are treated correctly. To recover the first value, the first a_1 is discarded and $\mathsf{a}_1\mathsf{a}_1$ is searched for, preserving only what is crossed.

$$\mathsf{pair}_{\mathsf{first}} = \mathbf{Comp}\left(\mathsf{decode} \left| \mathbf{Rec}\left(\widehat{\varepsilon} \left| \begin{array}{l} \mathbf{Comp}\left(\mathsf{if}_{\mathsf{a}_1\Sigma^*} \left| \begin{array}{l} \pi_2^1 \\ \widehat{\mathsf{a}_1} \\ \mathbf{Comp}\left(_{\mathsf{a}_1} \cdot \middle| \pi_2^2\right) \end{array}\right.\right) \\ \mathbf{Comp}\left(_{\mathsf{a}_2} \cdot \middle| \pi_2^2\right) \\ \mathbf{Comp}\left(_{\mathsf{a}_3} \cdot \middle| \pi_2^2\right) \end{array}\right.\right)\right.\right).$$

To recover the second value, the first a_1 is discarded and $\mathsf{a}_1\mathsf{a}_1$ is searched for, discarding what is crossed.

$$\mathsf{pair}_{\mathsf{second}} = \mathbf{Comp}\left(\mathbf{Rec}\left(\widehat{\varepsilon} \left| \begin{array}{l} \mathbf{Comp}\left(\mathsf{if}_{\mathsf{a}_1\Sigma^*} \left| \begin{array}{l} \pi_2^1 \\ \mathbf{Comp}\left(\mathsf{pair}_{\mathsf{first}} \middle| \pi_2^1\right) \\ \pi_2^2 \end{array}\right.\right) \\ \pi_2^2 \\ \pi_2^2 \end{array}\right.\right) \middle| \mathsf{suppress}_{\mathsf{a}_1?}\right).$$

This paring scheme extends straightforwardly to encode any tuple.

4 Primitive Recursion Without Concatenation

Let Σ-CL-PRec be the smallest set of functions containing the empty-word function, all the projections, and closed by the composition and the primitive recursion operators on Σ^*. A direct induction shows that:

Lemma 1. *The output of any word-function in* Σ-CL-PRec *must be a suffix of a word in the input.*

In particular, if the input is composed only of ε, then the output is ε. This limits the computing power and even constrains language recognition: unless a non-ε constant is provided, ε is accepted. This means that if ε is not in the language, a non-empty constant has to be provided in the input.

Since logical operators do not use concatenation, the set of decidable languages/relations is closed under union, intersection and complement (with a constant).

4.1 Some Algebraic Languages Decided in Σ-CL-PRec

Palindromes. Test for palindrome p. 6 does not use concatenation. This language is algebraic, non-ambiguous but not deterministic (it cannot be recognised by deterministic push-down automata, DPDA: it has to *guess* when the middle of the w is read).

Language $\mathsf{a}_1^n\mathsf{a}_2^n$. Function $\mathsf{test}_{\mathsf{a}_1^n\mathsf{a}_2^n}$ first considers the case of input ε (accepted). Otherwise, the input is not ε and is stored as a fail value. The first symbol has to be a_1 (otherwise fail) and then for each discarded a_1, a function that removes one a_2 (or fail) is used on the output.

Technical detail: $\mathsf{test}^{\mathsf{fail}}_{\mathsf{a}_1^n\mathsf{a}_2^{n+1}}$ consumes the first a_2 to know when a_2^n starts; to keep balance $\mathsf{test}_{\mathsf{a}_1^n\mathsf{a}_2^n}$ consumes the first a_1 before handling the rest of the word to $\mathsf{test}^{\mathsf{fail}}_{\mathsf{a}_1^n\mathsf{a}_2^{n+1}}$. The label fail in the name means that a fail value has to be provided as second argument. It differs from the meaning of else since the fail value might not be used to indicate failure.

$$\mathsf{test}^{\mathsf{fail}}_{\mathsf{a}_1^n\mathsf{a}_2^{n+1}} = \mathbf{Rec}\left(\mathsf{id}\;\middle|\;\begin{matrix}\mathbf{Comp}\left(\mathsf{suppress}^{\mathsf{else}}_{\mathsf{a}_2}\;\middle|\;\begin{matrix}\pi^2_3\\ \pi^3_3\end{matrix}\right)\\ \pi^1_3\\ \pi^3_3\end{matrix}\right),$$

$$\mathsf{test}_{\mathsf{a}_1^n\mathsf{a}_2^n} = \mathbf{Comp}\left(\mathbf{Rec}\left(\widehat{\varepsilon}\;\middle|\;\begin{matrix}\mathbf{Comp}\left(\mathsf{test}^{\mathsf{fail}}_{\mathsf{a}_1^n\mathsf{a}_2^{n+1}}\;\middle|\;\begin{matrix}\pi^1_3\\ \pi^3_3\end{matrix}\right)\\ \pi^3_3\\ \pi^3_3\end{matrix}\right)\;\middle|\;\begin{matrix}\mathsf{id}\\ \mathsf{id}\end{matrix}\right).$$

If the word is not in $\mathsf{a}_1^n\mathsf{a}_2^n$, then either the fail value is used or a $\mathsf{a}_1^n\mathsf{a}_2^n$ prefix is removed leaving a non-ε word.

This language is deterministic algebraic (can be recognised by DPDA).

Language $\mathtt{a}_1^n \mathtt{a}_2^n \mathtt{a}_1^m \cup \mathtt{a}_1^n \mathtt{a}_2^m \mathtt{a}_1^m$. On a word from $\mathtt{a}_1^n\mathtt{a}_2^n\mathtt{a}_1^m$, $\mathsf{test}_{\mathtt{a}_1^n\mathtt{a}_2^n}$ should return $\mathtt{a}_1^m$. So that the end of the test is carried out by removing remaining $\mathtt{a}_1$. Removing leading $\mathtt{a}_1^*$ is done with $\mathsf{suppress}_{\mathtt{a}_1^*}$. To avoid consuming one extra symbol (the first $\mathtt{a}_{\neq 1}$), one $\mathsf{suppress}_{\mathtt{a}_1?}$ is stacked for each $\mathtt{a}_1$ and then the composition is used on a copy of the input.

$$\mathsf{suppress}_{\mathtt{a}_1^*} = \mathbf{Comp}\left(\mathbf{Rec}\left(\widehat{\varepsilon}\,\middle|\,\begin{array}{l}\mathbf{Comp}\left(\mathsf{suppress}_{\mathtt{a}_1?}\,\middle|\,\pi_3^2\right)\\ \pi_3^3\\ \pi_3^3\end{array}\right)\middle|\,\begin{array}{l}\mathsf{id}\\ \mathsf{id}\end{array}\right),$$

$$\mathsf{test}_{\mathtt{a}_1^n\mathtt{a}_2^n\mathtt{a}_1^m} = \mathbf{Comp}\left(\mathsf{suppress}_{\mathtt{a}_1^*}\,\middle|\,\mathsf{test}_{\mathtt{a}_1^n\mathtt{a}_2^n}\right).$$

The language $\mathtt{a}_1^n\mathtt{a}_2^m\mathtt{a}_1^m$ is decided by removing all leading $\mathtt{a}_1$ and then using previous test (swapping $\mathtt{a}_1$ and $\mathtt{a}_2$): $\mathsf{test}_{\mathtt{a}_1^n\mathtt{a}_2^m\mathtt{a}_1^m} = \mathbf{Comp}\left(\mathsf{test}_{\mathtt{a}_1^n\mathtt{a}_2^n}\,\middle|\,\mathsf{suppress}_{\mathtt{a}_1^*}\right)$.

Since union of decidable languages is decidable, the algebraic language $\mathtt{a}_1^n\mathtt{a}_2^n\mathtt{a}_1^m \cup \mathtt{a}_1^n\mathtt{a}_2^m\mathtt{a}_1^m$ is decidable. This language is ambiguous.

4.2 Some Non-algebraic Languages Decided in Σ-CL-PRec

Languages $\mathtt{a}_1^n\mathtt{a}_2^n\mathtt{a}_1^n$. Since intersection of decidable languages is decidable, the language $\mathtt{a}_1^n\mathtt{a}_2^n\mathtt{a}_1^n = \mathtt{a}_1^n\mathtt{a}_2^n\mathtt{a}_1^m \cap \mathtt{a}_1^n\mathtt{a}_2^m\mathtt{a}_1^m$ is decidable. This language is not algebraic. Similarly, it is possible to prove that the languages $\mathtt{a}_1^n\mathtt{a}_2^n\mathtt{a}_1^n \cdots \mathtt{a}_1^n$ are all decidable.

Languages $\mathtt{a}_1^n\mathtt{a}_2^{P(n)}$ with P Polynomial with Positive Coefficients. The idea is to deal with functions that discard (or fail) the right amount of $\mathtt{a}_2$ according to the number of $\mathtt{a}_1$ for each monomial. So that the result is empty only if the sum matches.

For each monomial, a ternary function is defined. The first argument starts with $\mathtt{a}_1^n\mathtt{a}_{\neq 1}$ to provide the value for n. The second argument is the one to remove the $\mathtt{a}_2$ from. The third argument is returned if removing is not possible.

For constant monomial 3, the function is

$$\mathsf{remove}^{\mathsf{else}}_{\mathtt{a}_2^3} = \mathbf{Comp}\left(\mathsf{suppress}^{\mathsf{else}}_{\mathtt{a}_2}\,\middle|\,\begin{array}{l}\mathbf{Comp}\left(\mathsf{suppress}^{\mathsf{else}}_{\mathtt{a}_2}\,\middle|\,\begin{array}{l}\mathsf{suppress}^{\mathsf{else}}_{\mathtt{a}_2}\\ \pi_2^2\end{array}\right)\\ \pi_2^2\end{array}\right)$$

$$\mathsf{remove}_{\mathtt{a}_2^3} = \mathbf{Comp}\left(\mathsf{remove}^{\mathsf{else}}_{\mathtt{a}_2^3}\,\middle|\,\begin{array}{l}\pi_3^2\\ \pi_3^3\end{array}\right).$$

For the monomial $3x$, this is done x times:

$$\mathsf{remove}_{3\mathtt{a}_2^x} = \mathbf{Comp}\left(\mathbf{Rec}\left(\pi_3^2\,\middle|\,\begin{array}{l}\mathbf{Comp}\left(\mathsf{remove}^{\mathsf{else}}_{\mathtt{a}_2^3}\,\middle|\,\begin{array}{l}\pi_5^2\\ \pi_5^5\end{array}\right)\\ \pi_5^4\\ \pi_5^4\end{array}\right)\middle|\,\begin{array}{l}\pi_3^1\\ \pi_3^1\\ \pi_3^2\\ \pi_3^3\end{array}\right).$$

For the monomial $3x^2$, it is done x times again. The function $\mathsf{remove}_{3\mathtt{a}_2^{x^2}}$ is:

$$\textsf{\textbf{Comp}}\left(\textsf{\textbf{Rec}}\left(\pi_3^2 \left| \begin{array}{l} \textsf{\textbf{Comp}}\left(\textsf{\textbf{Rec}}\left(\pi_3^2 \left| \begin{array}{l} \textsf{\textbf{Comp}}\left(\textsf{remove}_{\mathsf{a}_2^3}^{\textsf{else}} \left| \begin{array}{l} \pi_2^5 \\ \pi_5^5 \end{array}\right.\right) \\ \pi_5^4 \\ \pi_5^4 \end{array}\right.\right) \left| \begin{array}{l} \pi_5^3 \\ \pi_5^3 \\ \pi_5^2 \\ \pi_5^5 \end{array}\right.\right) \\ \\ \pi_5^4 \\ \pi_5^4 \end{array}\right.\right) \left| \begin{array}{l} \pi_3^1 \\ \pi_3^1 \\ \pi_3^2 \\ \pi_3^3 \end{array}\right.\right).$$

Even though the definition looks involving, these are just nested for loops.

It is possible to design concatenation-less functions that yield each maximal suffixes of $\mathsf{a}_1^+\mathsf{a}_2^+\mathsf{a}_3^+\cdots\mathsf{a}_m^+$ of the form $\mathsf{a}_k^+\cdots\mathsf{a}_m^+$. Hence, all the languages $\mathsf{a}_1^+\mathsf{a}_2^+\cdots\mathsf{a}_i^n\cdots\mathsf{a}_j^{P(n)}\cdots\mathsf{a}_m^+$ (for given $i \neq j$ and P) are all decidable.

Using the same tools, it is also possible to test such languages as $\mathsf{a}_1^n\mathsf{a}_2^m\mathsf{a}_2^{P(n,m)}$ with P polynomial in 2 variables with positive coefficients. More than two variables is similarly possible.

5 Regular Languages are Decidable in Σ-CL-PRec with Multiple Recursion

The multiple recursion operator is usually synthesised with the use of a pairing function, i.e. a one-to-one function from $\Sigma^* \times \Sigma^*$ to Σ^*. Yet, no such function is available without concatenation since any pairing function would have to map $\{(\mathsf{a}_1^i, \mathsf{a}_1^j)\}_{0 \leq i,j<2}$ to four distinct values, but the only possible outputs are in $\{\varepsilon, \mathsf{a}_1\}$ (the suffixes). (Adding constants would no work for $\{(\mathsf{a}_1^i, \mathsf{a}_1^j)\}_{0 \leq i,j<k}$ for every k.)

Lemma 2. *There is no pairing function in Σ-*CL-PRec.

Multiple Recursion Operator on Σ. Let m and k be any positive numbers. Let $(g_i)_{1 \leq i \leq m}$ be k-ary functions and, for each a of Σ, $(h_{\mathsf{a},i})_{1 \leq i \leq m}$ be $(k+m+1)$-ary functions. The $(k+1)$-ary functions

$$(f_i)_{1 \leq i \leq m} = \textsf{\textbf{Rec}}^m\Big((g_i)_{1 \leq i \leq m}, (h_{\mathsf{a},i})_{\mathsf{a} \in \Sigma, 1 \leq i \leq m}\Big)$$

are uniquely defined by $\forall i, 1 \leq i \leq m$:

$$\begin{aligned} f_i(\varepsilon, \vec{y}) &= g_i(\vec{y}) \quad \text{and} \\ \forall \mathsf{a} \in \Sigma, \quad f_i(\mathsf{a} \cdot w, \vec{y}) &= h_{\mathsf{a},i}(w, f_1(w, \vec{y}), \cdots, f_m(w, \vec{y}), \vec{y}) \end{aligned}$$

where $\vec{y}$ represents k arguments.

The set Σ-CL-PRec* is defined like Σ-CL-PRec, but with the addition of the closure by the recursion operators of every arity. Lemma 1 extends to Σ-CL-PRec*: the output has to be a suffix of an input.

Regular Languages are Decidable in Σ-CL-PRec*. Let L be a regular language. It is decided by some deterministic finite automaton (Q, δ, q_0, A) where

Q is finite set of state, δ is the transition table, q_0 is the initial state, and A is the set of accepting states. We suppose that $\varepsilon \in L$ (otherwise add a constant to the input and complement).

Let the 2-ary functions $(f_q)_{q \in Q}$ be defined by multiple recursion from projections by:

$$\begin{aligned}
\forall q \in A, \quad & f_q(\varepsilon, w_1) = \widehat{\varepsilon}(w_1) = \varepsilon \\
\forall q \in Q \backslash A, \quad & f_q(\varepsilon, w_1) = \pi_1^1(w_1) = w_1 \\
\forall q \in Q, \quad \forall \mathsf{a} \in \Sigma, \quad & f_q(\mathsf{a} \cdot w, w_1) = \pi^i_{|Q|+2}\Big(w, (f_s(w, w_1))_{s \in Q}, w_1\Big) \\
& \qquad = f_r(w, w_1) \\
& \qquad \text{where}\, \delta(q, \mathsf{a}) = r \,\text{and}\, i \,\text{suitably chosen}
\end{aligned}$$

The transition table is encoded in the recursion. The following function decides L.

$$\mathsf{test}_L = \mathbf{Comp}\left(f_{q_0}, (\pi_1^1, \pi_1^1)\right)$$

6 Conclusion

Word-recursion is a rich context allowing to address words directly and to relate to complexity theory. Although forbidding concatenation seems limiting, it allows to decide non trivial languages. It is open whether all algebraic languages are decidable, and if not, which of them are not and why. More generally, a condition for a function to be (un)computable without concatenation that would rule out functions (e.g., equality) and languages is to be found.

Without concatenation it is still possible to check constrains expressed with a polynomial with positive coefficients. Although we advocate recursion on words, the range of integer languages decidable is also wide; e.g. by testing all possible splitting in two terms, the language $\{n + n^2 | n \in \mathbb{N}\}$ can be decided.

We conjecture that even though this class is restricted, there should be some undecidable properties. For example, emptiness of accepted language might be undecidable (using diophantine equations [8]).

Any function defined without concatenation, f, satisfies $|f(x_1, \cdots, x_k)| \leq \max(|x_1|, \cdots, |x_k|)$, so that this class is included in the level E_0 of the Grzegorczyk hierarchy (see [6] for definitions). Relatively to the relations/languages theses classes defined, we lack an example to show that the inclusion is strict. We conjecture that the height of recursion in the function definition provides a proper hierarchy inside the class.

Some of provided constructions rely on duplicating the input. We are wondering whether forbidding duplication leads to a non-trivial class. Otherwise, how can it be characterised?

We would like to close this article by addressing minimisation. The few operators for words in the literature are usually number representation based (related to the shortlex order) in settings where the successor is not a base function but a non-trivial word-function. We want to avoid the influence of numbers and refuse to impose a non-trivial order on words. In the number setting, one can consider the successor function to be just a function to provide from the current one the next value to test. We propose to take that point of view: that the minimisation operator requires another word-function to generate from the current one the next word to try (starting from the empty word), without any constraint on this function (does not have to onto, one-to-one or total, as long as it is in the class). Although it seems more complex, it corresponds to the update of variables in while loops.

References

1. Asser, G.: Primitive recursive word-functions of one variable. In: Börger, E. (ed.) Computation Theory and Logic. LNCS, vol. 270, pp. 14–19. Springer, Heidelberg (1987). https://doi.org/10.1007/3-540-18170-9_150
2. Bellantoni, S.J., Cook, S.A.: A new recursion-theoretic characterization of the polytime functions. Comput. Complex. **2**, 97–110 (1992). https://doi.org/10.1007/BF01201998
3. Calude, C., Sântean, L.: On a theorem of günter asser. Math. Log. Q. **36**(2), 143–147 (1990)
4. Cobham, A.: The intrinsic computational difficulty of functions. In: Bar-Hillel, Y. (ed.) Studies in Logic and the Foundations of Mathematics. In: Proceedings of the 1964 International Congress, North-Holland, pp. 24–30 (1965)
5. Cook, S.A., Kapron, B.M.: A survey of classes of primitive recursive functions. Electron. Colloquium Comput. Complex. 1 (2017). https://eccc.weizmann.ac.il/report/2017/001
6. von Henke, F.W., Rose, G., Indermark, K., Weihrauch, K.: On primitive recursive wordfunctions. Computing **15**(3), 217–234 (1975). https://doi.org/10.1007/BF02242369
7. Khachatryan, M.H.: On generalized primitive recursive string functions. Math. Probl. Comput. Sci. **43**, 42–46 (2015)
8. Matiyasevich, Y.: Hilbert's tenth problem and paradigms of computation. In: Cooper, S.B., Löwe, B., Torenvliet, L. (eds.) CiE 2005. LNCS, vol. 3526, pp. 310–321. Springer, Heidelberg (2005). https://doi.org/10.1007/11494645_39
9. Santean, L.: A hierarchy of unary primitive recursive string-functions. In: Dassow, J., Kelemen, J. (eds.) IMYCS 1990. LNCS, vol. 464, pp. 225–233. Springer, Heidelberg (1990). https://doi.org/10.1007/3-540-53414-8_45
10. Soare, R.I.: Computability and incomputability. In: Cooper, S.B., Löwe, B., Sorbi, A. (eds.) CiE 2007. LNCS, vol. 4497, pp. 705–715. Springer, Heidelberg (2007). https://doi.org/10.1007/978-3-540-73001-9_75
11. Vučkovi, V.: Recursive word-functions over infinite alphabets. Math. Log. Q. **13**(2), 123–138 (1970)

Clusters of Repetition Roots Forming Prefix Chains

Szilárd Zsolt Fazekas[1(✉)] and Robert Mercaş[2]

[1] Graduate School of Engineering Science, Akita University, Akita, Japan
szilard.fazekas@ie.akita-u.ac.jp

[2] Department of Computer Science, Loughborough University, Loughborough, UK
R.G.Mercas@lboro.ac.uk

Abstract. We investigate lower bounds on the size of clusters (sets of starting positions of occurrences) of common prefixes shared by repetition roots. Such lower bounds in terms of the constituent roots in the sets provide upper bounds on the number of distinct repetitions. In the case of distinct square roots which are totally ordered by the prefix relation it has been shown that there must be more occurrences of the common prefix than the number of roots. Here we develop the theory further by presenting the tools to extend the bounds to exponents higher than 2 and we show that they are optimal in the sense that any sequence of cluster sizes satisfying the lower bounds can be realized. We also take the next step towards the bounds on arbitrary (only partially prefix-ordered) sets of roots by proving a lower bound on unbordered prefixes shared by two overlapping prefix chains of roots.

1 Introduction

Repetitions in words are one of the most studied topic in word combinatorics [17], partly due to their various applications in string matching [5], molecular biology [11], or text compression [19]. The most basic repetition is xx, where x is a non-empty string. Such strings are also called, due to the form $xx = x^2$, *squares*.

A string is said to be square-free or repetition-free if it contains no squares. Combinatorics on words arguably started with the work of Thue [21,22] who showed that there exist square-free strings over ternary alphabets and cube-free ones over two letters. Over two letters, trivially every string of length at least 4 contains a square and it has also been shown that any sufficiently long binary string must contain at least three *distinct squares* [9].

A string of length n can have $\Theta(n^2)$ squares (just take a unary sequence). If the root x of each square xx must be primitive (not a repetition), one can still have at most $\Theta(n \log n)$ squares [5]. When the roots of the squares must be distinct, then the maximal number becomes linear in the length of the string. Fraenkel and Simpson proved [10] that the maximum number of distinct squares

S. Z. Fazekas—This Work Was Supported By JSPS KAKENHI Grant Number JP19K11815.

Published by Springer Nature Switzerland AG 2022
Y.-S. Han and G. Vaszil (Eds.): DCFS 2022, LNCS 13439, pp. 43–56, 2022.
https://doi.org/10.1007/978-3-031-13257-5_4

in a string is not more than twice the length of the string and they conjectured that the bound can be significantly improved:

Conjecture 1. The number of distinct squares in a length n word is less than n.

They also constructed lower bounds which asymptotically match the conjectured upper bound except for a sublinear term. We will use another simple lower bound construction by Jonoska, Manea and Seki [15] as our starting point for discussing optimality later on.

There have been several developments in the last 25 years on the topic. Some alternative and simple proofs of the $2n$ upper bound were found [12,13], after which the bound was improved to $2n-\Theta(\log n)$ [14]. Deza, Franek and Thierry [6] proved the best (peer-reviewed) bound as of now, $11n/6$, by a deep investigation of left aligned last occurrences of distinct squares. There was a claim of further improvement to $3n/2$ very recently [20], but it has not appeared in peer-reviewed publication to the best of our knowledge.

Regarding exponents larger than 2 it was shown [3] that for fixed integers $\ell > 2$, there can be no more than $\frac{n}{\ell-2}$ powers of exponent ℓ in a word of length n. For cubes, that is, $\ell = 3$ the bound was improved to $4n/5$ [4]. The study of repetitions of higher fixed exponents was inspired by the importance of counting runs, i.e., repetitions whose exponent is at least 2 and which cannot be extended in either direction without increasing the period. The bound on this number was conjectured to be less than the word's length [16] (not much after Fraenkel and Simpson's square conjecture was published) and recently proved to be so by a very elegant and simple argument [1].

There were other developments relevant to the question even though they did not necessarily improve upper bounds. By using square density increasing mappings it was shown that binary strings can achieve maximum density if the conjectured upper bound holds [18]. In the case of partial words (strings with holes) tight upper bounds have been proved depending on the number of holes [2]. Another recent paper [8] proposed a framework to integrate existing results and facilitate new ones in the analysis of distinguished positions of squares.

Our Contribution. Finally, the basis of our current work proposed another angle of attack using clusters of repetition roots [7]. The techniques used there extract global properties of occurrences of repetitions in a word from local ones and we continue that line of investigation. We group the repetitions by the partial order imposed on their roots by the prefix ordering. All repetitions whose roots share a common prefix are in one group and our aim is to show that there are 'many' occurrences of this common prefix forced by the occurrences of the repetitions. We are working toward proving the conjecture on the lower bound on the number of those prefixes which would imply Fraenkel and Simpson's. We will introduce notation and the line of attack in the next section. In Sect. 3 we generalize the lower bound technique used recently for prefix chains of squares, to the case of higher exponents. More specifically, we show that if two ℓ-powers are aligned at the end of their second or further root occurrence, then the shorter root must be non-primitive. In our previous work this was used to assign unique positions to primitively rooted squares, followed by a different assignment procedure for non-primitively rooted ones, so it forms the basis of lower bound results for prefix chains of repetition roots. Afterwards we discuss the optimality of the bounds obtained for squares. As opposed to the other bounds mentioned in the introduction, ours are tight in the sense that for each sequence of cluster sizes satisfying the bounds we can find a word and repetition roots in it which have those exact cluster sizes. We present a simple construction to achieve those bounds. We also show that a counting argument of similar flavor can be applied to runs whose suffixes of length equal to the run's period form a prefix chain. In Sect. 4 we develop the technique further by designating special occurrences of a shared unbordered prefix of roots in two overlapping prefix chains. The main result in that section is a counterpart of the theorem in Sect. 3: alignment of repetitions at their suitably defined anchor means that the shorter one is non-primitive. The challenge is that the anchor has to be defined differently in the case of root sets which are not linearly ordered by the prefix relation. We present a solution in the case when such a set is the union of two prefix chains with minimal elements that are unbordered.

2 Preliminaries

A *word* or *string* is a concatenation of letters from a *finite alphabet* Σ. The *empty word* ε is the word of length 0. For a word $w = xyz$, we call x a *prefix* (denoted by $x \leq_p w$, or $x <_p w$ if $x \neq w$) and z a *suffix* of w, while each of x, y, z are called *factors* of w. The word y is an inside factor of w if neither x nor z are empty. A factor is *proper* if it is non-empty and not equal to w. If $x = z$, then x is also a *border* of w. If two words u and v are not comparable by the prefix relation, we write $u <>_p v$. The longest common prefix of two words $u = xau'$ and $v = xbv'$ is $\mathbf{lcp}(u, v) = x$ if either au' or bv' is empty or otherwise $a \neq b$.

We call p a *period* of w if the letters repeat every p positions apart in w. The *minimal period* is given by the smallest such p. By $|w|_x$ we denote the number of times x occurs as a factor of w (including overlaps).

A *repetition* represents consecutive concatenations of the same word. An *ℓ-power* (*ℓ-repetition*) represents ℓ such repetitions of the same factor. If a word is not a repetition, then it is called *primitive*. Moreover, if $w = u^\ell$ is an ℓ-repetition we say that u is a *root* of w, and call u *the primitive root* of w when u is primitive.

For a word u and a prefix u' of u, all words $u^\ell u'$ with integer exponent $\ell \geq 0$ have period $|u|$. A word can have multiple periods, e.g., *ababa* has periods 2 and 4, since $ababa = (ab)^2a = (abab)^1a$. While repetitions are defined in terms of integer powers, rational powers are also possible. Namely, $u = t^k$ for some rational k, if $|u| = k|t|$ and $|t|$ is a period of u. For instance, the word *abcabca* is a fractional power of *abc* since $abcabca = (abc)^{\frac{7}{3}}$. A *run* is given by the positions in the word that contain a maximal repetitive factor with period at most half as long as the length of the factor (a repetition is maximal, if taking a previous or following position changes the period). In other words, a run is a factor that has an exponent at least 2, and which cannot be extended to either left or right. Finally, by t^ω we denote the infinite word consisting in consecutive repetitions of t.

We also recall the following well-known results about primitivity of words and multiple periods.

Lemma 1. *[17] A word w is primitive if and only if it occurs only twice in ww.*

Theorem 1 (Fine and Wilf). *[17] If a word w has periods p and q and $|w| \geq p+q-\gcd(p,q)$, then $\gcd(p,q)$ is also a period of w.*

2.1 Clusters of Repetition Roots

In this subsection we introduce clusters of repetition roots and explain the conjecture which is the final goal of our study.

When wanting to count all distinct ℓ-powers for a fixed ℓ, we denote by $\mathbf{clust}_w(u)$, for each factor u^ℓ of w, the set that contains the starting position of all suffixes having u as a prefix. We will call this set the *cluster* of u. Clearly, if an ℓ-repetition u^ℓ is a factor of a word, then the cluster of u is of size at least ℓ. As every word, and therefore every suffix starting with v also has u as prefix when $u <_p v$, the next observation is straightforward.

Observation 1. *For any two factors u and v of a word w, we have $u \leq_p v \Leftrightarrow \mathbf{clust}_w(v) \subseteq \mathbf{clust}_w(u) \Leftrightarrow \mathbf{clust}_w(u) \cap \mathbf{clust}_w(v) \neq \emptyset$ and $|u| \leq |v|$.*

In this paper we attempt to get closer to the following conjecture, which, if true, would give a general upper bound for integer exponent distinct repetitions:

Conjecture 2. [7] For any word w, any positive integer $\ell > 1$, and any set of words $S = \{u_1, u_2, \ldots, u_n\}$ such that, for all $i \in \{1, \ldots, n\}$, u_i^ℓ is a factor of w and $u_1 \leq_p u_i$, we have $|S| < \frac{1}{\ell-1}|w|_{u_1}$.

In the paper proposing the conjecture, it was proved for the case where $\ell = 2$ and $u_1 \leq_p \cdots \leq_p u_n$, that is, S is a set of roots of distinct squares, totally ordered by the prefix relation. Such a collection of square roots is called a *(prefix) chain* and with that, the result can be stated as

Theorem 2. *[7] For a word w and a prefix chain $S = \{u_1, u_2, \ldots, u_n\}$ of square roots of w, with $u_i \leq_p u_{i+1}$ for all $i \in \{1, \ldots, n-1\}$, we have $|S| < |w|_{u_1}$.*

In the next section we generalize the results necessary to prove Conjecture 2 for prefix chains of roots in the case of repetitions of arbitrary exponents. Due to the page limit we do not present the reassignment procedure, which allocates distinct positions to the non-primitively rooted repetitions. Compared to the results in [6,10,14,15], the bound in Theorem 2 is different because it is in a sense optimal, as we will argue at the end of Sect. 3. Furthermore, while the bounds on distinct repetitions would be direct corollaries of Conjecture 2, the converse does not hold.

3 Single Chains

In this section we show that the non-primitivity conditions on the roots of colliding powers used to prove Conjecture 2 in the special case of single chains of square roots, are valid for arbitrary exponent K. These are conceptually simple proofs following the argument of their counterparts for squares (Lemma 5 and Corollary 2 in [7]). Afterwards we discuss the optimality of the bound w.r.t. the existence of words $w, u_1, \ldots, u_n$ for every possibility of cluster sizes satisfying the bound. Finally we show that prefix chains of square roots at the end of runs can help find alternative techniques for counting maximal repetitions, too.

For a prefix $x \leq_p u$ and natural number $\ell \in \{2, \ldots, K\}$, we say that the (ℓ, x)-representative ((ℓ, x)-rep) of u^K is the longest prefix of u^ℓ which ends in x. Note that this x-rep is of length at least $(\ell - 1)|u| + |x|$. Formally, the (ℓ, x)-rep of u^K is $u^{\ell-1}u'x \leq_p u^K$ such that for all y we have that $u^{\ell-1}yx \leq_p u^\ell$ implies $|y| \leq |u'|$.

Let w be a word which contains u^K as a factor. For the leftmost occurrence in w of the (ℓ, x)-rep $u^{\ell-1}u'x$ of the K-power u^K, let u_s be its starting position and $u_m = u_s + (\ell - 1)|u|$.

We define the (ℓ, x)-*anchor* of u^K in w as the starting position of the rightmost occurrence of x in the first occurrence of the (ℓ, x)-rep of the power u^K in w. This (ℓ, x)-anchor is denoted by $\boldsymbol{\Psi}_w(u^\ell, x)$. If the (ℓ, x)-rep of u^K is $u^{\ell-1}u'x$, then $\boldsymbol{\Psi}_w(u^\ell, x) = u_s + (\ell - 1)|u| + |u'|$.

For example, in the word w below

$$\begin{array}{cccccccccccccccccccccccc} a & b & a & a & b & c & a & b & a & a & b & a & a & b & c & a & b & a & a & b & a & a & b & a \\ 1 & 2 & 3 & 4 & 5 & 6 & 7 & 8 & 9 & 10 & 11 & 12 & 13 & 14 & 15 & 16 & 17 & 18 & 19 & 20 & 21 & 22 & 23 & 24 \end{array}$$

we have the cube (3-power) $u = (aba)^3$ starting at position 16. The $(2, \boldsymbol{a})$-rep of u^3 is $aba\boldsymbol{a}ba = u^2$, first occurring at 7, so $\boldsymbol{\Psi}_w(u^2, a) = 7 + |abaab| = 12$. The $(2, \boldsymbol{ab})$-rep of u^3 is $aba\boldsymbol{ab}$, first occurring at 1, therefore $\boldsymbol{\Psi}_w(u^2, ab) = 1 + |aba| = 4$. The $(3, \boldsymbol{ab})$-rep of u^3 is $(aba)^2\boldsymbol{ab}$ whose only occurrence is at 16, meaning that $\boldsymbol{\Psi}_w(u^3, ab) = 16 + |(aba)^2| = 22$.

While the (ℓ, x) anchors are not exactly at the right edge of the repetitions u^ℓ, as we will see, when two repetitions are aligned by their anchors it has a similar consequence as if they were aligned at their right edge: the shorter one is non-primitive. We show that this is true for all pairs of coinciding anchors.

Lemma 2. *Let w be an arbitrary word with two K-powers u^K, v^K such that $u <_p v$, and let x be a common prefix of u and v. If there are $\ell, \ell' \in \{2, \ldots, K\}$ such that $\boldsymbol{\Psi}_w(u^\ell, x) = \boldsymbol{\Psi}_w(v^{\ell'}, x)$, then $u = t^k$ for some primitive word t with $|t| < |x|$ and $k \geq 2$. Moreover, $tu'x \leq_p v$, where $u'x$ is the longest prefix of u bordered by x.*

Proof. Assume $\boldsymbol{\Psi}_w(u^\ell, x) = \boldsymbol{\Psi}_w(v^{\ell'}, x)$. We distinguish three cases based on the relative positions of u_s, u_m and v_m, and will derive contradictions in all of them, except in the last case, when u is non-primitive with its root shorter than

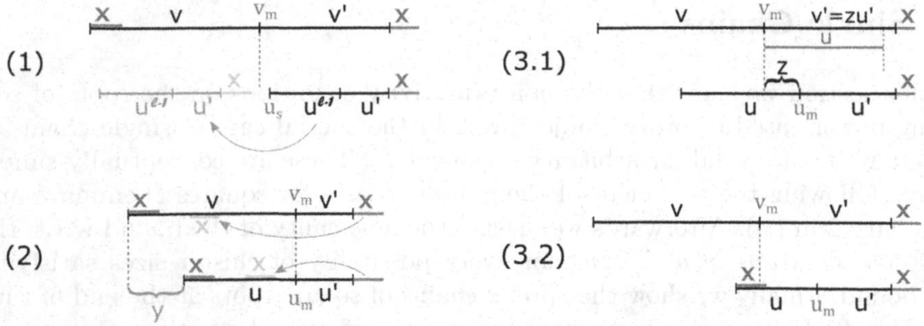

Fig. 1. The cases analyzed in Lemma 2.

x. Note that $v_m \leq u_m$ always holds, since $u \leq_p v$ implies $\mathbf{\Psi}_w(u^\ell, x) - u_m \leq \mathbf{\Psi}_w(v^{\ell'}, x) - v_m$. In what follows, let the (ℓ, x)-rep of u^K be $u^{\ell-1}u'x$.
(1) $v_m \leq u_s$, see Fig. 1(1). In this case the (ℓ, x)-rep of u^K is a factor of v, therefore it also occurs at $u_s - |v|$, a contradiction.
(2) $v_m = u_m$, see Fig. 1(2). This means that u is a suffix of v and since $|v| > |u|$, we have $v = yu$, for some non-empty word y. From $\mathbf{\Psi}_w(u^\ell, x) = \mathbf{\Psi}_w(v^{\ell'}, x)$, we get that the x-rep of v^K is $v^{\ell'-1}u'x$. However, $yu'x \leq_p v$ which means that the rightmost x occurrence in v is at least $|yu'|$ positions from its start, so

$$\mathbf{\Psi}_w(v^{\ell'}, x) \geq v_s + (\ell' - 1)|v| + |yu'| > v_s + (\ell' - 1)|v| + |u'| = \mathbf{\Psi}_w(v^{\ell'}, x),$$

a contradiction.
(3) $u_s < v_m < u_m$. Let the (ℓ', x)-rep of v^K be $v^{\ell'-1}zu'x$, where z is the non-empty word starting at v_m and ending at $u_m - 1$. Both $zu'x$ and u are prefixes of v, so they are prefixes of each other. If $zu'x \leq_p u$, then

$$\mathbf{\Psi}_w(u^\ell, x) \geq u_s + (\ell - 1)|u| + |zu'| > u_s + (\ell - 1)|u| + |u'| = \mathbf{\Psi}_w(u^\ell, x),$$

which is a contradiction. The only remaining possibility is if $u \leq_p zu'x$. Then, there is an occurrence of u at v_m and by Lemma 1 this means that u is not primitive. (see Fig. 1(3.1)).

Now let $u = t^k$, with t primitive and $k \geq 2$. If $|uu'| \geq |v|$ then a conjugate of v is a prefix of uu', because uu' is a factor of v^2. From here, v has period $|t|$ and the fact that t^k is its prefix and t is its suffix means that $v = t^m$ for some $m > k$. This, in turn, means that u^ℓ and hence the (ℓ, x)-rep of u^K occurs at position v_s, so the occurrence at u_s is not the leftmost, another contradiction.

We are left with the case $|uu'| < |v|$. We have an occurrence of x at $u_m - |u|$. If that x finishes before position v_m, that is, $v_m - |x| \geq u_m - |u|$, then there should be an occurrence of x located $|v|$ positions further to the right in v^K. That would give $\mathbf{\Psi}_w(v^{\ell'}, x) \geq u_m - |u| + |v| > u_m - |u| + |uu'| = \mathbf{\Psi}_w(u^\ell, x)$, contradicting $\mathbf{\Psi}_w(v^{\ell'}, x) = \mathbf{\Psi}_w(u^\ell, x)$. Hence, we get that $v_m - (u_m - |u|) < |x|$, which means $|t| < |x|$. (see Fig. 1(3.2)).

As x is a prefix of $u = t^k$, it has the form $x = t^r t'$ for some $r < k$ and $t' \leq_p t$. The longest prefix of $u = t^k$ bordered by x is $t^{k-1}t' = u'x$. As $u_m > v_m$, we get that $tt^{k-1}t' = tu'x \leq_p v$. □

Corollary 1. *Let $u_1^K, \ldots, u_n^K$ and $v_1^K, \ldots, v_n^K$ be powers in some word w with their roots all from the same chain and let x be a common prefix of those roots, such that for all $i \in \{1, \ldots, n\}$ there are $\ell_i, \ell'_i \in \{2, \ldots, K\}$ with $\mathbf{\Psi}_w(u_i^{\ell_i}, x) = \mathbf{\Psi}_w(v_i^{\ell'_i}, x)$. Then, there exists some primitive word t shorter than x, such that $u_i = t^{k_i}$ with $k_i \geq 2$, for all $i \in \{1, \ldots, n\}$.*

Proof. From Lemma 2, whenever the (ℓ_i, x)-anchor of u_i^K and the (ℓ'_i, x)-anchor of v_i^K coincide, there is some primitive t_i with $|t_i| < |x|$ such that $u_i = t_i^{k_i}$ with $k_i \geq 2$ and $t_i x$ is a prefix of v_i. Given that the roots of these powers form a prefix chain, we get that the words $t_i x$ also form a prefix chain, that is, for all $i, j \in \{1, \ldots, n\}$ either $t_i x \leq_p t_j x$ or $t_j x \leq_p t_i x$. Furthermore, since x is a common prefix of all the powers, we have $x \leq_p t_i x$, so x has period $|t_i|$, and therefore, trivially, so does $t_i x$. For any pair t_i, t_j, with $|t_i| \leq |t_j|$, we know that $t_i x \leq_p t_j x$, so $t_i x$ also has period $|t_j|$. Since $|t_i x| > |t_i| + |t_j| > |t_i| + |t_j| - \gcd(|t_i|, |t_j|)$, we can apply Theorem 1 and get that t_i and t_j have a common primitive root t. We already know that t_i and t_j are primitive, so $t_i = t_j = t$. □

Not surprisingly, the same anchor assignment procedure does not produce the desired conclusion if we apply it to powers whose roots are not linearly ordered by the prefix relation. The reason is that what we exploit in the proofs above is that aligning the right edge of powers whose roots are prefixes of each other results in (at least the shorter one of) them being non-primitive. However, right-aligning powers which merely share some prefix does not provide the same strict conclusion.

An alternative way of anchoring which might work for powers in two prefix chains with an overlapping part is to assign the symmetric difference of the chains by their longest common prefix, and anchoring the intersection by the shortest root as before. Further on we show a scheme which works in a special case when the shortest root is unbordered. Before moving on to that, however, we first discuss the sharpness of the bounds implied by our conjecture.

3.1 Optimality

Consider a chain of square roots $u_1 <_p \cdots <_p u_n$ as before. From Theorem 2 we already know that $|\mathbf{clust}(u_i)| \geq n - i + 2$, for all $i \in \{1, \ldots, n\}$, and trivially, $|\mathbf{clust}(u_{i-1})| \geq |\mathbf{clust}(u_i)|$, but it is natural to ask whether the bounds are optimal, that is, whether all possible combinations of cluster sizes satisfying those conditions can actually be realized in some string w. Using the lower bound construction in [15], we can easily illustrate the extremal cases. We are only interested in the situations where $|\mathbf{clust}_w(u_1)| = n + 1$ because we can trivially add further occurrences of all roots at the end of w to accommodate the other cases. When $|\mathbf{clust}_w(u_i)| = n - i + 2$, that is, the topmost cluster has size 2 and then each subsequent cluster is one larger than the previous, take $u_i = ab^{i-1}$ and the word $w = u_1u_2 \cdots u_nu_n$. The case $|\mathbf{clust}_w(u_1)| = |\mathbf{clust}_w(u_n)| = n + 1$ is realized by the roots $u_i = a^{n-1}ba^{i-1}$ and again a word of the form $u_1u_2 \cdots u_nu_n$.

From this starting point we can develop an algorithm to realize any combination of cluster sizes. The idea is to start from the case when all clusters are equal and then reduce the relevant clusters by adding further as to the end of their roots. We start out with $u_i = a^{n-1}ba^{i-1}$ as before and the word in which we realize the clusters will be the concatenation of all the u_i. At this point all clusters are equal to $n + 1$ and we set $r_i = i - 1$ for all $i \in \{1, \ldots, n\}$. We will refine iteratively the values r_i and in the end will set $u_i = a^{n-1}ba^{r_i}$. To remove the occurrence immediately preceding the k-th b from the clusters of each root u_i with $i \geq j$ we add $r_k + n - r_j$ many as to each such r_i. After updating the r_i in question, we keep repeating the removal as many times as necessary. To see whether the construction is correct, note that increasing r_i does not affect the cluster of any of the u_j with $j < i$. By adding $r_k + n - r_j$ to r_j we get that the unary a-tail of u_j is of length $r_k + n$ which is more than the distance between the k-th and $(k+1)$-th b in the word, removing all occurrences of u_j (and hence all longer roots, as well) starting before the k-th b.

For example, let the clusters of $u_1, \ldots, u_6$ be of length $7, 7, 5, 5, 3, 3$, respectively. This means $n = 6$, so initially we set $u_1 = a^5b$, $u_2 = a^5ba$, $u_3 = a^5ba^2$, $u_4 = a^5ba^3$, $u_5 = a^5ba^4$ and $u_6 = a^5ba^5$ and $r_i = i - 1$. First we need to remove the first occurrence of the clusters of $u_3, \ldots, u_6$, so we get $k = 1$ and $j = 3$. This means adding $r_k + n - r_j = 0 + 6 - 2 = 4$ to each r_i with $i \geq 3$. Now the r_i values are $0, 1, 6, 7, 8, 9$. Next we need to remove the occurrences preceding the second b from the same cluster so $k = 2$ and $j = 3$, and hence we need to add $r_k + n - r_j = 1 + 6 - 6 = 1$ to each of those r values, resulting in $0, 1, 7, 8, 9, 10$. Removing the next two occurrences, $k = 3$ and 4, respectively, from the clusters of u_5 and u_6 is by first adding $7 + 6 - 9 = 4$ to them and then $8 + 6 - 13 = 1$, respectively. The end result is $0, 1, 7, 8, 14, 15$, so the clusters are realized by the occurrences of $u_1 = a^5b$, $u_2 = a^5ba$, $u_3 = a^5ba^7$, $u_4 = a^5ba^8$, $u_5 = a^5ba^{14}$ and $u_6 = a^5ba^{15}$ in the word $u_1 \cdots u_6u_6$.

This construction is not optimal in the sense that in most cases there exist much shorter words w and $u_1, \ldots, u_n$ which have a chain of clusters satisfying the same conditions. We expect that investigating the shortest words which realize a combination of cluster sizes could lead to improvements in both lower and upper bounds on distinct repetitions.

3.2 Single Chains of Run Ending Squares

A related direction for expanding the theory of clusters is to find a proof of the upper bound on runs in terms of clusters. We present a brief argument for a simple bound for runs whose "ending squares" form a prefix chain. We cannot readily apply the technique used for distinct squares, because here multiple occurrences of a repetition have to be taken into account.

Consider a run $(a_1 \cdots a_n)^{\frac{k}{n}}$ in a word w, where $a_i \in \Sigma$, $k \geq 2n$, and $a_1 \cdots a_n$ is primitive. Let this run begin at some position i in w. The run ending square is the square starting at position $i+k-2n$ and ending at $i+k-1$. For example, if $w = aababaa$ and we consider the run $(ab)^{\frac{5}{2}}$ starting at $i = 2$ in w, then the run ending square is $baba$, which starts at $i + k - 2n = 3$ and ends at $i + k - 1 = 6$.

Each run has a run ending square, so an upper bound on their number is implicitly an upper bound on the number of runs. The crucial property of run ending squares uu is that the letter following uu in the word is different from the first letter of u. Consider roots of run ending squares $u <_p v \in \Sigma^*$, with a being their first letter. Although uu may occur followed by a, but in those cases it is not the suffix of a run with period $|u|$. An occurrence of uu in w is a run ending square if it is followed by some $b \neq a$ or if it is a suffix of w. Let the run ending occurrences of u^2 start at positions $i_1 < \cdots < i_k$. This means that $\{i_1, i_1+|u|, \ldots, i_k, i_k+|u|\} \subseteq \mathbf{clust}(u)$. However, for all $j \in \{1, \ldots, k-1\}$ we have $w[i_j+|u|] \neq w[i_j+2\cdot|u|]$, and $w[i_k+|u|] \neq w[i_k+2\cdot|u|]$ or $i_k+2\cdot|u| = |w|+1$. From here, for each $j \in \{1, \ldots, k\}$, at least one of the two positions i_j and $i_j+|u|$ is not in $\mathbf{clust}(v)$, so $|\mathbf{clust}(u)|-|\mathbf{clust}(v)| \geq k$. Applying this argument to consecutive roots in a prefix chain $u_1 <_p \cdots <_p u_n$, we get that $\mathbf{clust}(u_i)$ is larger than the number of all runs with run ending square u_j^2, $j \geq i$. However, similarly to the case of distinct powers, this argument does not extend easily to overlapping chains of run ending squares, so one either has to define roots differently for a run or figure out how to treat the case of run ending squares u^2, v^2, w^2 where u is a common prefix of v and w, but the latter two are incomparable.

4 Two Overlapping Chains

Using the anchor positions seen before one can prove the hypothesis for single chains in the general case. As a first extension of the bounds to multiple chains, we will prove a special case when two overlapping chains share an unbordered prefix, in terms of whose occurrences we can upper-bound the number of distinct roots in the two chains combined. Here we will use a type of argument relying on the fact that the prefixes in question are unbordered. First we look at some simple bounds for single chains which, although already obsolete because of Theorem 2, serve as simple demonstrations of the benefits afforded by considering unbordered prefixes.

We will need the following simple lemma establishing restrictions on the relative positions of the rightmost occurrences of two squares whose roots have the same cluster.

Lemma 3. *[7] Let $u^2 \neq v^2$ be two squares in some word w with $u \leq_p v$ and $\mathbf{clust}_w(u) = \mathbf{clust}_w(v)$. If their corresponding rightmost occurrences start at positions u_s and v_s, respectively, then $|u_s - v_s| \geq |u|$.*

We call S a *grounded chain* if the shortest u which is the root of a square occurring in w and is a common prefix of all elements of S, is also in S. For some $u_i, u_j \in S$, we call u_i^2 *covered* by u_j if $u_i <_p u_j \leq_p u_i^2$ or $u_i^2 \leq_p u_j$. The *shortest square root* of a grounded chain S is denoted by $\mathbf{ssr}(S)$ and represents the shortest element in S. Note that $\mathbf{ssr}(S)$ is not bordered. If it were, say $\mathbf{ssr}(S) =$

pqp, for some $p \neq \varepsilon$, then $\mathbf{ssr}(S)^2 = pqppqp$, contains p^2, so $p \in S$, which contradicts $\mathbf{ssr}(S)$ being the shortest element in S. Finally, for two different square roots x and u with $x <_p u$ denote $\mathbf{diff}(x, u) = |\mathbf{clust}(x)| - |\mathbf{clust}(u)|$.

Lemma 4. *For a grounded chain S, let m be the number of covered squares with roots in S and let $x = \mathbf{ssr}(S)$. Then, $|u_n|_x \geq m$.*

Proof. If a square u_i^2 is covered by some u_j, then x occurs at position $|u_i|$ in u_j and in all u_k, with $k > j$, because $u_j \leq_p u_k$. In fact, x occurs at position $|u_i|$ even in u_ℓ, for $i < \ell < j$, as $u_i \leq_p u_\ell \leq_p u_j$. □

Lemma 5. *For a grounded chain of square roots $S = \{u_1, \ldots, u_n\}$, with $x = \mathbf{ssr}(S)$, we have $\mathbf{diff}(x, u_i) + |u_i|_x < \mathbf{diff}(x, u_{i+1}) + |u_{i+1}|_x$.*

Proof. Since $u_i \leq_p u_{i+1}$, we have $|u_i|_x \leq |u_{i+1}|_x$, while $\mathbf{clust}(u_{i+1}) \subseteq \mathbf{clust}(u_i)$ gives $\mathbf{diff}(x, u_i) \leq \mathbf{diff}(x, u_{i+1})$, so both terms in the sum are non-decreasing. Moreover, at least one of them increases in each step: if u_{i+1} covers u_i^2, then $|u_i|_x < |u_{i+1}|_x$, while if it does not, then $|\mathbf{clust}(u_{i+1})| < |\mathbf{clust}(u_i)|$). □

Corollary 2. *For a grounded chain of square roots $S = \{u_1, \ldots, u_n\}$ with $x = \mathbf{ssr}(S)$ we have $n < \frac{3|\mathbf{clust}(x)|}{2} - 1$.*

Proof. Since $u_1 = x$ we have $\mathbf{diff}(x, x) = 0$ and $|u_1|_x = 1$. By Lemma 5, for each $i \in \{1, \ldots, n\}$, the sum $\mathbf{diff}(u_i, x) + |u_i|_x$ is strictly increasing, so $n < \mathbf{diff}(x, u_n) + |u_n|_x$. Since $|\mathbf{clust}(u_n)| \geq 2$, we have $\mathbf{diff}(u_n, x) = |\mathbf{clust}(x)| - |\mathbf{clust}(u_n)| \leq |\mathbf{clust}(x)| - 2$. Also, since u_n^2 occurs, the size of $\mathbf{clust}(x)$ is at least $2|u_n|_x$, that is, $|u_n|_x \leq \frac{\mathbf{clust}(x)}{2}$. Adding the two gives us the statement. □

By the above we have that, for a chain S, the number of clusters is bounded by $3n/2$, where $n = |\mathbf{clust}(\mathbf{ssr}(S))|$. Using Lemma 3 we can further refine this.

Proposition 1. *For a grounded chain of square roots $S = \{u_1, \ldots, u_n\}$ with $x = \mathbf{ssr}(S)$ we have $n < 4|\mathbf{clust}(x)|/3$.*

Proof. Let us look at the topmost level where two clusters are equal, that is, suppose $\mathbf{clust}(u) = \mathbf{clust}(v)$ for $u <_p v$ and for all y with $v <_p y$ there exists no z with $\mathbf{clust}(y) = \mathbf{clust}(z)$.

Since $\mathbf{clust}(u) = \mathbf{clust}(v)$, by Lemma 3 we have that $|\mathbf{clust}(u)| \geq 3$ and there are at least three non-overlapping occurrences of u. From here, if $x = \mathbf{ssr}(S)$, we get that $|u|_x \leq \frac{|\mathbf{clust}(x)|}{3}$, but the consecutive clusters above v are never equal, hence the number of clusters is at most $|\mathbf{clust}(x)|$ plus the number of times when two consecutive cluster are equal. The latter is at most $|u|_x$, hence we get that the number of clusters is at most $\frac{4 \cdot |\mathbf{clust}(x)|}{3}$. □

As the main focus of this section we present an adaptation of the technique we used for the upper bound on single chains, for showing that the combined size of two overlapping prefix chains of roots cannot be larger than the number of occurrences of their common prefix, *when that prefix is unbordered.* The latter qualification is an important one, even though we believe that this is a promising direction towards the full solution of the conjecture. The requirement that the prefix is unbordered not only means that we cannot deduce our conjecture for arbitrary base clusters, but also that we cannot generalize the result to multiple overlaps between multiple chains in a straightforward manner. This, in turn, means that a piece of the puzzle is still missing for the proof of Conjecture 2.

For easy referencing we will denote by different letters the roots which are in the shared part of the two chains and the differing parts of the chains, respectively. Let $X = \{x_1 <_p \cdots <_p x_k\}$ be the common part. The chains $U = \{u_1 <_p \cdots <_p u_m\}$ and $V = \{v_1 <_p \cdots <_p v_n\}$ are the differing parts, so we have $u_1 <>_p v_1$, and of course, as the x_i are the common part, $x_k <_p u_1$ and $x_k <_p v_1$. Since the result in this section does not yield a full proof of the conjecture yet anyway, we will only treat the case of squares instead of general K-powers, to simplify the exposition.

First we show a slightly stronger version of Lemma 1, where we do not necessarily need the whole word to occur three times in its square to imply its non-primitivity.

Lemma 6. *Let $t_1, \ldots, t_n$ with $n \geq 2$ be arbitrary words and let x be any unbordered word such that $|t_i|_x = 0$, for all $i \in \{1, \ldots, n\}$. Let P_i denote the product $xt_1xt_2 \cdots xt_i$. If*

$$|P_n^2|_{P_{n-1}x} > 2$$

then P_n is non-primitive.

Proof. Since x is unbordered and is not contained in t_i, we can reformulate the statement into an equivalent one over the alphabet containing the letters t_i, $i \in \{1, \ldots, n\}$ as follows: $|(t_1 \cdots t_n)^2|_{t_1 \cdots t_{n-1}} > 2$ implies that the word $t_1 \cdots t_n$ of length n is non-primitive. Since $P_{i-1}x$ occurs at least 3 times in P_i^2, we get that $t_1 \cdots t_{n-1}$ occurs at least three times in $(t_1 \cdots t_n)^2$. Let the second occurrence of $t_1 \cdots t_{n-1}$ start at the ith letter (with $i > 1$) of the square $(t_1 \cdots t_n)^2$. This means that $t_1 \cdots t_n$ has period $i - 1$ and therefore $r = t_1 \cdots t_{i-1} t_1 \cdots t_{n-1}$ also has period $i - 1$. At the same time r is the prefix of the square $(t_1 \cdots t_n)^2$, so it also has period n, moreover, its length is $n - 1 + (i - 1) = n + (i - 1) - 1$. From here by the Fine and Wilf theorem r has period $\gcd(i - 1, n)$ and we get that $t_1 \cdots t_n$ is not primitive which implies the statement. □

To describe the assignment of positions to squares we need some definitions first. For a given x, the *ℓ-level x-prefix* ((ℓ, x)-prefix) of a word z is a word z' such that

- $z' <_p z$, and
- $|z'|_x = \ell$.

Further, the *ℓ-level x-representative* ((ℓ, x)-rep) of a square z^2 is the longest prefix of z^2 bordered by the (ℓ, x)-prefix of z^2. The assignment will differ for u_i and v_j depending on the number of occurrences of x in them. Let us partition the roots in U based on whether they have more x's than $\mathbf{lcp}(u_1, v_1)$ or not, so

$U = U_= \cup U_>$ with $U_= = \{u \in U \mid |u|_x = |\mathbf{lcp}(u_1, v_1)|_x\}$ and $U_> = U \setminus U_=$. We partition V similarly into $V_=$ and $V_>$. Now we are ready to describe the assignment of anchors as follows:

- For all x_i^2 and *also for all* u_i^2, v_j^2 with $u_i \in U_=$ and $v_j \in V_=$, we set the x-rep as in the single chain case, i.e., the longest prefix of the square ending in x and start of the last x in the leftmost x-rep as the anchor.
- For the other u_i and v_j, we set the start of the last x in their leftmost occurring (ℓ, x)-rep as the anchor, where $\ell = |\mathbf{lcp}(u_1, v_1)|_x + 1$.

Lemma 7. *Let $u, v \in X \cup U \cup V$ be two distinct square roots. If the anchors of u^2 and v^2 coincide then the shorter between u and v is non-primitive.*

Proof. We have to check what happens when squares collide for each pairing of $X, U_=, U_>, V_=$ and $V_>$. These potentially 25 pairings reduce to 15 as the order does not matter, and can be treated in 7 groups, as we will see below. Like before, the starting position of the x-rep of an arbitrary square z^2 will be denoted by z_s and we set $z_m = z_s + |z|$.

1. $u \in U_>$ and $v \in V_>$: impossible, because in the x-rep of u^2 at the ℓth x before the anchor we have the (ℓ, x)-prefix starting, whereas in the x-rep of v^2 we would have the (ℓ, x)-prefix of v at the same position, but the two are incomparable by the prefix relation as they are longer than $\mathbf{lcp}(u_1, v_1)$.
2. $u \in U_>$ and $v \in U_>$ (analogous to pairing $(V_>, V_>)$): possible; the (ℓ, x)-prefix of u and v are the same, say y. In this case we can apply Lemma 2 as the y-anchors of u and v coincide, giving the non-primitivity of the shorter between the two with a primitive root of length less than u_1.
3. $u \in U_>$ and $v \in V_=$ (analogous to the pairing $(V_>, U_=)$): possible; in this case we have $u_s < v_s$. If $u_m \leq v_s$, then the x-rep of v^2 occurs earlier, a contradiction. If $u_s < v_s < u_m$, then we can apply Lemma 6 and we get that v is non-primitive.
4. $u \in U_>$ and $v \in U_=$ (analogous to the pairings $(V_>, V_=)$, $(U_>, X)$, $(V_>, X)$): possible; here the anchor of u is defined as the last x occurrence in a copy of its (ℓ, x)-prefix $u'x$, whereas the anchor of v is the last occurrence of x in its x-rep $vv'x$. As u contains more occurrences of x than v does, which has exactly as many as the $\mathbf{lcp}$ of u_1 and v_1, we get that $v'x <_p u'x$. Now we can apply Lemma 6 and conclude that v is non-primitive.
5. $u \in U_=$ and $v \in V_=$: impossible because the fact that $|u|_x = |v|_x$ implies $u_m = v_m$ which, in turn, also means $u_s = v_s$. However, at u_s we have an occurrence of u_1 and at v_s an occurrence of v_1, which are incomparable.
6. $u \in U_=$ and $v \in U_=$ (analogous to $(V_=, V_=)$): impossible, by an argument similar to the previous point. Since u and v have the same number of x occurrences, we get $u_m = v_m$ and then $u_s = v_s$ which implies $u = v$.
7. $u \in U_=$ and $v \in X$ (analogous to pairings $(V_=, X)$, (X, X)): possible; this is again a case where Lemma 2 applies as the anchors are all x-anchors, giving non-primitivity of v with root shorter than x.

All 15 cases have been listed above and all are either impossible or result in the non-primitivity of the shorter root. □

We obtained that the collision of anchors results in non-primitive shorter root. A reallocation of the non-primitively rooted squares is likely possible following the logic used for squares ([7] proof of Theorem 2). However, it is probably more technically involved in this overlapping case, and since we do not know how to generalize Lemma 7 to more chains with complex overlapping structure, it seems of limited use at the moment and we decided not to pursue it here due to the space restrictions. However, some manner of separately anchoring the chains based on their **lcp** with neighboring incomparable chains seems a promising way towards a final solution, so we expect that the analysis above will prove useful.

References

1. Bannai, H., I, T., Inenaga, S., Nakashima, Y., Takeda, M., Tsuruta, K.: The "runs" theorem. SIAM J. Comput. **46**(5), 1501–1514 (2017)
2. Blanchet-Sadri, F., Mercaş, R., Scott, G.: Counting distinct squares in partial words. Acta Cybern. **19**(2), 465–477 (2009)
3. Crochemore, M., Fazekas, S., Iliopoulos, C., Jayasekera, I.: Number of occurrences of powers in strings. Int. J. Found. Comput. Sci. **21**(4), 535–547 (2010)
4. Crochemore, M., Iliopoulos, C., Kubica, M., Radoszewski, J., Rytter, W., Waleń, T.: The maximal number of cubic runs in a word. J. Comput. System Sci. **78**(6), 1828–1836 (2012)
5. Crochemore, M., Rytter, W.: Squares, cubes, and time-space efficient string searching. Algorithmica **13**(5), 405–425 (1995)
6. Deza, A., Franek, F., Thierry, A.: How many double squares can a string contain? Disc. Appl. Math. **180**, 52–69 (2015)
7. Fazekas, S.Z., Mercaş, R.: Clusters of repetition roots: single chains. In: Bureš, T., et al. (eds.) SOFSEM 2021. LNCS, vol. 12607, pp. 400–409. Springer, Cham (2021). https://doi.org/10.1007/978-3-030-67731-2_29
8. Fazekas, S.Z., Seki, S.: Square network on a word. Theor. Comput. Sci. **894**, 121–134 (2021)
9. Fraenkel, A., Simpson, J.: How many squares must a binary sequence contain? Electron. J. Comb. **2**, R2 (1995)
10. Fraenkel, A., Simpson, J.: How many squares can a string contain? J. Comb. Theory Ser. A **82**(1), 112–120 (1998)
11. Gusfield, D.: Algorithms on Strings, Trees, and Sequences - Computer Science and Computational Biology. Cambridge University Press, Cambridge (1997)
12. Hickerson, D.: Less than $2n$ distinct squares in a word of length n (2003). Communicated by Dan Gusfield
13. Ilie, L.: A simple proof that a word of length n has at most $2n$ distinct squares. J. Comb. Theory Ser. A **112**(1), 163–164 (2005)
14. Ilie, L.: A note on the number of squares in a word. Theoret. Comput. Sci. **380**(3), 373–376 (2007)
15. Jonoska, N., Manea, F., Seki, S.: A stronger square conjecture on binary words. In: Geffert, V., Preneel, B., Rovan, B., Štuller, J., Tjoa, A.M. (eds.) SOFSEM 2014. LNCS, vol. 8327, pp. 339–350. Springer, Cham (2014). https://doi.org/10.1007/978-3-319-04298-5_30

16. Kolpakov, R., Kucherov, G.: Finding maximal repetitions in a word in linear time. In: Proceedings of 40th FOCS, pp. 596–604. IEEE Computer Society Press (1999)
17. Lothaire, M.: Combinatorics on Words. Cambridge University Press, Cambridge (1997)
18. Manea, F., Seki, S.: Square-density increasing mappings. In: Manea, F., Nowotka, D. (eds.) WORDS 2015. LNCS, vol. 9304, pp. 160–169. Springer, Cham (2015). https://doi.org/10.1007/978-3-319-23660-5_14
19. Storer, J.A.: Data Compression: Methods and Theory. Computer Science Press, Inc. (1988)
20. Thierry, A.: A proof that a word of length n has less than 1.5n distinct squares (2020). https://arxiv.org/abs/2001.02996
21. Thue, A.: Über unendliche Zeichenreihen. Kra. Vidensk. Selsk. Skrifter. I Mat. Nat. Kl. **7** (1906)
22. Thue, A.: Über die gegenseitige Lage gleicher Teile gewisser Zeichenreihen. Kra. Vidensk. Selsk. Skrifter. I Mat. Nat. Kl. **1** (1912)

Nearly k-Universal Words - Investigating a Part of Simon's Congruence

Pamela Fleischmann(✉), Lukas Haschke, Annika Huch, Annika Mayrock, and Dirk Nowotka

Kiel University, Kiel, Germany
{fpa,lha,dn}@informatik.uni-kiel.de,
{stu216885,stu217133}@mail.uni-kiel.de

Abstract. Determining the index of Simon's congruence is a long outstanding open problem. Two words u and v are called Simon congruent if they have the same set of scattered factors (also known as subwords or subsequences), which are parts of the word in the correct order but not necessarily consecutive, e.g., `oath` is a scattered factor of `logarithm` but `tail` is not. Following the idea of scattered factor k-universality (also known as k-richness), we investigate nearly k-universality, i.e., words where exactly one scattered factor of length k is absent. We present a full characterisation as well as the index of the congruence in this special case and the shortlex normal form for each such class. Moreover, we extend the definition to m-nearly k-universality (exactly m scattered factors of length k are absent), show some results for $m > 1$, and give a full combinatorial characterisation of m-nearly k-universal words which are additionally $(k-1)$-universal.

1 Introduction

Given a word w, a *scattered factor* (also known as *(scattered) substring or subword*) of w is a word, that is obtained by deleting letters from w while preserving the order, i.e., formally u of length $n \in \mathbb{N}_0$ is a scattered factor of w (denoted by $u \in \text{ScatFact}(w)$) if $w = v_1u[1]v_2u[2]...v_nu[n]v_{n+1}$ for existing (possibly empty) words $v_1, ..., v_{n+1}$. For instance, `flow`, `poor`, `wow` are scattered factors of `powerflower` but `rope`, `loop` are not scattered factors since the letters do not occur in the correct order in w. Therefore, scattered factors are a complexity measure for words (strings) in terms of existing or absent parts of information. Hence, scattered factors are not only of a theoretical interest, but a practical, too. When examining discrete data, e.g., protein sequences or incomplete or faulty transmissions of signals [7,11,23], scattered factors can be used as a representation [6,28]. Moreover, scattered factors can be found in some famous algorithmic problems like searching for longest (increasing) subsequences [1,3,4], shortest common supersequences [22], string-to-string correction problems [27], most unusual time series subsequence [18], fast subsequence matching in time-series databases [8]. Furthermore, there exist neural machine translations, which use rare words with subword units [25] or byte-level subwords [28].

Published by Springer Nature Switzerland AG 2022
Y.-S. Han and G. Vaszil (Eds.): DCFS 2022, LNCS 13439, pp. 57–71, 2022.
https://doi.org/10.1007/978-3-031-13257-5_5

In 1972, Simon defined the famous congruence relation regarding scattered factors in the context of piecewise testable events [26], today known as *Simon's congruence*: two words x and y are called *congruent w.r.t.* $k \in \mathbb{N}$ ($x \sim_k y$), iff x and y have the same set of scattered factors of length up to k, i.e., $\text{ScatFact}_\ell(x) = \text{ScatFact}_\ell(y)$ for all $\ell \leq k$, with the index denoting the length of the considered scattered factors. Thus, we have $\mathtt{aba} \sim_2 \mathtt{aabaa}$ and $\mathtt{aba} \not\sim_2 \mathtt{abab}$ since $\mathtt{bb}$ is a scattered factor of $\mathtt{abab}$ but not of $\mathtt{aba}$. A profound introduction into scattered factors and Simon's congruence can be found in [21, Section 6] by Sakarovich and Simon. Although $\sim_k$ is well studied from different perspectives with deep insights (cf. [9,21,26]), determining its index, i.e., determining $|\Sigma^*/\sim_k|$ for a given alphabet Σ and $k \in \mathbb{N}$, is still an open problem. Remarkable results regarding a normal form for congruence classes w.r.t. $\sim_k$ can also be found in [20,24]. In [14–16] the notion of k-richness was introduced in the context of piecewise testable languages: w is k-rich if $\text{ScatFact}_k(w) = \Sigma^k$. This notion coincides with the notion of k-universality introduced in [2] (therein also the relation of both is explained). The language of k-universal words was intensively investigated and characterised in [2,5,10]. One of the main insights of k-universal words is that a word w is k-universal iff w's arch factorisation [13] has k arches. Very recently, Gawrychowski et al. presented an algorithm to test Simon's congruence in time linear in the sum of the words' length [12]. This very important result is based on a new data structure called *Simon tree*. Pursuing the idea of k-universality, where the main focus is on the cardinality of a word's scattered factors set, one can define the sets $M_{i,k} = \{L \subseteq \Sigma^* \mid \exists w \in \Sigma^* : \text{ScatFact}_k(w) = L, |L| = i\}$ for all $1 \leq i \leq |\Sigma|^k$ which contain all languages of cardinality i occurring as a scattered factor set of some word w w.r.t. a length k. Thus, each such $L \in M_{i,k}$ represents a congruence class of $\sim_k$. A special subclass of $M_{|\Sigma|^k-m,k}$ has recently been studied from an algorithmic point of view in [19]. There the authors investigated shortest absent scattered factors (SAS) of words, i.e., for a given $(k-1)$-universal word w they determined the set of words with length k that are not scattered factors of w. If this set has cardinality m, we obtain a subset of $M_{|\Sigma|^k-m,k}$. This subset may be proper witnessed by the word $\mathtt{aabbb}$ which is 13-nearly 4-universal but not 3-universal.

Our Contribution. In this work, we investigate and characterise the set $M_{|\Sigma|^k-1,k}$ and give some insights into $M_{i,k}$ for some other $i < |\Sigma|^k - 1$. We call a word m-nearly k-universal if $|\text{ScatFact}_k(w)| = |\Sigma|^k - m$, i.e., k-universal words are 0-nearly k-universal in the new notion. We compute the shortlex normal form for each congruence class of 1-nearly k-universal words and present an algorithm which decides in linear time whether a word is 1-nearly k-universal that in contrast to [12] does not need additional data structures.

Structure of the Work. In Sect. 2 we give the basic definitions and notations. In Sect. 3 we present the results on 1-nearly k-universal words including the characterisation and the congruence classes w.r.t. $\sim_k$. The results for $m > 1$ including a combinatorial characterisation of m-nearly k-universal words which are also $(k-1)$-universal are presented in Sect. 4.

2 Preliminaries

Let $\mathbb{N}$ be the set of all natural numbers, $\mathbb{N}_0 = \mathbb{N} \cup \{0\}$, $[n] = \{1, \ldots, n\}$, and $[n]_0 := [n] \cup \{0\}$. An *alphabet* Σ is a non empty finite set whose elements are called *letters*. Set $\sigma = |\Sigma|$. A *word* is a finite sequence of letters from Σ. Let Σ^* be the set of all finite words over Σ with concatenation and the empty word ε as neutral element. Set $\Sigma^+ := \Sigma^* \setminus \{\varepsilon\}$. Let $w \in \Sigma^*$. For all $n \in \mathbb{N}_0$ define inductively, $w^0 = \varepsilon$ and $w^n = ww^{n-1}$. The *length* of w is the number of w's letters; thus $|\varepsilon| = 0$. For all $k \in \mathbb{N}_0$ set $\Sigma^k := \{w \in \Sigma^* \mid |w| = k\}$ and denote w's i^{th} letter by $w[i]$ and set $w[i..j] = w[i] \cdots w[j]$ if $i < j$, and ε if $i > j$ for all $i, j \in [|w|]$. Set $\text{alph}(w) = \{\mathtt{a} \in \Sigma \mid \exists i \in [|w|] : w[i] = \mathtt{a}\}$ as w's alphabet and for each $\mathtt{a} \in \Sigma$ set $|w|_{\mathtt{a}} = |\{i \in [|w|] \mid w[i] = \mathtt{a}\}|$. The word $u \in \Sigma^*$ is called a *factor* of w if there exist $x, y \in \Sigma^*$ such that $w = xuy$. In the case $x = \varepsilon$, we call u a *prefix* of w and *suffix* if $y = \varepsilon$. Let $\text{Fact}(w)$, $\text{Pref}(w)$ and $\text{Suff}(w)$, respectively, be the corresponding sets and let $\text{Pref}_i(w)$ denote the prefix of length i of w for all $i \in [|w|]_0$. Define the *reverse* of w by $w^R = w[|w|] \cdots w[1]$ and if $w = x_1^{k_1} x_2^{k_2} \cdots x_\ell^{k_\ell} \in \Sigma^*$ with $k_i, \ell \in \mathbb{N}$, $i \in [\ell]$, the *condensed form (print)* of w is defined by $\text{cond}(w) = x_1 \cdots x_\ell$ under the assumption that $x_j \neq x_{j+1}$ for $j \in [\ell - 1]$. Let $<_\Sigma$ be a total order on Σ and denote the *lexicographical order* on Σ^* by $<$. Define w_Σ as the word in Σ^σ with $w_\Sigma[i] <_\Sigma w_\Sigma[i+1]$ and $\text{alph}(w) = \Sigma$. A mapping $f : \Sigma^* \to \Sigma^*$ is called a *morphism* if $f(uv) = f(u)f(v)$ holds for all $u, v \in \Sigma^*$. Thus, a morphic mapping is already completely defined, if the images for all letters in Σ are given. If f is additionally bijective, f is called a morphic permutation. For further definitions see [21]. After these basic notations, we introduce the scattered factors.

Definition 1. *Let $w \in \Sigma^*$ and $n \in \mathbb{N}_0$. A word $u \in \Sigma^n$ is called a* scattered factor *of w ($u \in \text{ScatFact}(w)$) if there exist $v_1, \ldots, v_{n+1} \in \Sigma^*$ such that $w = v_1 u[1] v_2 u[2] \cdots v_n u[n]\, v_{n+1}$. Set $\text{ScatFact}_k(w) = \{u \in \text{ScatFact}(w) \mid |u| = k\}$.*

The words `cau`, `cafe`, `life` and `ufo` are all scattered factors of `cauliflower` but neither `flour` nor `row`. Tightly related to the notion of scattered factors is the famous *Simon congruence*.

Definition 2. *Two words $w, v \in \Sigma^*$ are* Simon congruent *w.r.t. $k \in \mathbb{N}_0$ ($w \sim_k v$) if $\text{ScatFact}_\ell(w) = \text{ScatFact}_\ell(v)$ for all $\ell \leq k$. Given $w \in \Sigma^*$, the word $u \in \Sigma^*$ is called* shortlex normal form *of w w.r.t. $\sim_k$ if $u \sim_k w$ and u is the lexicographically smallest word among the shortest words in w's congruence class $[w]_{\sim_k}$.*

Since $\text{ScatFact}_k(w) \subseteq \Sigma^k$ holds for all $k \in \mathbb{N}_0$, determining the index of Simon's congruence can be split into the parametrised problem on determining how many scattered factor sets - or equivalently how many different words - exist with $|\text{ScatFact}_k(w)| = \sigma^k - m$ for all $m \in \mathbb{N}_0$ (cf. [2,5,10] for $m = 0$).

Definition 3. *A word $w \in \Sigma^*$ is called m-*nearly *k-*universal *if $|\text{ScatFact}_k(w)| = \sigma^k - m$. If $m = 0$, we call w k-universal. Denote by $\iota(w)$ the* universality index, *i.e., the largest* $k \in \mathbb{N}_0$ *such that* w *is* k*-universal. We call 1-universal words,* $\mathrm{Univ}_{\Sigma,k}$*,* universal *and* 1*-nearly* k*-universal words,* $\mathrm{NUniv}_{\Sigma,k}$*,* nearly k-universal.

Remark 4. By definition, all k-universal words are congruent modulo k and a k-universal word $w \in \Sigma^*$ is also k'-universal for all $k' \leq k$.

In this work, we mainly investigate nearly k-universal words, thus words, where in comparison to Σ^k, exactly one word of length k is absent from the scattered factor set. In the unary alphabet ε is the only word which has $\sigma^k - 1 = 0$ scattered factors; therefore we only consider at least binary alphabets. Moreover, we assume $\Sigma = \mathrm{alph}(w)$ for a given w, if not stated otherwise.

Remark 5. Notice that $w \in \mathrm{NUniv}_{\Sigma,k}$ does not imply $w \in \mathrm{NUniv}_{\Sigma,k-1}$: we have $\mathtt{aba} \in \mathrm{NUniv}_{\Sigma,2}$ but by $\iota(\mathtt{aba}) = 1$, $\mathtt{aba}$ is not nearly 1-universal but 1-universal.

One of the main tools for the investigation of nearly k-universal words is the *arch factorisation* which was introduced by Hebrard [13]. In this factorisation a word is factorised into universal factors and a rest.

Definition 6. *For a word* $w \in \Sigma^*$ *the* arch factorisation *is given by* $w = \mathrm{ar}_1(w) \cdots \mathrm{ar}_k(w)\,\mathrm{r}(w)$ *for* $k \in \mathbb{N}_0$ *with*

(a) $\iota(\mathrm{ar}_i(w)) = 1$ *for all* $i \in [k]$*,*
(b) $\mathrm{ar}_i(w)[|\mathrm{ar}_i(w)|] \notin \mathrm{alph}(\mathrm{ar}_i(w)[1 \cdots |\mathrm{ar}_i(w)| - 1])$ *for all* $i \in [k]$*, and*
(c) $\mathrm{alph}(\mathrm{r}(w)) \subsetneq \Sigma$*.*

The words $\mathrm{ar}_i(w)$ *are called* arches *of* w *and* $\mathrm{r}(w)$ *is the* rest *of* w*. Define the* modus $\mathrm{m}(w) = \mathrm{ar}_1(w)[|\mathrm{ar}_1(w)|] \cdots \mathrm{ar}_k(w)[|\mathrm{ar}_k(w)|]$*. The* inner of the ith arch of w *is defined as the prefix of* $\mathrm{ar}_i(w)$ *such that* $\mathrm{ar}_i(w) = \mathrm{in}_i(w)\,\mathrm{m}(w)[i]$ *holds.*

To visualise the arch factorisation in explicit examples we use parenthesis. For example we write $(\mathtt{aab}) \cdot (\mathtt{bba}) \cdot \mathtt{a}$ to mark the two arches, namely $\mathtt{aab}$ and $\mathtt{bba}$ and the rest, $\mathtt{a}$, which is denoted without parenthesis.

Remark 7. The modus $\mathrm{m}(w)$ consists of all unique last letters of the arches and is therefore uniquely defined.

Based on the arch factorisation we define perfect universal words, which are words without a rest.

Definition 8. *We call a word* $w \in \Sigma^*$ perfect k-universal *if* $\iota(w) = k$ *and* $\mathrm{r}(w) = \varepsilon$*. The set of all these words with* $\mathrm{alph}(w) = \Sigma$ *is denoted by* $\mathrm{PUniv}_{\Sigma,k}$*.*

For the algorithmic results in Sect. 3 and 4 we use the standard computational model RAM with logarithmic word-size (see, e.g., [17]), i.e., we follow a standard assumption from stringology, if w is the input word for our algorithms, we assume $\Sigma = \mathrm{alph}(w) = \{1, 2, \ldots, \sigma\}$.

3 Nearly k-Universal Words

In this section we characterise $\mathrm{NUniv}_{\Sigma,k}$: we show that there exist exactly σ^k different classes w.r.t. $\sim_k$, i.e., for each word $v \in \Sigma^k$ there exists a word $w \in \Sigma^*$ such that $\mathrm{ScatFact}_k(w) = \Sigma^k \backslash \{v\}$. The first lemma proves that nearly k-universal words are $(k-1)$-universal and that all letters of Σ but one have to occur in the rest.

Lemma 9. *If* $w \in \mathrm{NUniv}_{\Sigma,k}$ *then* $\iota(w) = k-1$ *and* $|\,\mathrm{alph}(\mathrm{r}(w))| = \sigma - 1$.

Remark 10. Lemma 9 implies that the length of a nearly k-universal word is at least $k\sigma - 1$ since we have $k-1$ arches and a rest of length $\sigma - 1$. Moreover, for each nearly k-universal word w, there exists a unique letter $\mathtt{a}_w$ with $\mathrm{alph}(\mathrm{r}(w)) = \Sigma \backslash \{\mathtt{a}_w\}$. This implies $\mathrm{ScatFact}_k(w) = \Sigma^k \backslash \{\mathrm{m}(w)\mathtt{a}_w\}$ for $w \in \mathrm{NUniv}_{\Sigma,k}$.

The conditions of Lemma 9 do not suffice for a characterisation of $\mathrm{NUniv}_{\Sigma,k}$. Consider the word $w = (\mathtt{acb})\cdot\mathtt{ba}$ with $\iota(w) = 1$ and $\mathrm{alph}(\mathrm{r}(w)) = \{\mathtt{a}, \mathtt{b}\}$. We have $|\,\mathrm{ScatFact}_2(w)| = |\Sigma^2 \backslash \{\mathtt{cc}, \mathtt{bc}\}|$ and thus $w \notin \mathrm{NUniv}_{\Sigma,2}$. The following, naïve, but intuitive characterisation uses Remark 10: all words of length k ending in $\mathtt{a}_w$, but $\mathrm{m}(w)\mathtt{a}_w$, have to appear within the word (all others appear necessarily).

Proposition 11. *A word* w *is nearly* k*-universal iff* $\iota(w) = k-1$, $\mathrm{alph}(\mathrm{r}(w)) = \Sigma \backslash \{\mathtt{a}_w\}$, *and for all* $v \in \Sigma^k$ *with* $v[1..k-1] \neq \mathrm{m}(w)$ *and* $v[k] = \mathtt{a}_w$ *there exists* $i \in [k-1]$ *with* $v[i]v[i+1] \in \mathrm{ScatFact}_2(\mathrm{ar}_i(w))$.

We have $w = (\mathtt{accb}) \cdot (\mathtt{bac}) \cdot \mathtt{ab} \in \mathrm{NUniv}_{\Sigma,3}$ as $\mathtt{ac}, \mathtt{cc} \in \mathrm{ScatFact}_2(\mathrm{ar}_1(w))$ and $\mathtt{ac}, \mathtt{bc} \in \mathrm{ScatFact}_2(\mathrm{ar}_2(w))$. This characterisation is not very helpful since checking whether a word is nearly k-universal means to check all σ^{k-1} options for v. The following characterisation does not only provide an efficient way to check whether $w \in \mathrm{NUniv}_{\Sigma,k}$ but also builds the basis for an efficient algorithm regarding $\sim_k$. In beforehand, we prove that *cutting off* ℓ arches at the beginning of a nearly k-universal word, leads to a nearly $(k-\ell)$-universal word.

Lemma 12. *Let* $\ell \leq k-1$. *If* $w \in \mathrm{NUniv}_{\Sigma,k}$ *with* $w = \mathrm{ar}_1(w) \cdots \mathrm{ar}_{k-1}(w)\,\mathrm{r}(w)$, *then* $\mathrm{ar}_{\ell+1}(w)...\mathrm{ar}_{k-1}(w)\,\mathrm{r}(w) \in \mathrm{NUniv}_{\Sigma,k-\ell}$.

Remark 13. Notice that Lemma 12 is not applicable for arches in the middle: $(\mathtt{ab}) \cdot (\mathtt{aab}) \cdot \mathtt{b} \in \mathrm{NUniv}_{\Sigma,3}$ but $(\mathtt{ab}) \cdot \mathtt{b} \notin \mathrm{NUniv}_{\Sigma,2}$.

The following theorem captures our main combinatorial result: a suitable characterisation for nearly k-universal words serving as basis for the algorithms. Here, $\mathrm{ScatFact}_k(w^R) = \{u^R |\, u \in \mathrm{ScatFact}_k(w)\}$ plays an important role.

Theorem 14. *For* $w \in \Sigma^*$ *the following statements are equivalent*

1. $w \in \mathrm{NUniv}_{\Sigma,k}$,
2. $\iota(w) = k-1$, $|\,\mathrm{alph}(\mathrm{r}(w))| = \sigma - 1 = |\,\mathrm{alph}(\mathrm{r}(w^R))|$, *and*
   (a) *if* k *is even then there exist* $u_1, v_2 \in \mathrm{PUniv}_{\Sigma,\frac{k}{2}}$, $u_2, v_1 \in \mathrm{PUniv}_{\Sigma,\frac{k}{2}-1}$ *and* $x_i \in \Sigma^+$ *with* $|\,\mathrm{alph}(x_i)| = \sigma - 1$ *with* $w = u_i x_i v_i^R$ *for* $i \in [2]$.

(b) if k is odd then there exist $u, v \in \mathrm{PUniv}_{\Sigma,\frac{k-1}{2}}$, and $x \in \Sigma^+$ with $|\operatorname{alph}(x)| = \sigma - 1$ with $w = uxv^R$.

3. $\iota(w) = k - 1$, $|\operatorname{alph}(\mathrm{r}(w))| = \sigma - 1 = |\operatorname{alph}(\mathrm{r}(w^R))|$, and for all $\hat{k}, \tilde{k} \in \mathbb{N}$ with $\hat{k} + \tilde{k} + 1 = k$ there exist $u \in \mathrm{PUniv}_{\Sigma,\hat{k}}$, $v \in \mathrm{PUniv}_{\Sigma,\tilde{k}}$, and $x \in \Sigma^+$ with $|\operatorname{alph}(x)| = \sigma - 1$ such that $w = uxv^R$.

Proof. The implication 3. to 2. is immediate. Now, we prove 2. implies 1. We have to show that w is nearly k-universal under the three constraints. We know $\mathrm{m}(w)\mathtt{a}_w \notin \mathrm{ScatFact}_k(w)$ and let $y \in \Sigma^k \backslash \{\mathrm{m}(w)\mathtt{a}_w\}$. If $y[k] \neq \mathtt{a}_w$, we have immediately $y \in \mathrm{ScatFact}_k(w)$ by the second condition. Thus, assume $y[k] = \mathtt{a}_w$.

Case 1: k is even

Choose $u_1, u_2, v_1, v_2, x_1, x_2$ according to condition a. Since u_1 and v_2 are perfect $\frac{k}{2}$-universal and u_2 and v_1 are perfect $\frac{k}{2} - 1$-universal, we have $y\left[1..\frac{k}{2}\right] \in \mathrm{ScatFact}(u_1)$, $y\left[\frac{k}{2} + 2..k\right] \in \mathrm{ScatFact}(v_1^R)$, $y\left[1..\frac{k}{2} - 1\right] \in \mathrm{ScatFact}(u_2)$, and $y\left[\frac{k}{2} + 1..k\right] \in \mathrm{ScatFact}(v_2^R)$. Thus, if $y[\frac{k}{2} + 1] \in \operatorname{alph}(x_1)$ or $y[\frac{k}{2}] \in \operatorname{alph}(x_2)$, we have $y \in \mathrm{ScatFact}_k(w)$. Assume $y[\frac{k}{2} + 1] \notin \operatorname{alph}(x_1)$ and $y[\frac{k}{2}] \notin \operatorname{alph}(x_2)$. Since we have also proven the claim if two consecutive letters of y are in one arch of u_1, u_2, v_1, or v_2, we may assume that $y[1..\frac{k}{2} - 1] = \mathrm{m}(u_2)$ and $y = [\frac{k}{2} + 2..k] = \mathrm{m}(v_1)^R$. By $|\operatorname{alph}(x_1)| = \sigma - 1$, we have $y[\frac{k}{2} + 1] = \mathrm{m}(v_2)[\frac{k}{2}]$, and analogously by $|\operatorname{alph}(x_2)| = \sigma - 1$, we have $y[\frac{k}{2}] = \mathrm{m}(u_1)[\frac{k}{2}]$. Choose $i_1, i_2 \in [|w|]$ with $w[i_1] = \mathrm{m}(v_2)[\frac{k}{2}]$ and $w[i_2] = \mathrm{m}(u_1)[\frac{k}{2}]$. If $i_1 \geq i_2$, w would have at least $\iota(u_1) + \iota(v_2^R) = k$ arches - a contradiction (Fig. 1). Thus we have $i_1 < i_2$. This implies that $y[\frac{k}{2} + 1]$ has be chosen before $y[\frac{k}{2}]$ in w. This implies $\iota(w) < k - 1$ - a contradiction.

Case 2: k is odd

Choose u, v, x according to condition b. Since u and v are perfect $\frac{k-1}{2}$-universal, we have $y\left[1..\frac{k-1}{2}\right] \in \mathrm{ScatFact}(u)$ and $y\left[\frac{k-1}{2} + 2..k\right] \in \mathrm{ScatFact}(v)$. If $y[\frac{k-1}{2} + 1] \in \operatorname{alph}(x)$, the claim is proven. Thus, assume $y[\frac{k-1}{2} + 1] \notin \operatorname{alph}(x)$. Again we can also assume $y[1..\frac{k-1}{2}] = \mathrm{m}(u)$ and $y[\frac{k-1}{2} + 2..k] = \mathrm{m}(v)^R$. Since $|\operatorname{alph}(x)| = \sigma - 1$, we have $y[\frac{k-1}{2} + 1] = \mathrm{m}(w)[\frac{k-1}{2} + 1]$ which occurs after $\mathrm{m}(v)[\frac{k-1}{2}]$ in w. Again we obtain $\iota(w) < k - 1$ - a contradiction. Finally, we prove that 1. implies 3. Consider firstly w be nearly k-universal. Then the first two claims follow immediately by Lemma 9 and the fact that w^R is nearly k-universal. By $\iota(w) = k - 1$, we have $w, w^R \in \mathrm{Univ}_{\Sigma,k'}$ for all $k' \leq k - 1$. Let $\hat{k}, \tilde{k} \in \mathbb{N}_{<k}$ with $\hat{k} + \tilde{k} + 1 = k$. Thus, there exist $u \in \mathrm{PUniv}_{\Sigma,\hat{k}}$ and $v \in \mathrm{PUniv}_{\Sigma,\tilde{k}}$ with

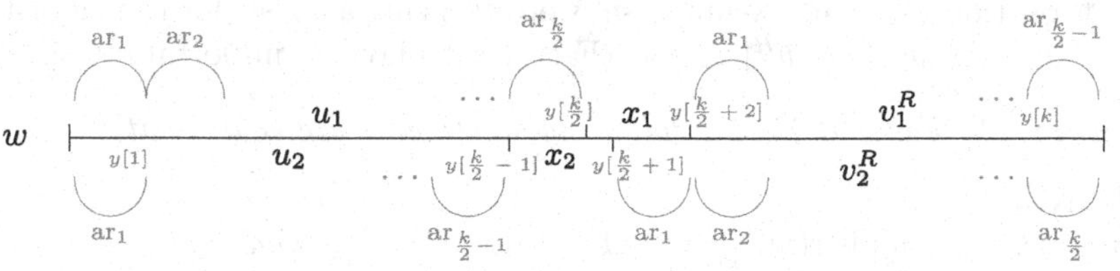

Fig. 1. The factorisation of w for even k where y's letters occur as the modus.

$u \in \text{Pref}(w)$ and $v \in \text{Pref}(w^R)$. Choose $x \in \Sigma^*$ with $w = uxv^R$. By Lemma 12, we get $xv^R \in \text{NUniv}_{\Sigma,k-\hat{k}}$. Thus, $vx^R \in \text{NUniv}_{\Sigma,k-\hat{k}}$. Applying Lemma 12 again, we obtain $x^R \in \text{NUniv}_{\Sigma,1}$. By Lemma 9 we get $|\text{alph}(x)| = \sigma - 1$. This concludes the proof. □

We have $w = (\mathtt{aab})\cdot(\mathtt{ba})\cdot(\mathtt{ab})\cdot\mathtt{a} \notin \text{NUniv}_{\Sigma,4}$ since the factorisation $(\mathtt{aab})(\mathtt{ba})\cdot \mathtt{a}\cdot((\mathtt{ab}))^R$ meets the requirements but the factorisation $(\mathtt{aab})\cdot\varepsilon\cdot((\mathtt{ab})(\mathtt{aab}))^R$ does not, witnessing that both are needed (cf. Theorem 14).

Corollary 15. *We have* $ww^R \in \text{NUniv}_{\Sigma,2k-1}$ *iff* $w \in \text{NUniv}_{\Sigma,k}$ *as well as* $waw^R \in \text{NUniv}_{\Sigma,2k-1}$ *with* $\mathtt{a} \in \Sigma$ *iff* $w \in \text{NUniv}_{\Sigma,k}$ *and* $\mathtt{a} \in \text{alph}(\text{r}(w))$.

With Theorem 14 we are able to solve the following two problems (for a given k) efficiently: decide whether $v \in \text{NUniv}_{\Sigma,k}$ and find for a given $u \in \Sigma^k$, $w \in \text{NUniv}_{\Sigma,k}$ such that $u \notin \text{ScatFact}_k(w)$. The latter one leads immediately to the index of Simon's congruence restricted to nearly k-universal words. Notice that for the first problem, a linear time algorithm is implicitly given in [12]: if w is a word of length n, the Simon tree can be constructed in time $\mathcal{O}(n)$ and in time $\mathcal{O}(k)$ the lexicographically smallest SAS can be determined; if there is only one SAS, we have $w \in \text{NUniv}_{\Sigma,k}$. The following algorithm only checks whether a word is nearly k-universal but does not need any additional data structures.

Proposition 16. *Given* $w \in \Sigma^*$, $k \in \mathbb{N}$, *we decide whether* $w \in \text{NUniv}_{\Sigma,k}$ *in time* $\mathcal{O}(|w|)$ *and compute if so the absent scattered factor.*

```
Data: Given w ∈ Σ* with arch factorisation and k ∈ ℕ.
Result: True, if w ∈ NUniv_{Σ,1,k}. False, otherwise.
if ι(w) ≠ k − 1 || |alph(r(w))| ≠ σ − 1 || |alph(r(w^R))| ≠ σ − 1 then
    return false;
else
    if k mod 2 == 0 then
        w_{v1} := (ar_{k/2}(w^R) ··· ar_{k−1}(w^R) r(w^R))^R ;  /* The index denotes
          the deleted archs of w's factorisation */
        w_{v2} := (ar_{k/2+1}(w^R) ··· ar_{k−1}(w^R) r(w^R))^R;
        return |alph(r(w_{v1}))| == σ − 1  &&  |alph(r(w_{v2}))| == σ − 1;
    else
        w_v := (ar_{(k−1)/2}(w^R) ··· ar_{k−1}(w^R) r(w^R))^R;
        return |alph(r(w_v))| == σ − 1;
    end
end
```

Algorithm 1: Testing nearly k-universality

Remark 17. With Theorem 14 nearly k-universal words can be constructed: if k is odd choose $u, v \in \text{PUniv}_{\Sigma,\frac{k-1}{2}}$ and x with $|\text{alph}(x)| = \sigma - 1$, then uxv^R is nearly k-universal. If k is even, choose $u, v \in \text{PUniv}_{\Sigma,\frac{k-1}{2}}$ and x_1, x_2 with $|\text{alph}(x_1)| = |\text{alph}(x_2)| = \sigma - 1$. Then, $ux_2yx_1v \in \text{NUniv}_{\Sigma,k}$ iff $y[|y|] \notin \text{alph}(x_2)$ and $y[1] \notin \text{alph}(x_1)$.

Now, we present an algorithm for the second problem. Please recall that $\Sigma_{\mathtt{a}} = \Sigma \backslash \{\mathtt{a}\}$ and $w_{\Sigma_{\mathtt{a}}}$ is the word containing all letters of $\Sigma_{\mathtt{a}}$ w.r.t. a predefined order $<_\Sigma$ on Σ. These words can be preprocessed in time $\mathcal{O}(\sigma)$ for all $\mathtt{a} \in \Sigma$. The intuitive candidate for $w \in \mathrm{NUniv}_{\Sigma,k}$ with $u \notin \mathrm{ScatFact}_k(w)$ is $w = w^2_{\Sigma_{u[1]}} u[1] \cdots w^2_{\Sigma_{u[k-1]}} u[k-1] w_{\Sigma_{u[k]}}$ but this is not the shortlex normal form: with $u = \mathtt{aaccb}$ the intuitive way leads to $(\mathtt{bcbca}) \cdot (\mathtt{bcbca}) \cdot (\mathtt{ababc}) \cdot (\mathtt{ababc}) \cdot \mathtt{ac}$ while the shortlex normal form is given by $(\mathtt{bca}) \cdot (\mathtt{bcca}) \cdot (\mathtt{abc}) \cdot (\mathtt{abbc}) \cdot \mathtt{ac}$.

Theorem 18. *Given $u \in \Sigma^k$ for $k \in \mathbb{N}$, one can compute $w \in \Sigma^*$ with $\mathrm{ScatFact}_k(w) = \Sigma^k \backslash \{u\}$ in time $\mathcal{O}(k)$. More precisely, there exists an algorithm needing k steps computing $w \in \mathrm{NUniv}_{\Sigma,k}$ in shortlex normal form (Fig. 2).*

Data: Given $u \in \Sigma^k$ with $\Sigma = \{\mathtt{a}_1, \dots \mathtt{a}_\sigma\}$.
Result: nearly k-universal word $w \in \Sigma^*$ with $\mathrm{ScatFact}_k(w) = \Sigma^k \setminus \{u\}$
$w := \varepsilon$;
$w_\Sigma = \mathtt{a}_1 \cdots \mathtt{a}_\sigma$;
for $i = 1$ *to* $k - 1$ **do**
  if $u[i] \neq u[i+1]$ **then**
    $w := w \cdot w_{\Sigma_{u[i]}} \cdot u[i+1] \cdot u[i]$;
  else
    $w := w \cdot w_{\Sigma_{u[i]}} \cdot u[i]$;
  end
end
$w := w \cdot w_{\Sigma_{u[k]}}$;
return w;

Algorithm 2: Computing $w \in \mathrm{NUniv}_{\Sigma,1,k}$ for $u \in \Sigma^k$ absent.

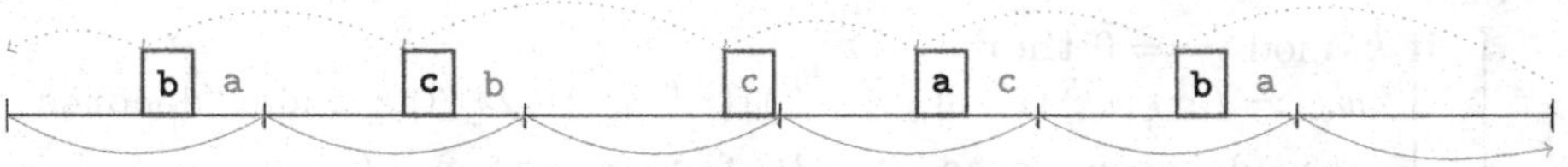

Fig. 2. Illustrating the algorithm of Theorem 18 for $u = \mathtt{abccab}$.

Let $u = \mathtt{abccab}$ and $\bullet$ represent placeholder. Since $u[1..5]$ is $\mathrm{m}(w)$, we get $(\bullet\mathtt{a}) \cdot (\bullet\mathtt{b}) \cdot (\bullet\mathtt{c}) \cdot (\bullet\mathtt{c}) \cdot (\bullet\mathtt{a})$. By $\mathrm{alph}(\mathrm{r}(w)) = \Sigma \backslash \{\mathtt{b}\}$, we get $(\bullet\mathtt{a}) \cdot (\bullet\mathtt{b}) \cdot (\bullet\mathtt{c}) \cdot (\bullet\mathtt{c}) \cdot (\bullet\mathtt{a}) \cdot \mathtt{ac}$. Including the arches of w^R we obtain $(\bullet\mathtt{ba}) \cdot (\bullet\mathtt{cb}) \cdot (\bullet\mathtt{c}) \cdot (\bullet\mathtt{ac}) \cdot (\bullet\mathtt{ba}) \cdot \mathtt{ac}$. Now, the $\bullet$ are replaced by the missing letters from each arch of w. Thus, we finaly get $(\mathtt{bcba}) \cdot (\mathtt{accb}) \cdot (\mathtt{abc}) \cdot (\mathtt{abac}) \cdot (\mathtt{bcba}) \cdot \mathtt{ac}$. Notice that we do not need to preprocess all $w_{\Sigma_{\mathtt{a}}}$ for all $\mathtt{a} \in \Sigma$ but only for all $\mathtt{a} \in \mathrm{alph}(\mathrm{m}(w))$.

Remark 19. Notice that the length of the resulting nearly k-universal word w depends on the given absent scattered factor $u \in \Sigma^k$. If $\sigma \geq 2$ and $\mathrm{cond}(u) = u_1 \cdots u_r$ for an $r \in \mathbb{N}$, we have $|w| = k\sigma + r - 2$. Thus, if u is unary, we have $|w| = k\sigma - 1$. For $k > 1$ and $\sigma > 2$, the shortlex normal form is strictly shorter than the intuitive candidate by $\sigma k - \sigma - 2k + 2$ letters.

Definition 20. *Given $u \in \Sigma^*$ and an order $<_\Sigma$ on Σ, let $w_u \in \mathrm{NUniv}_{\Sigma,k}$ denote the shortlex normal form w.r.t. $\sim_k$ with $u \notin \mathrm{ScatFact}_k(w_u)$.*

Corollary 21. *Given $k \in \mathbb{N}$, we have $|\mathrm{NUniv}_{\Sigma,k}/\sim_k| = \sigma^k$, i.e., restricting Simon's congruence to nearly k-universal words leads to σ^k different congruence classes.*

By Corollary 21 we know how many congruence classes in $\mathrm{NUniv}_{\Sigma,k}$ w.r.t. $\sim_k$ exist. Now we show when $w \sim_k w_u$ holds for $w \in \Sigma^*$, i.e., we characterise $[w_u]_{\sim_k}$. Therefore, we need some further insights into nearly k-universal words.

Lemma 22. *Given $w \in \mathrm{NUniv}_{\Sigma,k}$, we have $\mathrm{ar}_1(w)\cdots\mathrm{ar}_{i-1}(w)\alpha\,\mathrm{ar}_{i+1}(w)\cdots\mathrm{ar}_{k-1}(w)\beta \in \mathrm{NUniv}_{\Sigma,k}$ for all $i \in [k-1]$, if $\alpha[|\alpha|] = \mathrm{m}(w)[i]$, $\mathrm{alph}(\alpha[1..|\alpha|-1]) = \mathrm{alph}(\mathrm{in}_i(w))$, $\mathrm{in}_i(w) \in \mathrm{ScatFact}(\alpha[1..|\alpha|-1])$, $|\mathrm{r}(w)| \leq |\beta|$, and $\mathrm{alph}(\beta) = \mathrm{alph}(\mathrm{r}(w))$.*

Definition 23. *Let $P(w)$ be the set of all words obtainable from w by Lemma 22.*

Remark 24. Lemma 22 implies that for all $n \in \mathbb{N}$ and $u \in \Sigma^k$ with $n \geq |w_u|$ there exists $w \in \mathrm{NUniv}_{\Sigma,k} \cap \Sigma^n$, i.e., there are infinitely many words in $|[w_u]_{\sim_k}|$.

We are now able to give a characterisation of the congruence classes of $\sim_k$ in $\mathrm{NUniv}_{\Sigma,k}$. Since we know that for each $u \in \Sigma^k$ there exists one congruence class, we fix $u \in \Sigma^k$. We know so far that for each w obtained by the application of Lemma 22, we have $w \in [w_u]_{\sim_k}$. Notice that Lemma 22 cannot be generalised to an equivalence, since deleting letters from arches may violate the nearly k-universality: considering $w = (\mathtt{aab}) \cdot \mathtt{b}$ and deleting one $\mathtt{a}$ in the first arch, indeed does not change the modus, but it deletes $\mathtt{aa}$ and thus we have $|\mathrm{ScatFact}_2(\mathtt{abb})| < 3$. Recall that the output w_u of the algorithm in Theorem 18 is w.r.t. a given order $<_\Sigma$ on Σ, in particular $\mathrm{Pref}_{\sigma-1}(\mathrm{ar}_i(w_u))$, for all $i \in [k-1]$, is the lexicographically smallest word containing all letters of Σ but $\mathrm{m}(w)[i]$. Analogously, $\mathrm{r}(w_u)$ is the lexicographically smallest word containing all letters but $u[k]$. If we change this order, we obtain other words of the same length, which are all by Theorem 18 of minimal length. Moreover, if we choose different orders for each arch and for the rest, we still obtain a nearly k-universal word since the crucial point of Theorem 18 still holds. Thus, each such word can be obtained from w_u by applying some morphic permutation of Σ on $\mathrm{Pref}_{\sigma-1}(\mathrm{ar}_i(w_u))$ and $\mathrm{r}(w_u)$ for all $i \in [k-1]$.

Definition 25. *Let π_j, for $j \in [\sigma!]$, be the different morphic permutations on Σ and set $p_i = \mathrm{Pref}_{\sigma-1}(\mathrm{ar}_i(w_u))$ for all $i \in [k-1]$. Choose $s_1, \ldots, s_{k-1} \in \Sigma^*$ with $w_u = p_1 s_1 \cdots p_{k-1} s_{k-1}\,\mathrm{r}(w_u)$. Define the* basis *of $[w_u]_{\sim_k}$ by*

$$B_u = \{w \in \Sigma^* \mid \exists i_1, \ldots, i_k \in [\sigma!] : w = \pi_{i_1}(p_1)s_1 \cdots \pi_{i_{k-1}}(p_{k-1})s_{k-1}\pi_{i_k}(\mathrm{r}(w_u))\}.$$

Remark 26. For $u \in \Sigma^k$, we have $|B_u| = ((\sigma-1)!)^{k-1}(\sigma-1)!$.

Based on this B_u and Lemma 22, we can characterise $[w_u]_{\sim_k}$.

Theorem 27. *Given* $u \in \Sigma^k$, *we have* $[w_u]_{\sim_k} = \{w \in \Sigma^* \mid \exists v \in B_u : w \in P(v)\}$.

Proof. If $w \in P(v)$ for some $v \in B_u$, we have $w \in [w_u]_{\sim_k}$. Assume $w \in [w_u]_{\sim_k}$. Thus $w \in \mathrm{NUniv}_{\Sigma,k}$ and $\mathrm{m}(w)\mathtt{a}_w = u$. Now, we examine w's i^{th} arch for a fixed $i \in [k-1]$. We know $\mathrm{alph}(\mathrm{in}_i(w)) = \Sigma \backslash \{u[i]\}$. Let $u[i] \neq u[i+1]$. Suppose that $|\mathrm{in}_i(w)|_{u[i+1]} = 1$. Theorem 14 with $\hat{k} = i-1$ and $\tilde{k} = k-i$ implies that the $(k-i)^{\mathrm{th}}$-arch from v^R ends in this occurrence of $u[i+1]$, i.e., $u[i], u[i+1] \notin \mathrm{alph}(x)$. Since this is a contradiction to $w \in \mathrm{NUniv}_{\Sigma,k}$ we not only have $|\mathrm{in}_i(w)|_{u[i+1]} \geq 2$ but also Theorem 14 leads to $\mathrm{ar}_i(w) = \alpha_i u[i+1]\beta_i u[i]$ with $\mathrm{alph}(\alpha_i) = \Sigma \backslash \{u[i]\}$ and $\beta_i \in (\Sigma \backslash \{u[i]\})^*$. Thus, there exists $v_i \in \mathrm{ScatFact}_{\sigma-1}(\alpha_i)$ with $\mathrm{alph}(v) = \Sigma \backslash \{u[i]\}$ and a permutation π on Σ which morphically applied yields $\pi(v_i) = \mathrm{Pref}_{\sigma-1}(\mathrm{ar}_i(w_u))$. Since $\mathrm{alph}(\mathrm{r}(w)) = \Sigma \backslash \{u[k]\}$ we get similarly an r which is a permuation of $\mathrm{r}(w_u)$. This leads to $v = v_1 u[1] \cdots v[k-1]u[k-1]r \in B_u$. Adding all letters of α_i, β_i and $\mathrm{r}(w)$ not in v_i and r, resp., implies $w \in P(v)$. □

Let $u = \mathtt{abbc}$ and $\mathtt{a} < \mathtt{b} < \mathtt{c}$. By Theorem 18 we get $w_u = (\mathtt{bcba}) \cdot (\mathtt{acb}) \cdot (\mathtt{accb}) \cdot \mathtt{ab}$ and $w \in B_u$ iff $w = w_1 w_2 w_3 w_4$ with $w_1 \in \{\mathtt{bcba}, \mathtt{cbba}\}$, $w_2 \in \{\mathtt{acb}, \mathtt{cab}\}$, $w_3 \in \{\mathtt{accb}, \mathtt{cacb}\}$, $w_4 \in \{\mathtt{ab}, \mathtt{ba}\}$. Thus, we have 16 basis elements for u. Each of these words can be enriched by additional letters in the inner of an arch and the rest w.r.t. Lemma 22 to obtain all elements equivalent to w_u.

We finish this section with a third characterisation of nearly k-universal words that relies on Theorem 14 and Lemma 12 and illustrates the relation of w and w^R in $\mathrm{NUniv}_{\Sigma,k}$.

Proposition 28. *We have* $w \in \mathrm{NUniv}_{\Sigma,k}$ *iff* $\iota(w) = k-1$, $|\mathrm{alph}(\mathrm{r}(w))| = \sigma - 1$, *and* $\mathrm{ar}_2(w^R) \ldots \mathrm{ar}_{k-1}(w^R)\, \mathrm{r}(w^R) \in \mathrm{NUniv}_{\Sigma,k-1}$.

Notice that only the deletion of a reversed arch from the beginning leads to an equivalence. Deleting the first arch of w does not suffice for a characterisation as witnessed by $w = \mathtt{bcaabcab}$: indeed, we have $\iota(\mathtt{abcab}) = 1$, $\mathrm{alph}(\mathrm{r}(w)) = \Sigma \backslash \{\mathtt{c}\}$, and $\mathtt{abcab} \in \mathrm{NUniv}_{\Sigma,2}$ but we get $(\mathtt{bca}) \cdot (\mathtt{abc}) \cdot \mathtt{ab} \notin \mathrm{NUniv}_{\Sigma,3}$.

In this section, we presented in Theorem 14 a characterisation for nearly k-universal words. This combinatorial insight led to two linear time algorithms that check whether a word is nearly k-universal and compute the shortlex normal form for a given absent scattered factor. Both algorithms do not require further data structures. Based on this shortlex normal form we presented the congruence classes w.r.t. $\sim_k$ and characterised the classes fully (cf.Theorem 27).

4 m-Nearly k-Universal Words

For a full characterisation of Simon's congruence with this approach, all sets $M_{i,k}$ for a fixed k and $i \in [\sigma^k]$ have to be investigated. In this section, we give some first insights into $M_{i,k}$ for $i < \sigma^k - 1$, in particular, we consider m-nearly k-universal words, where m is not necessarily 1, i.e., we are interested in $w \in \Sigma^*$ with $|\mathrm{ScatFact}_k(w)| = \sigma^k - m$. Therefore, we extend our definitions.

Definition 29. *A word* $w \in \Sigma^*$ *is called* m-nearly k-universal, *if we have* $|\,\mathrm{ScatFact}_k(w)| = \sigma^k - m$. *Let* $\mathrm{NUniv}_{\Sigma,m,k}$ *denote the set of all* m*-nearly* k*-universal words.*

Implicitly, a subset of these words was investigated in [19]. There, the authors determine all shortest absent scattered factors, i.e., if $\iota(w) = k-1$ and $|\,\mathrm{ScatFact}_k(w)| = \sigma^k - m$, we have that $w \in \mathrm{NUniv}_{\Sigma,m,k}$. In contrast to nearly k-universal words, for $m > 1$, $\iota(w) = k-1$ does not necessarily hold as witnessed by $\mathtt{ababca} \in \mathrm{NUniv}_{\Sigma,14,3}$ with $\iota(\mathtt{ababca}) = 1 \neq 2$. Moreover, we have, for instance, $w = (\mathtt{accab}), w' = (\mathtt{abc}) \cdot \mathtt{a} \in \mathrm{NUniv}_{\Sigma,3,2}$ with $r(w) = \varepsilon$ and $|\,\mathrm{alph}(r(w'))| < \sigma - 1$. The results from Sect. 3 do not hold in general for $m > 1$: $w = (\mathtt{abc}) \cdot (\mathtt{bca}) \cdot \mathtt{bb} \in \mathrm{NUniv}_{\Sigma,7,3}$ but $(\mathtt{bca}) \cdot \mathtt{bb} \in \mathrm{NUniv}_{\Sigma,3,2} \neq \mathrm{NUniv}_{\Sigma,7,2}$ (cf. Lemma 12).

Thus, a thorough characterisation of $\mathrm{NUniv}_{\Sigma,m,k}$ is still open. Unfortunately, we cannot give such a characterisation but we present some first insights for $m \in \{2, \sigma^k - 2, \sigma^k - 1, \sigma^k\}$ as well as a full characterisation of the subclass established in [19] including the congruence classes of $\sim_k$ in this case. If $w \in \Sigma^k$, we have immediately $w \in \mathrm{NUniv}_{\Sigma,\sigma^k-1,k}$. Therefore, we have $|w| \geq k+1$ for all $w \in \mathrm{NUniv}_{\Sigma,m,k}$ with $m < \sigma^k - 1$.

Remark 30. Similar to $\mathrm{NUniv}_{\Sigma,0,k} = \mathrm{Univ}_{\Sigma,k}$, the set $\mathrm{NUniv}_{\Sigma,\sigma^k,k}$ provides exactly one equivalence class for $\sim_k$, since exactly the words strictly shorter than k do not have any scattered factor of length k.

Proposition 31. *For each* $k \in \mathbb{N}$, *we have* $|\mathrm{NUniv}_{\Sigma,\sigma^k-1,k}/\sim_k| = \sigma^k$.

If a word has exactly two scattered factors, the following lemma shows that we are immediately in the binary alphabet. This leads to the index proven in the following proposition.

Lemma 32. *If* $w \in \mathrm{NUniv}_{\Sigma,\sigma^k-2,k}$ *then* $|\,\mathrm{alph}(w)| = 2 = |\mathrm{cond}(w)|$.

Proposition 33. *For each* $k \in \mathbb{N}$, *we have* $|\mathrm{NUniv}_{\Sigma,\sigma^k-2,k}/\sim_k| = 2\binom{\sigma}{2}k$.

Proposition 33 shows that the formula determining the index of $\sim_k$ gets more complicated the farther m is from 0 or σ^k, resp. Now we show a similar result to Lemma 9 for $\mathrm{NUniv}_{\Sigma,2,k}$ backing the observation that the conditions on w get more complicated. Notice that, $w \in \mathrm{NUniv}_{\Sigma,\sigma-1,k}$ implies $\iota(w) = k-1$.

Proposition 34. *Let* $w \in \mathrm{NUniv}_{\Sigma,2,k}$ *with* $\sigma > 2$. *Then* $\iota(w) = k-1$ *and either* $|\,\mathrm{alph}(\mathrm{r}(w))| = |\,\mathrm{alph}(\mathrm{r}(w^R))| = \sigma - 1$, *or* $|\,\mathrm{alph}(\mathrm{r}(u))| = \sigma - 1$ *and* $|\,\mathrm{alph}(\mathrm{r}(u^R))| = \sigma - 2$ *for all* $u \in \{w, w^R\}$.

The remainder of this section presents results for arbitrary but fixed m. First, we give an estimation for the number of arches of an m-nearly k-universal word. In Sect. 3 we saw that for nearly k-universal words $\iota(w) = k-1$ holds. This does not hold for $m > 1$, witnessed by $(\mathtt{aab}) \cdot \mathtt{aa}, (\mathtt{ab}) \cdot (\mathtt{bba}) \in \mathrm{NUniv}_{\Sigma,4,3}$ and $\iota((\mathtt{aab}) \cdot \mathtt{aa}) = 1 \neq 2 = \iota((\mathtt{ab}) \cdot (\mathtt{bba}))$. Moreover, there is not just one fixed $\iota(w)$ which can be uniquely determined by m and k. A first estimation is presented in the following remark.

Remark 35. If $w \in \mathrm{NUniv}_{\Sigma,m,k}$ and $\sigma^{i-1} \leq m \leq \sigma^i - 1$, then $\iota(w) \geq k - i$. Suppose $\iota(w) < k - i$. Then there exists $v \in \Sigma^{k-i}$ with $v \notin \mathrm{ScatFact}_{k-i}(w)$. Thus, for all $v' \in \Sigma^i$ we have $vv' \notin \mathrm{ScatFact}_k(w)$ which are σ^i distinct words. Estimating the number of absent scattered factors results in $\sigma^k - m = |\,\mathrm{ScatFact}_k(w)| \leq \sigma^k - \sigma^i \leq \sigma^k - (\sigma^i - 1)$. Therefore, $m > \sigma^i - 1$ follows - a contradiction. By induction we get that for $m < \sigma^{i-1}$ there exists $j < i$ such that $m \leq \sigma^j - 1$. Thus, $\iota(w) \geq k - j$ which is a worst lower bound since $j < i$ and $\iota(w) < k$ for all $w \notin \mathrm{Univ}_{\Sigma,k}$.

We finish this section by characterising $\mathrm{NUniv}_{\Sigma,m,k} \cap \mathrm{Univ}_{\Sigma,k-1}$. Recently, in [19] Kosche et al. presented algorithmic results to enumerate absent scattered factors of $(k-1)$-universal words: given a word w with $\iota(w) = k - 1$, they inductively construct a tree structure (SAS-tree) that allows to efficiently query this (possibly) exponentially large set. The idea behind this construction is that for any $u \notin \mathrm{ScatFact}_k(w)$ and $i < k$ the letter $u[i]$ must occur in $\mathrm{ar}_i(w)$ and $u[i+1]$ must not, but can only be found in the following arch and only as a localised modus (otherwise u would not be absent since there are exactly $k - 1 - i$ succesive arches to choose the remaining letters from). For a combinatorial presentation of these conditions, we introduce a factorisation of these words that will be of use for the remainder of this section. Let from now on $w \in \mathrm{Univ}_{\Sigma,k-1}$. By $|\,\mathrm{alph}(\mathrm{r}(w^R))| < \sigma$, we have $\mathrm{r}(w)^R \in \mathrm{Pref}(\mathrm{ar}_1(w^R))$ and $\mathrm{m}(w^R)[1] \in \mathrm{alph}(\mathrm{ar}_{k-1}(w))$. Thus, choose $\alpha_{k-1}, \beta_{k-1} \in \Sigma^*$ with $\mathrm{ar}_{k-1}(w) = \alpha_{k-1}\beta_{k-1}$ and $\mathrm{ar}_1(w^R) = (\beta_{k-1}\,\mathrm{r}(w))^R$. With $\mathrm{alph}(\beta_{k-i}) \subseteq \Sigma$, inductively there exist $\alpha_i, \beta_i \in \Sigma^*$ such that $\mathrm{ar}_i(w) = \alpha_i\beta_i$ and $\mathrm{ar}_{k-i}(w^R) = (\beta_i\alpha_{i+1})^R$ with $\alpha_k = \mathrm{r}(w)$ and $\alpha_1 = \mathrm{r}(w^R)^R$, for all $i \in [k-1]$ (Fig. 3).

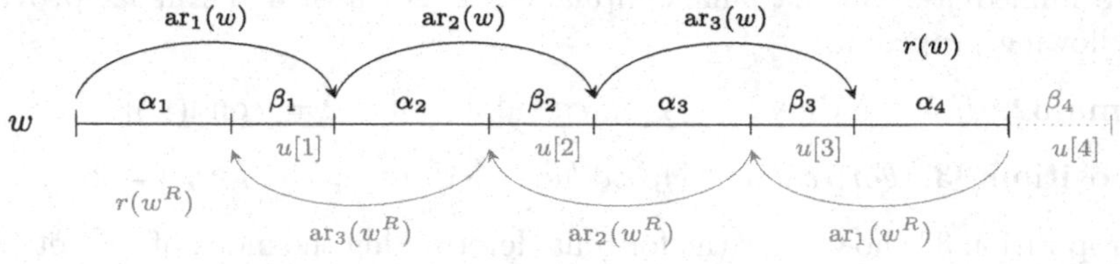

Fig. 3. α-β factorisation of w.

Proposition 36. *Let* $u \in \Sigma^k$. *Then* $u \notin \mathrm{ScatFact}_k(w)$ *iff* $u[1] \in \mathrm{alph}(\beta_1) \setminus \mathrm{alph}(\alpha_1)$, $u[i] \in \mathrm{alph}(\beta_i)$, $u[i]u[i+1] \notin \mathrm{ScatFact}_2(\beta_i\alpha_{i+1})$ *for all* $i \in [k-1]\setminus\{1\}$, *and* $u[k] \notin \mathrm{alph}(\mathrm{r}(w))$.

Given any $u \in \Sigma^k$, Proposition 36 allows to test whether $u \in \mathrm{ScatFact}_k(w)$. Due to the inductive nature of the conditions it cannot be used straightforwardly to compare words w, w' w.r.t. $\sim_k$. Thus, we introduce functions f_w mapping positions in w to their appropriate arches, $g_{w,l}$ for finding leftmost occurrences of letters within these arches l, and sets $M_{w,i}$ to capture the letters that can succeed $w[i]$ according to Proposition 36, and $M'_{w,i}$ to index them in w. Lastly, h_w is used to recursively count how many possible $u \notin \mathrm{ScatFact}_k(w)$ can exists.

Definition 37. *Let* $f_w : [|w|] \to [k]$ *such that* $f_w(i) = \ell$ *iff* w*'s* i^{th} *letter belongs to* $\mathrm{ar}_\ell(w)$, *for* $i \in [|w| - |\mathrm{r}(w)|]$, *and* $f_w(i) = k$ *otherwise. Moreover, define* $g_{w,\ell} : \Sigma \to [|w|]$ *by* $g_{w,\ell}(\mathtt{a}) = \min\{i \mid w[i] = \mathtt{a} \wedge f_w(i) = \ell\}$ *for all* $\ell \in [k-1]$. *Set* $M_{w,1} = \mathrm{alph}(\beta_1) \setminus \mathrm{alph}(\alpha_1)$ *and* $M_{w,j} = (\mathrm{alph}(\beta_{i+1}) \setminus \mathrm{alph}(\beta_i[j'+1..|\beta_i|]\alpha_{i+1})) \cap \mathrm{alph}(\beta_i[1..j'])$ *where* $f_w(j) = i$, $j' = j - (\sum_{l=1}^{i} |\mathrm{ar}_l(w)| + |\alpha_i|)$ *and* $\mathrm{alph}(\beta_k) = \Sigma \setminus \mathrm{alph}(\mathrm{r}(w))$, *as well as* $M'_{w,1} = g_{w,1}(M_{w,1})$ *and* $M'_{w,j} = g_{w,f(j)+1}(M_{w,j})$ *for all* $2 \leq j < \max\{m \mid f_w(m) < k\}$. *Let* $h_w(i) = \sum_{j \in M'_{w,i}} h_w(j)$ *for all* $i \in \{\ell \mid f_w(\ell) < k-1\}$ *and* $h_w(i) = |\Sigma \setminus \mathrm{alph}(\mathrm{r}(w))|$ *otherwise.*

Remark 38. Notice that by the definition of $\mathrm{m}(w)$ and Proposition 36, we have $\mathrm{m}(w)[i+1] \in M_{w,g_{w,f_w(i)}(\mathrm{m}(w)[i])}$ for all $i \in [k-2]$.

Proposition 39. *If* $w \in \mathrm{NUniv}_{\Sigma,m,k} \cap \mathrm{Univ}_{\Sigma,k-1}$ *then* $m = h_w(1)$.

Proof. Choose a sequence of numbers $\mathcal{I}_u \in \mathbb{N}^{k-1}$ such that $\mathcal{I}_u[1] \in M'_{w,1}$ and $\mathcal{I}_u[i+1] \in M'_{w,\mathcal{I}_u[i]}$ for all $i \in [k-1]$. Then for the word $u \in \Sigma^k$ such that $u[i] = w[\mathcal{I}_u[i]]$ for $i \in [k-1]$ and $u[k] \in \Sigma \setminus \mathrm{alph}(\mathrm{r}(w))$ we have

- $u[1] \in \mathrm{alph}(\beta_1) \setminus \mathrm{alph}(\alpha_1)$,
- $u[i] \in \beta_i$, $u[i]u[i+1] \notin \mathrm{ScatFact}_2(\beta_i\alpha_{i+1})$ for all $i \in [k-2]\setminus\{1\}$, and
- $u[k] \notin \mathrm{alph}(\mathrm{r}(w))$.

Thus, by Proposition 36, we have $u \notin \mathrm{ScatFact}_k(w)$. Then, calculating $h_w(1)$ recursively equals the number of possibilities to choose such sequences $\mathcal{I}_u$ and extend them with any letter $\mathtt{a}_w \notin \mathrm{r}(w)$. Each such sequence is associated to a different absent scattered factor u, i.e., $h(1)$ equals exactly the number m of length k absent scattered factors in w. □

The following lemma shows that $u \in \Sigma^k$ is absent in w, w' iff the sets of possible candidates for positions in β_i coincide for w and w' respectively.

Lemma 40. *Let* $w, w' \in \mathrm{Univ}_{\Sigma,k-1}$ *with* $\mathrm{alph}(\mathrm{r}(w')) \subseteq \mathrm{alph}(\mathrm{r}(w))$ *and* $u \in \Sigma^k$ *with* $u \notin \mathrm{ScatFact}_k(w)$. *Let* $\mathcal{I} \in [|w|]^{k-1}$ *with* $\mathcal{I}[1] \in M'_{w,1}$ *and* $\mathcal{I}[i+1] \in M'_{w,\mathcal{I}[i]}$ *such that* $u[1..k-1] = w[\mathcal{I}[1]] \cdots w[\mathcal{I}[k-1]]$. *Then* $u \notin \mathrm{ScatFact}_k(w')$ *iff there exist* $\mathcal{I}' \in [|w|]^{k-1}$ *with* $\mathcal{I}'[1] \in M'_{w',1}$ *and* $\mathcal{I}'[i+1] \in M'_{w',\mathcal{I}'[i]}$ *with* $u[1..k-1] = w'[\mathcal{I}'[1]] \cdots w[\mathcal{I}'[k-1]]$ *and* $u[i] \in M_{w,\mathcal{I}[i]} \cap M_{w',\mathcal{I}'[i]}$ *for all* $i \in [k-1]$.

For $w, w' \in \mathrm{Univ}_{\Sigma,k-1}$ and $u \in \Sigma^k$, let $C(u, w, w')$ be the predicate of the iff-conditions for $u \notin \mathrm{ScatFact}_k(w)$.

Theorem 41. *For all* $w, w' \in \mathrm{NUniv}_{\Sigma,m,k} \cap \mathrm{Univ}_{\Sigma,k-1}$, *we have* $w \sim_k w'$ *iff* $C(u, w, w')$ *and* $C(u, w', w)$ *for all* $u \in \Sigma^k$.

Notice that $w \sim_k w'$ is equivalent to $M_{w,j} = M_{w',j'}$ for all j, j' according to appropriate sequences $\mathcal{I}$ and $\mathcal{I}'$.

In this section we showed for some m how $\mathrm{NUniv}_{\Sigma,m,k}$ looks like and determined m for $w \in \mathrm{NUniv}_{\Sigma,m,k} \cap \mathrm{Univ}_{\Sigma,k-1}$ as well as $[w]_{\sim_k}$.

5 Conclusion

In this work, we pursued the approach to partition Σ^* w.r.t. the number of absent scattered factors of a given length k. This leads to the notion of m-nearly k-universal words, which are words where exactly m scattered factors of length k are absent. We have chosen this perspective to investigate the index of Simon's congruence $\sim_k$ and indeed we were able to fully characterise 1-nearly k-universal words and give the index as well as a characterisation of $\sim_k$ restricted to this subclass. Moreover, we gave some insights for $m > 1$, especially for $m \in \{2, \sigma^k - 1, \sigma^k - 2, \sigma^k\}$ (notice that $m = 0$ is fully investigated in [2]). Additionally in Sect. 4, we followed the idea from [19] from a combinatorial point of view, showing for instance that letters have the same dist-value in [19] iff they are in the same arch of w^R. By this approach we showed that m can be determined recursively for w with $\iota(w) = k - 1$ by investigating the overlaps of the arches from w and w^R. Moreover, we proved when two words w_1, w_2 with $\iota(w_1) = \iota(w_2) = k - 1$ fulfil $w_1 \sim_k w_2$.

Unfortunately, we were not able to give a full characterisation of $\mathrm{NUniv}_{\Sigma,m,k}$ for arbitrary m. A first step could be to determine $\iota(w)$ for $w \in \mathrm{NUniv}_{\Sigma,m,k}$. We conjecture that choosing $i \in [\sigma^k]$ such that $\sigma^i \leq m \leq \sigma^{i+1} - 1$ leads to $k - \lfloor \frac{m}{\sigma^i} \rfloor - 1 \leq \iota(w) \leq k - \lfloor \frac{m}{\sigma^i} \rfloor$. A subpartition of $\mathrm{NUniv}_{\Sigma,m,k}$ depending on $\iota(w)$ (as introduced in [19] and used in Sect. 4) could prove useful.

References

1. Baik, J., Deift, P., Johansson, K.: On the distribution of the length of the longest increasing subsequence of random permutations. J. Am. Math. Soc. **12**(4), 1119–1178 (1999)
2. Barker, L., Fleischmann, P., Harwardt, K., Manea, F., Nowotka, D.: Scattered factor-universality of words. In: Jonoska, N., Savchuk, D. (eds.) DLT 2020. LNCS, vol. 12086, pp. 14–28. Springer, Cham (2020). https://doi.org/10.1007/978-3-030-48516-0_2
3. Bergroth, L., Hakonen, H., Raita, T.: A survey of longest common subsequence algorithms. In: SPIRE, pp. 39–48. IEEE (2000)
4. Blumer, A., Blumer, J., Haussler, D., Ehrenfeucht, A., Chen, M.T., Seiferas, J.: The smallest automation recognizing the subwords of a text. Theor. Comp. Sci. **40**, 31–55 (1985)
5. Day, J., Fleischmann, P., Kosche, M., Koß, T., Manea, F., Siemer, S.: The edit distance to k-subsequence universality. In: STACS, vol. 187, pp. 25:1–25:19 (2021)
6. Do, D., Le, T., Le, N.: Using deep neural networks and biological subwords to detect protein s-sulfenylation sites. Brief. Bioinform. **22**(3) (2021)
7. Dress, A., Erdős, P.: Reconstructing words from subwords in linear time. Ann. Combinatorics **8**(4), 457–462 (2005)
8. Faloutsos, C., Ranganathan, M., Manolopoulos, Y.: Fast subsequence matching in time-series databases. ACM Sigmod Rec. **23**(2), 419–429 (1994)
9. Fleischer, L., Kufleitner, M.: Testing Simon's congruence. In: Proceedings of MFCS 2018, LIPIcs, vol. 117, pp. 62:1–62:13 (2018)
10. Fleischmann, P., Germann, S., Nowotka, D.: Scattered factor universality-the power of the remainder. preprint arXiv:2104.09063 (published at RuFiDim) (2021)

11. Fleischmann, P., Lejeune, M., Manea, F., Nowotka, D., Rigo, M.: Reconstructing words from right-bounded-block words. Int. J. Found. Comput. **32**, 1–22 (2021)
12. Gawrychowski, P., Kosche, M., Koß, T., Manea, F., Siemer, S.: Efficiently testing Simon's congruence. In: STACS, LIPIcs, vol. 187, pp. 34:1–34:18 (2021)
13. Hebrard, J.J.: An algorithm for distinguishing efficiently bit-strings by their subsequences. Theor. Comput. Sci. **82**(1), 35–49 (1991)
14. Karandikar, P., Kufleitner, M., Schnoebelen, P.: On the index of Simon's congruence for piecewise testability. Inf. Process. Lett. **115**(4), 515–519 (2015)
15. Karandikar, P., Schnoebelen, P.: The height of piecewise-testable languages with applications in logical complexity. In: Proceedings of CSL, LIPIcs, vol. 62, pp. 37:1–37:22 (2016)
16. Karandikar, P., Schnoebelen, P.: The height of piecewise-testable languages and the complexity of the logic of subwords. LICS **15**(2) (2019)
17. Kärkkäinen, J., Sanders, P., Burkhardt, S.: Linear work suffix array construction. J. ACM **53**(6), 918–936 (2006)
18. Keogh, E., Lin, J., Lee, S.H., Van Herle, H.: Finding the most unusual time series subsequence: algorithms and applications. KAIS **11**(1), 1–27 (2007)
19. Kosche, M., Koß, T., Manea, F., Siemer, S.: Absent subsequences in words. In: Bell, P.C., Totzke, P., Potapov, I. (eds.) RP 2021. LNCS, vol. 13035, pp. 115–131. Springer, Cham (2021). https://doi.org/10.1007/978-3-030-89716-1_8
20. Kátai-Urbán, K., Pach, P., Pluhár, G., Pongrácz, A., Szabó, C.: On the word problem for syntactic monoids of piecewise testable languages. Semigroup Forum **84**(2), 323–332 (2012)
21. Lothaire, M.: Combinatorics on Words. Cambridge Mathematical Library, Cambridge University Press, Cambridge (1997)
22. Maier, D.: The complexity of some problems on subsequences and supersequences. J. ACM (JACM) **25**(2), 322–336 (1978)
23. Maňuch, J.: Characterization of a word by its subwords. In: DLT, pp. 210–219. World Scientific (2000)
24. Pach, P.: Normal forms under Simon's congruence. Semigroup Forum **97**(2), 251–267 (2018)
25. Sennrich, R., Haddow, B., Birch, A.: Neural machine translation of rare words with subword units. preprint arXiv:1508.07909 (2015)
26. Simon, I.: Piecewise testable events. In: Brakhage, H. (ed.) GI-Fachtagung 1975. LNCS, vol. 33, pp. 214–222. Springer, Heidelberg (1975). https://doi.org/10.1007/3-540-07407-4_23
27. Wagner, R., Fischer, M.: The string-to-string correction problem. JACM **21**(1), 168–173 (1974)
28. Wang, C., Cho, K., Gu, J.: Neural machine translation with byte-level subwords. In: Proceedings of the AAAI Conference on Artificial Intelligence, vol. 34, pp. 9154–9160 (2020)

State Complexity of Binary Coded Regular Languages

Viliam Geffert(✉), Dominika Pališínová, and Alexander Szabari

Department of Computer Science, P. J. Šafárik University,
Jesenná 5, 04154 Košice, Slovakia
{viliam.geffert,alexander.szabari}@upjs.sk,
dominika.palisinova@student.upjs.sk

Abstract. For the given non-unary input alphabet Σ, a maximal prefix code h mapping strings over Σ to binary strings, and an optimal deterministic finite automaton (DFA) $\mathcal{A}$ with n states recognizing a language $\mathcal{L}$ over Σ, we consider the problem of how many states we need for an automaton $\mathcal{A}'$ that decides membership in $h(\mathcal{L})$, the binary coded version of $\mathcal{L}$. Namely, $\mathcal{A}'$ accepts binary inputs belonging to $h(\mathcal{L})$ and rejects binary inputs belonging to $h(\mathcal{L}^{\mathrm{C}})$, where $\mathcal{L}^{\mathrm{C}}$ is the complement of $\mathcal{L}$. The outcome on inputs that are not valid binary codes for any string in Σ^* can be arbitrary: $\mathcal{A}'$ may accept, reject, or halt in a "don't care" state. We show that any optimal deterministic don't care finite automaton (dcDFA) $\mathcal{A}'$ solving this promise problem uses at most $(\|\Sigma\|-1)\cdot n$ states but at least n states. We also show that, for each non-unary input alphabet Σ, there exists a maximal binary prefix code h such that, for each $n \geq 2$ and for each N in range from n to $(\|\Sigma\|-1)\cdot n$, there exists a language $\mathcal{L}$ over Σ such that the optimal DFA recognizing $\mathcal{L}$ uses exactly n states and any optimal dcDFA for solving the above promise problem uses exactly N states. Thus, we have the complete state hierarchy for deciding membership in the binary coded version of $\mathcal{L}$, with no magic numbers in between the lower and upper bounds.

Keywords: state complexity · finite automata · don't care automata · prefix codes · promise problems

1 Introduction

One of the earliest results in automata theory is the subset construction [16]: every n-state nondeterministic finite automaton (NFA) can be replaced by an equivalent deterministic finite automaton (DFA) using at most 2^n states. This raised later the question of whether it is possible, for a given number n, to find some $N \in \{n, \ldots, 2^n\}$ such that there is no optimal DFA with exactly N states, equivalent to some optimal NFA with exactly n states [10]; such numbers were named "magic". The problem was solved in [11], showing that there are no magic numbers for ternary languages, contrary to the unary languages [5]. Since then,

Supported by the Slovak grant contract VEGA 1/0177/21.

Published by Springer Nature Switzerland AG 2022
Y.-S. Han and G. Vaszil (Eds.): DCFS 2022, LNCS 13439, pp. 72–84, 2022.
https://doi.org/10.1007/978-3-031-13257-5_6

the magic numbers were studied for language operations, e.g., in [9], it was shown that, for the intersection of two languages, given by two DFAs with n and m states, we have no magic numbers in $\{1, \ldots, n{\cdot}m\}$. Such state hierarchies were studied for other operations as well [4,7,9,11].

From a different starting point, we are going to land in yet another complete state hierarchy with no magic numbers. Our initial motivation was the fact that most present-day computers store data in a binary coded form. This raises the following natural question: given a standard DFA $\mathcal{A}$ with n states for a regular language $\mathcal{L}$ over an input alphabet Σ, how many states we need to recognize $h(\mathcal{L})$, the binary coded version of $\mathcal{L}$? Clearly, the answer depends also on $h : \Sigma^* \to \{0,1\}^*$, the binary code in use. In most cases, we can work with the assumption that the *code* is a homomorphism, such that $h(\alpha_1) = h(\alpha_2)$ implies $\alpha_1 = \alpha_2$, so that each encoded string can be unambiguously decoded back. Since it is well known that regular languages are closed under *any* homomorphism (not necessarily a code—see e.g. [8, Sect. 4.2.3]), the situation seems clear at first glance:[1] construct an optimal DFA for $h(\mathcal{L})$.

However, if the automaton for $h(\mathcal{L})$ receives only inputs that are valid binary images of strings in Σ^*, the outcome on inputs that are not valid images can be quite arbitrary, which allows us to save some states. This brings us to a modified problem: given a code $h : \Sigma^* \to \{0,1\}^*$ and a standard DFA $\mathcal{A}$ with n states for $\mathcal{L} \subseteq \Sigma^*$, how many states we need for an automaton $\mathcal{A}'$ that accepts each $\beta \in h(\mathcal{L})$ and rejects each $\beta \in h(\mathcal{L}^{\mathrm{C}})$? Here $\mathcal{L}^{\mathrm{C}}$ denotes the complement of $\mathcal{L}$.

This approach is not completely new: in general, we are given a pair of disjoint languages $\langle \mathcal{L}^{\oplus}, \mathcal{L}^{\ominus} \rangle$ over the same alphabet Σ, called a *promise problem*, and we decide whether $w \in \mathcal{L}^{\oplus}$ or $w \in \mathcal{L}^{\ominus}$ by the use of a *don't care deterministic finite automaton* (dcDFA) which, besides accepting and rejecting states, may also use *neutral* or "don't care" states, otherwise it behaves like a standard DFA (see e.g. [6,13]). In our settings, $\mathcal{L}^{\oplus} = h(\mathcal{L})$ and $\mathcal{L}^{\ominus} = h(\mathcal{L}^{\mathrm{C}})$, where $h : \Sigma^* \to \{0,1\}^*$ is a code. We shall concentrate on the most common binary codes used in practice, that allow decoding by one-way deterministic finite-state transducers in real time and minimize $\sum_{a \in \Sigma} |h(a)|$, the sum of lengths of codewords. Such codes are called *maximal prefix codes* in literature [1,3]. (See Definition 1.)

This paper shows that, for each maximal prefix code $h : \Sigma^* \to \{0,1\}^*$ and each optimal DFA $\mathcal{A}$ with n states recognizing some $\mathcal{L}$ over the alphabet Σ, the binary promise problem $\langle h(\mathcal{L}), h(\mathcal{L}^{\mathrm{C}}) \rangle$ can be solved by a dcDFA $\mathcal{A}'$ using at most $(\|\Sigma\| - 1){\cdot}n$ states, but at least n states.[2] We also show that, for each non-unary input alphabet Σ, there exists a maximal binary prefix code h such that, for each $n \geq 2$ and each $N \in \{n, \ldots, (\|\Sigma\| - 1){\cdot}n\}$, there exists a language $\mathcal{L} \subseteq \Sigma^*$ such that the optimal DFA recognizing $\mathcal{L}$ uses exactly n states and any optimal dcDFA for solving $\langle h(\mathcal{L}), h(\mathcal{L}^{\mathrm{C}}) \rangle$ uses exactly N states.

[1] State complexity of homomorphisms depends on the length of the images of symbols and is somewhat difficult to define in the general case. Perhaps the only existing related result is the state complexity of projections (that is, homomorphisms mapping each symbol either to itself or to ε), which was determined to be $3/4{\cdot}2^n - 1$ in [12].

[2] Throughout the paper, $\|X\|$ denotes the cardinality of the set X.

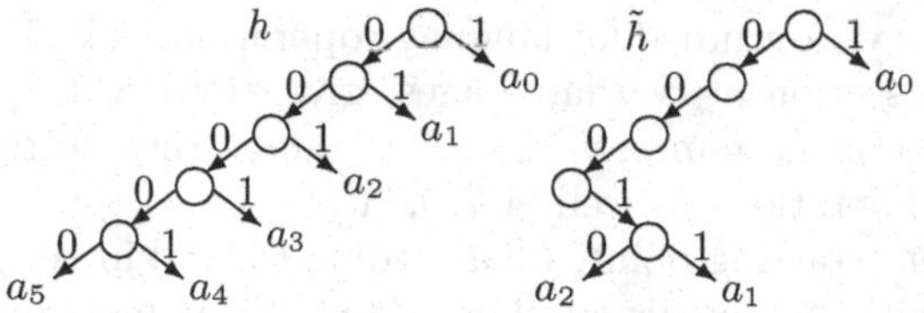

Fig. 1. Examples of homomorphisms establishing some binary prefix codes. Each homomorphism is displayed as a tree in which each leaf represents some a_i, a letter of the original input alphabet; the edges are labeled so that the path from the root to a_i gives the corresponding string $h(a_i)$. Internal nodes of the tree are related to prefixes of strings in $\{h(a) : a \in \Sigma\}$. The code h (left), defined by $h(a_0) = 1$, $h(a_1) = 01$, $h(a_2) = 001$, $h(a_3) = 0001$, $h(a_4) = 00001$, and $h(a_5) = 00000$, is maximal, while the code $\tilde{h}$ (right), with $\tilde{h}(a_0) = 1$, $\tilde{h}(a_1) = 00011$, and $\tilde{h}(a_2) = 00010$, is not—it can be extended, e.g., by defining $\tilde{h}(a_3) = 01$.

2 Preliminaries

Here we shall fix some basic definitions, notation, and preliminary properties. For more details, we refer the reader to [6,8], or any other standard textbooks.

Definition 1. *A* homomorphism *between strings over two alphabets is a mapping $h : \Sigma_1^* \to \Sigma_2^*$ preserving concatenation, i.e., $h(\alpha_1 \cdot \alpha_2) = h(\alpha_1) \cdot h(\alpha_2)$, for each $\alpha_1, \alpha_2 \in \Sigma_1^*$. The image of a language $L \subseteq \Sigma_1^*$ is $h(L) = \{h(\alpha) : \alpha \in L\} \subseteq \Sigma_2^*$.*

If $h(\alpha_1) = h(\alpha_2)$ implies that $\alpha_1 = \alpha_2$, then h is called a code.

h is a prefix code, *if no string in $h(\Sigma_1) = \{h(a) : a \in \Sigma_1\}$ is a proper prefix of another one. The code h is* maximal, *if there is no other code $h' : \Sigma_1'^* \to \Sigma_2^*$ (for some $\Sigma_1' \supseteq \Sigma_1$) such that $h'(\Sigma_1')$ is a proper superset of $h(\Sigma_1)$.*

Each homomorphism h is completely determined by the strings in $h(\Sigma_1)$, since $h(a_1 \cdots a_\ell) = h(a_1) \cdots h(a_\ell)$, for each $a_1, \ldots, a_\ell \in \Sigma_1$. In addition, if h is a code, each $\beta \in h(\Sigma_1^*)$ has a unique factorization into $\beta = \beta_1 \cdots \beta_\ell$, where $\ell \geq 0$ and $\beta_1, \ldots, \beta_\ell \in h(\Sigma_1)$. For examples of codes, see Fig. 1.

Prefix codes allow easy decoding by a one-way deterministic finite-state machine such that, for the given $\beta \in h(\Sigma_1^*)$, it computes the factorization of β into $h(a_1) \cdots h(a_\ell)$ and prints $a_1 \cdots a_\ell$ on the output in real time [1, Prop. 5.1.6].

Maximal codes minimize $\sum_{a \in \Sigma} |h(a)|$ and do not have "gaps" in images: each $\beta \in \Sigma_2^*$ can be extended to an image of some $\alpha \in \Sigma_1^*$, that is, to $\beta \cdot \beta' = h(\alpha)$, for some $\beta' \in \Sigma_2^*$ and some $\alpha \in \Sigma_1^*$, not excluding $\beta' = \varepsilon$.

Since we shall deal with *binary codes* only, we are going to simplify notation and write Σ instead of Σ_1 and fix $\Sigma_2 = \{0, 1\}$.

Definition 2. *A* don't care deterministic finite automaton (dcDFA) *is a 6-tuple $\mathcal{A} = \langle Q, \Sigma, q_{\text{I}}, f, F^{\oplus}, F^{\ominus} \rangle$, in which Q is a finite set of states; Σ is a finite input alphabet; $q_{\text{I}} \in Q$ is the initial state; $f : Q \times \Sigma \to Q$ is a transition function; $F^{\oplus} \subseteq Q$ is the set of* accepting *states; and $F^{\ominus} \subseteq Q$ the set of* rejecting *states, $F^{\oplus} \cap F^{\ominus} = \emptyset$. The remaining states are called* neutral *or "don't care" states.*

A (standard) deterministic finite automaton (DFA) *is a 5-tuple* $\mathcal{A} = \langle Q, \Sigma, q_{\rm I}, f, F\rangle$, *with* $F \subseteq Q$ *denoting the set of accepting states and* $Q\backslash F$ *the set of rejecting states; the remaining components have the same meaning as above.*

The transition function f can be extended to $f^*: Q \times \Sigma^* \to Q$ in a natural way, taking by definition $f^*(q, \varepsilon) = q$ and $f^*(q, \alpha a) = f(f^*(q, \alpha), a)$, for each $q \in Q$, $\alpha \in \Sigma^*$, and $a \in \Sigma$. To simplify notation, $f^*(q, \alpha) = q'$ shall sometimes be displayed in a more compact form $q \xrightarrow{\alpha} q'$.

A *promise problem* (see e.g. [6]) is a pair of disjoint languages $\langle \mathcal{L}^\oplus, \mathcal{L}^\ominus\rangle$ over the same alphabet Σ. The promise problem is *solved* by a dcDFA $\mathcal{A}$, if $\mathcal{A}$ accepts each $w \in \mathcal{L}^\oplus$ (that is, $f^*(q_{\rm I}, w) \in F^\oplus$) and rejects each $w \in \mathcal{L}^\ominus$ ($f^*(q_{\rm I}, w) \in F^\ominus$). We do not have to worry about the outcome on inputs belonging neither to $\mathcal{L}^\oplus$ nor to $\mathcal{L}^\ominus$: on such inputs, $\mathcal{A}$ may accept, reject, or halt in a neutral state.

$\mathcal{A}$ is *optimal* for $\langle \mathcal{L}^\oplus, \mathcal{L}^\ominus\rangle$, if it solves $\langle \mathcal{L}^\oplus, \mathcal{L}^\ominus\rangle$ and there is no dcDFA $\mathcal{A}'$ that solves $\langle \mathcal{L}^\oplus, \mathcal{L}^\ominus\rangle$ with fewer states than does $\mathcal{A}$.

If $\mathcal{L}^\oplus \cup \mathcal{L}^\ominus = \Sigma^*$, then $\mathcal{A}$ has no neutral reachable states and can be viewed as a standard DFA; we have the standard language recognition and say that $\mathcal{L}^\oplus$ is *recognized* by $\mathcal{A}$. The language $\mathcal{L}^\oplus$ is then usually denoted by $\mathcal{L}(\mathcal{A})$ and its complement $\mathcal{L}^\ominus$ by $\mathcal{L}(\mathcal{A})^{\rm C}$. In this case, the concept of optimal dcDFA coincide with the concept of minimal DFA for $\mathcal{L}^\oplus$.

Note that if a promise problem $\langle \mathcal{L}^\oplus, \mathcal{L}^\ominus\rangle$ can be solved by a dcDFA $\mathcal{A}$ with n states, it can also be solved by a standard dcDFA $\mathcal{A}'$ with n states, none of which is neutral: any neutral state could be set as accepting or rejecting, without affecting $\langle \mathcal{L}^\oplus, \mathcal{L}^\ominus\rangle$. This leaves us some degree of freedom, leading to different machines. Namely, if $\mathcal{A}$ uses k neutral reachable states, we obtain 2^k different automata solving the same promise problem, all of them of size at most n. These automata do not agree in acceptance/rejection on inputs not belonging to $\mathcal{L}^\oplus \cup \mathcal{L}^\ominus$. Thus, the given dcDFA can also be viewed as a more concise template representing these 2^k DFAs.

This is related to the following *separation problem*: given DFAs $\mathcal{A}^\oplus$ and $\mathcal{A}^\ominus$ for two disjoint languages $\mathcal{L}^\oplus$ and $\mathcal{L}^\ominus$, find a DFA $\mathcal{A}'$ with minimal number of states, such that $\mathcal{L}^\oplus \subseteq \mathcal{L}(\mathcal{A}')$ and $\mathcal{L}^\ominus \subseteq \mathcal{L}(\mathcal{A}')^{\rm C}$. In general, this problem is NP-complete [13, Thm. 9]. This was shown by a simple application of NP-completeness for a slightly different computational model (in which some transitions $f(q, a)$ may be undefined), presented in [14,15].

The next theorem will play the same role for don't care automata as the *fooling set technique* [2] for standard automata:

Theorem 1. *Let* $\mathcal{L}^\oplus$, $\mathcal{L}^\ominus$ *be two disjoint languages over the same alphabet* Σ. *Suppose there exist m-tuple* $X = \langle x_e\rangle_{e=1}^m$ *and* $\binom{m}{2}$*-tuple* $Y = \langle y_{e,\tilde{e}}\rangle_{e,\tilde{e}=1,\, e<\tilde{e}}^m$ *consisting of strings in* Σ^* *such that, for each* $e, \tilde{e} \in \{1, \ldots, m\}$, $e < \tilde{e}$,

(I) *both* $x_e{\cdot}y_{e,\tilde{e}}$ *and* $x_{\tilde{e}}{\cdot}y_{e,\tilde{e}}$ *are in* $\mathcal{L}^\oplus \cup \mathcal{L}^\ominus$,
(II) $x_e{\cdot}y_{e,\tilde{e}} \in \mathcal{L}^\oplus$ *if and only if* $x_{\tilde{e}}{\cdot}y_{e,\tilde{e}} \in \mathcal{L}^\ominus$.

Then any dcDFA solving the promise problem $\langle \mathcal{L}^\oplus, \mathcal{L}^\ominus\rangle$ *uses at least m states.*

Proof. Let $\mathcal{A} = \langle Q, \Sigma, q_{\text{I}}, f, F^{\oplus}, F^{\ominus} \rangle$, satisfying $F^{\oplus} \cap F^{\ominus} = \emptyset$, be an arbitrary dcDFA for solving $\langle \mathcal{L}^{\oplus}, \mathcal{L}^{\ominus} \rangle$. Suppose that $\mathcal{A}$ uses less than m states.

Now, for the given m-tuple $X = \langle x_1, x_2, \ldots, x_m \rangle$, let $q_1, q_2, \ldots, q_m$ denote the respective states reached by $\mathcal{A}$ on these inputs, that is, $q_{\text{I}} \xrightarrow{x_e} q_e$, for each $e \in \{1, \ldots, m\}$. But then, using a pigeonhole argument, some state must be repeated, i.e., we have $q_e = q_{\tilde{e}}$, for some $1 \leq e < \tilde{e} \leq m$. This implies that the computations on inputs $x_e \cdot y_{e,\tilde{e}}$ and $x_{\tilde{e}} \cdot y_{e,\tilde{e}}$ must end in the same state, denoted here by r. That is, we have the following computations: $q_{\text{I}} \xrightarrow{x_e} q_e \xrightarrow{y_{e,\tilde{e}}} r$ and $q_{\text{I}} \xrightarrow{x_{\tilde{e}}} q_{\tilde{e}} = q_e \xrightarrow{y_{e,\tilde{e}}} r$. There are now two possibilities:

First, let $x_e \cdot y_{e,\tilde{e}} \in \mathcal{L}^{\oplus}$. Then, using (II), we also have that $x_{\tilde{e}} \cdot y_{e,\tilde{e}} \in \mathcal{L}^{\ominus}$. This implies that the computation on $x_e \cdot y_{e,\tilde{e}}$ ends in $r \in F^{\oplus}$ and, at the same time, the computation on $x_{\tilde{e}} \cdot y_{e,\tilde{e}}$ in $r \in F^{\ominus}$. But this is a contradiction: $F^{\oplus} \cap F^{\ominus} = \emptyset$.

Second, let $x_e \cdot y_{e,\tilde{e}} \notin \mathcal{L}^{\oplus}$. Then, using (II), we have $x_{\tilde{e}} \cdot y_{e,\tilde{e}} \notin \mathcal{L}^{\ominus}$. Now, by (I), we see that $x_e \cdot y_{e,\tilde{e}} \in \mathcal{L}^{\ominus}$ and $x_{\tilde{e}} \cdot y_{e,\tilde{e}} \in \mathcal{L}^{\oplus}$. This leads to the same kind of contradiction as above, swapping the roles of $x_e \cdot y_{e,\tilde{e}}$ and $x_{\tilde{e}} \cdot y_{e,\tilde{e}}$. □

Note that, apart from providing the lower bound on the number of states, the *statement* of the above theorem does not deal with states in any dcDFA solving $\langle \mathcal{L}^{\oplus}, \mathcal{L}^{\ominus} \rangle$ but, rather, with *strings* in Σ^*. However, if there does exist a dcDFA $\mathcal{A}$ with m states for $\langle \mathcal{L}^{\oplus}, \mathcal{L}^{\ominus} \rangle$, that is, if the lower bound provided by Theorem 1 matches the upper bound, then one can establish a one-to-one correspondence between states in $\mathcal{A}$ and strings in $X = \langle x_1, x_2, \ldots, x_m \rangle$, with $Y = \langle y_{e,\tilde{e}} \rangle_{e,\tilde{e}=1,\, e<\tilde{e}}^{m}$ giving the pairwise distinguishability of states in $\mathcal{A}$. The standard fooling set technique (for DFAs) uses $y_{e,\tilde{e}_1} = y_{e,\tilde{e}_2} = \ldots$, with the condition (I) satisfied automatically.

3 Upper and Lower Bounds

We are now going to show that $(\|\Sigma\| - 1) \cdot n$ states are sufficient but n states necessary for a dcDFA that decides whether the given binary input is in $h(\mathcal{L})$ or in $h(\mathcal{L}^{\mathrm{C}})$, that is, for a dcDFA solving $\langle h(\mathcal{L}), h(\mathcal{L}^{\mathrm{C}}) \rangle$, the binary promise-problem version of $\mathcal{L}$. Here $h : \Sigma^* \to \{0,1\}^*$ is a maximal prefix code and $\mathcal{A}$ is an optimal DFA with n states, recognizing a language $\mathcal{L}$ over a non-unary alphabet Σ.

For the given code h, let us begin by fixing some additional notation for the *images of letters* and *proper prefixes*:

$$\begin{aligned} H &= \{h(a) : a \in \Sigma\}, \\ P &= \{\pi : \pi \cdot \beta \in H, \text{ for some } \beta \in \{0,1\}^+\}. \end{aligned} \tag{1}$$

Recall that h is a maximal prefix code. Thus, P includes the empty string ε, but no string from H. Next, if $\pi \in P$, then $\pi \cdot 0, \pi \cdot 1 \in P \cup H$ (see also Fig. 1). The next two theorems provide the upper and lower bounds.

Theorem 2. *Let $h : \Sigma^* \to \{0,1\}^*$ be a maximal binary prefix code and let $\mathcal{L}$ be a language over the non-unary alphabet Σ. Then, if $\mathcal{L}$ can be recognized by a DFA $\mathcal{A} = \langle Q, \Sigma, q_{\text{I}}, f, F \rangle$ with n states, the binary promise problem $\langle h(\mathcal{L}), h(\mathcal{L}^{\mathrm{C}}) \rangle$ can be solved by a dcDFA $\mathcal{A}'$ with at most $n' \leq (\|\Sigma\| - 1) \cdot n$ states.*

Proof (a sketch). The idea of the construction is to remember $q \in Q$, the current state of $\mathcal{A}$ at the moment when $\mathcal{A}$ has read $a_1 \cdots a_\ell \in \Sigma^*$, and $\pi \in P$, the prefix of a code for the next input symbol $a_{\ell+1}$, not completed yet. This leads to $Q' = Q \times P$, with $q'_{\mathrm{I}} = \langle q_{\mathrm{I}}, \varepsilon \rangle$, $F^{\oplus} = F \times \{\varepsilon\}$, and $F^{\ominus} = (Q \backslash F) \times \{\varepsilon\}$. Transitions in $\mathcal{A}'$ are defined as follows, for each $q \in Q$, $\pi \in P$, and $b \in \{0, 1\}$:

(I) $f'(\langle q, \pi \rangle, b) = \langle q, \pi b \rangle$, provided that $\pi \cdot b \in P$,
(II) $f'(\langle q, \pi \rangle, b) = \langle f(q, a), \varepsilon \rangle$, provided that, for some $a \in \Sigma$, $\pi \cdot b = h(a) \in H$.

□

The above construction can be updated so that it works for prefix codes that are not maximal. Then $\pi \in P$ does not imply that $\pi \cdot b$ is in $P \cup H$. In such cases, we can define $f'(\langle q, \pi \rangle, b) = q'_{\mathrm{E}}$, where q'_{E} is an additional trap state, in which we scan the rest of the input—the input can no longer be extended to a string in $h(\Sigma_1^*) = h(H^*)$. However, for such codes, $\|P\|$ is not bounded by $\|\Sigma\| - 1$.

Theorem 3. *Let $h : \Sigma^* \to \{0, 1\}^*$ be a binary prefix code (not necessarily maximal) and let $\mathcal{L}$ be a language over the alphabet Σ (not necessarily non-unary). Then, if the binary promise problem $\langle h(\mathcal{L}), h(\mathcal{L}^{\mathrm{C}}) \rangle$ can be solved by a dcDFA $\mathcal{A}' = \langle Q', \{0, 1\}, q'_{\mathrm{I}}, f', F^{\oplus}, F^{\ominus} \rangle$ with n' states, the language $\mathcal{L}$ can be recognized by a standard DFA $\mathcal{A} = \langle Q, \Sigma, q_{\mathrm{I}}, f, F \rangle$ with at most $n \le n'$ states.*

Proof. If, for some $q, q' \in Q'$ and $a \in \Sigma$, the original $\mathcal{A}'$ has a path beginning in q, ending in q', and reading from the input the string $h(a) \in H$ (introduced by (1)), we shall add the transition $q \xrightarrow{a} q'$ to $\mathcal{A}$. Recall that $\mathcal{A}'$ is deterministic and $h(a) = b_1 \cdots b_m$ is unique for each $a \in \Sigma$. But then $q' = f'^*(q, h(a))$ is also unique for each $q \in Q'$ and each $a \in \Sigma$, and hence $\mathcal{A}$ will be deterministic.

In addition, we can restrict the set of finite control states in $\mathcal{A}$ to states that can be reached from q'_{I} by reading some $\beta \in h(\Sigma^*) = H^*$, that is, to

$$R = \{f'^*(q'_{\mathrm{I}}, \beta) : \beta \in H^*\}. \tag{2}$$

Thus, $Q = R$, $q_{\mathrm{I}} = q'_{\mathrm{I}}$, and $F = R \cap F^{\oplus}$. Clearly, $R \subseteq F^{\oplus} \cup F^{\ominus}$, since no $\mathcal{A}'$ solving $\langle h(\mathcal{L}), h(\mathcal{L}^{\mathrm{C}}) \rangle$ halts in a neutral state on any $h(\alpha) \in h(\Sigma^*)$. Finally, let

$$f(q, a) = f'^*(q, h(a)), \text{ for each } q \in R \text{ and each } a \in \Sigma.$$

It is easy to see, for each $q, q' \in R$ and each $a \in \Sigma$, that $\mathcal{A}$ has a transition from q to q' reading the symbol $a \in \Sigma$ if and only if $\mathcal{A}'$ has a path connecting the same states and reading the string $h(a) \in H$. By a straightforward induction on the length of $\alpha \in \Sigma^*$, we have $q \xrightarrow{\alpha} q'$ in $\mathcal{A}$ if and only if $q \xrightarrow{h(\alpha)} q'$ in $\mathcal{A}'$.

Thus, if $\alpha \in \mathcal{L}$, then $h(\alpha) \in h(\mathcal{L})$ must be accepted by dcDFA $\mathcal{A}'$, which gives $q'_{\mathrm{I}} \xrightarrow{h(\alpha)} q'$ for some $q' \in F^{\oplus}$. Moreover, since $h(\alpha) \in H^*$, q' must also belong to R. But then, for $\mathcal{A}$, we have $q_{\mathrm{I}} = q'_{\mathrm{I}} \xrightarrow{\alpha} q'$ with $q' \in R \cap F^{\oplus} = F$, and hence α is accepted by $\mathcal{A}$. Similarly, if $\alpha \notin \mathcal{L}$, then $\mathcal{A}'$ has a path $q'_{\mathrm{I}} \xrightarrow{h(\alpha)} q'$ ending in $q' \in R \cap F^{\ominus}$. For $\mathcal{A}$, this gives $q_{\mathrm{I}} = q'_{\mathrm{I}} \xrightarrow{\alpha} q'$ ending in $q' \in R \backslash F^{\oplus} = R \backslash (R \cap F^{\oplus}) = Q \backslash F$, and hence α is rejected by $\mathcal{A}$.

Summing up, $\mathcal{A}$ is a standard DFA recognizing $\mathcal{L}$, with $n \le n'$ states. □

By combining Theorems 2 and 3, we get:

Theorem 4. *Let* $h: \Sigma^* \rightarrow \{0,1\}^*$ *be a maximal binary prefix code and let* $\mathcal{L}$ *be a language over the non-unary alphabet* Σ. *Then, if the optimal DFA* $\mathcal{A}$ *recognizing* $\mathcal{L}$ *uses* n *states, any optimal dcDFA* $\mathcal{A}'$ *solving the binary promise problem* $\langle h(\mathcal{L}), h(\mathcal{L}^{\mathrm{C}})\rangle$ *uses at least* n *states and at most* $(\|\Sigma\| - 1)\cdot n$ *states.*

Proof. The upper bound is a direct consequence of Theorem 2: this theorem does not necessarily produce a dcDFA that is optimal, however, it does guarantee $(\|\Sigma\|-1)\cdot n$ states for $\mathcal{A}'$. The lower bound follows from Theorem 3: suppose that $\langle h(\mathcal{L}), h(\mathcal{L}^{\mathrm{C}})\rangle$ can be solved by $\mathcal{A}'$ with $n' < n$ states. But then, by this theorem, we could obtain a standard DFA recognizing $\mathcal{L}$ with fewer states than n, which is a contradiction, since $\mathcal{A}$ is optimal. □

4 The Hierarchy

We are now ready to establish the complete state hierarchy and provide a witness language for each N between n and $(\|\Sigma\| - 1)\cdot n$. First, for the given

$$\Sigma = \{a_0, a_1, \ldots, a_d\}, \text{ where } d = \|\Sigma\| - 1 \geq 2,$$

define a maximal binary prefix code $h_\Sigma : \Sigma^* \rightarrow \{0,1\}^*$ as follows:

$$\begin{aligned} h_\Sigma(a_j) &= 0^j 1, \text{ for } j \in \{0, \ldots, d-1\}, \\ h_\Sigma(a_d) &= 0^d. \end{aligned} \tag{3}$$

Second, for the given Σ and any given

$$n \geq 2, \quad g \in \{0, \ldots, n\}, \quad k \in \{0, \ldots, d-2\}, \tag{4}$$

define a DFA $\mathcal{A}_{\Sigma,n,g,k} = \langle Q, \Sigma, q_{\mathrm{I}}, f, F\rangle$ with the state set $Q = \{0, \ldots, n-1\}$, $q_{\mathrm{I}} = 0$, $F = \{0\}$, and the following transitions:

$$\begin{aligned} f(i,a) &= (i+1) \bmod n, && \text{if } i < g \text{ and } a \in \Sigma, \\ f(g,a) &= (g+1) \bmod n, && \text{if } g \leq n-2 \text{ and } a \in \{a_0, \ldots, a_k\} \cup \{a_d\}, \\ &= (g+2) \bmod n, && \text{if } g \leq n-2 \text{ and } a \in \{a_{k+1}, \ldots, a_{d-1}\}, \\ f(i,a) &= (i+1) \bmod n, && \text{if } i > g \text{ and } a \in \Sigma \backslash \{a_d\}, \\ &= i, && \text{if } i > g \text{ and } a = a_d. \end{aligned} \tag{5}$$

There are two special cases. The first one is $g = n-1$, with no states $i \in Q$ satisfying $i > g$. Moreover, this case differs in one value, namely, in $f(g, a_d)$:

$$\begin{aligned} f(g,a) &= (g+1) \bmod n = 0, \text{ if } g = n-1 \text{ and } a \in \{a_0, \ldots, a_k\}, \\ &= (g+2) \bmod n = 1, \text{ if } g = n-1 \text{ and } a \in \{a_{k+1}, \ldots, a_d\}. \end{aligned} \tag{6}$$

The second special case is $g = n$, with no states $i \in Q$ satisfying $i > g$ or $i = g$. Thus, the condition $i < g$ is satisfied automatically for each $i \in Q$, which reduces (5)–(6) above to $f(i,a) = (i+1) \bmod n$ for each $i \in Q$ and each $a \in \Sigma$.

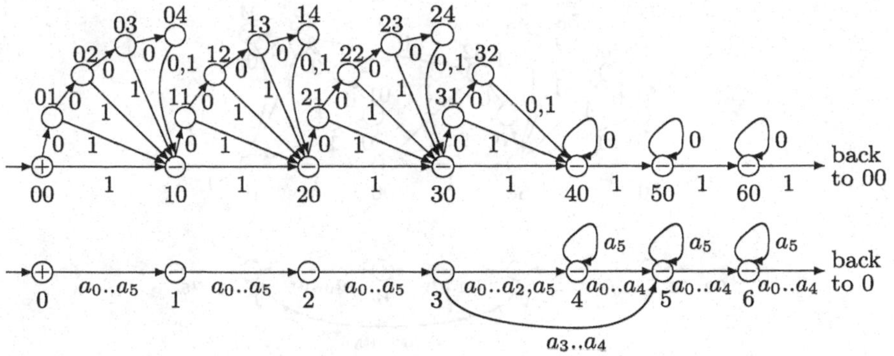

Fig. 2. Examples of a DFA $\mathcal{A}_{\Sigma,n,g,k}$ (bottom) and the corresponding dcDFA $\mathcal{A}'_{\Sigma,n,g,k}$ (top), if $\Sigma = \{a_0, \ldots, a_5\}, d = 5, n = 7, g = 3$, and $k = 2$. Accepting states are tagged by "+", rejecting states by "−", and neutral don't care states by no sign. To simplify notation for $\mathcal{A}'_{\Sigma,n,g,k}$, the ordered pairs "$\langle i, j\rangle$" are displayed here in the form "ij".

Examples of h_Σ, $\mathcal{A}_{\Sigma,n,g,k}$, and subsequent $\mathcal{A}'_{\Sigma,n,g,k}$ are displayed in Fig. 1 (left), Fig. 2 (bottom), and Fig. 2 (top), respectively, for $d = 5$, $n = 7$, $g = 3$, and $k = 2$. The special case of $g = n - 1$ is illustrated by Fig. 3.

Finally, for the given Σ, n, g, k satisfying (4), consider a dcDFA $\mathcal{A}'_{\Sigma,n,g,k} = \langle Q', \{0,1\}, q'_\mathrm{I}, f', F^\oplus, F^\ominus\rangle$, *not* constructed for $\mathcal{A}_{\Sigma,n,g,k}$ by the use of Theorem 2, but defined as follows. First, let $Q' = Q_0 \cup \ldots \cup Q_{n-1}$, where

$$\begin{aligned} Q_i &= \{\langle i,0\rangle, \ldots, \langle i, d-1\rangle\}, \text{ for } i \in \{0,\ldots,g-1\},\\ Q_g &= \{\langle g,0\rangle, \ldots, \langle g,k\rangle\},\\ Q_i &= \{\langle i,0\rangle\}, \qquad\qquad \text{for } i \in \{g+1,\ldots,n-1\}. \end{aligned} \tag{7}$$

There are no sections Q_i with $i > g$, if $g = n - 1$, and no section Q_g, if $g = n$, in accordance with the two special cases for $\mathcal{A}_{\Sigma,n,g,k}$.

Now, let $q'_\mathrm{I} = \langle 0,0\rangle, F^\oplus = \{\langle 0,0\rangle\}$, and $F^\ominus = \{\langle 1,0\rangle, \langle 2,0\rangle, \ldots, \langle n-1,0\rangle\}$. Transitions are defined as follows:

$$\begin{aligned} f'(\langle i,j\rangle,1) &= \langle (i+1) \bmod n, 0\rangle, && \text{for each } \langle i,j\rangle \in Q',\\ f'(\langle i,j\rangle,0) &= \langle i, j+1\rangle, && \text{if } i < g \text{ and } j < d-1,\\ &= \langle (i+1) \bmod n, 0\rangle, && \text{if } i < g \text{ and } j = d-1,\\ f'(\langle g,j\rangle,0) &= \langle g, j+1\rangle, && \text{if } j < k,\\ &= \langle (g+1) \bmod n, 0\rangle \quad = \langle g+1, 0\rangle, && \text{if } g \le n-2 \text{ and } j = k,\\ &= \langle (g+1) \bmod n, j+1\rangle = \langle 0, k+1\rangle, && \text{if } g = n-1 \text{ and } j = k,\\ f'(\langle i,0\rangle,0) &= \langle i,0\rangle, && \text{if } i > g. \end{aligned} \tag{8}$$

Note that also here the case of $g = n - 1$ is different. (See also Fig. 3).

Lemma 1. *Let h_Σ, $\mathcal{A}_{\Sigma,n,g,k}$, and $\mathcal{A}'_{\Sigma,n,g,k}$ be the binary code, DFA, and dcDFA defined above. Then $\mathcal{A}'_{\Sigma,n,g,k}$ solves the binary promise problem $\langle h_\Sigma(\mathcal{L}(\mathcal{A}_{\Sigma,n,g,k})), h_\Sigma(\mathcal{L}(\mathcal{A}_{\Sigma,n,g,k})^\mathrm{C})\rangle$.*

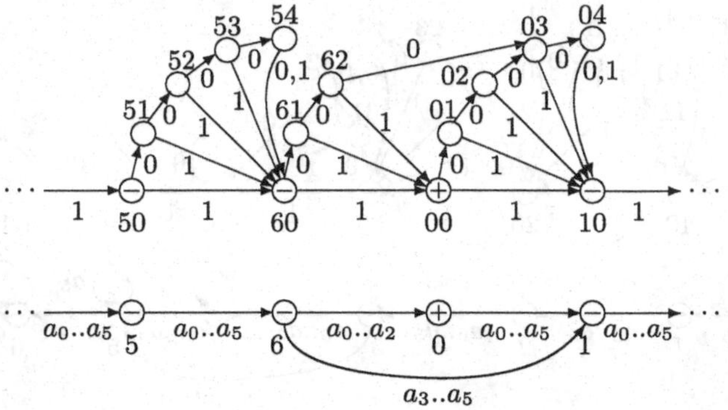

Fig. 3. Examples of $\mathcal{A}_{\Sigma,n,g,k}$ and $\mathcal{A}'_{\Sigma,n,g,k}$ for the special case of $g = n - 1$, namely, for $\Sigma = \{a_0, \ldots, a_5\}, d = 5, n = 7,\ g = n - 1 = 6$, and $k = 2$ (graph rotated, so that the state $g = n - 1$ is not displayed at the right end).

Proof. First, it is not too hard to see that if $\mathcal{A}_{\Sigma,n,g,k}$ has a transition $i \xrightarrow{a} i'$, then $\mathcal{A}'_{\Sigma,n,g,k}$ has the corresponding computation path $\langle i, 0\rangle \xrightarrow{h_\Sigma(a)} \langle i', 0\rangle$. This can be shown by consulting (3) and by comparing all transitions presented by (5), (6), and (8), for each $i \in Q$ and each $a \in \Sigma$:

- $f(i, a) = (i + 1) \bmod n$, if $i < g$ and $a \in \Sigma$ (which covers the case of $g = n$):
  - $\langle i, 0\rangle \xrightarrow{0^j} \langle i, j\rangle \xrightarrow{1} \langle (i+1) \bmod n, 0\rangle$, for $h_\Sigma(a) = 0^j1, j \in \{0, \ldots, d-1\}$,
  - $\langle i, 0\rangle \xrightarrow{0^{d-1}} \langle i, d - 1\rangle \xrightarrow{0} \langle (i + 1) \bmod n, 0\rangle$, for $h_\Sigma(a) = 0^d$.
- $f(g, a) = (g + 1) \bmod n$, if $g \le n - 2$ and $a \in \{a_0, \ldots, a_k\} \cup \{a_d\}$:
  - $\langle g, 0\rangle \xrightarrow{0^j} \langle g, j\rangle \xrightarrow{1} \langle (g + 1) \bmod n, 0\rangle$, for $h_\Sigma(a) = 0^j1,\ j \in \{0, \ldots, k\}$,
  - $\langle g, 0\rangle \xrightarrow{0^k} \langle g, k\rangle \xrightarrow{0} \langle g + 1, 0\rangle \xrightarrow{0^{d-k-1}} \langle g + 1, 0\rangle = \langle (g + 1) \bmod n, 0\rangle$, for $h_\Sigma(a) = 0^d$.
- $f(g, a) = (g + 2) \bmod n$, if $g \le n - 2$ and $a \in \{a_{k+1}, \ldots, a_{d-1}\}$:
  - $\langle g, 0\rangle \xrightarrow{0^k} \langle g, k\rangle \xrightarrow{0} \langle g + 1, 0\rangle \xrightarrow{0^{j-k-1}} \langle g + 1, 0\rangle \xrightarrow{1} \langle (g + 2) \bmod n, 0\rangle$, for $h_\Sigma(a) = 0^j1,\ j \in \{k + 1, \ldots, d - 1\}$.
- $f(i, a) = (i + 1) \bmod n$, if $i > g$ and $a \in \Sigma \backslash \{a_d\}$:
  - $\langle i, 0\rangle \xrightarrow{0^j} \langle i, 0\rangle \xrightarrow{1} \langle (i+1) \bmod n, 0\rangle$, for $h_\Sigma(a) = 0^j1, j \in \{0, \ldots, d-1\}$.
- $f(i, a) = i$, if $i > g$ and $a = a_d$:
  - $\langle i, 0\rangle \xrightarrow{0^d} \langle i, 0\rangle$, for $h_\Sigma(a) = 0^d$.

The same can be seen for different transitions in the case of $g = n - 1$:

- $f(g, a) = (g + 1) \bmod n = 0$, if $g = n - 1$ and $a \in \{a_0, \ldots, a_k\}$:
  - $\langle g, 0\rangle \xrightarrow{0^j} \langle g, j\rangle \xrightarrow{1} \langle (g + 1) \bmod n, 0\rangle$, for $h_\Sigma(a) = 0^j1,\ j \in \{0, \ldots, k\}$.
- $f(g, a) = (g + 2) \bmod n = 1$, if $g = n - 1$ and $a \in \{a_{k+1}, \ldots, a_d\}$:
  - $\langle g, 0\rangle \xrightarrow{0^k} \langle g, k\rangle \xrightarrow{0} \langle 0, k+1\rangle \xrightarrow{0^{j-k-1}} \langle 0, j\rangle \xrightarrow{1} \langle 1, 0\rangle = \langle (g+2) \bmod n, 0\rangle$, for $h_\Sigma(a) = 0^j1,\ j \in \{k + 1, \ldots, d - 1\}$,
  - $\langle g, 0\rangle \xrightarrow{0^k} \langle g, k\rangle \xrightarrow{0} \langle 0, k + 1\rangle \xrightarrow{0^{d-k-2}} \langle 0, d - 1\rangle \xrightarrow{0} \langle 1, 0\rangle = \langle (g + 2) \bmod n, 0\rangle$, for $h_\Sigma(a) = 0^d$.

Now, by induction on the length of $\alpha = a_{i_1}\cdots a_{i_\ell} \in \Sigma^*$, we easily obtain that the computation path $i \xrightarrow{\alpha} i'$ in $\mathcal{A}_{\Sigma,n,g,k}$ implies the existence of the corresponding path $\langle i,0\rangle \xrightarrow{h_\Sigma(\alpha)} \langle i',0\rangle$ for $\mathcal{A}'_{\Sigma,n,g,k}$, for each $i,i' \in Q$ and each $\alpha \in \Sigma$.

Thus, if $\mathcal{A}_{\Sigma,n,g,k}$ has a path $q_\text{I} = 0 \xrightarrow{\alpha} 0 \in F$, then $\mathcal{A}'_{\Sigma,n,g,k}$ has the corresponding path $q'_\text{I} = \langle 0,0\rangle \xrightarrow{h_\Sigma(\alpha)} \langle 0,0\rangle \in F^\oplus$, and hence $h_\Sigma(\alpha)$ is accepted by $\mathcal{A}'_{\Sigma,n,g,k}$, if $\alpha \in \mathcal{L}(\mathcal{A}_{\Sigma,n,g,k})$. On the other hand, if this path in $\mathcal{A}_{\Sigma,n,g,k}$ halts in some $i' \neq 0$, that is, in some $i' \in Q\backslash F$, the corresponding path in $\mathcal{A}'_{\Sigma,n,g,k}$ will halt in $\langle i',0\rangle \in F^\ominus$, and hence $h_\Sigma(\alpha)$ is rejected by $\mathcal{A}'_{\Sigma,n,g,k}$, if $\alpha \in \mathcal{L}(\mathcal{A}_{\Sigma,n,g,k})^\text{C}$.

Therefore, $\mathcal{A}'_{\Sigma,n,g,k}$ is a valid dcDFA for solving the binary promise problem $\langle h_\Sigma(\mathcal{L}(\mathcal{A}_{\Sigma,n,g,k})), h_\Sigma(\mathcal{L}(\mathcal{A}_{\Sigma,n,g,k})^\text{C})\rangle$. □

$\mathcal{A}'_{\Sigma,n,g,k}$ uses fewer states than dcDFA obtained by the use of Theorem 2, but it may accept/reject some binary inputs that are not images of any $\alpha \in \Sigma^*$. That is, it does not necessarily halt in a neutral state on such inputs.

Lemma 2. *Let $\mathcal{A}_{\Sigma,n,g,k}$ be the DFA defined above. Then $\mathcal{A}_{\Sigma,n,g,k}$ is optimal and uses exactly n states.*

Proof. Using (5) and (6), we see that $f(i,a_0) = (i+1) \bmod n$, for each $i \in Q = \{0,\ldots,n-1\}$, not excluding the special cases of $g = n-1$ or $g = n$. Since $q_\text{I} = 0$ and $F = \{0\}$, $a_0^e \in \mathcal{L}(\mathcal{A}_{\Sigma,n,g,k})$ if and only if e is an integer multiple of n.

This implies that $\mathcal{A}_{\Sigma,n,g,k}$ cannot be replaced by an equivalent DFA using fewer states: such DFA would accept a_0^n by a computation path $r_0 \xrightarrow{a_0} r_1 \xrightarrow{a_0} r_2 \xrightarrow{a_0} \cdots \xrightarrow{a_0} r_n$ along which some state would be repeated, which gives a valid accepting computation path for some a_0^e with $0 < e < n$, a contradiction. □

Lemma 3. *Let h_Σ, $\mathcal{A}_{\Sigma,n,g,k}$, and $\mathcal{A}'_{\Sigma,n,g,k}$ be the binary code, DFA, and dcDFA defined above. Then $\mathcal{A}'_{\Sigma,n,g,k}$ is optimal for solving the binary promise problem $\langle h_\Sigma(\mathcal{L}(\mathcal{A}_{\Sigma,n,g,k})), h_\Sigma(\mathcal{L}(\mathcal{A}_{\Sigma,n,g,k})^\text{C})\rangle$ and uses exactly $m = (\|\Sigma\|-1)\cdot g + (k+1) + (n-g-1)$ states, if $g \leq n-1$, but exactly $m = (\|\Sigma\|-1)\cdot n$ states, if $g = n$.*

Proof. By Lemma 1, $\mathcal{A}'_{\Sigma,n,g,k}$ solves the given promise problem and, by (7), it uses $m = d\cdot g + (k+1) + (n-g-1)$ states, if $g \leq n-1$. For $g = n$, all sections Q_i are of equal size d in (7), which gives $m = d\cdot n$. Since $d = \|\Sigma\| - 1$, the upper bound for $m = \|Q'\|$ follows.

We only have to show that this bound cannot be reduced. Let $\langle i,j\rangle, \langle\tilde{\imath},\tilde{\jmath}\rangle$ represent two arbitrary—but different—states in Q', that is, either $i < \tilde{\imath}$, or $i = \tilde{\imath}$ but $j < \tilde{\jmath}$. For $i = \tilde{\imath}$ we have two subcases, depending on whether $i < g$ or $i = g$. (There are no pairs of different states with $i = \tilde{\imath} > g$; this condition implies $j = \tilde{\jmath} = 0$, by (7). We do not consider $i > \tilde{\imath}$, or $i = \tilde{\imath}$ with $j > \tilde{\jmath}$ either—the roles of $\langle i,j\rangle, \langle\tilde{\imath},\tilde{\jmath}\rangle$ can be swapped). Let us now define the following binary strings:

$$\begin{aligned}
x_{\langle i,j\rangle} &= 1^i\cdot 0^j, && \text{for each } \langle i,j\rangle \in Q',\\
y_{\langle i,j\rangle\langle\tilde{\imath},\tilde{\jmath}\rangle} &= 1\cdot 1^{n-i-1}, && \text{if } 0 \leq i < \tilde{\imath} \leq n-1,\\
y_{\langle i,j\rangle\langle i,\tilde{\jmath}\rangle} &= 0^{d-\tilde{\jmath}}1\cdot 1^{n-i-1}, && \text{if } 0 \leq i < g \text{ and } 0 \leq j < \tilde{\jmath} \leq d-1,\\
y_{\langle g,j\rangle\langle g,\tilde{\jmath}\rangle} &= 0^{k+1-\tilde{\jmath}}1\cdot 1^{n-g-1}, && \text{if } g \leq n-1 \text{ and } 0 \leq j < \tilde{\jmath} \leq k.
\end{aligned} \tag{9}$$

It can be seen from (8) that each state $\langle i,j\rangle \in Q'$ is reached by reading $x_{\langle i,j\rangle}$ from the input: $q'_{\mathrm{I}} = \langle 0,0\rangle \xrightarrow{1^i} \langle i \bmod n, 0\rangle = \langle i,0\rangle \xrightarrow{0^j} \langle i,j\rangle$.

If $g = n-1$, we get $y_{\langle g,j\rangle\langle g,\bar{\jmath}\rangle} = 0^{k+1-\bar{\jmath}}1$, if $g = n$, we do not define $y_{\langle g,j\rangle\langle g,\bar{\jmath}\rangle}$.

We are now going to show that *(i)* both $x_{\langle i,j\rangle}\cdot y_{\langle i,j\rangle\langle \bar{\imath},\bar{\jmath}\rangle}$ and $x_{\langle \bar{\imath},\bar{\jmath}\rangle}\cdot y_{\langle i,j\rangle\langle \bar{\imath},\bar{\jmath}\rangle}$ are valid binary images of some strings in Σ^*, i.e., both of them are in $h_\Sigma(\Sigma^*)$, and that *(ii)* the computation of $\mathcal{A}'_{\Sigma,n,g,k}$ on $x_{\langle i,j\rangle}\cdot y_{\langle i,j\rangle\langle \bar{\imath},\bar{\jmath}\rangle}$ starts in $q'_{\mathrm{I}} = \langle 0,0\rangle$ and ends in $\langle 0,0\rangle \in F^{\oplus}$, while the computation on $x_{\langle \bar{\imath},\bar{\jmath}\rangle}\cdot y_{\langle i,j\rangle\langle \bar{\imath},\bar{\jmath}\rangle}$ starts in $q'_{\mathrm{I}} = \langle 0,0\rangle$ and ends in some $\langle i',0\rangle \in F^{\ominus}$, with $i' \neq 0$. Taking into account (i), this gives that $x_{\langle i,j\rangle}\cdot y_{\langle i,j\rangle\langle \bar{\imath},\bar{\jmath}\rangle} \in h_\Sigma(\mathcal{L}(\mathcal{A}_{\Sigma,n,g,k}))$ and $x_{\langle \bar{\imath},\bar{\jmath}\rangle}\cdot y_{\langle i,j\rangle\langle \bar{\imath},\bar{\jmath}\rangle} \in h_\Sigma(\mathcal{L}(\mathcal{A}_{\Sigma,n,g,k})^{\mathrm{C}})$. These statements can be shown by analyzing all cases, using (9), (3), and (8) (see also Figs. 2 and 3):

- If $0 \le i < \bar{\imath} \le n-1$, and hence $0 < \bar{\imath} - i \le n-1$, with $j,\bar{\jmath} \in \{0,\ldots,d-1\}$:
  - $x_{\langle i,j\rangle}\cdot y_{\langle i,j\rangle\langle \bar{\imath},\bar{\jmath}\rangle} = 1^i\cdot 0^j\cdot 1\cdot 1^{n-i-1} = h_\Sigma(a_0^i\cdot a_j\cdot a_0^{n-i-1})$,
    $\langle 0,0\rangle \xrightarrow{1^i0^j} \langle i,j\rangle \xrightarrow{1} \langle (i+1) \bmod n, 0\rangle \xrightarrow{1^{n-i-1}} \langle 0,0\rangle$,
  - $x_{\langle \bar{\imath},\bar{\jmath}\rangle}\cdot y_{\langle i,j\rangle\langle \bar{\imath},\bar{\jmath}\rangle} = 1^{\bar{\imath}}\cdot 0^{\bar{\jmath}}\cdot 1\cdot 1^{n-i-1} = h_\Sigma(a_0^{\bar{\imath}}\cdot a_{\bar{\jmath}}\cdot a_0^{n-i-1})$,
    $\langle 0,0\rangle \xrightarrow{1^{\bar{\imath}}0^{\bar{\jmath}}} \langle \bar{\imath},\bar{\jmath}\rangle \xrightarrow{1} \langle (\bar{\imath}+1) \bmod n, 0\rangle \xrightarrow{1^{n-i-1}} \langle \bar{\imath}-i,0\rangle \neq \langle 0,0\rangle$.
- If $0 \le i < g$ and $0 \le j < \bar{\jmath} \le d-1$, and hence $1 \le j+d-\bar{\jmath} \le d-1$:
  - $x_{\langle i,j\rangle}\cdot y_{\langle i,j\rangle\langle i,\bar{\jmath}\rangle} = 1^i\cdot 0^j\cdot 0^{d-\bar{\jmath}}1\cdot 1^{n-i-1} = h_\Sigma(a_0^i\cdot a_{j+d-\bar{\jmath}}\cdot a_0^{n-i-1})$,
    $\langle 0,0\rangle \xrightarrow{1^i0^j} \langle i,j\rangle \xrightarrow{0^{d-\bar{\jmath}}} \langle i,j+d-\bar{\jmath}\rangle \xrightarrow{1} \langle (i+1) \bmod n, 0\rangle \xrightarrow{1^{n-i-1}} \langle 0,0\rangle$,
  - $x_{\langle i,\bar{\jmath}\rangle}\cdot y_{\langle i,j\rangle\langle i,\bar{\jmath}\rangle} = 1^i\cdot 0^{\bar{\jmath}}\cdot 0^{d-\bar{\jmath}}1\cdot 1^{n-i-1} = h_\Sigma(a_0^i\cdot a_d\cdot a_0^{n-i})$,
    $\langle 0,0\rangle \xrightarrow{1^i0^{\bar{\jmath}}} \langle i,\bar{\jmath}\rangle \xrightarrow{0^{d-1-\bar{\jmath}}} \langle i,d-1\rangle \xrightarrow{0} \langle (i+1) \bmod n, 0\rangle \xrightarrow{1^{n-i}} \langle 1,0\rangle$.
- If $g \le n-1$ and $0 \le j < \bar{\jmath} \le k$, and hence $1 \le j+k+1-\bar{\jmath} \le k$:
  - $x_{\langle g,j\rangle}\cdot y_{\langle g,j\rangle\langle g,\bar{\jmath}\rangle} = 1^g\cdot 0^j\cdot 0^{k+1-\bar{\jmath}}1\cdot 1^{n-g-1} = h_\Sigma(a_0^g\cdot a_{j+k+1-\bar{\jmath}}\cdot a_0^{n-g-1})$,
    $\langle 0,0\rangle \xrightarrow{1^g0^j} \langle g,j\rangle \xrightarrow{0^{k+1-\bar{\jmath}}} \langle g,j{+}k{+}1{-}\bar{\jmath}\rangle \xrightarrow{1} \langle (g{+}1) \bmod n, 0\rangle \xrightarrow{1^{n-g-1}} \langle 0,0\rangle$,
  - $x_{\langle g,\bar{\jmath}\rangle}\cdot y_{\langle g,j\rangle\langle g,\bar{\jmath}\rangle} = 1^g\cdot 0^{\bar{\jmath}}\cdot 0^{k+1-\bar{\jmath}}1\cdot 1^{n-g-1} = h_\Sigma(a_0^g\cdot a_{k+1}\cdot a_0^{n-g-1})$,
    $\langle 0,0\rangle \xrightarrow{1^g0^{\bar{\jmath}}} \langle g,\bar{\jmath}\rangle \xrightarrow{0^{k-\bar{\jmath}}} \langle g,k\rangle$, with two different ways to continue:
    if $g \le n-2$, then $\langle g,k\rangle \xrightarrow{0} \langle g+1,0\rangle \xrightarrow{1^{n-g}} \langle (n+1) \bmod n, 0\rangle = \langle 1,0\rangle$,
    if $g = n-1$, then $\langle g,k\rangle \xrightarrow{0} \langle 0,k+1\rangle \xrightarrow{1^{n-g}} \langle (n-g) \bmod n, 0\rangle = \langle 1,0\rangle$.

Summing up, we have constructed m-tuple $X = \langle x_{\langle i,j\rangle}\rangle_{\langle i,j\rangle\in Q'}$ and $\binom{m}{2}$-tuple $Y = \langle y_{\langle i,j\rangle\langle \bar{\imath},\bar{\jmath}\rangle}\rangle_{\langle i,j\rangle,\langle \bar{\imath},\bar{\jmath}\rangle\in Q',\, \langle i,j\rangle\neq\langle \bar{\imath},\bar{\jmath}\rangle}$, where $m = \|Q'\|$, consisting of binary strings such that, for each pair $\langle i,j\rangle \neq \langle \bar{\imath},\bar{\jmath}\rangle$,

- both $x_{\langle i,j\rangle}\cdot y_{\langle i,j\rangle\langle \bar{\imath},\bar{\jmath}\rangle}$ and $x_{\langle \bar{\imath},\bar{\jmath}\rangle}\cdot y_{\langle i,j\rangle\langle \bar{\imath},\bar{\jmath}\rangle}$ are in
  $h_\Sigma(\Sigma^*) = h_\Sigma(\mathcal{L}(\mathcal{A}_{\Sigma,n,g,k})) \cup h_\Sigma(\mathcal{L}(\mathcal{A}_{\Sigma,n,g,k})^{\mathrm{C}})$,
- $x_{\langle i,j\rangle}\cdot y_{\langle i,j\rangle\langle \bar{\imath},\bar{\jmath}\rangle} \in h_\Sigma(\mathcal{L}(\mathcal{A}_{\Sigma,n,g,k}))$ and $x_{\langle \bar{\imath},\bar{\jmath}\rangle}\cdot y_{\langle i,j\rangle\langle \bar{\imath},\bar{\jmath}\rangle} \in h_\Sigma(\mathcal{L}(\mathcal{A}_{\Sigma,n,g,k})^{\mathrm{C}})$.

But then, by Theorem 1, any dcDFA solving the binary promise problem $\langle h_\Sigma(\mathcal{L}(\mathcal{A}_{\Sigma,n,g,k})), h_\Sigma(\mathcal{L}(\mathcal{A}_{\Sigma,n,g,k})^{\mathrm{C}})\rangle$ must use at least $m = \|Q'\|$ states, which gives that $\mathcal{A}'_{\Sigma,n,g,k}$ is optimal. □

Theorem 5. *For each non-unary input alphabet Σ, there exists a maximal binary prefix code $h:\Sigma^*\rightarrow\{0,1\}^*$ such that, for each $n \ge 2$ and each value $N \in \{n,\ldots,(\|\Sigma\|-1)\cdot n\}$, there exists a language $\mathcal{L} \subseteq \Sigma^*$ such that the optimal DFA recognizing $\mathcal{L}$ uses exactly n states and any optimal dcDFA for solving $\langle h(\mathcal{L}), h(\mathcal{L}^{\mathrm{C}})\rangle$, the binary promise-problem version of $\mathcal{L}$, uses exactly N states.*

Proof. Let us handle the pathological case of $\Sigma = \{a_0, a_1\}$ first. There are only two maximal prefix codes in this case, both of them are bijections from $\{a_0, a_1\}$ to $\{0,1\}$, and none of them can change the state complexity of any language. This corresponds to the fact that here $N \in \{n, \ldots, (\|\Sigma\| - 1)\cdot n\} = \{n\}$.

Now, for the given Σ, with $\|\Sigma\| \geq 3$, let us fix $h = h_\Sigma$, as introduced by (3). Next, the witness language $\mathcal{L}$ depends on Σ and on the given values n and N:

First, if $N \leq (\|\Sigma\| - 1)\cdot n - 1 = d\cdot n - 1$, we can take $\mathcal{L} = \mathcal{L}(\mathcal{A}_{\Sigma,n,g,k})$, using the following parameters:

$$g = \lfloor (N - n)/(d - 1) \rfloor, \;\; k = (N - n) \bmod (d - 1).$$

Clearly, $g \leq \lfloor (d\cdot n - 1 - n)/(d - 1) \rfloor = \lfloor n - \frac{1}{d-1} \rfloor = n - 1$ and $k \leq d - 2$. By Lemma 2, $\mathcal{A}_{\Sigma,n,g,k}$ is the optimal DFA for recognizing $\mathcal{L}$, using exactly n states. Similarly, by Lemma 3, $\mathcal{A}'_{\Sigma,n,g,k}$ is optimal dcDFA for solving $\langle h_\Sigma(\mathcal{L}), h_\Sigma(\mathcal{L}^{\mathrm{C}})\rangle$ and uses exactly $m = d\cdot g + (k + 1) + (n - g - 1)$ states. This gives $m = d\cdot g + (k+1) + (n - g - 1) = (d-1)\cdot g + k + n = (d-1)\cdot \lfloor (N - n)/(d - 1) \rfloor + (N - n) \bmod (d - 1) + n = (N - n) + n = N$ states, using the fact that $a\cdot \lfloor b/a \rfloor + b \bmod a = b$.

Second, if $N = (\|\Sigma\| - 1)\cdot n$, take $\mathcal{L} = \mathcal{L}(\mathcal{A}_{\Sigma,n,g,k})$ with $g = n$ and $k = 0$. (Here $\mathcal{A}_{\Sigma,n,g,k}$ does not actually depend on k.) Again, by Lemma 2, $\mathcal{A}_{\Sigma,n,g,k}$ is optimal and uses exactly n states and, by Lemma 3, $\mathcal{A}'_{\Sigma,n,g,k}$ is optimal for solving $\langle h_\Sigma(\mathcal{L}), h_\Sigma(\mathcal{L}^{\mathrm{C}})\rangle$, this time with exactly $m = (\|\Sigma\| - 1)\cdot n = N$ states. □

5 Concluding Remarks

By a more careful analysis of the construction in Theorem 3, we see that it does not increase the number of accepting or rejecting states. As a direct consequence, if the optimal DFA $\mathcal{A}$ recognizing $\mathcal{L}$ uses $n^\oplus$ accepting and $n^\ominus$ rejecting states (neither of these values can be reduced, since the optimal $\mathcal{A}$ is unique), then any optimal dcDFA $\mathcal{A}'$ solving the binary promise problem $\langle h(\mathcal{L}), h(\mathcal{L}^{\mathrm{C}})\rangle$ must use at least $n^\oplus$ accepting and at least $n^\ominus$ rejecting states. But all states in $\mathcal{A}'$ that cannot be reached from q'_{I} by reading some $\beta \in h(\Sigma^*)$ can be made neutral (see also (2) in the proof of Theorem 3). This will only change acceptance/rejection to "don't care" answers on *some* inputs not belonging to $h(\Sigma^*)$.

This allows to establish some kind of pseudo-isomorphism between $\mathcal{A}$ and $\mathcal{A}'$. (Proof omitted here due to space constraints, to appear in a journal version.) Namely, there exists a bijective function $t\colon Q \to F^\oplus \cup F^\ominus$ that maps q_{I} to q'_{I}, F to $F^\oplus$, and $Q \backslash F$ to $F^\ominus$, preserving the machine's transitions, i.e., $t(f(q,a)) = f'^*(t(q), h(a))$, for each $q \in Q$ and $a \in \Sigma$. However, such pseudo-isomorphism does not exclude, for some transition $q \xrightarrow{a} q'$ in $\mathcal{A}$, passing through some state $t(q'') \in F^\oplus \cup F^\ominus$ along the corresponding path $t(q) \xrightarrow{h(a)} t(q')$ in $\mathcal{A}'$—even more than once in the meantime.[3]

[3] This phenomenon can be seen in Fig. 2, where we have "3" $\xrightarrow{a_4}$ "5" for $\mathcal{A}_{\Sigma,n,g,k}$. Since $h(a_4) =$ "00001", this corresponds to $t($"3"$) =$ "30" $\xrightarrow{00001}$ "50" $= t($"5"$)$ for $\mathcal{A}'_{\Sigma,n,g,k}$, passing twice through $t($"4"$) =$ "40".

There are more open questions in the related area than the known answers. As an example, we do not know the cost of binary coded intersection; the same holds for other basic operations with regular languages. It can be expected that answers may depend also on the code h in use, and we expect some anomalies for prefix codes that are not maximal.

References

1. Berstel, J., Perrin, D., Reutenauer, C.: Codes and Automata. Cambridge University Press, Cambridge (2010)
2. Birget, J.-C.: Intersection and union of regular languages and state complexity. Inform. Process. Lett. **43**, 185–190 (1992)
3. Bruyère, V.: Maximal codes with bounded deciphering delay. Theoret. Comput. Sci. **84**, 53–76 (1991)
4. Čevorová, K.: Kleene star on unary regular languages. In: Jurgensen, H., Reis, R. (eds.) DCFS 2013. LNCS, vol. 8031, pp. 277–288. Springer, Heidelberg (2013). https://doi.org/10.1007/978-3-642-39310-5_26
5. Geffert, V.: Magic numbers in the state hierarchy of finite automata. Inform. Comput. **205**, 1652–1670 (2007)
6. Goldreich, O.: On promise problems: a survey. In: Goldreich, O., Rosenberg, A.L., Selman, A.L. (eds.) Theoretical Computer Science. LNCS, vol. 3895, pp. 254–290. Springer, Heidelberg (2006). https://doi.org/10.1007/11685654_12
7. Holzer, M., Rauch, C.: The range of state complexities of languages resulting from the cascade product—the unary case (extended abstract). In: Maneth, S. (ed.) CIAA 2021. LNCS, vol. 12803, pp. 90–101. Springer, Cham (2021). https://doi.org/10.1007/978-3-030-79121-6_8
8. Hopcroft, J., Motwani, R., Ullman, J.: Introduction to Automata Theory, Languages, and Computation. Addison-Wesley, Boston (2001)
9. Hricko, M., Jirásková, G., Szabari, A.: Union and intersection of regular languages and descriptional complexity. In: Proceedings of Descriptional Complexity of Formal Systems, pp. 170–181. IFIP & University, Milano (2005)
10. Iwama, K., Kambayashi, Y., Takaki, K.: Tight bounds on the number of states of DFA's that are equivalent to n-state NFA's. Theoret. Comput. Sci. **237**, 485–494 (2000)
11. Jirásková, G.: Magic numbers and ternary alphabet. Internat. J. Found. Comput. Sci. **22**, 331–344 (2011)
12. Jirásková, G., Masopust, T.: On a structural property in the state complexity of projected regular languages. Theoret. Comput. Sci. **449**, 93–105 (2012)
13. Moreira, N., Pighizzini, G., Reis, R.: Optimal state reductions of automata with partially specified behaviors. Theoret. Comput. Sci. **658**, 235–245 (2017)
14. Paull, M.C., Unger, S.H.: Minimizing the number of states in incompletely specified sequential switching functions. IRE Trans. Electron. Comput. **3**, 356–367 (1959)
15. Pfleeger, C.P.: State reduction in incompletely specified finite-state machines. IEEE Trans. Comput. **C–22**, 1099–1102 (1973)
16. Rabin, M., Scott, D.: Finite automata and their decision problems. IBM J. Res. Develop. **3**, 114–125 (1959)

Reset Complexity and Completely Reachable Automata with Simple Idempotents

Stefan Hoffmann(✉)

Informatikwissenschaften, FB IV, Universität Trier, Trier, Germany
hoffmanns@informatik.uni-trier.de

Abstract. Every regular ideal language is the set of synchronizing words of some automaton. The reset complexity of a regular ideal language is the size of such an automaton with the minimal number of states. The state complexity is the size of a minimal automaton recognizing a regular language in the usual sense. There exist regular ideal languages whose state complexity is exponentially larger than its reset complexity. We call an automaton sync-maximal, if the reset complexity of the ideal language induced by its set of synchronizing words equals the number of states of the automaton and the gap between the reset complexity and the state complexity of this language is maximal possible. An automaton is completely reachable, if we can map the whole state set to any non-empty subset of states (for synchronizing automata, it is only required that the whole state set can be mapped to a singleton set). We first state a general structural result for sync-maximal automata. This shows that sync-maximal automata are closely related to completely reachable automata. We then investigate automata with simple idempotents and show that for these automata complete reachability and sync-maximality are equivalent. Lastly, we find that for automata with simple idempotents over a binary alphabet, subset reachability problems that are PSPACE-complete in general are solvable in polynomial time.

Keywords: finite automata · synchronization · set of synchronizing words · automata with simple idempotents · completely reachable automata · sync-maximal automata

1 Introduction

Let Σ be a *finite set of symbols* and Σ^* be the *free monoid* with neutral element ε (called the *empty word*). *Languages* are subsets of Σ^*. A language $I \subseteq \Sigma^*$ is an *ideal language* if $x, y \in \Sigma^*$ and $u \in I$ imply $xuy \in I$. A *(semi-)automaton* is a triple $\mathcal{A} = (Q, \Sigma, \delta)$ where Q is *finite set of states* and $\delta : Q \times \Sigma \to Q$ a (totally defined) *transition function*. Here, we simplify our notation by not mentioning δ explicitly, i.e., we write $q.a$ when applying the transition function δ to the state $q \in Q$ and letter $a \in \Sigma$ and we write an automaton as a 2-tuple $\mathcal{A} = (Q, \Sigma)$.

Published by Springer Nature Switzerland AG 2022
Y.-S. Han and G. Vaszil (Eds.): DCFS 2022, LNCS 13439, pp. 85–99, 2022.
https://doi.org/10.1007/978-3-031-13257-5_7

The transition function is extended to a function $Q \times \Sigma^* \to Q$ (denoted by the dot notation as well) by setting $q.\varepsilon = q$ and $q.ua = (q.u).a$ for $u \in \Sigma^*$, $a \in \Sigma$ and $q \in Q$. Furthermore, we extend it to subsets $S \subseteq Q$ by setting $S.u = \{q.u \mid q \in S\}$ for $u \in \Sigma^*$.

A language $L \subseteq \Sigma^*$ is a *regular language* if there exists an automaton $\mathcal{A} = (Q, \Sigma)$ and $q_0 \in Q$ and $F \subseteq Q$ such that $L = \{u \in \Sigma^* : q_0.u \in F\}$. We say the automaton $\mathcal{A}$ *accepts* (or *recognizes*) the language L. For a regular language $L \subseteq \Sigma^*$ we denote by $\mathrm{sc}(L) = \min\{|Q| : \mathcal{A} = (Q, \Sigma) \text{ accepts } L\}$ the *state complexity* of L.

Set $\mathrm{Syn}(\mathcal{A}) = \{u \in \Sigma^* \mid |Q.u| = 1\}$, the *set of synchronizing words* of $\mathcal{A}$ (which is an ideal language). If $\mathrm{Syn}(\mathcal{A}) \neq \emptyset$, the automaton is called *synchronizing*. For every n-state automaton $\mathcal{A}$ we have $\mathrm{sc}(\mathrm{Syn}(\mathcal{A})) \leqslant 2^n - n$ [15]. We call $\mathcal{A}$ *sync-maximal* if $\mathrm{sc}(\mathrm{Syn}(\mathcal{A}))$ equals $2^n - n$. If $I \subseteq \Sigma^*$ is a regular ideal language, then it is precisely the set of synchronizing words of the automaton with the least number of states accepting it [9,15]. The *reset complexity* of I is

$$\mathrm{rc}(I) = \min\{|Q| : \mathcal{A} = (Q, \Sigma) \text{ with } I = \mathrm{Syn}(\mathcal{A})\},$$

i.e., the least number of states such that I is realized as the set of synchronizing word of an automaton. We have $\mathrm{rc}(I) \leqslant \mathrm{sc}(I)$. There are known families of ideal languages I_n associated to synchronizing automata such that $\mathrm{sc}(I_n) = 2^n - n$ but $\mathrm{rc}(I_n) = n$ [15]. For example, the set of synchronizing words of the *Černý family* of automata $\mathcal{C}_n = (Q_n, \{a, b\})$ defined by Černý [6] for $n > 1$ by

$$i.a = \begin{cases} i & \text{if } i < n, \\ 1 & \text{if } i = n; \end{cases} \qquad i.b = \begin{cases} i+1 & \text{if } i < n, \\ 1 & \text{if } i = n. \end{cases}$$

The automaton $\mathscr{C}_n$ is shown in Fig. 1.

Hence, describing regular ideal languages as the set of synchronizing words can be exponentially more succinct than the usual notion of acceptance by automata.

For $L \subseteq \Sigma^*$, let $||L|| = \min\{|u| \mid u \in L\}$ be the length of a shortest word in L. In combinatorial automata theory (and also in related applications, see [19] for a survey in the context of model-based testing), the question on the length of shortest synchronizing words arises. The *Černý conjecture* states that for an n-state automaton $\mathcal{A}$ we have $||\,\mathrm{Syn}(\mathcal{A})|| \leqslant (n-1)^2$. For the n-state automata $\mathcal{C}_n$ from Fig. 1 we have $||\,\mathrm{Syn}(\mathcal{C}_n)|| = (n-1)^2$. The best general upper bound proven so far is cubic in the number of states [21]. For more information and further references, see the recent survey [22]. Investigating the length of shortest words in regular ideal languages yields a natural approach to the Černý conjecture, more precisely it is equivalent to the statement that $\mathrm{rc}(I) \geqslant \sqrt{||I||} + 1$ for every regular ideal language $I \subseteq \Sigma^*$.

In fact, the connection between regular ideal languages and synchronizing automata is even deeper. It can be shown that every regular ideal language equals the set of synchronizing word of a strongly connected automaton [16].

Automata with simple idempotents have been introduced in [18] and it has been shown that a shortest synchronizing word has at most quadratic length for these automata.

Overview and Contribution. In Sect. 2 we introduce automata with simple idempotents and further notation that was not already introduced in the introduction. Then we make the conditions for sync-maximality more precise. Example 1 gives an automaton that is completely reachable, but not sync-maximal.

Section 3 discusses completely reachable automata.

In Sect. 4 we determine the structure of sync-maximal automata. Our results show that both notions are closely connected, as every sync-maximal automaton contains a completely reachable subautomaton. In Example 2 we give automata that are sync-maximal but not completely reachable.

Then in Sect. 5 we investigate automata with simple idempotents. Hence, this chapter is concerned with the reset complexity of ideal languages induced by automata with simple idempotents. However, we do not mention ideal languages anymore, but rather express our result directly with automata (ideal languages were introduced in the introduction to give a broader context of our results). We show that an automaton with simple idempotents that is completely reachable is sync-maximal. Note that Example 2 and Example 3 give automata with simple idempotents that are sync-maximal, but not completely reachable. However, for strongly connected automata with simple idempotents, it follows that complete reachability and sync-maximality are equivalent.

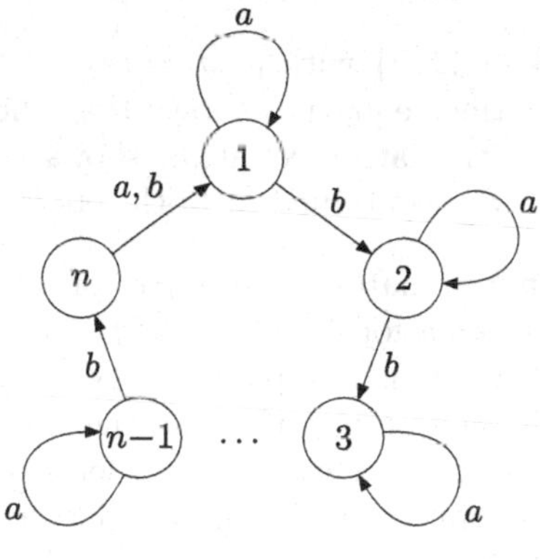

Fig. 1. The automaton $\mathcal{C}_n$

2 Some More Notation and Preliminary Results

Let $f : X \to Y$ be a function. Here, function application is written on the right, i.e., xf or $(x)f$ denotes the function f applied to x. The same applies to the extension to subsets, i.e., if $S \subseteq X$, then $(S)f$ and Sf denote the set $\{xf \mid x \in S\}$. In this respect, if $g : Y \to Z$ is another function, the *function composition* fg is the function $x(fg) = (xf)g$, i.e. f is applied first. This "right action notation" deviates from the more usual "left action notation" $f(x)$ used in formal language theory. We chose this notation as, in our opinion, it makes certain algebraic manipulations in Sect. 5 easier to read, as it conforms better with the way function composition is defined and read from left to right. This notation[1] is actually quite common in more algebraic approaches, for example, in [1].

For $n \geqslant 0$, we set $[0] = \emptyset$ and $[n] = \{1, \ldots, n\}$ if $n > 0$. If $f : [n] \to [n]$ is a permutation, i.e., a bijective mapping, then $f^{-1} : [n] \to [n]$ denotes the *inverse mapping* with $xff^{-1} = xf^{-1}f = x$ for all $x \in [n]$.

For algebraic notions as semigroup, monoid, generating set etc., we refer to the literature, e.g., the textbook [14]. By $\mathcal{T}_n$ we denote the *transformation monoid of all mappings on a finite set* of cardinality n.

Sets with precisely k elements are called *k-sets*, and 1-sets are also called *singleton sets.*

For $f : X \to Y$ with X, Y finite, the *defect* is $|X \setminus \{xf \mid x \in X\}|$.

A mapping $f : X \to X$ on a finite set X is a *simple idempotent (mapping)* if it has defect one and for each $x \in X$ we have $xff = xf$. Note that a simple idempotent mapping is completely specified by the two points $x \in X$ and xf with $xf \neq x$. In Sect. 5 we need the following "cancellation property" of simple idempotent mappings.

Lemma 1. *Let $f : [n] \to [n]$ be a simple idempotent mapping and $A, B \subseteq [n]$ with $|A| = |B|$. If $Af = Bf$ and there exist $x \in A$, $y \in B$ such that $xf \neq x$ and $yf \neq y$, then $A = B$ and $x = y$.*

Remark 1. Let $f : \{1,2\} \to \{1,2\}$ with $(1)f = (2)f = 2$. Then $\{1\}f = \{1,2\}f$ and $\{1\}f = \{2\}f$. The former equation shows that the assumption $|A| = |B|$ is necessary in Lemma 1, the latter equation shows the assumption that the element that is moved by f is contained in both sets is necessary.

Let $\mathcal{A} = (Q, \Sigma)$ be an automaton. The *defect* of a letter $a \in \Sigma$ is the defect of the induced function $q \mapsto q.a$ for $q \in Q$. A *simple idempotent letter* is a letter that induces a simple idempotent mapping on the states, and a *permutational letter* is a letter that induces a permutation on the state set. The automaton $\mathcal{A}$ is an *automaton with simple idempotents* if every letter is either a permutational letter or a simple idempotent letter. A subset $S \subseteq Q$ defines (or induces) a *subautomaton* if $s.a \in S$ for each $s \in S$ and $a \in \Sigma$. In this case, the set S together with the transition function restricted to S in the arguments and the image gives a totally defined function, i.e., we can regard it as an automaton on its own.

The *transformation monoid of the automaton* $\mathcal{A}$ is the monoid generated by the mappings $q \mapsto q.a$ for $q \in Q$ induced by each letter $a \in \Sigma$ on the state set.

---

[1] Note that we actually mix both notations, as we write certain operators (which are never composed here), for example $\mathrm{Syn}(\mathcal{A})$, in the other convention. But this is also done in the literature, for example [1], and should pose no problem.

A state $t \in Q$ is *reachable* from another state $s \in Q$ if there exists $u \in \Sigma^*$ such $s.u = t$. A *strongly connected component* is a maximal subset of states such that for every two states in this subset are reachable from each other. The automaton $\mathcal{A}$ is *strongly connected* if Q is a strongly connected component.

An automaton $\mathcal{A}$ is minimal [13] for $\{u \in \Sigma^* \mid q_0.u \in F\}$ with $q_0 \in Q$ and $F \subseteq Q$ if and only if every state is reachable from q_0 and every pair of distinct state $q, q' \in Q$ is *distinguishable*, which means that there exists $u \in \Sigma^*$ such that precisely one of the two states $q.u$ and $q'.u$ is final, i.e., the following holds true: $q.u \in F$ if and only if $q'.u \notin F$.

The *power automaton* is $\mathcal{P}_{\mathcal{A}} = (\{S \mid \emptyset \neq S \subseteq Q\}, \Sigma)$ where the transition function of $\mathcal{P}_{\mathcal{A}}$ is the transition function of $\mathcal{A}$ extended to subsets. The automaton $\mathcal{A}$ is *completely reachable*, if every non-empty subset is reachable from the state Q in the power automaton of $\mathcal{A}$. Setting $F = \{\{q\} \mid q \in Q\}$, as $\mathrm{Syn}(\mathcal{A}) = \{u \in \Sigma^* \mid Q.u \in F\}$, the power automaton accepts $\mathrm{Syn}(\mathcal{A})$. The states in F can be merged into a single state to get another automaton accepting $\mathrm{Syn}(\mathcal{A})$. Hence, $\mathrm{sc}(\mathrm{Syn}(\mathcal{A})) \leqslant 2^n - n$.

Translating the condition of minimality of an automaton to the specific language $\mathrm{Syn}(\mathcal{A})$ and the power automaton, we find that the sync-maximality of $\mathcal{A}$ is equivalent to the following two conditions:

1. Every non-empty subset with at least two states is reachable in $\mathcal{P}_{\mathcal{A}}$ and at least one singleton subset is reachable in $\mathcal{P}_{\mathcal{A}}$.
2. For any two non-empty and distinct subsets $S, T \subseteq Q$ with $\min\{|S|, |T|\} \geqslant 2$ there exists a word $u \in \Sigma^*$ such that precisely one of the two subsets $T.u$ and $S.u$ is a singleton subsets, i.e., both subset are distinguishable (in $\mathcal{P}_{\mathcal{A}}$).

In [10, Lemma 3.1] (and a little more general in [12, Theorem 7]) it was shown that distinguishability of states in the power automaton with respect to $\mathrm{Syn}(\mathcal{A})$ can be simplified by only considering 2-sets.

Proposition 2. *Let $\mathcal{A} = (Q, \Sigma)$. Then all states in the power automaton $\mathcal{P}_{\mathcal{A}}$ are distinguishable if and only if all 2-sets are distinguishable in $\mathcal{P}_{\mathcal{A}}$.*

Example 1. The automaton (see Fig. 2) with the state set $Q = \{1, 2, 3\}$, input letters $a_{[1]}, a_{[2]}, a_{[3]}, a_{[1,2]}$ and transition function given by

$$i.a_{[1]} = \begin{cases} 2 & \text{if } i = 1, 2, \\ 3 & \text{if } i = 3; \end{cases} \qquad i.a_{[2]} = \begin{cases} 1 & \text{if } i = 1, 2, \\ 3 & \text{if } i = 3; \end{cases}$$

$$i.a_{[3]} = \begin{cases} 1 & \text{if } i = 1, 2, \\ 2 & \text{if } i = 3; \end{cases} \qquad i.a_{[1,2]} = 3 \ \text{ for all } \ i = 1, 2, 3.$$

is taken from [3, Example 2] as an example of a completely reachable automaton. However, it is not sync-maximal as the two 2-sets $\{1, 3\}$ and $\{2, 3\}$ are not distinguishable.

Next, we introduce two decision problems that have been investigated in [2,3,17]. Subsets as in the latter problem were called *totally extensible* in [2], and in [17] the problem was called the *global inclusion problem for non-initial automata*.

Definition 3. Reachable Subset
Input: $\mathcal{A} = (Q, \Sigma)$ and $\emptyset \neq S \subseteq Q$.
Question: Exists $w \in \Sigma^*$ with $Q.w = S$?

Definition 4. Sync-Into-Subset
Input: $\mathcal{A} = (Q, \Sigma)$ and $S \subseteq Q$.
Question: Exists $w \in \Sigma^*$ with $Q.w \subseteq S$?

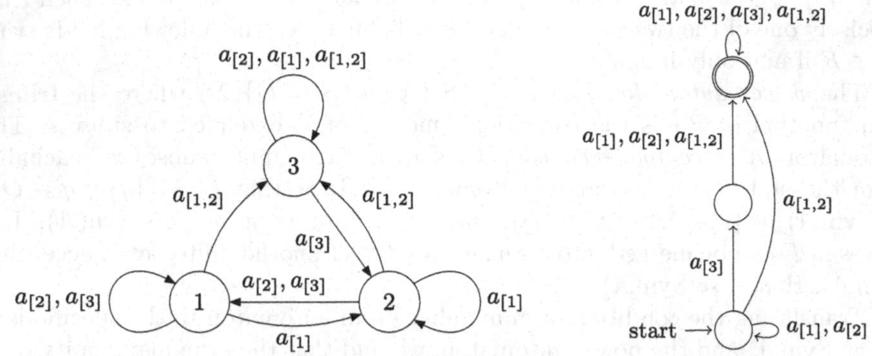

Fig. 2. Left: A completely reachable automaton (taken from [3, Example 2]) that is not sync-maximal. Right: A minimal automaton for the set of synchronizing words.

Lastly, we mention the following easy facts [10] that will be used without special mentioning.

Lemma 5. *A strongly connected sync-maximal automaton is completely reachable. A completely reachable automaton is strongly connected.*

3 Completely Reachable Automata

The notion of a completely reachable automaton was introduced in [3], based on a sufficient condition for the reachability of all subsets in circular automata [7]. This sufficient condition was generalized in this very first work [3], and later extended to a characterization with more general constructions in [4]. An extended version of [3,4] (and with further results) is under submission and a preliminary version available on arXiv [5]. Complete reachability has been used in [10] to characterize primitive permutation groups.

Given a finite automaton and two subsets of states, it is complete for deterministic polynomial space to check if there exists a word mapping one subset onto the other, see [3,17]. This implies that complete reachability can be checked in non-deterministic polynomial space by checking if a given automaton is not completely reachable in the following way: non-deterministically guess a non-empty subset and check if it is reachable from the whole state set, if not, then the automaton is not completely reachable. By Savitch's theorem [20] this problem is solvable in deterministic polynomial space as well, which implies that complete reachability is decidable in deterministic polynomial space. However, the precise computational complexity of deciding complete reachability is an open problem [3–5].

With Proposition 2, which yields a polynomial time procedure to check distinguishability of all non-empty subset [10, Corollary 3.2], we get the next result.

Proposition 6. *Deciding if a given automaton is sync-maximal can be done in polynomial space.*

In [8] a completely reachable automaton with letters of defect one was given for which the sufficient condition from [3] is not fulfilled, which was meant to be a counter-example to a conjecture from [3]. However, with another result from [8, Theorem 20] it can be deduced that complete reachability is decidable in polynomial time for automata with simple idempotents.

Theorem 7. *For automata $\mathcal{A} = (Q, \Sigma)$ with simple idempotents it is decidable in polynomial time if they are completely reachable.*

Proof (sketch). In [3] a sufficient (graph-theoretical) condition for complete reachability was stated, and in [8] it was shown that this sufficient condition can be checked in polynomial time. Furthermore [8, Theorem 20] states that the following implies the mentioned sufficient condition: For every proper non-empty $S \subseteq Q$ there exists $w \in \Sigma^*$ with $S = Q.w$ and $w_1, w_2 \in \Sigma^*$ with $w = w_1 w_2$ such that $|Q.w| + 1 = |Q.w_1|$ and w_2 has defect one. Now, it can be shown that this is fulfilled for completely reachable automata with simple idempotents. Combining these facts yields the claim. □

4 The Structure of Sync-Maximal Automata

Here, we determine the structure of sync-maximal automata. We show that they are either completely reachable or consist of precisely two strongly connected components, where one contains only a single "dangling state" and the other component forms a completely reachable subautomaton.

Theorem 8. *Let $\mathcal{A} = (\Sigma, Q)$ be an n-state semi-automaton with $n \geqslant 3$. If $\mathcal{A}$ is sync-maximal, i.e., the smallest recognizing automaton for* Syn($\mathcal{A}$) *has $2^n - n$ states, then either $\mathcal{A}$ is completely reachable or all of the the following statements hold true:*

1. *$|\Sigma| \geqslant 3$,*
2. *we have two strongly connected components $\{q\}$, $q \in Q$, and $S = Q \setminus \{q\}$,*
3. *there exists $a \in \Sigma$ with[2] $q.a \in S$ and such that $q'.a \neq q.a$ for at least one state $q' \in S$,*
4. *there exists $b \in \Sigma$ having defect one and $c \in \Sigma \setminus \{b\}$ with $q.b = q.c = q$,*
5. *if $|\Sigma| = 3$ and $n \geqslant 4$, then the letter b cyclically permutes S.*

[2] Observe that as $\{q\}$ and S are strongly connected components, the condition $q.a \in S$ implies that the state q is not reachable from any state in S and so $Q.u \neq \{q\}$ for all $u \in \Sigma^*$.

Proof. As $\text{Syn}(\mathcal{A}) \neq \emptyset$, there must exist a state $s \in Q$ and a synchronizing word $w \in \Sigma^*$ such that $Q.w = \{s\}$. Let $S \subseteq Q$ be the strongly connected component containing s. As $q.w = s$ for every $q \in Q$, this strongly connected component is uniquely determined for any choice of a state s such that there exists a word $w \in \Sigma^*$ with $Q.w = \{s\}$. Furthermore, it has the property that, once entered, we cannot leave S, i.e., $S.u \subseteq S$ for all $u \in \Sigma^*$. However, this implies $S \cap Q.u \neq \emptyset$ for every $u \in \Sigma^*$. Hence, no non-empty subset of $Q \backslash S$ is reachable. As by assumption every non-empty subset with at least two elements is reachable, we find $|S| = |Q|$ or $|S| = |Q| - 1$.

In the first case, $\mathcal{A}$ is strongly connected. This implies that if at least one singleton subset is reachable, then all singleton subsets are reachable and so $\mathcal{A}$ is completely reachable.

In the second case, we can write $Q = S \cup \{q\}$ with $q \notin S$. Note that in this case $\mathcal{A}$ is not completely reachable, as $\{q\}$ is not reachable. As $Q.w \in S$, there exists at least one letter mapping q into S.

Let $s, t \in S$ be two arbitrary distinct states. Consider the states $\{q, s\}$ and $\{q, t\}$ in the power automaton. They must be distinguishable, i.e., there must exist a word $u \in \Sigma^*$ mapping precisely one, say $\{q, s\}$, to a singleton set but not the other. Then $S.u \subseteq S$ and we can write $u = u'au''$ with $u', u'' \in \Sigma^*$ and $a \in \Sigma$ such that $q.ua \in S$ and $q.u = q$ and so $q.a \in S$. We must have $|\{q, t\}.ua| = 2$, which implies $t.a \neq q.a$.

Now, suppose $n \geqslant 3$. Then we must have at least two distinct letters $b, c \in \Sigma$ such that $q.b = q.c = q$. To see this, consider a non-empty subset $T \subseteq S$ with $|T| = n - 2$. The subset $T \cup \{q\}$ must be reachable. This is only possible if there exists a letter $b \in \Sigma$ with $q.b = q$ (recall $q \notin S.u$ for each $u \in \Sigma^*$) having defect one, for if every letter fixing q permutes the states or has defect at least two, then no subset of the form $T \cup \{q\}$ with $|T| = n - 2$ is reachable.

Next, consider a subset $T' \cup \{q\}$ with $|T'| = n - 2$ such that $T' \cup \{q\} \neq Q.b$. We cannot use the letter a to reach the subset $T' \cup \{q\}$ as $q \notin Q.a$. Let $i \geqslant 2$. Then $|Q.b^i| \leqslant n - 1$ and $|Q.b^i| = n - 1$ implies, as $Q.b^i \subseteq Q.b$, that $Q.bb = Q.b$. So, there must exist a third letter $c \in \Sigma \backslash \{a, b\}$ with $q.c = q$ to reach the subset $T' \cup \{q\}$.

Lastly, suppose $\Sigma = \{a, b, c\}$. Then a is the only letter such that $q.a \in S$. Furthermore, for each $q' \in S$ the subset $\{q\} \cup S \backslash \{q'\}$ must be reachable. If $Q.ub$ contains q and has size $n - 1$, then, as $Q.ub \subseteq Q.b$, we must have $Q.ub = Q.b$. If $|Q.c| \leqslant n$ and $n \geqslant 3$, then $Q.c$ must be a subset of size $n - 1$ to reach another subset not equal to $Q.b$ of size $n - 1$. However, as shown before for the letter b, if $Q.cc$ has size $n-1$, then $Q.cc = Q.c$. So, if $n \geqslant 4$ there exists a subset of size $n-1$ that is not reachable and hence in this case we must have $|Q.c| = n$. Putting all the arguments together, every subset of size $n-1$ containing q must be reachable by a word of the form bc^i for some $i \geqslant 0$. Let $q' \in S$ such that $Q.b = Q \backslash \{q'\}$ and choose $q'' \in S$. Then there exists $i \geqslant 0$ such that $Q.bc^i = Q \backslash \{q''\}$. As c permutes the states, this implies $q'.c = q''$. However, a single permutation that maps all states in S onto each other is only possible if this permutation induces a single cycle on these states and we conclude that c cyclically permutes the states in S. □

In case a sync-maximal automaton is not completely reachable, then we can show that one strongly connected component forms a completely reachable subautomaton.

Theorem 9. *Let $\mathcal{A} = (Q, \Sigma)$ be a sync-maximal automaton that is not completely reachable. Suppose $q \in Q$ is the "dangling state" that exists according to Theorem 8. Then the states in $Q\backslash\{q\}$ form a strongly connected, completely reachable and sync-maximal subautomaton.*

We can use sync-maximal and completely reachable automata to construct sync-maximal automata that are not completely reachable by adding a dangling state, as done in the next example.

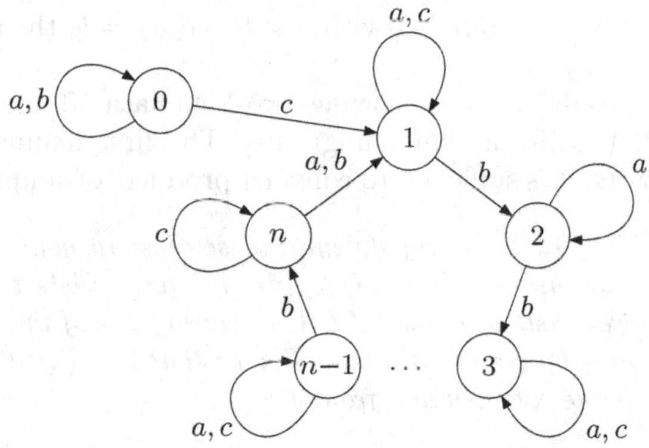

Fig. 3. The automaton $\mathcal{A}_n$ from Example 2

Example 2. We derive from the Černý family a new family of automata by adjoining an additional state and a new letter (see Fig. 3) that give sync-maximal, but not completely reachable (as they are not strongly connected) automata. Let $\mathcal{A}_n = (\{0, 1, \ldots, n\}, \{a, b, c\})$ with

$$i.a = \begin{cases} i & \text{if } i < n, \\ 1 & \text{if } i = n; \end{cases} \quad i.b = \begin{cases} 0 & \text{if } i = 0, \\ i+1 & \text{if } 0 < i < n, \\ 1 & \text{if } i = n. \end{cases} \quad i.c = \begin{cases} 1 & \text{if } i = 0, \\ i & \text{if } i \neq 0. \end{cases}$$

Observe that the automaton induced on the states $\{1, \ldots, n\}$ and by the letters $\{a, b\}$ is precisely the Černy automaton $\mathcal{C}_n$. The Černy automata are completely reachable and sync-maximal (which is implied by results from [11], but also by Theorem 12 of the present work). Hence, all non-empty subsets of $\{1, \ldots, n\}$ are distinguishable. If $S, T \subseteq \{0, 1, \ldots, n\}$ are non-empty and distinct, and at least one, say S, contains the state 0, we can distinguish them the following way: (1) If $0 \notin T$, then choosing any word from $\{a, b\}^*$ that maps T to a singleton distinguishes S and T, as it maps S to a 2-set. (2) If $0 \in T$, then write $S = \{0, s\}$

and $T = \{0, t\}$. By assumption $s \neq t$. There exists $m > 0$ such that $s.b^m = 1$. Then $t.b^m \neq 1$. Hence $S.b^m c = \{1\}$ and $T.b^m a = \{1, t.b^m\}$ is a 2-set. So, S and T are distinguishable.

5 Automata with Simple Idempotents

A strongly connected sync-maximal automaton is also completely reachable [10, Lemma 3.3]. Here, we show that if an automaton with simple idempotents is completely reachable, then it is sync-maximal. Hence, for strongly connected automata with simple idempotents, complete reachability and sync-maximality are equivalent.

Let $f : [n] \to [n]$ be a mapping and $g : [n] \to [n]$ be a permutation, then the *conjugate of f by g*, written f^g, is the mapping given by $f^g = g^{-1} f g$. Note that if f is a simple idempotent mapping with $a \neq b$ and $af = b$, then f^g is a simple idempotent mapping ag to bg.

Crucial for our result are the following two Lemmata 10 and 11 formulated in the language of transformation semigroups. The first lemma says that for reachability of subsets, it is sufficient to consider products of simple idempotents.

Lemma 10. *Let $T \leqslant \mathcal{T}_n$ be a transformation semigroup generated by permutations and simple idempotents and $S \subseteq [n]$. If there exists $t \in T$ such that $S = ([n])t$, then there exists a product $t' \in T$ of conjugates of the generators that are simple idempotents by permutations in T such that $S = ([n])t'$. In particular, t' is a product of simple idempotents from T.*

Proof. Write $t = g_1 f_1 g_2 f_2 g_3 \cdots f_{n-1} g_n f_n g_{n+1}$ where the f_i are the simple idempotents from the generating set and the g_i are permutations generated by the permutations in the generating set. Then (this relation was already observed in [1])

$$\begin{aligned} t = g_1 f_1 g_2 f_2 g_3 \cdots f_{n-1} g_n g_{n+1} f_n^{g_{n+1}} &= g_1 f_1 g_2 f_2 g_3 \cdots g_{n-1} g_n g_{n+1} f_{n-1}^{g_n g_{n+1}} f_n^{g_{n+1}} \\ &= \ldots = g_1 g_2 \cdots g_{n+1} f_1^{g_2 g_3 \cdots g_n g_{n+1}} f_2^{g_3 \cdots g_n g_{n+1}} \cdots f_{n-1}^{g_n g_{n+1}} f_n^{g_{n+1}}. \end{aligned}$$

Now, as $g_1 g_2 \cdots g_{n+1}$ is a permutation, we have $([n])(g_1 g_2 \cdots g_{n+1}) = [n]$. Hence, if we set $t' = f_1^{g_2 g_3 \cdots g_n g_{n+1}} f_2^{g_3 \cdots g_n g_{n+1}} \cdots f_{n-1}^{g_n g_{n+1}} f_n^{g_{n+1}}$ we have $S = ([n])t'$. Each conjugate f_i^g where g is a permutation is simple idempotent. Observe that the number of simple idempotent in the resulting product of t' is the same as the number of simple idempotents used in t. □

Next, we give a sufficient condition for the distinguishability of 2-sets.

Lemma 11. *Let $T \leqslant \mathcal{T}_n$ be a transformation semigroup generated by permutations and simple idempotents and containing a constant map. Then for every two distinct 2-sets there exists an element in T mapping precisely one 2-set to a singleton but not the other.*

Proof. Let $\{a,b\},\{c,d\} \subseteq [n]$ be distinct 2-sets. By assumption and Lemma 10, there exists a product of simple idempotents $f \in T$ such that $|\{a,b\}f| = 1$ or $|\{c,d\}f| = 1$. Choose the element f that is expressible as a shortest possible product of simple idempotents, i.e. $f = f_1 \cdots f_m$ with m is minimal, the f_i are simple idempotent mappings and $|\{a,b\}f| = 1$ or $|\{c,d\}f| = 1$.

Assume $|(\{a,b\})f| = |(\{c,d\})f| = 1$.

The function f_m has defect one. Hence the two elements mapped to a single element are unique. By the choice of f as a minimal product and as f_m is applied at the end, we can conclude that $|\{a,b\}(f_1 \cdots f_{m-1})| = |\{c,d\}(f_1 \cdots f_{m-1})| = 2$ and $\{a,b\}(f_1 \cdots f_{m-1}) = \{c,d\}(f_1 \cdots f_{m-1})$.

Let $i \in \{1,\ldots,m-1\}$. Set $h_i = f_1 \cdots f_i$ and let h_0 denote the identity transformation. Assume $\{a,b\}h_i = \{a,b\}h_{i+1}$, then $|\{a,b\}(h_i f_{i+2} \cdots f_m)| = 1$ and f can be written as a product of $m-1$ simple idempotents, contradicting the minimal length of the product. Similarly, we must have $\{c,d\}h_i \neq \{c,d\}h_{i+1}$. Hence, for every $i \in \{0,1,\ldots,m-1\}$ we have

$$\{a,b\}h_i \neq \{a,b\}h_{i+1} \text{ and } \{c,d\}h_i \neq \{c,d\}h_{i+1}. \tag{1}$$

Now, for $i \in \{1,\ldots,m-1\}$, suppose $\{a,b\}h_i = \{c,d\}h_i$. Set $A = \{a,b\}h_{i-1}$ and $B = \{c,d\}h_{i-1}$. By Eq. (1), we have $A \neq Af$ and $B \neq Bf$. So there exist $x \in A$, $y \in B$ such that $xf_i \neq x$ and $yf_i \neq y$. By Lemma 1 we can conclude $A = B$. So, inductively, as $\{a,b\}h_{m-1} = \{c,d\}h_{m-1}$, we find $\{a,b\} = \{c,d\}$. However, this contradicts our assumption that both 2-sets are distinct and so we cannot have that both are mapped to a singleton. □

If we consider the transformation monoid of a given automaton with simple idempotents, Proposition 2 and Lemma 11 directly give the main result of this section.

Theorem 12. *Let $\mathcal{A} = (Q,\Sigma)$ be an automaton with simple idempotents. Then if $\mathcal{A}$ is completely reachable, then it is sync-maximal.*

As every strongly connected sync-maximal automaton is completely reachable, we get the next corollary.

Corollary 13. *Let $\mathcal{A} = (Q,\Sigma)$ be a strongly connected automaton with simple idempotents. Then $\mathcal{A}$ is completely reachable if and only if it is sync-maximal.*

By Theorem 8, every sync-maximal automaton over a binary alphabet is completely reachable, which implies that the automaton is strongly connected. This yields the next corollary.

Corollary 14. *Let $\mathcal{A}$ be an automaton with simple idempotents over a binary alphabet. Then $\mathcal{A}$ is completely reachable if and only if it is sync-maximal.*

The equivalence between complete reachability and sync-maximality holds only for strongly connected automata with simple idempotents and for automata over a binary alphabet. Example 2 gives automata with simple idempotents over a ternary alphabet that are sync-maximal but not completely reachable. Next, we give a different example.

Example 3. Here, we give further examples an automata with simple idempotents that are sync-maximal but not completely reachable. Let the automaton $\mathcal{A} = (\{0, 1, \ldots, n\}, \{a, b, c, d\})$ be such that

$$i.a = \begin{cases} 1 & \text{if } i = 0, \\ i & \text{if } i > 0; \end{cases} \qquad i.b = \begin{cases} 1 & \text{if } i = 2, \\ i & \text{if } i \neq 1; \end{cases}$$

$$i.c = \begin{cases} 1 & \text{if } i = 2, \\ 2 & \text{if } i = 1, \\ i & \text{if } i \notin \{1, 2\}; \end{cases} \qquad i.d = \begin{cases} i+1 & \text{if } i \notin \{0, n\}, \\ 0 & \text{if } i = 0, \\ 1 & \text{if } i = n. \end{cases}$$

Then $\mathcal{A}$ is an automaton with simple idempotents. As $\mathcal{A}$ is not strongly connected, it is not completely reachable. However, it is sync-maximal. This follows as the letters d and c generate the full symmetric group on $\{1, 2, \ldots, n\}$. Let $\{q_1, q_2\}, \{p_1, p_2\}$ be two distinct 2-sets. If $\{q_1, q_2\}, \{p_1, p_2\} \subseteq \{1, 2, \ldots, n\}$, then there exists a word $u \in \{c, d\}^*$ such that $\{q_1, q_2\}.u = \{1, 2\}$ and $\{p_1, p_2\}.u \neq \{1, 2\}$ and the word ub maps $\{1, 2\}$ to $\{2\}$ and $\{p_1, p_2\}$ to another 2-set. Otherwise, at least one subset contains 0, say, without loss of generality, $0 \in \{q_1, q_2\}$ and $q_1 = 0$. Let $u \in \{c, d\}^*$ be a word such that $q_2.u = 1$. Then $\{q_1, q_2\}.ua = \{1\}$ as $\{q_1, q_2\}.u = \{0, 1\}$. Furthermore, $\{p_1, p_2\}.ua$ is a 2-set. If $0 \notin \{p_1, p_2\}$, this is clear as ua permutes the states $\{1, \ldots, n\}$. If $0 \in \{p_1, p_2\}$, then $q_2 \notin \{p_1, p_2\}$, which implies $\{0, 1\} = \{p_1, p_2\}.u \neq \{q_1, q_2\}.u$ and hence $|\{q_1, q_2\}.u| = 2$.

Example 4. Here, we give an infinite family of synchronizing automata with simple idempotents over a binary alphabet that are neither sync-maximal nor completely reachable. Let $\mathcal{A} = (\{0, 1, \ldots, n\}, \{a, b\})$ with

$$i.a = \begin{cases} n & \text{if } i = n-1, \\ i & \text{if } i \neq n-1; \end{cases} \qquad i.b = \begin{cases} n & \text{if } i = n, \\ i+1 \bmod n & \text{if } i \in \{0, \ldots, n-1\}; \end{cases}$$

The word $a(ba)^{n-2}$ synchronizes $\mathcal{A}$. However, $\mathcal{A}$ is not completely reachable as it is not strongly connected, which implies, by Theorem 8, as it is over a binary alphabet, that it is not sync-maximal.

Lastly, we state that the problems Sync-Into-Subset and Reachable Subset are solvable in polynomial time for automata with simple idempotents over a binary alphabet. This is based on the following lemma about the structure of the reachable subsets in automata with simple idempotents.

Lemma 15. *Let $\Sigma = \{a, b\}$ and $\mathcal{A} = (Q, \Sigma)$ be an automaton with $Q = \{0, 1, \ldots, n-1\}$ and $q.b = (q+1) \bmod n$ and $a \in \Sigma$ be a simple idempotent letter with a state $q \in Q$ such that $\delta(q, a) \neq q$. Let $d > 0$ be the greatest common divisor of n and the number*[3] *$0 < r \leqslant n$ with $q.a = q.b^r$. Then for $S \subseteq Q$ we have $Q.u = S$ for some $u \in \Sigma^*$ if and only if $S = A_0 \cup \ldots \cup A_{d-1}$ for non-empty subsets $A_i \subseteq Q$ such that $s \in A_i$ implies $s \equiv i \pmod{d}$.*

[3] The case $r = n$ is a borderline case as it essentially implies that a acts as the identity. However, the statement entails it with $S = Q$ being the only reachable subset.

Proposition 16. *For automata with simple idempotents over a binary alphabet, the problems* SYNC-INTO-SUBSET *and* REACHABLE SUBSET *are solvable in polynomial time.*

6 Conclusion

We have introduced the sync-maximal automata and determined their structure. They are closely connected to completely reachable automata in the sense that they are either completely reachable or contain a completely reachable subautomaton. Furthermore, in a sync-maximal automaton all subsets with at least two states are reachable.

A natural question is how sync-maximality relates to the length of shortest synchronizing words. Intuitively, it means the set of synchronizing words is a "complicated" set, and one might expect that this might yield lower bounds on shortest possible paths in the power automaton. However, we can clearly construct automata with very short synchronizing words that are sync-maximal by adding to an existing automaton that is sync-maximal a single letter that maps everything to a single state, as the property of sync-maximality is retained when adding letters. But such a construction feels rather artificial, and a natural question is then what happens if we do not have arbitrary many letters at hand or the letters have to fulfill a certain property (like being idempotent or only having a certain defect). What can we say about lower bounds for shortest synchronizing words for automata over a binary alphabet, or only having the least number of letters of a certain type yielding a sync-maximal automaton on the given state set? For an upper bound, note that for completely reachable automata over a binary alphabet, the Černý conjecture has been confirmed in [5]. As sync-maximal automata over a binary alphabet are completely reachable by Theorem 8, sync-maximal automata over a binary alphabet also fulfill Černý's conjecture.

Furthermore, we have shown that a completely reachable automaton with simple idempotents must be sync-maximal. Hence, for strongly connected automata over simple idempotents being completely reachable is equivalent to sync-maximality. It is known that as soon as the transformation monoid of an automaton contains a primitive permutation group, it is both completely reachable and sync-maximal [10]. But what properties on the letters do we need to retain this equivalence (or simply that complete reachability already implies sync-maximality) that are more general than being either a permutation or a simple idempotent? In our method of proof, we used the idempotency (i.e., $q.aa = q.a$ for each state $q \in Q$) and the fact that the letters have defect one. But what when letters of defect more than one are involved? What about letters that instead of being idempotent fulfill the property $Q.aa = Q.a$, i.e., the image $Q.a$ is permuted by a?

Acknowledgement. I thank the anonymous reviewers for careful reading, spotting typos and unclear formulations, and pointers to the literature. In particular, I thank one reviewer for spotting an error in the original formulation and proof of Theorem 8, which has been fixed, and another reviewer for giving a very easy argument related to checking complete reachability.

References

1. Araújo, J., Bentz, W., Cameron, P.J.: Groups synchronizing a transformation of non-uniform kernel. Theor. Comput. Sci. **498**, 1–9 (2013). https://doi.org/10.1016/j.tcs.2013.06.016
2. Berlinkov, M.V., Ferens, R., Szykula, M.: Preimage problems for deterministic finite automata. J. Comput. Syst. Sci. **115**, 214–234 (2021). https://doi.org/10.1016/j.jcss.2020.08.002
3. Bondar, E.A., Volkov, M.V.: Completely reachable automata. In: Câmpeanu, C., Manea, F., Shallit, J. (eds.) DCFS 2016. LNCS, vol. 9777, pp. 1–17. Springer, Cham (2016). https://doi.org/10.1007/978-3-319-41114-9_1
4. Bondar, E.A., Volkov, M.V.: A characterization of completely reachable automata. In: Hoshi, M., Seki, S. (eds.) DLT 2018. LNCS, vol. 11088, pp. 145–155. Springer, Cham (2018). https://doi.org/10.1007/978-3-319-98654-8_12
5. Bondar, E.A., Casas, D., Volkov, M.V.: Completely reachable automata: an interplay between automata, graphs, and trees. CoRR abs/2201.05075 (2022). https://arxiv.org/abs/2201.05075
6. Černý, J.: Poznámka k. homogénnym experimentom s konecnými automatmi. Mat. fyz. čas SAV **14**, 208–215 (1964)
7. Don, H.: The Černý conjecture and 1-contracting automata. Electron. J. Comb. **23**(3), P3.12 (2016)
8. Gonze, F., Jungers, R.M.: Hardly reachable subsets and completely reachable automata with 1-deficient words. J. Autom. Lang. Comb. **24**(2–4), 321–342 (2019). https://doi.org/10.25596/jalc-2019-321
9. Gusev, V.V., Maslennikova, M.I., Pribavkina, E.V.: Finitely generated ideal languages and synchronizing automata. In: Karhumäki, J., Lepistö, A., Zamboni, L. (eds.) WORDS 2013. LNCS, vol. 8079, pp. 143–153. Springer, Heidelberg (2013). https://doi.org/10.1007/978-3-642-40579-2_16
10. Hoffmann, S.: Completely reachable automata, primitive groups and the state complexity of the set of synchronizing words. In: Leporati, A., Martín-Vide, C., Shapira, D., Zandron, C. (eds.) LATA 2021. LNCS, vol. 12638, pp. 305–317. Springer, Cham (2021). https://doi.org/10.1007/978-3-030-68195-1_24
11. Hoffmann, S.: State complexity of the set of synchronizing words for circular automata and automata over binary alphabets. In: Leporati, A., Martín-Vide, C., Shapira, D., Zandron, C. (eds.) LATA 2021. LNCS, vol. 12638, pp. 318–330. Springer, Cham (2021). https://doi.org/10.1007/978-3-030-68195-1_25
12. Hoffmann, S.: Sync-maximal permutation groups equal primitive permutation groups. In: Han, Y., Ko, S. (eds.) DCFS 2021. LNCS, vol. 13037, pp. 38–50. Springer, Cham (2021). https://doi.org/10.1007/978-3-030-93489-7_4
13. Hopcroft, J.E., Ullman, J.D.: Introduction to Automata Theory, Languages, and Computation. Addison-Wesley Publishing Company, Boston (1979)
14. Howie, J.M.: Fundamentals of Semigroup Theory. Oxford University Press, Oxford (1996)

15. Maslennikova, M.I.: Reset complexity of ideal languages over a binary alphabet. Int. J. Found. Comput. Sci. **30**(6–7), 1177–1196 (2019). https://doi.org/10.1142/S0129054119400343
16. Reis, R., Rodaro, E.: Ideal regular languages and strongly connected synchronizing automata. Theor. Comput. Sci. **653**, 97–107 (2016). https://doi.org/10.1016/j.tcs.2016.09.026
17. Rystsov, I.K.: Polynomial complete problems in automata theory. Inf. Process. Lett. **16**(3), 147–151 (1983). https://doi.org/10.1016/0020-0190(83)90067-4
18. Rystsov, I.K.: Estimation of the length of reset words for automata with simple idempotents. Cybern. Syst. Anal. **36**(3), 339–344 (2000). https://doi.org/10.1007/BF02732984
19. Sandberg, S.: 1 homing and synchronizing sequences. In: Broy, M., Jonsson, B., Katoen, J.-P., Leucker, M., Pretschner, A. (eds.) Model-Based Testing of Reactive Systems. LNCS, vol. 3472, pp. 5–33. Springer, Heidelberg (2005). https://doi.org/10.1007/11498490_2
20. Savitch, W.J.: Relationships between nondeterministic and deterministic tape complexities. J. Comput. Syst. Sci. **4**(2), 177–192 (1970). https://doi.org/10.1016/S0022-0000(70)80006-X
21. Shitov, Y.: An improvement to a recent upper bound for synchronizing words of finite automata. J. Autom. Lang. Combin. **24**(2–4), 367–373 (2019). https://doi.org/10.25596/jalc-2019-367
22. Volkov, M.V., Kari, J.: Černý's conjecture and the road colouring problem. In: Éric Pin, J. (ed.) Handbook of Automata Theory, vol. I, pp. 525–565. European Mathematical Society Publishing House (2021)

On the Descriptional Complexity of the Direct Product of Finite Automata

Markus Holzer(✉) and Christian Rauch

Institut für Informatik, Universität Giessen, Arndtstr. 2, 35392 Giessen, Germany
{holzer,christian.rauch}@informatik.uni-giessen.de

Abstract. In [4] the descriptional complexity of certain automata products of two finite state devices, for reset, permutation, permutation-reset, and finite automata was investigated. Although an almost complete picture emerged for the magic number problem, there were several open problems related to the direct product, also called cross product, of finite automata, in particular for permutation and permutation-reset devices. We solve these left open problems and show (i) that for two permutation-reset automata of n- and m-states the whole range $[1, nm]$ of state complexities is obtainable for the direct product, if the automata have at least a quaternary input alphabet, while (ii) for binary input alphabet this is not the case, and (iii) for the direct product of a permutation and a permutation-reset automaton the number $\alpha = 2$ is always magic if n and m fulfill some property, i.e., cannot be obtained by the direct product of any automata of this kind. Moreover, our results can be seen as a generalization of previous results in [7] for the intersection operation on automata.

1 Introduction

The direct or cross product of automata is well known from the intersection and union construction from automata theory. It is only a special case of more complex automata operations, which were recently studied from a descriptional complexity perspective in [4]. In general, a product of automata is obtained by series (cascading), parallel, and/or feedback composition of automata. In the direct product there is no communication between the component automata, while for instance, in the cascade product that is yet another well known product of automata, the second automaton receives along with the input letter also the state of the first automaton. For the hierarchy of automata products of increasing feedback dependencies the magic number problem was almost completely classified for all meaningful product types of two automata on the classes of reset (RFA), permutation (PFA), permutation-reset (PRFA), and deterministic finite state automata in general (DFA)—see Table 1 for the results on the direct product. Let us explain how to interpret the "yes" and "no" entries within the table: a "no" means that there are no magic numbers, i.e., the whole range $[1, nm]$ of state complexities can be reached by m- and n-state automata of the appropriate type not including reset automata if the input alphabet is at least

Published by Springer Nature Switzerland AG 2022
Y.-S. Han and G. Vaszil (Eds.): DCFS 2022, LNCS 13439, pp. 100–111, 2022.
https://doi.org/10.1007/978-3-031-13257-5_8

Table 1. The magic number problem for the direct product of different types of automata. A "no" entry indicates that there are no magic numbers and the whole induced interval of state complexities can be reached, while a "yes" entry gives rise to at least one state complexity that cannot be reached, i.e., a magic number. If not specified elsewhere all automata have an input alphabet of size at least two.

Direct product	RFA	PFA	PRFA	DFA
RFA	no	no	no	no
PFA		yes	yes	no
PRFA			no, if $\|\Sigma\| \geq 4$ yes, if $\|\Sigma\| = 2$	no
DFA				no

binary. For instance, the "no" entry for the direct product of DFAs is due to [7] and all other "no" entries are from [4]. On the other hand, a "yes" entry indicates that at least one magic number α exists under the same condition on the input alphabet as mentioned above, i.e., it cannot be reached by a direct product of appropriate automata of m- and n-states, respectively. The "yes" entry in the PFA-PFA cell is due to [4].

The gray shaded entries in Table 1 are the results that are presented here. Previously in [4] magic numbers for these cases were announced, which where found by exhaustive computer programs for small values of m, n, and α. To be more precise,

- $\alpha = 2$ is magic, for $n = m = 3$ and alphabets of size at most three for the direct product of a PFA and PRFA, and
- $\alpha = 8$ is magic, for $n = m = 3$ and at most binary alphabets[1] for the direct product of two PRFAs.

A complete understanding of the magic number problem for both cases is missing in [4]. We partially close this gap and show the following results: (i) $\alpha = 2$ is magic for m and n both odd and at least three for binary input alphabets in case of the direct product of a PFA and a PRFA. For larger alphabets the value α remains magic, but we can only prove it for fixed $n = 3$ and odd m at least three. (ii) For the direct product of two PRFAs we first show that no magic numbers exist if the input alphabet is at least four. Whether this result is optimal w.r.t. the input alphabet size is left open, but we can narrow the search for the answer to a small interval of numbers for the outcome of the direct product for two given permutation-reset input automata. In passing we show that the above mentioned result for $\alpha = 8$ is best possible w.r.t. the input alphabet size, because with three letters this number is obtainable for $n = m = 3$—see Example 1. In the light of [7] and the previously obtained results of the authors on automata products the existence of magic numbers is expected, because if several restrictions are

[1] In [4] there is a misprint on the alphabet size, which was said to be at most three.

being imposed on automata, then, sooner or later, some values of the state complexity become unreachable. However these results solve the main open issues from [4] and thus complete the overall picture of automata products on finite automata. Nevertheless, certain fine grain details on the question whether a particular value α is magic or not for the direct product of the automata under consideration are still open and await solution.

The paper is organized as follows: next we introduce the necessary notations on automata and the direct product. Then we start our investigation and first give an overview on the previously obtained results on the direct product of automata w.r.t. the magic number problem. Then we prove our new results and finally we conclude with an open problem and topics for further investigations.

2 Preliminaries

We recall some definitions on finite automata as contained in [3]. A *deterministic finite automaton* (DFA) is a quintuple $A = (Q, \Sigma, \cdot, q_0, F)$, where Q is the finite set of *states*, Σ is the finite set of *input symbols*, $q_0 \in Q$ is the *initial state*, $F \subseteq Q$ is the set of *accepting states*, and the *transition function* $\cdot$ maps $Q \times \Sigma$ to Q. The *language accepted* by the DFA A is defined as $L(A) = \{ w \in \Sigma^* \mid q_0 \cdot w \in F \}$, where the transition function is recursively extended to a mapping $Q \times \Sigma^* \to Q$ in the usual way. Obviously, every letter $a \in \Sigma$ induces a mapping from the state set Q to Q by $q \mapsto q \cdot a$, for every $q \in Q$. A DFA is *unary* if the input alphabet Σ is a singleton set, that is, $\Sigma = \{a\}$, for some input symbol a. Moreover, a DFA is said to be a *permutation-reset* automaton (PRFA) if every input letter induces either a permutation or a constant mapping on the state set. If every letter of the automaton induces only permutations on the state set, then we simply speak of a *permutation* automaton (PFA). Finally, a DFA is said to be a *reset* automaton (RFA) if every letter induces either the identity or a constant mapping on the state set. The class of reset, permutation, permutation-reset, and deterministic automata in general are referred to as **RFA**, **PFA**, **PRFA**, and **FA**, respectively. It is obvious that the inclusions $X\mathbf{FA} \subseteq \mathbf{PRFA} \subseteq \mathbf{FA}$, where $X \in \{\mathbf{P}, \mathbf{R}\}$, hold. Moreover, it is not hard to see that the classes **RFA** and **PFA** are incomparable.

The direct product of two DFAs, also known as the *cross product*, $A = (Q_A, \Sigma, \cdot_A, q_{0,A}, F_A)$ and $B = (Q_B, Q_A \times \Sigma, \cdot_B, q_{0,B}, F_B)$, denoted by $A \times B$, is defined as the automaton[2]

$$A \times B = (Q_A \times Q_B, \Sigma, \cdot, (q_{0,A}, q_{0,B}), F_A \times F_B),$$

where the transition function is given by

$$(q, p) \cdot a = (q \cdot_A a, p \cdot_B a),$$

for $q \in Q_A$, $p \in Q_B$, and $a \in \Sigma$. Observe, that the transitions of A and B depend only on Σ. We say that A is the *first automaton* and B the *second automaton*

[2] In [4] the direct product was referred to as ν_0-product and with $\circ_{\nu_0}$ notated. This naming originates from the hierarchy of automata products studied in automata networks, see, e.g., [2].

in the product. Observe, that although the statements to come on the direct product explicitly refer to first and second automaton of a certain type, these types can be obviously commuted, since in the direct product the order of the operand automata is not relevant to the product automaton (up to isomorphism). For the choice of the final set of states of the direct product automaton we follow the lines of [1] and the forerunner papers [4–6]. One observes, that the device $A \times B$ accepts the intersection of the language accepted by A and B.

We give a small example.

Example 1. Consider the PRFA $A = (\{q_0, q_1, q_2\}, \{a, b, c, d\}, \cdot_A, q_0, \{q_0, q_2\})$, where

$$\begin{array}{lll} q_0 \cdot_A a = q_0, & q_1 \cdot_A a = q_1, & q_2 \cdot_A a = q_2, \\ q_0 \cdot_A b = q_0, & q_1 \cdot_A b = q_1, & q_2 \cdot_A b = q_2, \\ q_0 \cdot_A c = q_2, & q_1 \cdot_A c = q_2, & q_2 \cdot_A c = q_2, \\ q_0 \cdot_A d = q_0, & q_1 \cdot_A d = q_2, & q_2 \cdot_A d = q_1. \end{array}$$

Then let

$$B = (\{p_0, p_1, p_2\}, \{a, b, c, d\}, \cdot_B, p_0, \{p_0, p_2\}),$$

be the PRFA, where

$$\begin{array}{lll} p_0 \cdot_B a = p_2, & p_1 \cdot_B a = p_2, & p_2 \cdot_B a = p_2, \\ p_0 \cdot_B b = p_0, & p_1 \cdot_B b = p_1, & p_2 \cdot_B b = p_2, \\ p_0 \cdot_B c = p_1, & p_1 \cdot_B c = p_0, & p_2 \cdot_B c = p_2, \\ p_0 \cdot_B d = p_0, & p_1 \cdot_B d = p_1, & p_2 \cdot_B d = p_2. \end{array}$$

The automata A and B are depicted in Fig. 1 on the top and lower right, respectively. It is easy to see that both automata are minimal.

By construction the ν_0-product of A and B is given by

$$A \times B = (\{q_0, q_1, q_2\} \times \{p_0, p_1, p_2\}, \{a, b, c, d\}, \cdot, (q_0, p_0), \{q_0, q_2\} \times \{p_0, p_2\}),$$

where the transitions of the initially reachable states

$$(q_0, p_0), (q_0, p_2), (q_1, p_0), (q_1, p_1), (q_1, p_2), (q_2, p_0), (q_2, p_1), (q_2, p_2),$$

can be deduced from Fig. 1, too, on the lower left. By inspection no initially reachable states in $A \times B$ are equivalent and (q_0, p_1) is not reachable. Hence, the minimal DFA accepting $L(A \times B)$ has $\alpha = 8$ states. One may have noticed that the letter b induces the identity mapping on all involved automata. The transitions of the letters a, b, c, and d are chosen such that in $A \times B$ the letter a maps every state onto the last row, the letter b induces a cycle in the first column of specific length (here one), the letters b and c map the states in the last column without (q_{n-1}, p_{m-1}) transitively onto each other and the letter d forms row-wise cycles of a specific length (here two) beginning in the last column. □

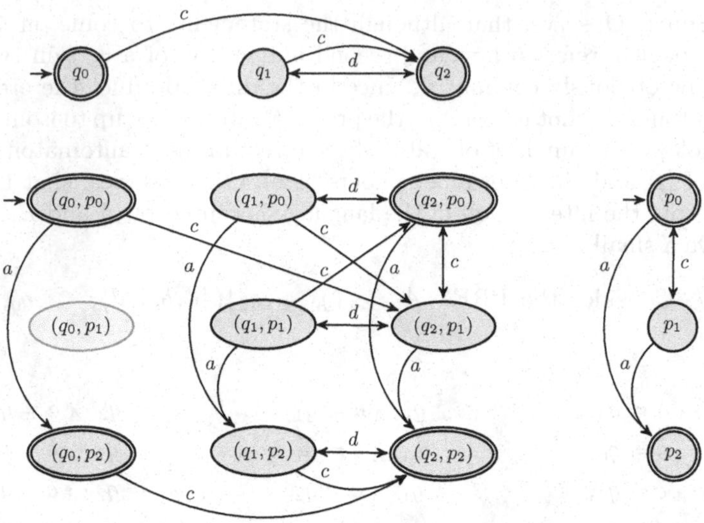

Fig. 1. The example automata A and B both with input alphabet $\{a, b, c, d\}$ on the top and lower right, respectively. For a better representability not all transitions of the automata are shown. In particular, this is the case for the automaton $A \times B$, where only the transitions of the initially reachable states are shown. Additionally no self-loops are shown. For instance, letter a acts as the identity on the state set of A. The direct-product $A \times B$ is depicted on the lower left.

When considering the descriptional complexity of the product of two automata, we limit ourselves to the case where the involved automata are non-trivial, i.e., they have more than one state. Thus, in the following we only consider non-trivial automata. It is easy to see that $n \cdot m$ states are sufficient for any product of an n-state and m-state automaton.

3 Results

First let us recall what is known from the literature for the magic number problem of the direct product, which is the following question: which numbers of states of the minimal DFA for the direct product of two minimal automata of state size n and m are reachable? Whenever a number is *not* obtainable, it is called "magic". Obviously the answer to this question depends on the types of the involved input automata. The following results are known:

1. In [7] it was shown that if the input automata are arbitrary deterministic finite automata the whole range $[1, nm]$ can be reached (DFA-DFA case), and
2. all combinations of RFAs, PFAs, PRFAs, and DFAs were considered in [4], where the following results were shown:

(a) Whenever a RFA is involved in the direct product (RFA-RFA, RFA-PFA, RFA-PRFA, and RFA-DFA case) no magic numbers exist and the whole interval can be reached. Note that minimal RFAs have state size at most two.
(b) For the PFA-PFA case the answer to the magic number problem is "yes", because magic numbers were already identified for the more complex cascade product of permutation automata.
(c) For the cases PFA-PRFA and PRFA-PRFA magic numbers were identified only by exhaustive computer programs for small cases of m, n, and α. In particular, for the direct product of a PFA and a PRFA the value $\alpha = 2$ is magic for $n = m = 3$ and alphabets of size at most three.
(d) Finally, no magic numbers exist for the PFA-DFA case and thus for the more general PRFA-DFA case.

Thus, only the PFA-PRFA and PRFA-PRFA lack a complete theoretical understanding, since in this case only computer determined evidence for magic numbers were given. In the forthcoming we close this gap in the affirmative of the magic number problem. We start our investigation with the PFA-PRFA case. As mentioned above $\alpha = 2$ was identified magic for $n = m = 3$ and alphabets of size at most three by a computer program.[3] Already in [4] it was conjectured that $\alpha = 2$ is magic whenever m and n are odd and at least three. The next lemma shows that this is actually the case for binary alphabets.

Lemma 2. *Let $n, m \geq 3$ be both odd. Then there exists no minimal binary n-state PRFA A and no minimal binary m-state PFA B such that the minimal DFA for the language $L(A \times B)$ has 2 states.*

Proof. We prove the statement by contradiction. Therefore assume to the contrary that there is a minimal n-state PRFA A and a minimal m-state PFA B such that the minimal DFA for the language $L(A \times B)$ has two states.

First we prove that A is neither a RFA nor a PFA. In case A is a RFA, i.e., all input letters are resets, we obtain a contradiction on the minimality of A, because every minimal RFA has at most two states [6], but A is a minimal device with at least 3 states. Hence, not all letters of the input alphabet of A are resets. Next assume that A is a PFA. In [6] it was shown that for every α in $[2, nm]$ that is coprime to n, there *does not* exist a minimal n-state PFA A and a minimal m-state PFA B such that the minimal DFA accepting the language of the cascade product of A and B has α states. Since the direct product is a special case of the cascade product this result also holds if the direct product ν_0 is considered. Thus, one letter, say a, of the input alphabet of A induces a reset on the state set Q_A of A and the other letter, say b, induces a permutation on Q_A. For convenience let Q_B refer to the state set of B. Thus, the input alphabet of A and also B, since we consider the direct product, is equal to $\Sigma = \{a, b\}$.

[3] Surprisingly the computer program also reveals that every other number in the range $[1, nm] = [1, 9]$ is reachable.

Next we define the state sets

$$Q_{A,1} := \{q_0 \cdot w \mid w \in \Sigma^* \text{ for } w \text{ inducing a permutation on } Q_A\},$$

and

$$Q_{A,2} := \{q_0 \cdot w \mid w \in a\Sigma^*\},$$

for q_0 being the initial state of A. Clearly this results in the properties

$$Q_{A,1} \cdot a = \{q_0 \cdot a\} \subseteq Q_{A,2}, \qquad Q_{A,2} \cdot a = \{q_0 \cdot a\} \subseteq Q_{A,2},$$
$$Q_{A,1} \cdot b = Q_{A,1}, \qquad Q_{A,2} \cdot b = Q_{A,2},$$

and

$$Q_A = Q_{A,1} \cup Q_{A,2},$$

where the union is not necessarily disjoint. Observe, that $Q_{A,2}$ contains at least one state, since a is the reset letter. Moreover, note that for every word $w \in \Sigma^*$ which induces a permutation there is a word $w^{-1} \in \Sigma^*$ which induces the inverse permutation on the state set of A. Therefore either $Q_{A,1}$ is a subset of $Q_{A,2}$ or the two sets are disjoint. Since n is at least equal to three the first case can only appear for $|Q_{A,2}| \geq 3$. Nevertheless the argumentation to come for the case $|Q_{A,2}| \geq 3$ does not require $Q_{A,1}$ and $Q_{A,2}$ to be disjoint. We want to mention that in all cases b permutes the states of $Q_{A,2}$ transitively because A is a binary device. Now we are ready to consider the following cases for $Q_{A,2}$, where we will conclude a contradiction in each case:

1. Case $|Q_{A,2}| = 1$. Let $Q_{A,2} = \{q\}$, for some state q in Q_A. We first assume that q is an accepting state. So the set $\{q\} \times Q_B$ induces a PFA which is isomorphic to B up to the initial state. Since B is minimal the states in $\{q\} \times Q_B$ cannot contain any equivalent states which contradicts $\alpha = 2$. Thus q has to be non-accepting which implies that all states in $\{q\} \times Q_B$ are equivalent. This implies the existence of an accepting state in the set $Q_{A,1} \times Q_B$ which is initially reachable. Since there is at least one reachable state in $A \times B$ for each state q' in $Q_{A,1}$, which has q' as its first component the assumption that only one state of $Q_{A,1} \times Q_B$ is reachable implies that $Q_{A,1}$ consists of one state. Indeed this gives us that $|Q_{A,1} \cup Q_{A,2}| = 1 + 1 = 2$, which is a contradiction to $2 < n = |Q_A|$. Therefore there are at least two states of $Q_{A,1} \times Q_B$ reachable. But on the other hand the states in $Q_{A,1}$ have to contain an accepting and a non-accepting state. Therefore an accepting state and a non-accepting state in $Q_{A,1} \times Q_B$ is reachable. Since there is a word $w \in \Sigma^*$ which maps the non-accepting state in $Q_{A,1} \times Q_B$ onto an accepting state the reachable states in $Q_{A,1} \times Q_B$ cannot contain a state equivalent to the reachable states of $\{q\} \times Q_B$. Therefore the minimal DFA for the language $A \times B$ has at least three states which is a contradiction to α equal to two.
2. Case $|Q_{A,2}| = 2$. Clearly $Q_{A,2}$ contains one accepting and one non-accepting state, because otherwise the above described closure properties of $Q_{A,2}$ contradicts the minimality of A.

We claim that each state in $Q_{A,2} \times Q_B$ is reachable in $A \times B$. Since B is a PFA for each pair of states p and p' there is a word w in $\Sigma^* a$ which maps p onto p'. Let q' be the image of the reset induced by a in A. Therefore every state (q, p) is mapped onto (q', p') for q being a state of A. Clearly this implies that all states in $\{q'\} \times Q_B$ are reachable in $A \times B$. Since every letter induces a permutation on Q_B and since for every state q in $Q_{A,2}$ there is a word which maps q' onto q the claim follows.
The b-cycles of the state set $Q_{A,2} \times Q_B$ can be interpreted as unary cyclic PFAs $P_0, P_1, \ldots, P_k$, for some $k \geq 0$. Recall that a cyclic automaton consists of one cycle. Observe, that there is an accepting state in one of the PFAs $P_0, P_1, \ldots, P_k$, say this is P_i. Additionally there must also be a non-accepting state in P_i which has the non-accepting state of $Q_{A,2}$ as its first component.
In [6] it was shown that for every (non-)minimal PFA there exists a number x such that every of its states is equivalent to x states. Therefore this also holds for each of the PFAs $P_0, P_1, \ldots, P_k$. Since all accepting states of a PFA P_i and all non-accepting states are equivalent this implies that the number of accepting and non-accepting states has to be equal in P_i. On the other hand all of the non-accepting states of all the PFAs are equivalent which implies that all PFAs must contain an accepting state and a non-accepting state. This holds because if P_i contains only non-accepting states and P_j contains an accepting state there is a word $w \in b^*$ which maps a non-accepting state of P_i onto a non-accepting state P_i and a non-accepting state of P_j onto an accepting state of P_j. In conclusion this means that for each of the PFAs $P_0, P_1, \ldots, P_k$ the number of accepting and non-accepting states has to be equal. Because the union of their state sets is equal to $Q_{A,2} \times Q_B$ we observe that $Q_{A,2} \times Q_B$ contains $|Q_{A,2} \times Q_B|/2$ accepting states.
This is a contradiction to the fact that only the half of the states in $Q_{A,2}$, i.e., only one, is accepting and Q_B contains at least one non-accepting state[4] which implies that the number of accepting states in $Q_{A,2} \times Q_B$ is strictly less than $|Q_{A,2} \times Q_B|/2$. We want to mention that this causes a contradiction in all cases since there cannot be a single PFA P_0, for $k = 0$, with two states because $|Q_{A,2} \times Q_B| = 2 \cdot |Q_B|$ is at least equal to six.

3. Case $|Q_{A,2}| \geq 3$. We use the notation as in the previous case, in particular the b-cycle PFAs $P_0, P_1, \ldots, P_k$, and argue along similar lines up to the contradiction in the last paragraph. Recall that each of the PFAs $P_0, P_1, \ldots, P_k$ contains an accepting and a non-accepting state.
Since all accepting (non-accepting, respectively) states are equivalent it is easy to understand that this is only possible if the finality of the states in each cycle alternates. The first components appear in the states of P_i in the same ordering as in $Q_{A,2}$. The ordering of $Q_{A,2}$ may occur multiple times in P_i but this will not matter for our reasoning. Indeed this implies that without loss of generality every state which is on an even position in $Q_{A,2}$ is accepting. There have to be also accepting states on odd positions in $Q_{A,2}$

[4] This is due to the fact that B is minimal and $|Q_B|$ is at least three.

or $|Q_{A,2}|$ because otherwise all accepting and all non-accepting states in $Q_{A,2}$ would be equivalent which would contradict the minimality of A. In both cases there are consecutive states in $Q_{A,2}$ which are accepting.
We show that the finality of the states in each b-cycle of B alternates, too. It is already known that every state in $Q_{A,2} \times Q_B$ is reachable. If p and p' are non-accepting states of B such that $p \cdot b = p'$ we obtain that for $q \cdot b = q'$ the states (q, p) and (q', p') are also non-accepting and that $(q, p) \cdot b = (q', p')$. Indeed this would contradict the fact that the finality of the states in each P_i alternates. If p and p' are accepting states of B such that $p \cdot b = p'$ we obtain that for $q \cdot b = q'$ the states (q, p) and (q', p') are also accepting if q and q' are accepting[5] and that $(q, p) \cdot b = (q', p')$. Again this would contradict the fact that the finality of the states in each P_i alternates.
Additionally we observe that each b-cycle of B has at least two states because otherwise there would be a PFA P_i which is either isomorphic to the PFA induced by $Q_{A,2}$ up to the initial state or which is a cycle of length $|Q_{A,2}|$ of non-accepting states. The first case contradicts the fact that all accepting states are equivalent in P_i and we proved already that the latter case is ruled out.
It is not hard to see that the ordering of $Q_{A,2}$ is the same ordering as for the first components of the states in each of the PFAs $P_0, P_1, \ldots, P_k$. Recall that there is an accepting state q in $Q_{A,2}$ which is followed by an accepting state. Since we have shown that every state in $Q_{A,2} \times Q_B$ is initially reachable we know that there is a reachable state (q, p) that is accepting. Since the finality of the states in all b-cycles of B alternates we obtain that the cycle of (q, p) contains two consecutive non-accepting states which is a contradiction to the fact that the finality of the states in each of the PFAs $P_0, P_1, \ldots, P_k$ alternates. □

By a careful inspection of the statement of the previous lemma we show that it can be improved to alphabets of arbitrary size restricting one automaton to three states. We have to leave open whether a more general improvement is possible.

Theorem 3. *Let $n = 3$ and m be odd with $m \geq 3$. Then there* does not *exist a minimal n-state PRFA A and no minimal m-state PFA B such that the minimal DFA for the language $L(A \times B)$ has 2 states.*

Proof. We prove this statement by showing that for $n = 3$ the reasoning of the proof of Lemma 2 is also valid for arbitrary alphabet size greater or equal to two. Therefore we use the same notation as in the previous proof which was mainly guided by the size of the state set $Q_{A,2}$, a subset of Q_A, the state set of the PRFA A.

By inspecting of the case $|Q_{A,2}| = 1$ of the previous proof we obtain that it only requires the input alphabet to contain the letters a and b which implies

[5] As mentioned before the existence of these states is guaranteed by the minimality of A.

that there can be arbitrary many other letters in the input alphabet. The cases $|Q_{A,2}| = 2$ and $|Q_{A,2}| \geq 3$ rely on the fact that there is letter b which induces a permutation and acts transitively on the set $Q_{A,2}$, e.g., it forms a cycle on $Q_{A,2}$. We prove now that the argument is also true for all alphabets with at least two elements if $n = 3$. To this end we consider two cases depending on the size of $Q_{A,2}$:

1. Case $|Q_{A,2}| = 2$. The proof that there is a letter that permutes the states of $Q_{A,2}$ non-trivially is shown by contradiction. Assume to the contrary that all letters which induce a permutation act on $Q_{A,2}$ trivially. Since $n = 3$ and $|Q_{A,2}| = 2$ we know that $|Q_{A,1}| = 1$ and $Q_{A,1} = Q_A \backslash Q_{A,2}$. Due to the definition of $Q_{A,1}$ we know that every permutation fixes the sole state in $Q_{A,1}$. This implies that every permutation induces the identity on $Q_A = Q_{A,1} \cup Q_{A,2}$. So A is a RFA which is a contradiction to the fact that A is minimal and has three states.
2. Case $|Q_{A,2}| \geq 3$. We distinguish three subcases with respect of the size of $Q_{A,1}$; note that in fact $|Q_{A,2}| = 3$, since $n = 3$:
   (a) Subcase $|Q_{A,1}| = 1$. We observe that the arguments used in the case $|Q_{A,2}| = 2$ of the proof of Lemma 2 imply for the case $|Q_{A,2}| = 3$ under consideration that all states of $A \times B$ are initially reachable because $n = 3$. One finds that there are three states of $A \times B$ which have the single state of $Q_{A,1}$ as their first component. These may contain zero, one, or two accepting states depending on the finality of the sole state in $Q_{A,1}$ and the number of accepting states of B. These three states are either transitively mapped onto each other which makes them inequivalent if at least one of them is accepting or one of these states, say q, is only mapped onto itself by permutations. We will show the contradiction for the second case because if all three states are transitively permuted and non-accepting they are equivalent while they are inequivalent to every non-accepting state that is mapped onto an accepting state by a permutation. Indeed this causes a contradiction in a similar fashion like it will for the case that q is only mapped onto itself. So q is not mapped onto either an accepting or a non-accepting state. Since A is not an RFA there must be a permutation c which acts non-trivially on the state set of A. Furthermore, letter c has to permute two states of different finalities to preserve the minimality of A. Thus, one of the cycles induced by c in $A \times B$ contains a non-accepting and an accepting state while q is a fixpoint of c. These three states cannot be equivalent because there is a word in c^* which maps them onto states of different finality. This implies that the minimal DFA accepting $L(A \times B)$ has at least three states which is a contradiction.
   (b) Subcase $|Q_{A,1}| = 2$. It is not hard to see that the arguments in the previous subcase can also be used for $|Q_{A,1}| = 2$, if we exchange q in the reasoning above by the state $\tilde{q}$ in $Q_A \backslash Q_{A,1}$ and by observing that $\tilde{q}$ is also mapped onto itself by every permutation.
   (c) Subcase $|Q_{A,1}| \geq 3$—By a similar reasoning as for the size of $Q_{A,2}$ together with $n = 3$ we are actually in the case $|Q_{A,1}| = 3$. Since $|Q_{A,1}| =$

3 either there is a permutation that permutes $Q_{A,1} = Q_{A,2}$ transitively or there are at least two non-trivial unequal permutations on that set. Due to the fact that they are non-trivial each of them must permute at least two elements while each of them permutes less than $|Q_{A,2}| = 3$ elements. Obviously they have order two, e.g., they are transpositions. Additionally they have one element in common since they permute $Q_{A,2}$ which has only three elements. So the composition of the two transposition has order three and therefore permutes $Q_{A,2}$ transitively.

Therefore all possible cases lead to a contradiction. □

Next we consider the PRFA-PRFA case. Here also at least one magic number was announced in [4] with the help of a computer program. This number is $\alpha = 8 = nm - 1$, for $n = m = 3$ and alphabet of size at most two. In fact, if the alphabet size is large enough, we show that no magic number in the PRFA-PRFA case exists. Due to the lack of space the proof of the following statement has to be omitted.

Theorem 4. *Let $n, m \geq 2$. Then for every α with $1 \leq \alpha \leq nm$, there exists a quaternary minimal n-state PRFA A and a quaternary minimal PRFA B such that the minimal DFA for the language $L(A \times B)$ has α states.*

Now the question arises whether the above theorem is best possible w.r.t. the input alphabet size. For alphabet size two $\alpha = 8$ is magic as mentioned above for $n = m = 3$. Unfortunately, this is not true anymore if we consider alphabets of size at least three, which is shown next for the more general case of $\alpha = nm - 1$ for large enough m and n.

Lemma 5. *Let $n, m \geq 3$. Then for $\alpha = nm - 1$, there exists a ternary minimal n-state PRFA A and a ternary minimal PRFA B such that the minimal DFA for the language $L(A \times B)$ has α states. This results holds true even if one automaton is a PFA.*

Proof. Define the PRFA

$$A = (\{q_0, q_1, \ldots, q_{n-1}\}, \{a, b, c\}, \cdot_A, q_0, \{q_0, q_{n-1}\})$$

with

$$\begin{aligned} q_{n-1} \cdot_A a &= q_{n-2}, \\ q_{n-2} \cdot_A a &= q_{n-1}, \\ q_i \cdot_A b &= q_1, && \text{for } 0 \leq i \leq n-1 \\ q_i \cdot_A c &= q_{i+1}, && \text{for } 1 \leq i \leq n-3 \\ q_{n-2} \cdot_A c &= q_1, \end{aligned}$$

where all not explicitly mentioned transitions are self-loops. Moreover, let

$$B = (\{p_0, p_1, \ldots, p_{m-1}\}, \{a, b, c\}, \cdot_B, p_0, \{p_0, p_{m-1}\}),$$

be the PRFA, where

$$\begin{aligned} p_{m-2} \cdot_A b &= p_{m-1}, \\ p_{m-1} \cdot_A b &= p_{m-2}, \\ p_i \cdot_A c &= p_{i+1 \bmod (m-1)}, \qquad \text{for } 0 \leq i \leq m-2 \end{aligned}$$

where all not explicitly mentioned transitions are self-loops. The minimality of both automata are immediate. Observe, that B is even a permutation automaton. The argumentation that the minimal automata that accepts the language $L(A \times B)$ requires exactly $\alpha = nm - 1$ states is left to the interested reader. □

The previous lemma does not answer the question whether Theorem 4 is best possible for the stated alphabet size. A careful inspection of the proof of Theorem 4 together with the previous lemma and results in [4] reveal that optimality is given if there is a number in the interval

$$[\max\{n + 2m - 1, m + 2n - 1\}, nm - 2]$$

that is magic for the PRFA-PRFA case for ternary alphabet size. Hopefully further research will give an answer to this question.

References

1. Ae, T.: Direct or cascade product of pushdown automata. J. Comput. Syst. Sci. **14**(2), 257–263 (1977)
2. Dömösi, P., Nehaniv, C.L.: Algebraic Theory of Automata Networks: An Introduction. SIAM (2005)
3. Harrison, M.A.: Introduction to Formal Language Theory. Addison-Wesley, Boston (1978)
4. Holzer, M., Rauch, C.: More on the descriptional complexity of products of finite automata. In: Han, Y.S., Ko, S.K. (eds.) DCFS 2021. LNCS, vol. 13037, pp. 76–87. Springer, Cham (2021). https://doi.org/10.1007/978-3-030-93489-7_7
5. Holzer, M., Rauch, C.: The range of state complexities of languages resulting from the cascade product—the general case (extended abstract). In: Moreira, N., Reis, R. (eds.) DLT 2021. LNCS, vol. 12811, pp. 229–241. Springer, Cham (2021). https://doi.org/10.1007/978-3-030-81508-0_19
6. Holzer, M., Rauch, C.: The range of state complexities of languages resulting from the cascade product—the unary case (extended abstract). In: Maneth, S. (ed.) CIAA 2021. LNCS, vol. 12803, pp. 90–101. Springer, Cham (2021). https://doi.org/10.1007/978-3-030-79121-6_8
7. Hricko, M., Jirásková, G., Szabari, A.: Union and intersection of regular languages and descriptional complexity. In: Mereghetti, C., Palano, B., Pighizzini, G., Wotschke, D. (eds.) Proceedings of the 7th Workshop on Descriptional Complexity of Formal Systems, pp. 170–181. Universita degli Studi di Milano, Como (2005)

Operations on Subregular Languages and Nondeterministic State Complexity

Michal Hospodár[1(✉)], Peter Mlynárčik[1,2], and Viktor Olejár[1,3]

[1] Mathematical Institute, Slovak Academy of Sciences, Košice, Slovakia
hosmich@gmail.com, olejar@saske.sk
[2] Faculty of Humanities and Natural Sciences, University of Prešov, Prešov, Slovakia
[3] Department of Computer Science, P. J. Šafárik University, Košice, Slovakia

Abstract. We study the nondeterministic state complexity of basic regular operations on subregular language families. In particular, we focus on the classes of combinational, finitely generated left ideal, group, star, comet, two-sided comet, ordered, and power-separating languages, and consider the operations of intersection, union, concatenation, power, Kleene star, reversal, and complementation. We get the exact complexity in all cases, except for complementation of group languages where we only have an exponential lower bound. The complexity of all operations on combinational languages is given by a constant function, except for the k-th power where it is $k+1$. For all considered operations, the known upper bounds for left ideals are met by finitely generated left ideal languages. The nondeterministic state complexity of the k-th power, star, and reversal on star languages is n. In all the remaining cases, the nondeterministic state complexity of all considered operations is the same as in the regular case, although sometimes we need to use a larger alphabet to describe the corresponding witnesses.

1 Introduction

The fields of study at the intersection of mathematics and computer science, known as formal language theory and automata theory, contain a rich history of publications interesting both from a practical and theoretical point of view. One of the primary investigated language classes in the field, regular languages, have a number of combinatorial, algebraic, and computational properties still prominently investigated today. The topic of interest in this publication are the notions of nondeterministic finite automata (NFA) accepting some subregular languages and operational state complexity.

The definition of NFAs originates from the seminal paper by Rabin and Scott [15]. A conversion procedure to deterministic finite automata (DFA) called "subset construction" was provided as well, showing that an NFA with n states can be simulated by a DFA with at most 2^n states. This model is connected to the measure of nondeterministic state complexity of a given language L, which

Research supported by VEGA grant 2/0132/19 and grant APVV-15-0091.

Published by Springer Nature Switzerland AG 2022
Y.-S. Han and G. Vaszil (Eds.): DCFS 2022, LNCS 13439, pp. 112–126, 2022.
https://doi.org/10.1007/978-3-031-13257-5_9

represents the number of states of the smallest NFA accepting L. The nondeterministic state complexity of a given regular operation is the nondeterministic state complexity of the language resulting from this operation, considered as a function of the sizes of NFAs for operands. A more rigorous investigation of this measure comes from Holzer and Kutrib [8] for the Boolean operations, concatenation, iteration, and reversal.

By restricting the operands to certain subclasses of regular languages, it turns out that the resulting nondeterministic state complexities of these operations might differ from the general case to various degrees. This observation motivated several publications focusing on specific subregular language classes. Han *et al.* [5,6] considered the complexities of some of the mentioned basic operations for prefix-free and suffix-free languages. Additional results were provided for star-free languages by Holzer *et al.* [9], for union-free languages by Jirásková and Masopust [14], and recently Hospodár *et al.* [12] examined various subclasses of convex languages.

In this paper, we continue with such investigations focusing on the operations of intersection, union, concatenation, power, Kleene star, reversal, and complementation. We consider the language classes mainly from [2], more specifically combinational languages, finitely generated left ideals, group languages, stars, comets, two-sided comets, ordered languages, and power-separating languages.

We get the exact complexity for each pair of operation and class except for complementation on group languages where we obtain only a lower bound. For combinational languages, the complexity does not depend on the size of input NFAs. In most other cases, the complexity is the same as for regular languages, except for finitely generated left ideals where the complexity of all operations is the same as for general left ideals [12]. To get lower bounds, instead of commonly used fooling sets for regular languages, we rather use fooling sets for MNFAs consisting of pairs of a reachable and a co-reachable set for each state. Then, we only test the emptiness of intersection of finite sets instead of deciding whether or not a string is in a language.

2 Preliminaries

We assume that the reader is familiar with the standard notation and definitions in formal language and automata theory. For details and a more thorough introduction, refer to [10].

We denote the set of positive integers by $\mathbb{N}$. Let Σ be a non-empty *alphabet* of symbols. Then Σ^* denotes the set of all strings over Σ, including the empty string ε. A *language* over Σ is any subset of Σ^*.

The *reversal of a string* w over Σ denoted w^R is defined as $\varepsilon^R = \varepsilon$ if $w = \varepsilon$, and $w^R = a_n a_{n-1} \cdots a_2 a_1$ if $w = a_1 a_2 \cdots a_{n-1} a_n$ with $a_i \in \Sigma$. The *reversal of a language* L is the language $L^R = \{w^R \mid w \in L\}$. The *complement* of a language L over Σ is the language $L^c = \Sigma^* \setminus L$. The *intersection* of languages K and L is the language $K \cap L = \{w \mid w \in K \text{ and } w \in L\}$, while the *union* of K and L is $K \cup L = \{w \mid w \in K \text{ or } w \in L\}$. The *concatenation* of languages K

and L is the language $KL = \{uv \mid u \in K \text{ and } v \in L\}$. For a given positive integer k, the *k-th power* of a language L is the language $L^k = LL^{k-1}$ with $L^0 = \{\varepsilon\}$. The *positive closure* of a given language L is $L^+ = \bigcup_{k\geq 1} L^k$, while the *Kleene star* of L is defined as $L^* = \bigcup_{k\geq 0} L^k$ and it is equal to $\{\varepsilon\} \cup L^+$. We use the notation of *regular expressions* over Σ in a standard way with $\emptyset$ (empty set), ε, and each $\sigma \in \Sigma$ being regular expressions; furthermore if r and s are regular expressions, then rs (concatenation), $r+s$ (union), and r^* (star) are also regular expressions. For a regular expression r, the expression r^k denotes the k-th power of the language of r, and $r^{\leq k}$ denotes the expression $r^0 + r^1 + \cdots r^k$.

A *nondeterministic finite automaton with multiple initial states* (MNFA) is a quintuple $M = (Q, \Sigma, \cdot, I, F)$ where Q is a finite non-empty set of *states*, Σ is a finite set of input symbols (*i.e.*, *input alphabet*), $I \subseteq Q$ is the set of *initial states*, $F \subseteq Q$ is the set of *final (accepting) states*, and $\cdot\colon Q \times \Sigma \to 2^Q$ is the *transition function* which can be naturally extended to the domain $2^Q \times \Sigma^*$. The language accepted by the MNFA M is $L(M) = \{w \in \Sigma^* \mid I \cdot w \cap F \neq \emptyset\}$. If R and S are two sets of states of M, then $R \xrightarrow{\sigma} S$ denotes that $R \cdot \sigma = S$.

An MNFA whose set of initial states is a singleton is called a *nondeterministic finite automaton* (NFA). An NFA is a *(complete) deterministic finite automaton* (DFA) if $|q \cdot \sigma| = 1$ for each $q \in Q$ and each $\sigma \in \Sigma$; in such a case, $\cdot$ is a mapping from $Q \times \Sigma$ to Q. A non-final state q with transitions (q, σ, q) for each σ in Σ is called a *dead state.*

A given language L is called *regular* if and only if there exists an MNFA M for which $L = L(M)$. Two MNFAs A and B are *equivalent* if they accept the same language. Every MNFA $M = (Q, \Sigma, \cdot, I, F)$ can be converted into an equivalent complete DFA $\mathcal{D}(M) = (2^Q, \Sigma, \cdot, I, \{S \in 2^Q \mid S \cap F \neq \emptyset\})$, by the *subset construction* [10] where $\cdot$ is the extension of the transition function of M to the domain $2^Q \times \Sigma$. The DFA $\mathcal{D}(M)$ is referred to as the *subset automaton.*

The *reverse* of an MNFA M, denoted M^R, is the MNFA obtained from M by reversing all transitions and by swapping the roles of initial and final states. A subset S of states of M for which exists a string w such that $I \cdot w = S$ is called *reachable* in M. If a set is reachable in M^R, we say it is *co-reachable* in M.

Sometimes we allow an MNFA to have ε-transitions, and then a set S is reached from a set R on a symbol σ if $S = E(\{q \cdot \sigma \mid q \in R\})$ where $E(P)$ is the set of states reachable from a state in the set P via ε-transitions.

The *nondeterministic state complexity of a regular language* L, denoted by $\text{nsc}(L)$, is the smallest number of states in any NFA for L. The *nondeterministic state complexity of a unary regular operation* $^\circ$ is a mapping from $\mathbb{N}$ to $\mathbb{N}$ defined as

$$n \mapsto \max\{\text{nsc}(L^\circ) \mid L \text{ is accepted by an } n\text{-state NFA}\}.$$

The *nondeterministic state complexity of a binary regular operation* $\circ$ is a mapping from $\mathbb{N}^2$ to $\mathbb{N}$ defined as

$$(m, n) \mapsto \max\{\text{nsc}(K \circ L) \mid K, L \text{ accepted by } m\text{-state and } n\text{ -state NFAs, resp.}\}.$$

In order to obtain lower bounds on the nondeterministic state complexity of regular languages, the so-called fooling set method is usually used. A set of pairs of strings $\{(x_i, y_i) \mid 1 \le i \le n\}$ is called a *fooling set* for some given language L if (1) $x_i y_i \in L$ for each i, and (2) if $i \neq j$, then $x_i y_j \notin L$ or $x_j y_i \notin L$. It is well known that if $\mathcal{F}$ is a fooling set for the given regular language L, then $\text{nsc}(L) \ge |\mathcal{F}|$ [1, Lemma, p. 188].

To describe fooling sets for languages can be tedious and checking whether or not a string $x_i y_j$ is in L may be hard. To avoid such difficulties, we use the technique of fooling sets for MNFAs where to each state of a given MNFA M, we assign a pair of subsets of the state set of M.

Definition 1. *Let $M = (Q, \Sigma, \cdot, I, F)$ be an MNFA. A set $\{(R_q, C_q) \mid q \in Q\}$, where R_q and C_q are subsets of Q, is a* fooling set for the MNFA M *if for all states p, q,*

(1) R_q is reachable and C_q is co-reachable in M,
(2) $q \in R_q \cap C_q$,
(3) if $p \neq q$, then $R_p \cap C_q = \emptyset$ or $R_q \cap C_p = \emptyset$.

Notice that by the definition above, a fooling set for $L(M)$ exists if and only if a fooling set for M of the same size exists; if each set R_q is reached by x_q and each set C_q is co-reached by y_q, then $\{(x_q, y_q^R) \mid q \in Q\}$ is a fooling set for $L(M)$, and vice versa. Therefore, we immediately get the following observation.

Lemma 2 (**[11, Lemma 4]**, **[12, Lemma 4]**). *Let $M = (Q, \Sigma, \cdot, I, F)$ be an MNFA such that at least one of the following conditions holds:*

(a) there exists a fooling set $\{(R_q, C_q) \mid q \in Q\}$,
(b) each singleton subset of Q is reachable and co-reachable in M.

Then $\text{nsc}(L(M)) \ge |Q|$. □

To describe a fooling set for the complement of a language may be cumbersome, *cf.* [13, Theorem 5]. The condition in the following lemma guarantees the existence of such a fooling set.

Lemma 3 (**[12, Proposition 6]**). *Let L be a language accepted by an NFA in which k subsets of the state set are reachable and each of their complements is co-reachable. Then* $\text{nsc}(L^c) \ge k$. □

So if we prove that each subset of states of an NFA A is both reachable and co-reachable, then $\text{nsc}(L(A)^c) = 2^n$. Notice that the reachability of all subsets in the NFA M from [13, Theorem 5] can be easily shown, and since M is isomorphic to its reverse, so can be the co-reachability. This immediately gives a lower bound 2^n for the complement of $L(M)$.

The union of two NFAs of m and n states is accepted by an $(m+n)$-state MNFA. To get an NFA for union, one more state may be needed. However, we cannot construct a fooling set for union of size $m+n+1$ since we already have an MNFA of size $m+n$. A similar observation works for reversal as well. In [14, Lemma 4], a modified fooling set method has been described. Now we present it using the reachable and co-reachable sets instead of strings.

Lemma 4 ($\mathcal{ST}$-Lemma, *cf.* [11, Lemma 8]). *Let Q be a set of states. Let $\mathcal{S}$ and $\mathcal{T}$ be disjoint sets of pairs of subsets of Q and let U and V be two subsets of Q such that $\mathcal{S} \cup \mathcal{T}$, $\mathcal{S} \cup \{(I, U)\}$, and $\mathcal{T} \cup \{(I, V)\}$ are fooling sets for the MNFA $M = (Q, \Sigma, \cdot, I, F)$. Then* $\text{nsc}(L(M)) \geq |\mathcal{S}| + |\mathcal{T}| + 1$. □

Next, we introduce the language classes considered in this paper. These languages were already examined to some extent in [2], with the exception of group languages which were investigated in [7]. A language L is

- combinational (class abbreviation CB): if $L = \Sigma^* H$ for $H \subseteq \Sigma$;
- finitely generated left ideal (FGLID): if $L = \Sigma^* H$ for some finite language H (in [2] called noninitial definite);
- left ideal (LID): if $L = \Sigma^* L$ (in [2] called ultimate definite);
- group language (GRP): if it is accepted by a permutation DFA (equivalently, if the minimal DFA for L is a permutation one);
- star (STAR): if $L = G^*$ for a regular language G [3] (equivalently, $L = L^*$);
- comet (COM): if $L{=}G^* H$ for some regular languages G, H with $G{\notin}\{\emptyset, \{\varepsilon\}\}$;
- two-sided comet (2COM): if $L{=}EG^* H$ for regular E, G, H with $G{\notin}\{\emptyset, \{\varepsilon\}\}$;
- ordered (ORD): if it is accepted by a (possibly non-minimal) DFA with ordered states such that $p \preceq q$ implies $p \cdot \sigma \preceq q \cdot \sigma$ for each symbol σ [17];
- star-free (SFREE): if L is constructable from finite languages, concatenation, union, and complementation (equivalently, if L has an aperiodic DFA) [16];
- power-separating (PSEP): if for every x in Σ^* there exists an integer m such that $\bigcup_{i \geq m}\{x^i\} \subseteq L$ or $\bigcup_{i \geq m}\{x^i\} \subseteq L^c$ [18].

We have CB $\subsetneq$ FGLID $\subsetneq$ LID, STAR $\subsetneq$ COM $\subsetneq$ 2COM, and ORD $\subsetneq$ STFR $\subsetneq$ PSEP [2]; the only star language that is not a comet is $\{\varepsilon\}$.

3 Results

In this section, we gradually present our obtained results by lemmas individually focusing on the considered operations and language classes. They are grouped together based on their proof structure, with summarizing tables included in the Conclusions section. We proceed with the proposition considering all operations on the class of combinational languages. This class is special since every combinational language has nondeterministic state complexity at most two.

Proposition 5. *Let $m, n \geq 2$. Let K and L be combinational languages over Σ accepted by m-state and n-state NFAs. Then*

(1) $\text{nsc}(K), \text{nsc}(L) \leq 2$,
(2) $\text{nsc}(K \cap L), \text{nsc}(K \cup L), \text{nsc}(L^R) \leq 2$, *and this bound is tight if* $|\Sigma| \geq 1$,
(3) $\text{nsc}(L^*), \text{nsc}(L^c) \leq 2$, *and this bound is tight if* $|\Sigma| \geq 2$,
(4) $\text{nsc}(KL) \leq 3$ *and* $\text{nsc}(L^k) \leq k + 1$, *and these bounds are tight if* $|\Sigma| \geq 1$.

The next two lemmas consider intersection and union on finitely generated left ideal languages.

Lemma 6. *Let $m,n \geq 3$ and $\Sigma = \{a_1, a_2, \ldots, a_{m-1}, b_1, b_2, \ldots, b_{n-1}, c, d, e\}$. Let A, B, C, and D be the NFAs from Fig. 1. Then $L(A)$, $L(B)$, $L(C)$, and $L(D)$ are finitely generated left ideal languages such that* $\text{nsc}(L(A) \cap L(B)) = mn$ *and* $\text{nsc}(L(C) \cup L(D)) = m + n - 1$.

Proof. First we consider intersection. We can get an NFA accepting a finite generator of $L(A)$ from A by removing loops in the initial state, adding final states $m+1, m+2, \ldots, 2m$ connected through transitions $m+1 \xrightarrow{b_j} m+2 \xrightarrow{b_j} \cdots \xrightarrow{b_j} 2m$ for each j, and adding transitions $(q, \sigma, m+1)$ for each transition (q, σ, m) in A. A similar construction can be done for B. Hence $L(A)$ and $L(B)$ are finitely generated left ideals. Consider the product automaton $A \times B$ for $L(A) \cap L(B)$. For each (i,j) in $\{1,2,\ldots,m\} \times \{1,2,\ldots,n\}$, define the following sets:

$[i,j] \;= \{1,2,\ldots,i\} \times \{1,2,\ldots,j\}$ if $1 \leq i \leq m-1$ and $1 \leq j \leq n-1$;
$[\![i,n]\!] = \{1,2,\ldots,i\} \times \{1,n\}$ if $1 \leq i \leq m-1$;
$[\![m,j]\!] = \{1,m\} \times \{1,2,\ldots,j\}$ if $1 \leq j \leq n-1$;
$[\![m,n]\!] = \{1,m\} \times \{1,2,\ldots,n\}$.

To each state (i,j) in $A \times B$, we assign a pair of sets $R_{i,j}$ and $C_{i,j}$ as follows:

$$(R_{i,j}, C_{i,j}) = \begin{cases} ([i,j], \{(i,j)\}), & \text{if } 1 \leq i \leq m-1 \text{ and } 1 \leq j \leq n-1; \\ ([\![i,n]\!], \{(i,n-1),(i,n)\}), & \text{if } 1 \leq i \leq m-1 \text{ and } j = n; \\ ([\![m,j]\!], \{(m-1,j),(m,j)\}), & \text{if } i = m \text{ and } 1 \leq j \leq n-1; \\ ([\![m,n]\!], \{(m,n)\}), & \text{if } i = m \text{ and } j = n. \end{cases}$$

It can be shown that the set $\{(R_{i,j}, C_{i,j}) \mid 1 \leq i \leq m \text{ and } 1 \leq j \leq n\}$ is a fooling set for $A \times B$ of size mn. Hence $\text{nsc}(K \cap L) = mn$ by Lemma 2(a).

Now we consider union. We have $L(C) = (a+b+c+d)^* a (a+b)^{m-2} a^* = (a+b+c+d)^* a (a+b)^{m-2} a^{\leq m-1}$, so $L(C)$ is a finitely generated left ideal. By a similar argument, the language $L(D)$ is a finitely generated left ideal as well. Construct the NFA N for $L(C) \cup L(D)$ from automata C and D by omitting the state 0 and by adding the transition $(1, c, m+1)$. For each state of N, define the following pairs of sets:

$$(R_i, C_i) = \begin{cases} (\{1,i\}, \{i\}), & \text{if } 1 \leq i \leq m+n-2 \text{and } i \neq m; \\ (\{1,i\}, \{i-1,i\}), & \text{if } i \in \{m, m+n-1\}. \end{cases}$$

Then $\{(R_i, C_i) \mid 1 \leq i \leq m+n-1\}$ is a fooling set for the NFA N of size $m+n-1$. Hence $\text{nsc}(L(C) \cup L(D)) = m+n-1$ by Lemma 2(a). □

The next lemma considers intersection, union, and concatenation on the class of group languages; notice that we use the same witnesses for all three operations.

Lemma 7. *Let $m,n \geq 2$. Let A and B be the NFAs from Fig. 2. Then $L(A)$ and $L(B)$ are group languages, and* $\text{nsc}(L(A) \cap L(B)) = mn$, $\text{nsc}(L(A) \cup L(B)) = m+n+1$, *and* $\text{nsc}(L(A)L(B)) = m+n$.

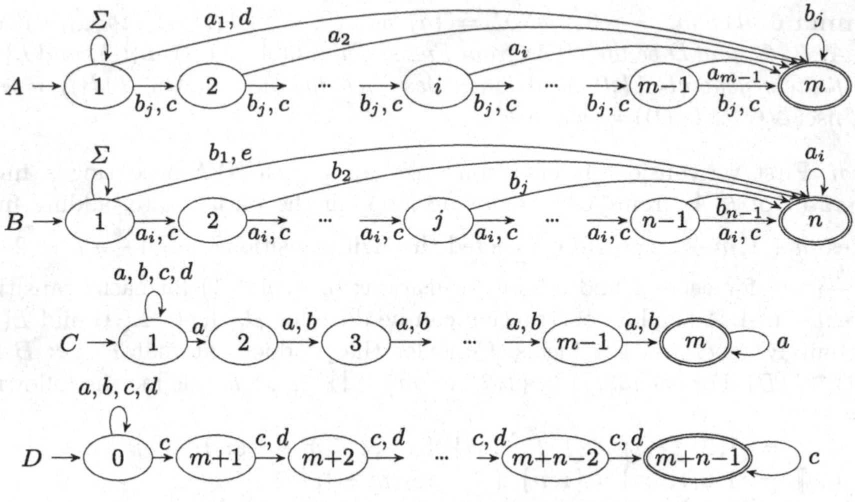

Fig. 1. Finitely generated left ideal witnesses for intersection and for union.

Proof. In the product automaton for $L(A) \cap L(B)$, each singleton set is reachable and co-reachable, so $\text{nsc}(L(A) \cap L(B)) = mn$ by Lemma 2(b).

In the case of union, we may assume that $m \leq n$. Construct the MNFA M for $L(A) \cup L(B)$ in the standard way. In M, each set $\{p_i, q_j\}$ is reachable and co-reachable. For each state q of M, we define the pair of sets (R_q, C_q) as follows:
$(R_{p_i}, C_{p_i}) = (\{p_i, q_{(i-1) \bmod m}\}, \{p_i, q_{(i-2) \bmod m}\})$,
$(R_{q_j}, C_{q_j}) = (\{q_j, p_{(j+2) \bmod m}\}, \{q_j, p_{(j+1) \bmod m}\})$.
Then $\mathcal{S} = \{(R_{p_i}, C_{p_i}) \mid i = 0, 1, \ldots, m-1\}$, $\mathcal{T} = \{(R_{q_j}, C_{q_j}) \mid j = 0, 1, \ldots, n-1\}$, $I = \{p_0, q_0\}$, $U = \{q_0, p_1\}$, and $V = \{p_0, q_{m-2}\}$ satisfy the conditions of Lemma 4, so $\text{nsc}(L(A) \cup L(B)) = m + n + 1$.

To get an NFA N for $L(A)L(B)$ from NFAs A and B, add the transition $(p_{m-1}, \varepsilon, q_0)$, and make the state p_{m-1} non-final and the state q_0 non-initial. Then the set $\{(\{p_i\}, \{p_i, q_{n-1}\}) \mid 0 \leq i \leq m-2\} \cup \{(\{p_{m-1}, q_0\}, \{p_{m-1}, q_{n-1}\})\} \cup \{(\{p_0, q_0\}, \{p_{m-1}, q_0\})\} \cup \{(\{p_0, q_j\}, \{q_j\}) \mid 1 \leq j \leq n-1\}$ is a fooling set for N of size $m + n$, so $\text{nsc}(L(A)L(B))$ by Lemma 2(a). $\square$

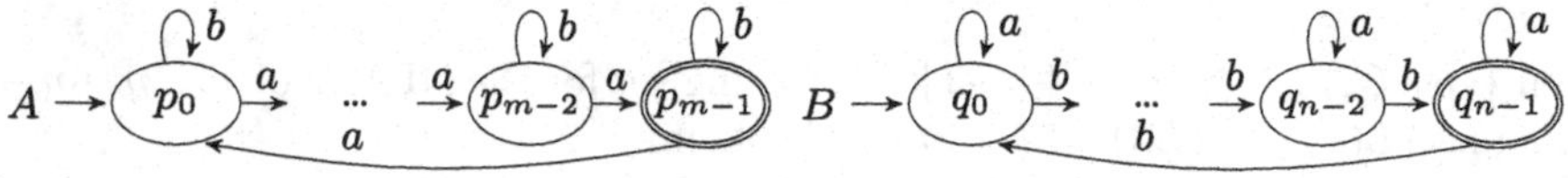

Fig. 2. Binary group witnesses for intersection, union, and concatenation.

To get star witnesses, construct the NFAs A' and B' from A and B in Fig. 2 by making the initial state final and all other states non-final. Then $L(A')$ and $L(B')$ are star languages. Moreover, all the sets from the proof above are still reachable and co-reachable, so we have $\mathrm{nsc}(L(A') \cap L(B')) = mn$ and $\mathrm{nsc}(L(A') \cup L(B')) = m + n + 1$. The concatenation of star languages $(a^m)^*$ and $(b^n)^*$ has nondeterministic state complexity $m + n$, as shown in [8, Theorem 7]. The next lemma considers intersection, union, and concatenation on ordered languages.

Lemma 8. *Let $m, n \geq 2$, $K = (b^*a)^{m-1}b^*$, and $L = (a^*b)^{n-1}a^*$. Then K and L are ordered languages accepted by m-state and n-state NFAs,* $\mathrm{nsc}(K \cap L) = mn$, $\mathrm{nsc}(K \cup L) = m + n + 1$, *and* $\mathrm{nsc}(KL) = m + n$.

Proof. The languages K and L are accepted by DFAs A and B from Fig. 3. In the product automaton $A \times B$ for $K \cap L$, each singleton set is reachable and co-reachable. This gives the tight lower bound mn by Lemma 2(b).

Let M be the MNFA containing all states and transitions of A and B. Then $L(M) = K \cup L$. In the MNFA M, the initial set is $\{p_1, q_1\}$, and each singleton set is both reachable and co-reachable by a string in a^*b^* or in b^*a^*. Let $\mathcal{S} = \{(\{p_i\}, \{p_i\}) \mid 1 \leq i \leq m\}$, $\mathcal{T} = \{(\{q_j\}, \{q_j\}) \mid 1 \leq j \leq n\}$. $I = \{p_1, q_1\}$, $U = \{q_1\}$, and $V = \{p_1\}$. Then the sets $\mathcal{S} \cup \mathcal{T}$, $\mathcal{S} \cup \{(I, U)\}$, and $\mathcal{T} \cup \{(I, V)\}$ are fooling sets for $A \cup B$. Hence $\mathrm{nsc}(K \cup L) = m + n + 1$ by Lemma 4.

Construct the NFA N from M by adding the transition (p_m, ε, q_1), making the state q_1 non-initial, and making the state p_m non-final. Then $L(N) = KL$, and the set $\{(\{p_i\}, \{p_i\}) \mid 1 \leq i \leq m - 1\} \cup \{(\{p_m, q_1\}, \{p_m\})\} \cup \{(\{q_1\}, \{p_m, q_1\})\} \cup \{(\{q_j\}, \{q_j\}) \mid 2 \leq j \leq n\}$ is a fooling set for N. Hence $\mathrm{nsc}(KL) = m + n$. □

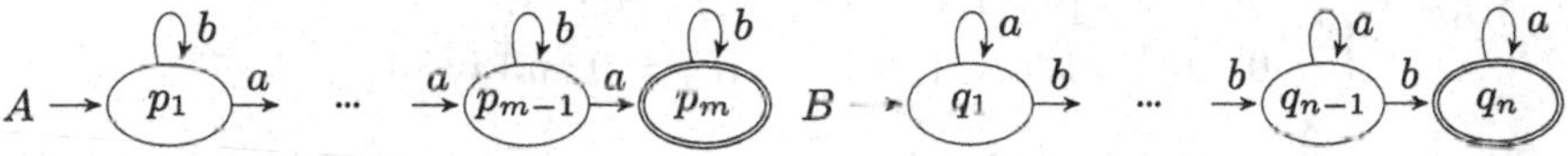

Fig. 3. Binary ordered witnesses for intersection, union, and concatenation.

In what follows, we consider the unary operations of the k-th power, star, reversal, and complementation. We start with the class of star languages.

Lemma 9. *Let L be a star language. Then $L^k = L^* = L$ and* $\mathrm{nsc}(L^R) = \mathrm{nsc}(L)$.

Proof. We have $L^k \subseteq L^* = L$ by definition. To show that $L \subseteq L^k$, let $w \in L$. Since $L = L^*$, we have $\varepsilon \in L$. Set $u_1 = w$ and $u_2 = u_3 = \cdots = u_k = \varepsilon$. Then $w = u_1 u_2 \cdots u_k$ with $u_i \in L$, so $w \in L^k$. Thus $L^k = L^* = L$.

For reversal, notice that each star language is accepted by an NFA A with a single final state which is the initial state. Then L^R is accepted by the NFA A^R which has the same number of states and the same initial and final state. Hence $\mathrm{nsc}(L^R) \leq \mathrm{nsc}(L)$. Since $(L^R)^R = L$, we have $\mathrm{nsc}(L^R) = \mathrm{nsc}(L)$. □

The language $(a^{n-1}b)^*a^{n-1}$ is a comet and ordered language and it meets the upper bound kn on the complexity of the k-th power if $n \geq 2$ [4, Theorem 3]. Now we consider the k-th power on the class of group languages and we show that the complexity in this class is kn as well.

Lemma 10. *Let $k \geq 2$ and $n \geq 3$. Let A be the binary NFA from Fig. 4. Then $L(A)$ is a group language and* $\operatorname{nsc}(L(A)^k) = kn$.

Proof. Construct the NFA N for $L(A)^k$ from k copies of A in the standard way; assume that the copies are numbered from 1 to k and the state j in the i-th copy is denoted (i,j). For each state (i,j) with $j \neq n-1$, set

$$R_{i,j} = \{(i,j)\} \cup \{(i-\ell, (j-\ell) \bmod (n-1)) \mid 1 \leq \ell \leq i-1\},$$

that is, in $R_{i,j}$ we have states $(i,j), (i-1,j-1), (i-2,j-2), \ldots$ where the second component is modulo $n-1$. Next, set

$$\begin{aligned} R_{i,n-1} = &\{(p,q) \mid q \leq n-3 \text{ and } (p,q) \in R_{i,n-2}\} \cup \\ &\{(p,n-1) \mid (p,n-2) \in R_{i,n-2}\} \cup \{(i+1,0)\}, \end{aligned}$$

that is, to get $R_{i,n-1}$, we move each state of $R_{i,n-2}$ in column $n-2$ to the corresponding state in column $n-1$, and we add the state $(i+1,0)$, so we have $R_{i,n-2} \xrightarrow{b} R_{i,n-1}$. Moreover $R_{i,n-1} \xrightarrow{b} R_{i,n-2} \cup \{(i+1,0)\} = R_{i+1,0}$.

Denote by $[\![i,j]\!]$ the set $\{(i,j),(i+2,j),\ldots,(i+2p,j)\}$ where $i+2p$ is either $k-1$ or k, that is, the set containing the state j in copies $i, i+2, \ldots, i+2p$. Set

$$C_{i,j} = \begin{cases} [\![i,j]\!] \cup [\![i+1,n-1]\!], & \text{if } 1 \leq j \leq n-2 \text{ or } (i,j)=(1,0); \\ [\![i,n-1]\!] \cup [\![i+1,n-2]\!], & \text{if } j = n-1; \\ [\![i,0]\!] \cup [\![i-1,n-1]\!], & \text{if } j=0 \text{ and } i \neq 1. \end{cases}$$

The set $\{(R_{i,j}, C_{i,j}) \mid 1 \leq i \leq k \text{ and } 0 \leq j \leq n-1\}$ is a fooling set for N of size kn. Hence $\operatorname{nsc}(L(A)^k) = kn$ by Lemma 2(a). □

It was shown in [8, Theorem 9] that for the language $L = (a^n)^*a^{n-1}$, we have $\operatorname{nsc}(L^*) = n+1$. Since L is a group and comet language, L^+ is ordered, and $(L^+)^* = L^*$, the nondeterministic state complexity of star in the classes of group, comet, and ordered languages is $n+1$. The next lemma shows that the complexity of star on finitely generated left ideal languages is $n+1$ as well.

Lemma 11. *Let $n \geq 4$. Let $K = (a+b)^*a^{n-2}(a+b)a^*$. Then K is a finitely generated left ideal language accepted by an n-state NFA, and* $\operatorname{nsc}(K^*) = n+1$.

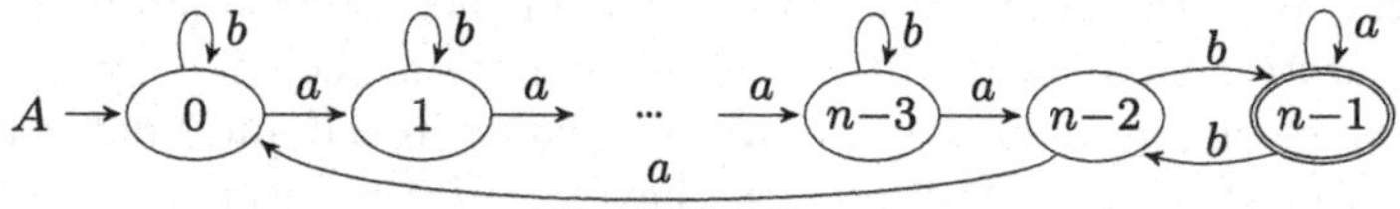

Fig. 4. A binary group witness for power meeting the upper bound kn.

Proof. Since we have $(a+b)^*a^{n-2}(a+b)a^* = (a+b)^*a^{n-2}(a+b)a^{\le n-1}$, the language K is a finitely generated left ideal accepted by the NFA A from Fig. 5. Construct the MNFA A^* for $L(A)^*$ by adding a new initial and final state 0 and the transitions $(n-1,a,1),(n-1,b,1),(n,a,1)$. To each state i of A^*, we assign the following pair of sets:

$$(R_i, C_i) = \begin{cases} (\{0,1\},\{0,n\}), & \text{if } i = 0; \\ (\{1,2,\dots,i\},\{i\}), & \text{if } 1 \le i \le n-1; \\ (\{1,n\},\{n-1,n\}), & \text{if } i = n. \end{cases}$$

Then $\{(R_i,C_i) \mid 0 \le i \le n\}$ is a fooling set for A^*. Hence $\text{nsc}(L(A)^*) = n+1$. □

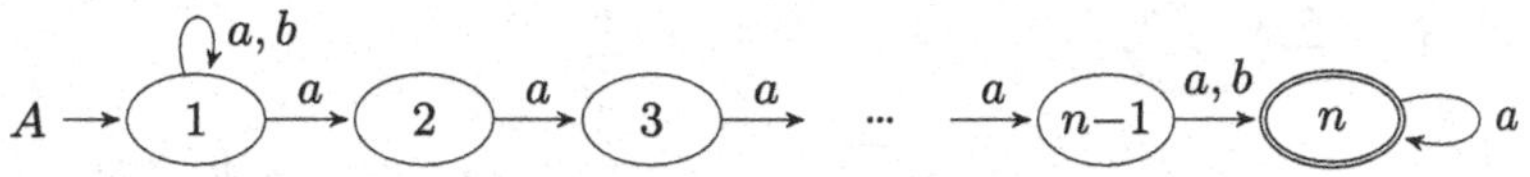

Fig. 5. A binary finitely generated left ideal witness for star meeting the bound $n+1$.

The following two lemmas consider the reversal on classes of finitely generated left ideal and group languages.

Lemma 12. *Let $n \ge 4$. Consider the NFAs A and B from Fig. 6 and the language $L = (a^{n-1}b)^*a^{\le n-1}$. Then $L(A)$ is a finitely generated left ideal language, $L(B)$ is a group language, L is a comet and ordered language accepted by an n-state NFA, and we have* $\text{nsc}(L(A)^R) = \text{nsc}(L(B)^R) = \text{nsc}(L^R) = n+1$.

Proof. In the lemma statement, we consider three witness languages. We present the proofs gradually, starting with $L(A) = (a+b+c)^*(c+(cc+a^{n-3}(a+b))a^*) = (a+b+c)^*(c+(cc+a^{n-3}(a+b))a^{\le n-2})$, so $L(A)$ is a finitely generated left ideal. For each state i of A^R, define the sets

$$R_i = \begin{cases} \{i\}, & \text{if } 1 \le i \le n-1; \\ \{n-1,n\}, & \text{if } i = n, \end{cases} \qquad C_i = \begin{cases} \{1,3,4,\dots,i\}, & \text{if } 3 \le i \le n-1, \\ \{1\} \cup \{i\}, & \text{if } i \in \{1,2,n\}. \end{cases}$$

Next, let $\mathcal{S} = \{(R_i,C_i) \mid 1 \le i \le 2\}$, $\mathcal{T} = \{(R_i,C_i) \mid 3 \le i \le n\}$, $I = \{2,n\}$, $U = \{1,n\}$, and $V = \{1,2\}$. Then $\mathcal{S} \cup \mathcal{T}$, $\mathcal{S} \cup \{(I,U)\}$, and $\mathcal{T} \cup \{(I,V)\}$ satisfy the conditions of Lemma 4, so $\text{nsc}(L(A)^R) = n+1$.

Now let us consider the witness for reversal on group languages, i.e., NFA B, which is actually a DFA. Since the symbols a and b perform permutations on the state set of B, the language $L(B)$ is a group language. Consider the following pairs of subsets of states of B:

$$(R_i, C_i) = \begin{cases} (\{i,i+1\},\{i\}), & \text{if } 1 \le i \le n-1; \\ (\{n,2\},\{n\}), & \text{if } i = n, \end{cases}$$

and set $\mathcal{S} = \{(R_i, C_i) \mid i = 1, 2, \ldots, n-1\}$, $\mathcal{T} = \{(R_n, C_n)\}$, $I = \{n, 1\}$, $U = \{n\}$, and $V = \{1\}$. Then $\mathcal{S} \cup \mathcal{T}$, $\mathcal{S} \cup \{(I, U)\}$, and $\mathcal{T} \cup \{(I, V)\}$ satisfy the conditions of Lemma 4, so $\operatorname{nsc}(L(B)^R) = n + 1$.

Finally, consider the comet language $L = (a^{n-1}b)^* a^{\leq n-1}$. It is accepted by the NFA C shown in Fig. 6. To get an ordered DFA for L from C, add the dead states 0 and $n{+}1$ and the transitions $(n, a, n{+}1)$ and $(i, b, 0)$ for $i = 1, 2, \ldots, n-1$. Hence L is ordered. In C, each singleton set $\{i\}$ is reachable by a^{i-1}, and in C^R, the initial set is $I = \{1, 2, \ldots, n\}$ and each singleton set $\{i\}$ is reachable by ba^{n-i}. Set $\mathcal{S} = \{(\{1\}, \{1\})\}$, $\mathcal{T} = \{(\{i\}, \{i\}) \mid 2 \leq i \leq n\}$, $U = \{2\}$, and $V = \{1\}$. Then $\mathcal{S} \cup \mathcal{T}$, $\mathcal{S} \cup \{(I, U)\}$, and $\mathcal{T} \cup \{(I, V)\}$ are fooling sets for C^R. It follows that $\operatorname{nsc}(L^R) = n + 1$ by Lemma 4. □

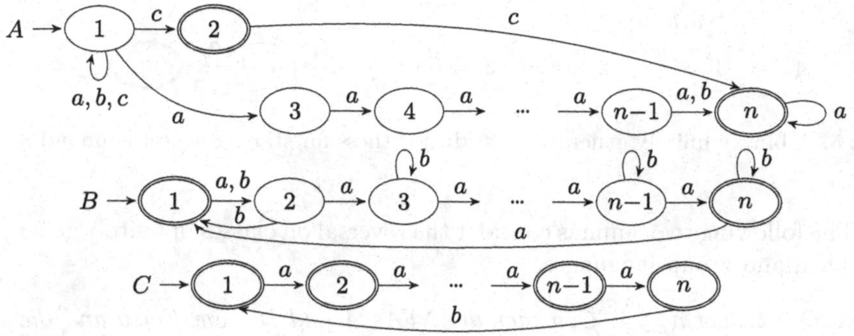

Fig. 6. A finitely generated left ideal, group, and ordered witnesses for reversal.

In the last two lemmas, we consider complementation. The upper bound on left ideals is known to be 2^{n-1} [12, Theorem 37(1)] and we provide a finitely generated witness for this bound. For stars and ordered languages, the complexity is 2^n, and for group language, we have a hyperpolynomial lower bound $\binom{n-1}{\lfloor n/2 \rfloor}$.

Lemma 13. *Let* $n \geq 3$. *Let* A, B, C *be the NFAs from Fig. 7;* $a_{i..j}$ *denotes the transitions on* $a_i, a_{i+1}, \ldots, a_j$. *Then* $L(A)$ *is a finitely generated left ideal,* $L(B)$ *is a star language,* $L(C)$ *is ordered, and we have* $\operatorname{nsc}(L(A)^c) = 2^{n-1}$ *and* $\operatorname{nsc}(L(B)^c) = \operatorname{nsc}(L(C)^c) = 2^n$.

Proof. We provide a proof only for the ordered witness $L(C)$. In the subset automaton $\mathcal{D}(C)$, let us assign the value $p_S = 2^{i_1} + 2^{i_2} + \cdots + 2^{i_k}$ to a set $S = \{i_1, i_2, \ldots, i_k\}$ with $n-1 \geq i_1 > i_2 > \cdots > i_k \geq 0$. It follows from the transitions defined in the NFA C that in $\mathcal{D}(C)$, we have $p_S \xrightarrow{a} \lfloor p_S/2 \rfloor$, $p_S \xrightarrow{b} 0$ if $p_S \in \{0, 1\}$ and $p_S \xrightarrow{b} 2^{n-1} + \lfloor p_S/2 \rfloor$ otherwise, and $p_S \xrightarrow{c_j} p_S$ if $j \notin S$ or $0 \in S$, and $p_S \xrightarrow{c_j} p_S + 1$ otherwise. Since all these transformations preserve the order of states in $\mathcal{D}(C)$ given by their corresponding values, the language $L(C)$ is ordered.

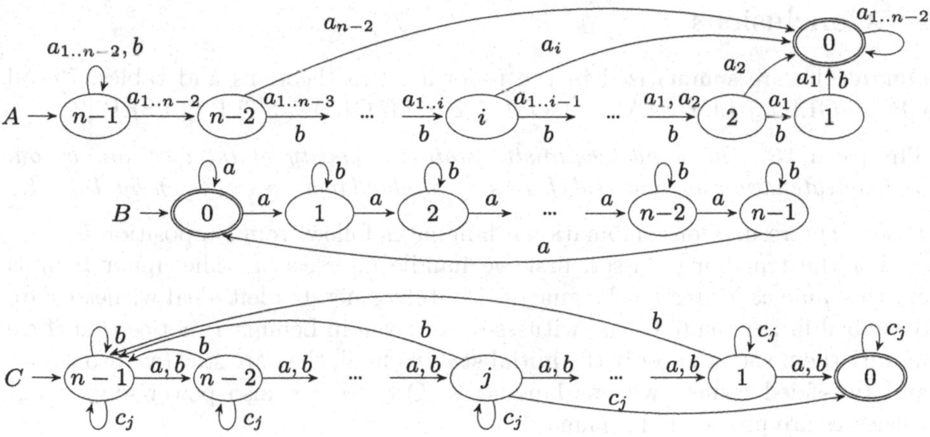

Fig. 7. Finitely generated left ideal, star, and ordered witnesses for complementation.

In C, the empty set and each singleton set is reachable by a string in a^*. Each set $\{n-1\} \cup S$ of size k is reached from the set $\{i+1 \mid i \in S\}$ of size $k-1$ by b, and each set S with $n-1 \notin S$ of size k is reached from a set of size k containing $n-1$ by a string in a^*. This proves the reachability of all subsets in C by induction. To get co-reachability, we use the symbols c_j. The empty set and each singleton set is co-reachable by a string in a^*. Each set S with $0 \in S$ and $\max S = j$ is co-reached from $S \setminus \{j\}$ by c_j. Each set S with $0 \notin S$ is co-reached from a set of the same size containing 0 by a string in a^*. It follows that all sets are co-reachable. Hence by Lemma 3, we have $\text{nsc}(L(C)^c) = 2^n$. □

Lemma 14. *Let* $n \geq 4$. *Let* M *be the binary MNFA from Fig. 8 with* $k = \lfloor n/2 \rfloor$. *Then* $L(M)$ *is a group language with* $\text{nsc}(L(M)) \leq n$ *and* $\text{nsc}(L(M)^c) = \binom{n-1}{k}$.

Proof. Since in M, the symbols a and b form a generator of all permutations on states from 1 to $n-1$, each subset of $\{1, 2, \ldots, n-1\}$ of size k is reachable and each subset of $\{1, 2, \ldots, n-1\}$ of size $n-1-k$ is co-reachable in M. In total we have $\binom{n-1}{k} = \binom{n-1}{\lfloor n/2 \rfloor}$ reachable sets and their co-reachable complements. This gives the lower bound for $\text{nsc}(L(M)^c)$ by Lemma 3. To get an equivalent n-state NFA A from M, add the initial state 0, make all other states non-initial, and add transitions $(0, b, i)$ and $(0, a, i+1)$ for each $i = 1, 2, \ldots, k$. Then $\text{nsc}(L(A)^c) = \text{nsc}(L(M)^c) \geq \binom{n-1}{\lfloor n/2 \rfloor}$. □

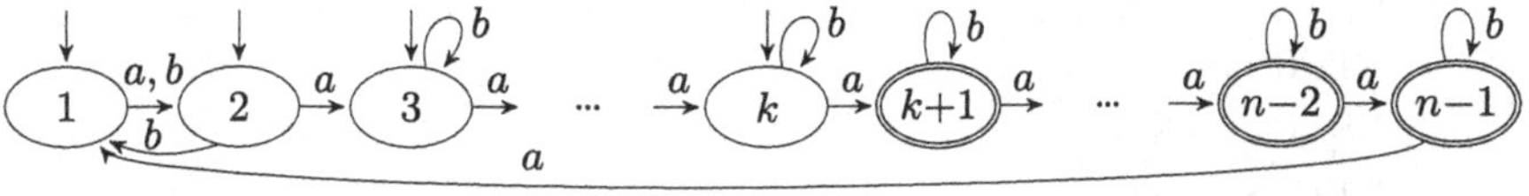

Fig. 8. A binary group language meeting the lower bound $\binom{n-1}{\lfloor n/2 \rfloor}$ for complementation.

4 Conclusions

Our results are summarized in the following two theorems and tables. Recall CB $\subsetneq$ FGLID $\subsetneq$ LID, STAR $\subsetneq$ COM $\subsetneq$ 2COM, ORD $\subsetneq$ STFR $\subsetneq$ PSEP [2].

Theorem 15. *The nondeterministic state complexity of intersection, union, and concatenation on some subclasses of regular languages is given by Table 1.*

Proof. The results for combinational languages follow from Proposition 5.

For the remaining classes, first we handle intersection. The upper bounds are the same as for regular languages. Finitely generated left ideal witnesses are described in Lemma 6. Group witnesses are given in Lemma 7; notice that if we modify them such that only the initial state is final, they are star (so also comet and two-sided comet) witness languages. Ordered (so also power-separating) witnesses are provided in Lemma 8.

Now consider union. The finitely generated left ideals from Lemma 6 meet the upper bound for left ideals. In the remaining classes, the upper bounds are the same as in the regular case. Group witnesses that can be modified to star (so also comet and two-sided comet) languages are described in Lemma 7. Ordered (so also power-separating) witnesses are given by Lemma 8.

Finally we discuss concatenation. The result for finitely generated left ideals follows from [12, Theorem 16] where it is shown that the upper bound for left ideals is $m + n - 1$; the unary witnesses a^*a^{m-1} and a^*a^{n-1} described in this theorem are finitely generated left ideals. In all the remaining cases, we have the regular upper bounds. The group witnesses are given in Lemma 7. A proof using the same fooling set as for the group languages works also for the star (so also comet and two-sided comet) witnesses $(a^m)^*$ and $(b^n)^*$, cf. [8, Theorem 7]. The ordered (so also power-separating) witnesses are defined in Lemma 8. □

Table 1. Results for binary operations; ◇ means the witness from above can be used.

	$K \cap L$	$\|\Sigma\|$	$K \cup L$	$\|\Sigma\|$	KL	$\|\Sigma\|$
CB	2	1	2	1	3	1
FGLID	mn	$m+n+1$	$m+n-1$	4	$m+n-1$	1
LID [12]	mn	2	$m+n-1$	2	◇	
GRP	mn	2	$m+n+1$	2	$m+n$	2
STAR	mn	2	$m+n+1$	2	$m+n$	2
COM	◇		◇		◇	
2COM	◇		◇		◇	
ORD	mn	2	$m+n+1$	2	$m+n$	2
STFR [9]	◇		◇		◇	
PSEP	◇		◇		◇	
REG [8]	mn	2	$m+n+1$	2	$m+n$	2

Theorem 16. *The nondeterministic state complexity of power, star, reversal, and complementation on some subclasses of regular languages is given by Table 2.*

Proof. The results for combinational languages follow from Proposition 5. Now let us examine the remaining classes.

First we consider the k-th power. The upper bound $k(n-1)+1$ for left ideals is met by the unary finitely generated left ideal a^*a^{n-1} [11, Theorem 12(c)]. The tight upper bound for star languages is n by Lemma 9. The general upper bound kn is met by the group language described in Lemma 10. The ordered language $(a^{n-1}b)^*a^{n-1}$ is also a comet (and two-sided comet) language and it meets the upper bound kn as shown in [4, Theorem 3].

The complexity of the star and reversal operations on star languages is n by Lemma 9. For the other classes, the upper bound $n+1$ for star is met by binary finitely generated left ideal language from Lemma 11 which is also a comet and two-sided comet language, by unary group and comet language $(a^n)^*a^{n-1}$, and by unary ordered (so also power-separating) language $(a^{n-1}+a^n)^*a^{n-1}$, as shown in [8, Theorem 9]. This upper bound for reversal is met by a ternary finitely generated left ideal language, a binary group language, and the binary comet and ordered language $(a^{n-1}b)^*a^{\leq n-1}$, as shown in Lemma 12.

The upper bound 2^{n-1} for complement on left ideals from [12, Theorem 37(1)] is met by the finitely generated left ideal over an alphabet of size $n-1$ from Lemma 13. The regular upper bound 2^n is met by a binary star (so also comet and two-sided comet) language and by ordered language over an alphabet of size $n+1$, as shown in Lemma 13, and by the binary star-free (so also power-separating) language from [9, Theorem 5]. Finally, a binary group language meeting the lower bound $\binom{n-1}{\lfloor n/2 \rfloor}$ for complementation is described in Lemma 14. □

Table 2. Results for unary operations;◇ means the witness from above can be used.

	L^k	$\|\Sigma\|$	L^*	$\|\Sigma\|$	L^R	$\|\Sigma\|$	L^c	$\|\Sigma\|$
CB	$k+1$	1	2	2	2	1	2	2
FGLID	$k(n-1)+1$	1	$n+1$	2	$n+1$	3	2^{n-1}	$n-1$
LID [12]	◇		◇		$n+1$	2	2^{n-1}	2
GRP	kn	2	$n+1$	1	$n+1$	2	$\geq \binom{n-1}{\lfloor n/2 \rfloor}$	2
STAR	n	1	n	1	n	1	2^n	2
COM	kn	2	$n+1$	1	$n+1$	2	◇	
2COM	◇		◇		◇		◇	
ORD	kn	2	$n+1$	1	$n+1$	2	2^n	$n+1$
STFR [9]	◇		◇		◇		2^n	2
PSEP	◇		◇		◇		◇	
REG	kn [4]	2	$n+1$ [8]	1	$n+1$ [13]	2	2^n [13]	2

References

1. Birget, J.: Intersection and union of regular languages and state complexity. Inf. Process. Lett. **43**(4), 185–190 (1992). https://doi.org/10.1016/0020-0190(92)90198-5
2. Bordihn, H., Holzer, M., Kutrib, M.: Determination of finite automata accepting subregular languages. Theor. Comput. Sci. **410**(35), 3209–3222 (2009). https://doi.org/10.1016/j.tcs.2009.05.019
3. Brzozowski, J.A.: Roots of star events. J. ACM **14**(3), 466–477 (1967). https://doi.org/10.1145/321406.321409
4. Domaratzki, M., Okhotin, A.: State complexity of power. Theor. Comput. Sci. **410**(24–25), 2377–2392 (2009). https://doi.org/10.1016/j.tcs.2009.02.025
5. Han, Y.S., Salomaa, K.: Nondeterministic state complexity for suffix-free regular languages. Electron. Proc. Theor. Comput. Sci. **31**, 189–196 (2010). https://doi.org/10.4204/eptcs.31.21
6. Han, Y.S., Salomaa, K., Wood, D.: Nondeterministic state complexity of basic operations for prefix-free regular languages. Fundam. Inform. **90**, 93–106 (2009). https://doi.org/10.3233/FI-2009-0008
7. Hoffmann, S.: State complexity bounds for the commutative closure of group languages. In: Jirásková, G., Pighizzini, G. (eds.) DCFS 2020. LNCS, vol. 12442, pp. 64–77. Springer, Cham (2020). https://doi.org/10.1007/978-3-030-62536-8_6
8. Holzer, M., Kutrib, M.: Nondeterministic descriptional complexity of regular languages. Int. J. Found. Comput. Sci. **14**(6), 1087–1102 (2003). https://doi.org/10.1142/S0129054103002199
9. Holzer, M., Kutrib, M., Meckel, K.: Nondeterministic state complexity of star-free languages. Theor. Comput. Sci. **450**, 68–80 (2012). https://doi.org/10.1016/j.tcs.2012.04.028
10. Hopcroft, J.E., Ullman, J.D.: Introduction to Automata Theory, Languages and Computation. Addison-Wesley, Boston (1979)
11. Hospodár, M.: Power, positive closure, and quotients on convex languages. Theor. Comput. Sci. **870**, 53–74 (2021). https://doi.org/10.1016/j.tcs.2021.02.002
12. Hospodár, M., Jirásková, G., Mlynárčik, P.: Nondeterministic complexity in subclasses of convex languages. Theor. Comput. Sci. **787**, 89–110 (2019). https://doi.org/10.1016/j.tcs.2018.12.027
13. Jirásková, G.: State complexity of some operations on binary regular languages. Theor. Comput. Sci. **330**(2), 287–298 (2005). https://doi.org/10.1016/j.tcs.2004.04.011
14. Jirásková, G., Masopust, T.: Complexity in union-free regular languages. Int. J. Found. Comput. Sci. **22**(07), 1639–1653 (2011). https://doi.org/10.1142/S0129054111008933
15. Rabin, M.O., Scott, D.: Finite automata and their decision problems. IBM J. Res. Dev. **3**(2), 114–125 (1959). https://doi.org/10.1147/rd.32.0114
16. Schützenberger, M.P.: On finite monoids having only trivial subgroups. Inf. Control **8**(2), 190–194 (1965). https://doi.org/10.1016/S0019-9958(65)90108-7
17. Shyr, H.J., Thierrin, G.: Ordered automata and associated languages. Tamkang J. Math. **5**, 9–20 (1974)
18. Shyr, H.J., Thierrin, G.: Power-separating regular languages. Math. Syst. Theory **8**(1), 90–95 (1974). https://doi.org/10.1007/BF01761710

On Simon's Congruence Closure of a String

Sungmin Kim[1], Yo-Sub Han[1(✉)], Sang-Ki Ko[2(✉)], and Kai Salomaa[3]

[1] Department of Computer Science, Yonsei University, 50 Yonsei-Ro, Seodaemun-Gu, Seoul 03722, Republic of Korea
{rena_rio,emmous}@yonsei.ac.kr

[2] Department of Computer Science and Engineering, Kangwon National University, 1 Kangwondaehak-gil, Chuncheon-si, Gangwon-do 24341, Republic of Korea
sangkiko@kangwon.ac.kr

[3] School of Computing, Queen's University, Kingston, ON K7L 3N6, Canada
ksalomaa@cs.queensu.ca

Abstract. Two strings are Simon's $\sim_k$-congruent if they have the same set of subsequences of length at most k. We study the Simon's congruence closure of a string, which is regular by definition. Given a string w over an alphabet Σ, we present an efficient DFA construction that accepts all $\sim_k$-congruent strings with respect to w. We also present lower bounds for the state complexity of the Simon's congruence closure. Finally, we design a polynomial-time algorithm that answers the following open problem: "given a string w over a fixed-sized alphabet, an integer k and a (regular or context-free) language L, decide whether there exists a string $v \in L$ such that $w \sim_k v$." The problem is NP-complete for a variable-sized alphabet.

Keywords: Simon's congruence · State complexity · Finite automata · Shortlex normal forms

1 Introduction

Simon's congruence $\sim_k$ is a relation on strings such that two strings are $\sim_k$-congruent if they have the same set $\mathbb{S}_k$ of subsequences of length at most k [12]. For example, strings $w_1 = ababac$ and $w_2 = aabbac$ are $\sim_2$-congruent since $\mathbb{S}_2(w_1) = \mathbb{S}_2(w_2)$. However, they are not $\sim_3$-congruent because $bab \in \mathbb{S}_3(w_1)$ but $bab \notin \mathbb{S}_3(w_2)$.

Given two strings w_1 and w_2, the MaxSimK problem is to compute the largest k for which $w_1 \sim_k w_2$. After Hébrard [7] presented a linear-time algorithm for MaxSimK over a binary alphabet, it was a long standing open problem to find a generalized optimal algorithm. Garel [5] presented an algorithm based on finite automata running in $O(|\Sigma||w_2|)$ for a special case when $w_2 = w_1 a$ for a symbol a. Fleischer and Kufleitner [3] and Barker et al. [1] suggested using binary search on k by repetitively testing for $w_1 \sim_k w_2$ using a linear decision algorithm. Recently, Gawrychowski et al. [6] proposed the first linear-time optimal

Published by Springer Nature Switzerland AG 2022
Y.-S. Han and G. Vaszil (Eds.): DCFS 2022, LNCS 13439, pp. 127–141, 2022.
https://doi.org/10.1007/978-3-031-13257-5_10

algorithm over general alphabets using novel data structures called Simon-Trees, and settled the MaxSimK problem for two strings. Then, as future work, they proposed the following problems between a string w and a regular or context-free language L.

- LangSimK: Decide whether there exists a string $v \in L$ such that $w \sim_k v$.
- MaxLangSimK: Find the maximum k for which there exists a string $v \in L$ such that $w \sim_k v$.

The motivation for our research is to find an efficient solution for LangSimK and MaxLangSimK. We tackle the problem by constructing a deterministic finite-state automaton (DFA) that recognizes a set $\text{Closure}_k(w)$ of strings that are $\sim_k$-congruent with w. For example, $\text{Closure}_2(aba) = L(a^+ba^+)$. While it is obvious that $\text{Closure}_k(w)$ is regular, the number of possible subsequences $|\mathbb{S}_k(w)|$ is exponential in $|\Sigma|$. Indeed, Karandikar et al. [9] proved that the number of equivalence classes $|\{\text{Closure}_k(w) \mid w \in \Sigma^*\}|$ is in $2^{\Theta(k^{|\Sigma|-1})\log k}$. This leads us to study an efficient automaton construction for the language $\text{Closure}_k(w)$ for a given string w and an integer k.

The Simon's congruence closure is closely related to the permutation operation (the commutative closure). The permutation set of a string w (or a language L) is defined to be the set of all strings w' that have the same Parikh vectors with w (or any string in L). For instance, $\text{Closure}_1(w) = \text{perm}(L)$ holds if $L = \{u \mid u \in \Sigma^* w_1 \Sigma^* w_2 \cdots \Sigma^* w_{|w|} \Sigma^*, w = w_1 w_2 \cdots w_{|w|}, \text{ and } \Sigma = \cup_{i=1}^{|w|}\{w_i\}\}$. Cho et al. [2] studied the state complexity of the permutation operation on finite languages as the permutation operation is not regularity-preserving. Recently, Hoffman [8] extended the result to the permutation operation on *alphabetical pattern constraints (APC)* that are defined as union of the form $\Sigma_0^* a_1 \Sigma_1^* \cdots a_n \Sigma_n^*$ with $\Sigma_0, \ldots, \Sigma_n \subseteq \Sigma$. Another topic related to Simon's congruence is the k-binomial equivalence relation $\equiv_k$ [4,10] that takes the number of occurrences of each subsequence into account when computing the equivalence classes. Freydenberger et al. [4] presented two polynomial algorithms for testing k-binomial equivalence between two strings. In case of $k = 2$, Lejeune et al. [10] proposed an algorithm to enumerate all words in the k-binomial closure of string w.

We present a DFA construction that is polynomial in $|w|$ and k. The main idea of the construction is to reverse a normalization algorithm, which computes the lexicographically smallest string among the shortest strings in $\text{Closure}_k(w)$ [3]. Then, using the resulting DFA A_w for $\text{Closure}_k(w)$, we efficiently solve LangSimK by intersecting A_w and a given regular or context-free language L and checking its emptiness; the intersection is exactly the set of all strings from L that are $\sim_k$-congruent with w. Finally, we efficiently solve MaxLangSimK by repeating the procedure $\log|w|$ times.

2 Preliminaries

Basic Definitions and Notation. Let Σ be a finite alphabet and Σ^* be the set of all strings over Σ. A language is a subset of Σ^*. The cardinality of a finite set S is denoted by $|S|$. Given a string w, we use $|w|$ to denote the length of w. A *nondeterministic finite-state automaton* (NFA) is a machine defined by a tuple $A = (Q, \Sigma, \delta, Q_0, F)$, where Σ is a finite alphabet, Q is a finite set of states, $Q_0 \subseteq Q$ is a set of initial states, $F \subseteq Q$ is a set of final states and δ is a transition function from $Q \times \Sigma$ into 2^Q. The automaton A is *deterministic* (a DFA) if Q_0 is a singleton set and δ is a partial function $Q \times \Sigma \to Q$. The size $|A|$ of a DFA A is the number of states. We use $L(A)$ to denote the language recognized by A.

The state complexity sc(L) of a regular language L is the size of the minimal DFA recognizing L [15]. For more background in automata theory, the reader may refer to the textbook [14].

Positions, Rankers and Coordinates. For a string w of size n, a *true position* of w refers to an integer $i \in [0, n-1]$ that maps to a 0-indexed character $w[i]$ in w. Similarly, an *in-between position* of w is an integer $j \in [0, n]$ that maps to a space at the beginning, between two consecutive characters or at the end of w. The notation for a *substring* $w[i : j]$ uses two in-between positions i and j to represent the sequence of characters between i and j. For example, a string $w = abc$ has 3 true positions such that $w[0] = a, w[1] = b$ and $w[2] = c$, and has 4 in-between positions $\{0, 1, 2, 3\}$. Then, we have $w[1 : 3] = bc$ because the in-between position 1 is the space between a and b and the in-between position 3 is the space after c. A *ranker* is a function that indicates the next occurrence of a character in a given string [11,13]. An *X-ranker* X_σ is a binary operator that takes an in-between position i and a string w as arguments and returns an in-between position $j > i$ such that $w[j-1] = \sigma$ and $w[i : j-1]$ does not contain σ. For instance, when $i = 3$ and $w = abcaacba$, we have $3X_bw = 7$. Symmetrically, a *Y-ranker* Y_σ is a binary operator that takes an in-between position i and a string w as arguments and returns an in-between position $j < i$ such that $w[j] = \sigma$ and $w[j+1 : i]$ does not contain σ. The default position argument for X- and Y-rankers is 0 and n, respectively. We call a sequence of rankers a *ranker chain*. We process a ranker chain from left to right. For example, for $w = aabbaaddc$ and a ranker chain $r = X_bX_aX_dX_d$, we have $r(w) = 0X_bX_aX_dX_dw = 3X_aX_dX_dw = 5X_dX_dw = 7X_dw = 8$. The *length* of a ranker chain is the number of operations. Fleischer and Kufleitner [3] defined the *X-coordinate* $\mathrm{X}(w, i)$ of a true position i to be the length of the shortest X-ranker chain r_X that satisfies $0r_Xw = i + 1$. Similarly, they defined the *Y-coordinate* $\mathrm{Y}(w, i)$ of a true position i is the length of the shortest Y-ranker chain r_Y such that $nr_Yw = i$. The pair of X- and Y-coordinates forms an *attribute* of a true position i. For $w = aabbaaddc$ and a true position 4, the shortest X-ranker chain returning 5 is X_bX_a and the shortest Y-ranker chain returning 4 is Y_aY_a. The attribute of position 4 is $(2, 2)$.

Simon's Congruence. A *subsequence* u of a string w is a string that satisfies $u = w[i_1]w[i_2]\cdots w[i_k]$ for positions $0 \leq i_1 < i_2 < \cdots < i_k \leq |w| - 1$. Let $\mathbb{S}_k(w)$ denote the set of all subsequences u of w such that $|u| \leq k$. We say that two strings w_1 and w_2 are *$\sim_k$-congruent* if $\mathbb{S}_k(w_1) = \mathbb{S}_k(w_2)$. The congruence relation $\sim_k$ is called *Simon's Congruence.* Now, for a string w and an integer k, we can define the Simon's congruence closure, $\text{Closure}_k(w)$, of w to be a set of strings that are $\sim_k$-congruent with w; namely, $\text{Closure}_k(w) = \{x \in \Sigma^* \mid x \sim_k w\}$. We define the shortlex normal form string $\text{ShortLex}_k(w)$ to be the lexicographically smallest string among the shortest strings in $\text{Closure}_k(w)$. Fleischer and Kufleitner [3] presented an $O(|\Sigma||w|)$-time algorithm to obtain $\text{ShortLex}_k(w)$, and Barker et al. [1] designed an improved $O(|w|)$-time algorithm. The core idea of both algorithms is to repeatedly remove positions that satisfy $\text{X}(w, i) + \text{Y}(w, i) > k + 1$. When no more eliminations are possible, the algorithm radix-sorts consecutive positions that have the same attribute such that the sum of X- and Y-coordinates equal $k+1$. The result is the lexicographically smallest string among the shortest strings in $\text{Closure}_k(w)$. We call this procedure the *shortlex normalization algorithm*. The following is a key property for the correctness of the algorithm.

Proposition 1 ([3]). *Let* $w = u\sigma v$ *with* $|u| = i$ *and* $\sigma \in \Sigma$. *If* $\text{X}(w, i)+\text{Y}(w, i) > k + 1$, *then* $u\sigma v \sim_k uv$.

If k is clear in the context, we use the shorthand notation w_s to indicate $\text{ShortLex}_k(w)$. We use w_p to denote an arbitrary permutation of w_s that is $\sim_k$-congruent with w_s. Thus, the shortlex normalization algorithm can be considered as a process that first converts w into w_p by deleting unnecessary symbols in w, then transforms w_p into w_s by relocating symbols in w_p to obtain the lexicographically smallest string.

3 Main Contributions

Our contributions are three-fold as follows. First, we show that given a string w, the state complexity of a DFA recognizing $\text{Closure}_k(w)$ is bounded from above by a linear function of the length $|w_s|$ of the shortlex normal form string of w. We establish the bound by presenting an efficient DFA construction. Recall that $|w_s| \leq |w|$ and we can obtain w_s from w in $O(|w|)$ time [1]. Second, we consider the lower bound for the state complexity, and demonstrate that the lower bound is linear in $|w_s|$ for a fixed-size alphabet but is exponential for a variable-sized alphabet. Lastly, we provide polynomial-time algorithms for the two open problems LangSimK and MaxLangSimK in Gawrychowski et al. [6] using our DFA construction for a fixed-sized alphabet. We also prove that, for a variable-sized alphabet, the problem is NP-complete.

3.1 Vectors and Blocks

Our first ingredient is *vectors*. Intuitively, vectors represent potential X- and Y-coordinates if a character is inserted in the middle of a given string. This is because we consider inserting characters between existing characters as long as it does not change the set of subsequences of length up to k. We give formal definitions of potential X- or Y-coordinates, and vectors.

Definition 1. *For a string w, an in-between position i and a character $\sigma \in \Sigma$, let $z = w[0:i]\sigma w[i:n]$ be a string obtained by inserting σ at position i. We define* the potential attribute *of i to be $(\hat{X}(w,i,\sigma), \hat{Y}(w,i,\sigma))$, where $\hat{X}(w,i,\sigma) = \mathrm{X}(z,i)$ and $\hat{Y}(w,i,\sigma) = \mathrm{Y}(z,i)$ are the* potential X- and Y-coordinate, *respectively.*

With the potential attributes, we can define Σ-indexed arrays of potential attributes for a specific string w and in-between position i:

Definition 2. *Given a string w over Σ and an in-between position i, we define the X-vector $\overrightarrow{X}(w,i)$ and the Y-vector $\overrightarrow{Y}(w,i)$ to be the array of potential X- and Y-coordinates defined as follows:*

$$\overrightarrow{X}(w,i)[\sigma] = \hat{X}(w,i,\sigma) \text{ and } \overrightarrow{Y}(w,i)[\sigma] = \hat{Y}(w,i,\sigma).$$

Additionally, k-bound X- and Y-vectors $\overrightarrow{X}_k(w,i)$ and $\overrightarrow{Y}_k(w,i)$ are X- and Y-vectors with each element capped at $k+1$:

$$\overrightarrow{X}_k(w,i)[\sigma] = \min(k+1, \overrightarrow{X}(w,i)[\sigma]),$$
$$\overrightarrow{Y}_k(w,i)[\sigma] = \min(k+1, \overrightarrow{Y}(w,i)[\sigma]).$$

Example 1. Consider a string $w = abcababc$. For an in-between position $i = 5$ and a character $\sigma = a$, we have $z = w[0:i]\sigma w[i:n] = abcabaabc$. Since $X_c X_b X_a$ is one of the shortest X-rankers that reach the in-between position $i+1$ on z and $Y_a Y_a$ is one of the shortest Y-rankers that reach the in-between position i on z, we have that $\overrightarrow{X}(w,5)[a] = \hat{X}(w,5,a) = 3$ and $\overrightarrow{Y}(w,5)[a] = \hat{Y}(w,5,a) = 2$.

The k-bound X- and Y-vectors $\overrightarrow{X}_k$ and $\overrightarrow{Y}_k$ serve as states in our DFA construction. At each input, the character inserting mechanism checks whether the sum of potential X- and Y-coordinates exceeds $k+1$ for that input. This reverses the deletion process of the shortlex normalization algorithm. In other words, X- and Y-vectors help restore w from w_p with the character insertion. Algorithm 1 shows the relationship between bound vectors.

Algorithm 1. $\mathrm{Iter}(x \in \{1, 2, \ldots, k+1\}^{|\Sigma|}, \sigma \in \Sigma)$

1: $x[\sigma] \leftarrow \mathtt{min}(x[\sigma]+1, k+1)$
2: **for** $\sigma' \in \Sigma$ **do**
3: $\quad x[\sigma'] \leftarrow \mathtt{min}(x[\sigma], x[\sigma'])$
4: **end for**
5: **return** x

The function $\mathrm{Iter}(x,\sigma)$ simulates an iteration of the X-coordinate computation function of the shortlex normalization algorithm, with the exception that each vector cell is capped at $k+1$ and no X-coordinate is remembered. Thus,

$$\mathrm{Iter}(\overrightarrow{X}_k(w,i), w[i]) = \overrightarrow{X}_k(w,i+1) \text{ and } \mathrm{Iter}(\overrightarrow{Y}_k(w,i+1), w[i]) = \overrightarrow{Y}_k(w,i)$$

for $i \in [0, n-1]$. Also, each call of Iter() uses the min operation exactly $|\Sigma|+1$ times and, thus, the function takes $\Theta(|\Sigma|)$ time.

Our second ingredient is *saturated blocks*. We use saturated blocks to indicate maximal substrings in the shortest string w_p such that any permutation within a saturated block does not result in the change in the set of subsequences.

Definition 3. *We define a* block B *of a string* w_p *to be a maximal range of true positions such that for positions* $i, j \in B$*, we have* $\mathrm{X}(w_p, i) = \mathrm{X}(w_p, j)$ *and* $\mathrm{Y}(w_p, i) = \mathrm{Y}(w_p, j)$*. A block* B *is* saturated *if* $\mathrm{X}(w_p, i) + \mathrm{Y}(w_p, i) = k+1$ *for positions* $i \in B$*.*

Checking for saturated blocks and computing Y-vectors for all permutations within each block of $\mathrm{ShortLex}_k(w)$ reverses the sorting process of the shortlex normalization algorithm. In other words, the saturated blocks help identify all permutations w_p that map to w_s when the characters in each saturated block are relocated in lexicographical order. Note that a saturated block remains a saturated block when permuted. From the definition of a saturated block, we observe the following property.

Observation 1. *Each symbol in* Σ *occurs at most once in a saturated block.*

Next, we use saturated blocks to establish conditions that yield the same vectors. The following statement shows that there can be multiple permutations that yield the same vector.

Lemma 1. *Given a string* w_p *and an integer* k*, let* $w_p = uv_1v_2y$ *such that positions for* v_1v_2 *form a saturated block. Let strings* x_1 *and* x_2 *be permutations of* v_1 *and* v_2*, respectively. Then,* $\overrightarrow{X}(uv_1v_2y, |uv_1|) = \overrightarrow{X}(ux_1x_2y, |ux_1|)$ *and* $\overrightarrow{Y}(uv_1v_2y, |uv_1|) = \overrightarrow{Y}(ux_1x_2y, |ux_1|)$*.*

Proof. For any $\sigma \in \Sigma$, let $z_v = uv_1\sigma v_2y$ and $z_x = ux_1\sigma x_2y$. Also, let RX_σ be one of the shortest X-ranker chains that satisfies $RX_\sigma z_v = |uv_1|+1$. We show that there exists an X-ranker chain of length equal to RX_σ and yields $|ux_1|+1$ on string z_x. Showing the above proves $\hat{X}(uv_1v_2y, |uv_1|, \sigma) = \hat{X}(ux_1x_2y, |ux_1|, \sigma)$ as the permutation relation between v_1 and x_1 is symmetric. First, if $Rz_v \in [0, |u|]$, then σ does not occur in string $u[Rz_v : |u|]v_1$. Thus, σ does not occur in string $u[Rz_x : |u|]x_1$ as well. It follows that RX_σ is an X-ranker chain that yields $|ux_1|+1$ on string z_x. Otherwise, the X-ranker chain R yields $Rz_v \in [|u|+1, |u|+|v_1|]$. If σ does not occur in v_1, then σ does not occur in x_1. Thus, RX_σ yields $|ux_1|+1$ on string z_x. If σ does occur in v_1, then recall that all positions in v_1 have the same attributes by the definition of a saturated block. Hence, we may assume that $R = R_1X_\sigma$ for an X-ranker chain R_1 since the length of RX_σ stays minimal. We have $R_1z_x = R_1z_v \in [0, |u|]$ by Observation 1, while there exists a single σ in $z_v[R_1z_v : |uv_1|]$. Note that σ also occurs only once in $z_x[R_1z_x : |ux_1|]$. Thus, RX_σ is indeed an X-ranker chain that yields $|ux_1|+1$ on string z_x. We have shown that $\hat{X}(uv_1v_2y, |uv_1|, \sigma) = \hat{X}(ux_1x_2y, |ux_1|, \sigma)$. Since the equation holds for all $\sigma \in \Sigma$, we have $\overrightarrow{X}(uv_1v_2y, |uv_1|) = \overrightarrow{X}(ux_1x_2y, |ux_1|)$. It follows from symmetry that $\overrightarrow{Y}(uv_1v_2y, |uv_1|) = \overrightarrow{Y}(ux_1x_2y, |ux_1|)$.

□

Now we define the set of all Y-vectors that can be produced by all possible permutations w_p of w_s.

Definition 4. *The set $\mathbb{Y}(w_s)$ for a shortlex form string w_s is the set of Y-vectors $\overrightarrow{Y}(w_p, i)$ for all in-between positions $i \in [0, |w_s|]$ and all permutations w_p of w_s such that $w_s \sim_k w_p$. Namely,*

$$\mathbb{Y}(w_s) = \{\overrightarrow{Y}(w_p, i) \mid |w_p| = |w_s|, w_p \sim_k w_s, i = 0, 1, \ldots, |w_s|\}.$$

By Lemma 1, for positions $0 \leq i \leq |w_s|$, multiple permutations of w_s map to a single element of $\mathbb{Y}(w_s)$. From a topological perspective, all Y-vectors in $\mathbb{Y}(w_s)$ form a directed acyclic graph when connected using the Iter() function. Only one Y-vector $[1, 1, \ldots, 1]$ has an in-degree of 0. Moreover, only Y-vectors for a saturated block may have an out-degree greater than 1. Finally, Lemma 1 proves that the graph should converge into a single Y-vector at the end of the saturated block. From these results, we obtain the following bound on $|\mathbb{Y}(w_s)|$.

Lemma 2. $|\mathbb{Y}(w_s)|$ *is at most* $\frac{2^{|\Sigma|}|w_s|}{|\Sigma|} + 1$.

Proof. For a string w_s in shortlex normal form, let a_i be the number of true positions in w_s that is a member of a block of length i, for $1 \leq i \leq |\Sigma|$. We can rewrite

$$2^{|\Sigma|} \times \frac{|w_s|}{|\Sigma|} = 2^{|\Sigma|} \frac{\sum_{i=1}^{|\Sigma|} a_i}{|\Sigma|} = \sum_{i=1}^{|\Sigma|} \frac{2^{|\Sigma|}}{|\Sigma|} a_i.$$

On the other hand, we have

$$|\mathbb{Y}(w_s)| - 1 \leq \sum_{i=1}^{|\Sigma|} ((2^i - 1) \times \frac{a_i}{i}) \leq \sum_{i=1}^{|\Sigma|} \frac{2^i}{i} a_i,$$

where the first inequality comes from the assumption that all blocks are saturated blocks. Finally, by subtracting the two results, we obtain

$$\sum_{i=1}^{|\Sigma|} (\frac{2^{|\Sigma|}}{|\Sigma|} - \frac{2^i}{i}) a_i \geq 0$$

since $\frac{2^{|\Sigma|}}{|\Sigma|} \geq \frac{2^i}{i}$ and $a_i \geq 0$ for all $i \geq 1$. Thus, we have $|\mathbb{Y}(w_s)| - 1 \leq \frac{2^{|\Sigma|}|w_s|}{|\Sigma|}$. On the other hand, there exists a shortlex form string w_s with $|\mathbb{Y}(w_s)| \in \Omega(\frac{2^{|\Sigma|}|w_s|}{|\Sigma|})$. Consider string $w = (\sigma_1 \sigma_2 \ldots \sigma_{|\Sigma|})^k$ for $\Sigma = \{\sigma_1, \sigma_2, \ldots, \sigma_{|\Sigma|}\}$. For each true position $ik + j \in [0, |w| - 1]$ with $j \in [0, |\Sigma| - 1]$, we have $\mathrm{X}(w, ik + j) = i$ and $\mathrm{Y}(w, ik+j) = (k+1) - i$, thus every position satisfies $\mathrm{X}(w, ik+j) + \mathrm{Y}(w, ik+j) = k+1$. Hence $w = w_s$. Note that we have $\frac{|w_s|}{|\Sigma|}$ saturated blocks of length $|\Sigma|$ and, thus, we have $\frac{(2^{|\Sigma|}-1)|w_s|}{|\Sigma|} + 1$ unique Y-vectors for w_s. Therefore, the bound is tight and $|\mathbb{Y}(w_s)| \in \Theta\left(\frac{2^{|\Sigma|}|w_s|}{|\Sigma|}\right)$. □

Similarly, we can compute $\mathbb{Y}(w_s)$ in time linear in $|w_s|$ as follows.

Lemma 3. *Given a positive integer k and a string w_s in shortlex normal form with respect to k, we can compute $\mathbb{Y}(w_s)$ in $O(2^{|\Sigma|}|w_s|)$ time.*

Proof. For every Y-vector in $\mathbb{Y}(w_s)$, each cell does not contain a value greater than $k+1$ because w_s is in shortlex normal form. Thus, all Y-vectors in $\mathbb{Y}(w_s)$ can be treated as a k-bound Y-vector. We prove by induction on the in-between positions of w_s.

Basis: position $i = |w_s|$. We have $\overrightarrow{Y}_k(w_s, i) = \overrightarrow{Y}_k(w_p, i) = [1, 1, \ldots, 1] \in \{1, 2, \ldots, k+1\}^{|\Sigma|}$ for all w_p of w_s. Note that the starting Y-vector is unique.

Induction: position $i < |w_s|$ and we have computed all the values for positions greater than i for all w_p of w_s. We can use the Iter() function to obtain the Y-vectors for position i from the Y-vectors for position $i+1$. Recall that the Iter() function takes $O(|\Sigma|)$ time. If the Y-vector for position i is singular, we simply use $\overrightarrow{Y}_k(w_s, i) = \text{Iter}(\overrightarrow{Y}_k(w_s, i+1), w[i])$. Otherwise, i must belong to a saturated block. Based on Lemma 1, we can use dynamic programming for each combination of characters to fetch a Y-vector for which corresponding character set is one character shorter. Thus, each Y-vector can be computed in $\Theta(|\Sigma|)$ time with the Iter() function and there are $\Theta\left(\frac{2^{|\Sigma|}|w_s|}{|\Sigma|}\right)$ unique Y-vectors by Lemma 2. Thus, the overall time to compute all Y-vectors is bound by $\Theta(2^{|\Sigma|}|w_s|)$. □

Finally, we bound the length of $\text{ShortLex}_k(w)$ in terms of k and $|\Sigma|$ as follows.

Lemma 4. $|\text{ShortLex}_k(w)| \leq \binom{k+|\Sigma|}{|\Sigma|} - 1$.

Proof. Given an alphabet $\Sigma = \{\sigma_1, \sigma_2, \ldots, \sigma_{|\Sigma|}\}$ and an integer k, let i and j be integers for $i \in [1, |\Sigma|]$ and $j \in [0, k]$. We define a string $M(i, j)$ by the following recurrence relation:

- if $i = 1$, then $M(i, j) = (\sigma_1)^j$.
- if $i > 1$, then $M(i, 0) = \lambda$ and $M(i, j) = M(i-1, j)\sigma_i M(i, j-1)$.

Thus,

- $|M(1, j)| = j$
- $|M(i, 0)| = 0$
- $|M(i, j)| = |M(i-1, j)| + |M(i, j-1)| + 1$

Consider the string $w = M(|\Sigma|, k)$. Starting with X-vector $[1, 1, \ldots, 1]$, we have $\frac{(k+|\Sigma|)\ldots(k+1)}{|\Sigma|!} - 1$ calls of Iter() until we reach X-vector $[k+1, k+1, \ldots, k+1]$ at the end of string w. At this point, the sum of the X- and Y-coordinates of the next input will exceed $k+1$ because the X-coordinate alone equals $k+1$. Moreover, the string exploits the fact that we can push the maximum values in an X-vector up to $k+1$ before they are capped by another lower value. This extensive search of possible X-vectors ensures there are no shortlex form strings under the relation $\sim_k$ which are longer than w. Solving the recurrence relation, we have $|M(|\Sigma|, k)| = \binom{k+|\Sigma|}{|\Sigma|} - 1$. Thus, $|\text{ShortLex}_k(w)| \in O\left(\binom{k+|\Sigma|}{|\Sigma|}\right)$. Note that the bound becomes $O\left(\frac{(k+|\Sigma|)\ldots(k+1)}{|\Sigma|!}\right) = O\left(k^{|\Sigma|}\right)$ when $|\Sigma|$ is constant. □

We use the bounds for $|\mathbb{Y}(w_s)|$ and $|\text{ShortLex}_k(w)|$ to obtain the bounds for the DFA state complexity and design polynomial-time algorithms for LangSimK and MaxLangSimK.

3.2 DFA Construction

From the shortlex normalization algorithm, we know that a true position of a string $x \in \text{Closure}_k(w)$ is either an eliminated position or a permuted position. For permuted positions, the DFA state's Y-vector component has an out-transition to the next Y-vector if the first character of the unread part of w_p matches the input. For eliminated positions, on the other hand, the state's Y-vector component has an out-transition to the same Y-vector if the sum of the potential X- and Y-coordinates exceeds $k + 1$. The X-vector component of each state is always updated following the Iter() function. This helps us to keep track of the current k-bound X- and Y-vector and check if any insertions are allowed. Given a string w_s in shortlex normal form, we construct a DFA $A = (Q, \Sigma, \delta, s, F)$, where

- $Q = K^{|\Sigma|} \times \mathbb{Y}(w_s)$ where $K = \{1, 2, \ldots, k+1\}$. For notational convenience, we regard state q as a two-dimensional array for which $q[0]$ represents a k-bound X-vector and $q[1]$ represents a Y-vector in $\mathbb{Y}(w_s)$.
- δ consists of the following transitions:
  1. **Consuming transitions.** For all $\sim_k$-congruent permutations w_p of w_s and all true positions $i = 0, 1, \ldots, |w_s| - 1$, any state $q = [x, \overrightarrow{Y}(w_p, i)]$ has a transition $\delta(q, w_p[i]) = [\text{Iter}(x, w_p[i]), \overrightarrow{Y}(w_p, i+1)]$. Note that the transitions are deterministic, since $\overrightarrow{Y}(w_{p_1}, i) = \overrightarrow{Y}(w_{p_2}, i)$ and $w_{p_1}[i] = w_{p_2}[i]$ implies $\overrightarrow{Y}(w_{p_1}, i+1) = \overrightarrow{Y}(w_{p_2}, i+1)$. These transitions are called "consuming transitions" because they "consume" characters in w_p.
  2. **Inserting transitions.** For all states $q = [x, \overrightarrow{Y}(w_p, i)]$ and all characters $\sigma \in \Sigma$ that satisfy the following conditions:
     - $q[0][\sigma] + q[1][\sigma] > k + 1$ and
     - $\delta(q, \sigma)$ is not defined as a consuming transition,

     we have $\delta(q, \sigma) = [\text{Iter}(x, \sigma), \overrightarrow{Y}(w_p, i)]$. These transitions are called "inserting transitions" because they "insert" characters into w_p to make some string z such that $w_p \sim_k z$.
  3. **Sink transitions.** Any other undefined transitions go to the implied sink state.
- $s = [\overrightarrow{X}_k(w_s, 0), \overrightarrow{Y}(w_s, 0)]$.
- $F = \{q \in Q \mid q[1] = \overrightarrow{Y}(w_s, |w_s|)\}$.

Example 2. For our running example $w = abcababc$ and $k = 3$, the X- and Y-coordinates are written above each character as follows:

$$\begin{array}{cccccccc} 1\,3 & 1\,3 & 1\,2 & 2\,2 & 2\,2 & 3\,1 & 3\,1 & 2\,1 \\ a & b & c & a & b & a & b & c \end{array}$$

Note that w is already in shortlex normal form. Observe that the true positions can be partitioned into five blocks $B_0 = \{0,1\}, B_1 = \{2\}, B_2 = \{3,4\}, B_3 = \{5,6\}$, and $B_4 = \{7\}$. Blocks B_0, B_2 and B_3 are saturated blocks since the sum of X- and Y-coordinates equal 4. We compute $\mathbb{Y}(w_s)$ using the algorithm in the proof of Lemma 3 and obtain the following result.

$$\begin{array}{cc} & \begin{array}{cccccccccccc} 0 & 1 & 1' & 2 & 3 & 4 & 4' & 5 & 6 & 6' & 7 & 8 \end{array} \\ \mathbb{Y}(w_s) = \begin{array}{c} a \\ b \\ c \end{array} & \begin{bmatrix} 4 & 3 & 4 & 3 & 3 & 2 & 3 & 2 & 1 & 2 & 1 & 1 \\ 4 & 4 & 3 & 3 & 3 & 3 & 2 & 2 & 2 & 1 & 1 & 1 \\ 3 & 3 & 3 & 3 & 2 & 2 & 2 & 2 & 2 & 2 & 2 & 1 \end{bmatrix} \end{array}$$

The columns represent Y-vectors. The labels on the top row are the in-between positions, and labels with a prime indicate the Y-vectors obtained from the $\sim_k$-congruent permutation of w. This example has a single alternative Y-vector for each saturated block because every saturated block has at most two elements.

Given a string w, let A_w be the resulting DFA of the proposed construction in Sect. 3.2 for $\text{Closure}_k(w)$. The construction guarantees that X-vector transitions are always simulated by the Iter() function. From the Y-vector perspective, on the other hand, the DFA A_X in Fig. 1 is a cross-section of A_w representing the Y-vectors and transitions among them. The DFA A_X is a cross-section in the sense that A_w consists of $(k+1)^{|\Sigma|}$ copied layers of A_X's states, with each layer representing a k-bound X-vector. Moreover, transitions in A_w are defined between states in different layers instead of states within the same cross-section DFA layer. A state in A_w has a consuming out-transition whenever the corresponding state in A_X has an out-transition to a different state in A_X (blue transitions in Fig. 1). On the other hand, a state in A_w has an inserting out-transition only when the corresponding state in A_X has a self-looping transition (red transitions in Fig. 1) and the sum of potential coordinates for an input symbol exceeds $k+1$. Note that inserting transitions for a character c in Fig. 1 do not exist because $|\text{ShortLex}_k(w)|_c < k$. Each state has subscripts that match each column label.

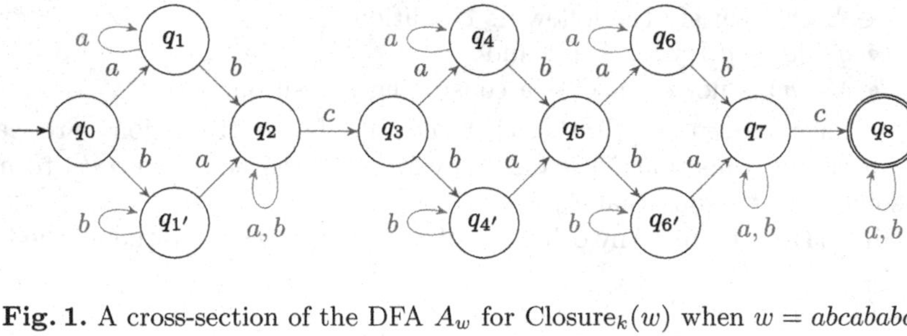

Fig. 1. A cross-section of the DFA A_w for $\text{Closure}_k(w)$ when $w = abcababc$.

We can use the cross-section DFA A_X along with a k-bound X-vector starting at $[1, 1, \ldots, 1]$ to simulate computations in A_w. For each input character σ, the

k-bound X-vector $\overrightarrow{X}_k$ is updated with the Iter() function. Before this update, however, we first check whether the current state in A_X has a valid transition reading σ. If the transition in A_X is defined between two different states, then we move on to the next state in A_X while we consume a character from some w_p using a consuming transition in A_w. If the transition is self-looping in A_X and the k-bound X-vector and Y-vector's sum for σ exceeds $k+1$, then we stay in the same state in A_X while we use an inserting transition in A_w. If both conditions fail, then A_w rejects the string.

We next prove the correctness of the DFA construction.

Lemma 5. *The constructed DFA A recognizes* $\text{Closure}_k(w)$.

Proof. We prove the statement by showing the equality between $L(A)$ and $\text{Closure}_k(w)$.

First, we show that if $x \in L(A)$, then $x \in \text{Closure}_k(w)$. If $x \in L(A)$, then there exists a computation $(s, x) \vdash_A \cdots \vdash_A (f, \lambda)$, where $f \in F$. Note that no sink transition can be used in this computation since the sink state is not a final state. For a configuration in this computation, let i and c be the number of inserting and consuming transitions used until arriving at that configuration, respectively. Since each single-step computation computes Iter() for $q[0]$ and the automaton is a DFA, the $(i+c)^{\text{th}}$ state q satisfies $q[0] = \overrightarrow{X}_k(x, i+c)$. Moreover, for all consuming transitions used, let w_p be the permutation of $\text{ShortLex}_k(w)$ used in generating those transitions. By construction, q satisfies $q[1] = \overrightarrow{Y}(w_p, c)$. Performing induction on the reverse order of computation steps, we prove that the property $x \sim_k x[0 : i + c]w_p[c : |w_p|]$ remains invariant.

Basis: Start from the last configuration (f, λ). Then $q = f$, $i + c = |x|$ and $c = |w_p|$. Thus, $x[0 : i + c]w_p[c : |w_p|] = x \sim_k x$ since $\sim_k$ is reflexive.

Induction: Let $(q_1, \sigma z)$ be the current configuration and $(q_1, \sigma z) \vdash_A (q_2, z)$ be a single-step computation in the given computation sequence. If the transition used is a consuming transition, then $q_1[1] = \overrightarrow{Y}_k(w_p, c)$ and $q_2[1] = \overrightarrow{Y}_k(w_p, c+1)$. Moreover, by construction, we have that $w_p[c] = x[i + c] = \sigma$. So, we have $x[0 : i + c]w_p[c : |w_p|] = x[0 : i + c + 1]w_p[c + 1 : |w_p|] \sim_k x$ by the induction hypothesis. Otherwise, if the transition used is an inserting transition, we have that $\text{X}(x[0 : i+c+1]w_p[c : |w_p|], i+c) + \text{Y}(x[0 : i+c+1]w_p[c : |w_p|], i+c) > k+1$. By Proposition 1, we have $x[0 : i + c]w_p[c : |w_p|] \sim_k x[0 : i + c + 1]w_p[c : |w_p|]$, and by the induction hypothesis, $x[0 : i + c]w_p[c : |w_p|] \sim_k x$.

End condition: Eventually the current configuration must become (s, x), with $i = j = 0$. Then, the invariant $x[0 : i+c]w_p[c : |w_p|] \sim_k x$ implies $w_p \sim_k x$. Therefore, it is guaranteed that a string accepted by A should exist in $\text{Closure}_k(w)$.

Next, we prove the other direction; if $x \in \text{Closure}_k(w)$, then $x \in L(A)$. From a string $x \in \text{Closure}_k(w)$, by applying the repeated deletion process of the shortlex normalization algorithm, we can obtain a shortest string $x_p \sim_k x$. Without loss of generality, assume that we erase the last occurrences of consecutive same symbols. For example, if we can erase two a's in string $bbaaaabb$, we erase true positions 4 and 5 rather than erasing true positions 2 and 3. We show that x is accepted by A by induction on the computation steps and proving that the property $q = [\overrightarrow{X}_k(x, i+c), \overrightarrow{Y}(x_p, c)]$ remains invariant, where i is the number of inserting transitions used and c is the number of consuming transitions used.

Basis: Start from the initial configuration (s, x). Since no transitions were used until now, $i = c = 0$. By construction, we have $s = [\overrightarrow{X}_k(x, 0), \overrightarrow{Y}(x_p, 0)]$.

Induction: Let $(q, x[i + c : |x|])$ be the current configuration. By the induction hypothesis, we have $q = [\overrightarrow{X}_k(x, i+c), \overrightarrow{Y}(x_p, c)]$. Assume that true position $i+c$ of x was not erased in obtaining x_p. By definition, there exists a consuming transition that reads $x[i + c] = x_p[c]$ and goes to state $q' = [\overrightarrow{X}_k(x, i + c + 1), \overrightarrow{Y}(x_p, c + 1)]$ because x_p is a permutation of w_s. Thus, the target property remains invariant. Otherwise, true position $i + c$ of x was erased in x_p. Since $x[0 : i + c]x_p[c : |x_p|] \sim_k x[0 : i + c + 1]x_p[c : |x_p|]$, we have that $\overrightarrow{X}_k(x[0 : i + c]x_p[c : |x_p|], i + c)[x[i + c]] + \overrightarrow{Y}(x[0 : i + c]x_p[c : |x_p|], i + c)[x[i + c]] > k + 1$ by Proposition 1. Since the consuming transition case was handled previously and we assumed that elimination of consecutive characters happen as late as possible, there must exist an inserting transition that reads $x[i + c]$ and goes to state $q' = [\overrightarrow{X}_k(x, i + c + 1), \overrightarrow{Y}(x_p, c)]$. Thus, the target property remains invariant.

End condition: The computation will use exactly $|x|$ transitions since there are no λ-transitions in a DFA. Also, the computation will use exactly $|x_p|$ consuming transitions since the induction implies that consuming transitions will be used if and only if a true position has not been erased in x_p. Finally, the induction shows that sink transitions are not used. Thus, after reading the last input character, the computation will halt at configuration (f, λ) where $f = [\overrightarrow{X}_k(x, |x|), \overrightarrow{Y}(x_p, |x_p|)] \in F$. Thus, DFA A accepts all strings in $\text{Closure}_k(w)$. This concludes the proof that $L(A) = \text{Closure}_k(w)$. □

3.3 State Complexity for $\text{Closure}_k(w)$

We investigate the state complexity $\text{sc}(\text{Closure}_k(w))$ of a DFA recognizing the Simon's congruence closure of a string w. First, we present an upper bound of the state complexity.

Theorem 1. *Given a string w over Σ and an integer k, the minimal DFA for* $\text{Closure}_k(w)$ *needs at most*

$$O\left(\frac{(2k+2)^{|\Sigma|} \times \binom{k+|\Sigma|}{|\Sigma|}}{|\Sigma|}\right)$$

states.

Proof. From the DFA construction in Sect. 3.2, we know that the resulting DFA has exactly $(k+1)^{|\Sigma|}|\mathbb{Y}(w_s)|$ states. Since $|\mathbb{Y}(w_s)|$ is at most $\frac{2^{|\Sigma|}|\text{ShortLex}_k(w)|}{|\Sigma|}+1$ (from Lemma 2) and $|\text{ShortLex}_k(w)|$ is no more than $\binom{k+|\Sigma|}{|\Sigma|}-1$ (from Lemma 4), we have

$$(k+1)^{|\Sigma|}|\mathbb{Y}(w_s)| \in O\left(\frac{(2k+2)^{|\Sigma|}\binom{k+|\Sigma|}{|\Sigma|}}{|\Sigma|}\right).$$

□

Next, we present two lower bounds for $\text{sc}(\text{Closure}_k(w))$. We obtain the first lower bound from the fact that the DFA should be able to recognize all permutations of a saturated block of length at most $|\Sigma|$, and the second lower bound from the distinguishability of vectors in $\mathbb{Y}(w_s)$.

Lemma 6. *Given a string w over Σ, the minimal DFA recognizing* $\text{Closure}_k(w)$ *needs at least $(k+1)^{|\Sigma|}$ states in the worst-case.*

Proof. By the definition of $\text{Closure}_k(w)$, the following equation always holds for a string $w = (\sigma_1\sigma_2\ldots\sigma_{|\Sigma|})^k$ of length $k|\Sigma|$ over $\Sigma = \{\sigma_1, \sigma_2, \ldots, \sigma_{|\Sigma|}\}$:

$$\text{Closure}_k(w) = \text{perm}(\sigma_1^k\sigma_2^k\ldots\sigma_{|\Sigma|}^k),$$

where $\text{perm}(z) = \{u \in \Sigma^* \mid |u|_\sigma = |z|_\sigma \forall\sigma \in \Sigma\}$. It is already known that we need at least $(k+1)^{|\Sigma|}$ states to recognize $\text{Closure}_k(w)$ from the recent result by Hoffmann [8] on the state complexity of the permutation operation on alphabetical pattern constraints. □

Lemma 7. *Given a string w over Σ, the minimal DFA recognizing* $\text{Closure}_k(w)$ *needs at least $|\mathbb{Y}(w_s)|$ states. Moreover, $|\mathbb{Y}(w_s)|$ is at most $\frac{2^{|\Sigma|}}{|\Sigma|} \times \binom{k+|\Sigma|}{|\Sigma|}$.*

Proof. Let $L = \text{Closure}_k(w)$ and w_{p_1}, w_{p_2} be two different permutations of $\text{ShortLex}_k(w)$. For two positions i and j, we have $\overrightarrow{Y}(w_{p_1}, i) \neq \overrightarrow{Y}(w_{p_2}, j)$ if and only if $w_{p_1}[: i]$ is not a permutation of $w_{p_2}[: j]$. Without loss of generality, we can decompose $w_{p_1} = xz_1$ and $w_{p_2} = yz_2$ such that $|z_1| \leq |z_2|$ and x is not a permutation of y. Then, $xz_1 \in \text{Closure}_k(w)$ but $yz_1 \notin \text{Closure}_k(w)$ because:

- if $|z_1| = |z_2|$, then w_{p_1} and w_{p_2} are cut in the middle of a saturated block B. Since x is not a permutation of y, there must exist characters that are included in portions of y and z_1 that correspond to B. Thus, yz_1 is not a permutation of w_{p_1}. Since $|yz_1| = |w_{p_1}|$ and yz_1 is not a permutation of $\text{ShortLex}_k(w)$, we have $yz_1 \notin \text{Closure}_k(w)$.
- if $|z_1| < |z_2|$, then $|yz_1| < |\text{ShortLex}_k(w)|$. By the definition of shortlex normal form, there does not exist a shorter string than $\text{ShortLex}_k(w)$ in $\text{Closure}_k(w)$. Hence $yz_1 \notin \text{Closure}_k(w)$.

This implies $\overrightarrow{Y}(xz_1, |x|) \neq \overrightarrow{Y}(yz_2, |y|) \Rightarrow x \not\equiv_L y$, where $\equiv_L$ is the Nerode equivalence. Thus, the number of states in the minimal DFA recognizing L is bounded from below by $\Omega(|\mathbb{Y}(w_s)|)$. Using Lemmas 2 and 4, we can bound the cardinality of $|\mathbb{Y}(w_s)|$ by $O\left(\frac{2^{|\Sigma|}}{|\Sigma|} \times \binom{k+|\Sigma|}{|\Sigma|}\right)$. □

Note that the bound in Lemma 6 is independent of the length of w whereas the bound in Lemma 7 depends on the length of the shortlex form of w. The bound is tight if $k = 1$. From these two lemmas, we establish the following lower bound.

Theorem 2. *Given a string w over Σ and an integer k, the minimal DFA for $\text{Closure}_k(w)$ needs at least*

$$\max\left\{(k+1)^{|\Sigma|} \text{ or } \frac{2^{|\Sigma|}|\text{ShortLex}_k(w)|}{|\Sigma|}\right\}$$

states.

We are now ready to tackle LangSimK and MaxLangSimK.

Theorem 3. *Given an integer k, a string w and a context-free language L over Σ, we can solve* LangSimK *and* MaxLangSimK *in polynomial time if Σ is a fixed-sized alphabet. For a variable-sized alphabet,* LangSimK *is NP-complete when L is either regular or context-free.*

Proof (sketch). Our algorithm is to construct a DFA $AC_k(w)$ for $\text{Closure}_k(w)$ and check the emptiness of the intersection between $AC_k(w)$ and L. Recall that $AC_k(w)$ has at most $O\left(\frac{(2k+2)^{|\Sigma|}|w_s|}{|\Sigma|}\right)$ states. Therefore, for a fixed-sized alphabet, we solve the problems in polynomial time. We solve LangSimK by computing the maximum k by the binary search between 1 and $|w|$.

For a variable-sized alphabet, we can reduce the Hamiltonian path problem to LangSimK when L is regular. We can also show that the problem still lies in NP when L is context-free. □

4 Conclusions

We have presented an efficient DFA construction that accepts $\text{Closure}_k(w)$. Moreover, we have presented upper and lower bounds of the state complexity of the Simon's congruence closure of a string. Finally, based on the finding that the problem LangSimK is NP-complete, we have presented efficient algorithms for solving LangSimK and MaxLangSimK under the assumption that $|\Sigma|$ is constant. For future works, we plan to investigate more efficient automata construction for $\text{Closure}_k(w)$ as well as tighten the bounds for $\text{sc}(\text{Closure}_k(w))$. We suspect that finding tighter bounds require extensive research on the distribution and properties of shortlex normal form strings with respect to the congruence relation $\sim_k$. Moreover, another interesting follow-up research topic is extending our construction to efficiently recognize the Simon's congruence closure $\text{Closure}_k(L)$ of a language L or the general k-binomial congruence closure of a string.

Acknowledgments. We wish to thank the referees for letting us know related references and providing valuable suggestions that improve the presentation of the paper. This research was supported by the NRF grant funded by MIST (NRF-2020R1A4A3079947).

References

1. Barker, L., Fleischmann, P., Harwardt, K., Manea, F., Nowotka, D.: Scattered factor-universality of words. In: Jonoska, N., Savchuk, D. (eds.) DLT 2020. LNCS, vol. 12086, pp. 14–28. Springer, Cham (2020). https://doi.org/10.1007/978-3-030-48516-0_2
2. Cho, D., Goč, D., Han, Y., Ko, S., Palioudakis, A., Salomaa, K.: State complexity of permutation on finite languages over a binary alphabet. Theor. Comput. Sci. **682**, 67–78 (2017)
3. Fleischer, L., Kufleitner, M.: Testing Simon's congruence. In: 43rd International Symposium on Mathematical Foundations of Computer Science, pp. 62:1–62:13 (2018)
4. Freydenberger, D.D., Gawrychowski, P., Karhumäki, J., Manea, F., Rytter, W.: Testing k-binomial equivalence. Multidisciplinary Creativity: homage to Gheorghe Paun on his 65th birthday, pp. 239–248 (2015)
5. Garel, E.: Minimal separators of two words. In: Apostolico, A., Crochemore, M., Galil, Z., Manber, U. (eds.) CPM 1993. LNCS, vol. 684, pp. 35–53. Springer, Heidelberg (1993). https://doi.org/10.1007/BFb0029795
6. Gawrychowski, P., Kosche, M., Koß, T., Manea, F., Siemer, S.: Efficiently testing simon's congruence. In: 38th International Symposium on Theoretical Aspects of Computer Science, vol. 187, pp. 34:1–34:18 (2021)
7. Hébrard, J.: An algorithm for distinguishing efficiently bit-strings by their subsequences. Theor. Comput. Sci. **82**(1), 35–49 (1991)
8. Hoffmann, S.: State complexity of permutation and related decision problems on alphabetical pattern constraints. In: Maneth, S. (ed.) CIAA 2021. LNCS, vol. 12803, pp. 115–126. Springer, Cham (2021). https://doi.org/10.1007/978-3-030-79121-6_10
9. Karandikar, P., Kufleitner, M., Schnoebelen, P.: On the index of simon's congruence for piecewise testability. Inf. Process. Lett. **115**(4), 515–519 (2015)
10. Lejeune, M., Rigo, M., Rosenfeld, M.: The binomial equivalence classes of finite words. Int. J. Algebra Comput. **30**(07), 1375–1397 (2020)
11. Schwentick, T., Thérien, D., Vollmer, H.: Partially-ordered two-way automata: a new characterization of DA. In: Kuich, W., Rozenberg, G., Salomaa, A. (eds.) DLT 2001. LNCS, vol. 2295, pp. 239–250. Springer, Heidelberg (2002). https://doi.org/10.1007/3-540-46011-X_20
12. Simon, I.: Piecewise testable events. In: Brakhage, H. (ed.) GI-Fachtagung 1975. LNCS, vol. 33, pp. 214–222. Springer, Heidelberg (1975). https://doi.org/10.1007/3-540-07407-4_23
13. Weis, P., Immerman, N.: Structure theorem and strict alternation hierarchy for FO^2 on words. Logical Meth. Comput. Sci. **5**(3), 1–23 (2009)
14. Wood, D.: Theory of Computation. Harper & Row, New York (1987)
15. Yu, S., Zhuang, Q., Salomaa, K.: The state complexities of some basic operations on regular languages. Theor. Comput. Sci. **125**(2), 315–328 (1994)

Approximate NFA Universality Motivated by Information Theory

Stavros Konstantinidis[1(✉)], Mitja Mastnak[1], Nelma Moreira[2], and Rogério Reis[2]

[1] Saint Mary's University, Halifax, NS, Canada
s.konstantinidis@smu.ca, mmastnak@cs.smu.ca
[2] CMUP and DCC, Faculdade de Ciências da Universidade do Porto, Rua do Campo Alegre, 4169-007 Porto, Portugal
{nelma.moreira,rogerio.reis}@fc.up.pt

Abstract. In coding and information theory, it is desirable to construct maximal codes that can be either variable length codes or error control codes of fixed length. However deciding code maximality boils down to deciding whether a given NFA is universal, and this is a hard problem (including the case of whether the NFA accepts all words of a fixed length). On the other hand, it is acceptable to know whether a code is 'approximately' maximal, which then boils down to whether a given NFA is 'approximately' universal. Here we introduce the notion of a $(1-\varepsilon)$-universal automaton and present polynomial randomized approximation algorithms to test NFA universality and related hard automata problems, for certain natural probability distributions on the set of words. We also conclude that the randomization aspect is necessary, as approximate universality remains hard for any fixed polynomially computable ε.

1 Introduction

It is well-known that NFA universality is a PSPACE-hard problem and that block NFA universality (whether an NFA of some fixed length words accepts all the words of that length) is a coNP-hard problem. Here we consider polynomial approximation algorithms for these NFA problems by considering the concept of an approximate universal NFA, or block NFA, where for instance 95% of all words are accepted by the NFA. In general, for some *tolerance* $\varepsilon \in (0,1)$, we assume that we are happy to know that an NFA is at least $(1-\varepsilon)$ universal. While approximate universality is still hard, it allows us to consider polynomial randomized algorithms that return an incorrect answer with small probability. Inspired from [14, pg 72], we view estimating the universality index of an NFA as the problem of estimating the parameter of some population.

Our motivation for defining the concept of approximate universality comes from the problem of generating codes (whether variable length codes, or fixed

Research supported by NSERC, Canada (Discovery Grants of S.K. and of M.M.) and by CMUP through FCT project UIDB/00144/2021.

Published by Springer Nature Switzerland AG 2022
Y.-S. Han and G. Vaszil (Eds.): DCFS 2022, LNCS 13439, pp. 142–154, 2022.
https://doi.org/10.1007/978-3-031-13257-5_11

length error control codes) that are maximal, where on the one hand the question of deciding maximality is hard, but on the other hand it is acceptable to generate codes that are maximal within a tolerance ε, [4,12]. For infinite languages, we define approximate universality relative to some probability distribution on the set of words. This idea is consistent with our interpretation of languages in the context of coding and information theory where words are in fact abstractions of physical network signals or magnetic polarities, [10,13], and the amount of energy they require should not be exponential. Our work falls under the general framework of problems about parameter estimation or approximate counting [1,6,14], however, we are not aware of the application of this framework in hard NFA problems, especially in the case where the NFA accepts an infinite language.

Main Results and Structure of the Paper. The next section contains basic notions including concepts of probability distributions on the nonnegative integers, in particular the three distributions: uniform, Lambert and Dirichlet. The Dirichlet distribution is a good substitute for the 'fictitious' uniform distribution on the nonnegative integers [7]. **Section** 3 discusses what a polynomial randomized approximation (PRAX) algorithm should be for the case of a hard decision problem on NFAs. The necessity for PRAX-like algorithms for NFA universality is discussed. **Section** 4 is about probability distributions on words over some alphabet $\mathtt{A}_s = \{0, 1, \ldots, s\}$ such that the length sets of these distributions follow the above three distributions on the nonnegatives. **Section** 5 considers whether an NFA $\boldsymbol{a}$ is universal relative to a maximum language $\mathtt{M}$ (i.e., whether $\mathtt{L}(\boldsymbol{a}) = \mathtt{M}$), and takes the approach that $\mathtt{M}$ is the domain of a probability distribution W on the set of words, in which case the universality index $W(\boldsymbol{a})$ of $\boldsymbol{a}$ is the probability that a word selected from the distribution W belongs to $\mathtt{L}(\boldsymbol{a})$. Then, $\boldsymbol{a}$ is $p\%$-universal relative to W, if $W(\boldsymbol{a}) \geq p\%$. The section closes with two simple random processes about estimating the universality index of NFAs. **Section** 6 gives PRAX algorithms for three hard NFA problems. **Section** 7 defines what a tractable length distribution (on the nonnegatives) is and gives a PRAX algorithm for whether a given NFA is universal relative to any fixed, but arbitrary, tractable word distribution (including the word distributions that are based on the Lambert and Dirichlet length distributions). The last section contains a few concluding remarks.

2 Basic Notation and Background Information

We use the notation $\mathbb{N}$ for the set of positive integers, $\mathbb{N}_0$ for the nonnegative integers, and $\mathbb{N}^{>x}$ for the positive integers greater than x, where x is any real number. We assume the reader to be familiar with basics of formal languages and finite automata [9,15]. Our arbitrary alphabet will be $\mathtt{A}_s = \{0, 1, \ldots, s-1\}$ for some positive integer s. Then, we use the following notation

$\boldsymbol{\varepsilon}$ = empty word, $|w|$ = length of word w

$\mathtt{A}_s^\ell$ = all words of length ℓ, $\mathtt{A}_s^{\leq \ell}$ = all words of length at most ℓ

DFA = all DFAs (deterministic finite automata)

NFA = all NFAs (nondeterministic finite automata)

ADFA = all acyclic DFAs (accepting finite languages)

BNFA = all block NFAs = NFAs accepting languages of a fixed word length.

$\mathsf{BNFA}[s]$ = all block NFAs over the alphabet $\mathtt{A}_s$.

$|\boldsymbol{a}|$ = the size of the NFA $\boldsymbol{a}$ = number of states plus the number of transitions.

$\mathtt{L}(\boldsymbol{a})$ = the language accepted by the NFA, or DFA, $\boldsymbol{a}$.

Next we list some decision problems about automata that are known to be hard, or easily shown to be hard.

$\mathsf{UNIV\_NFA} = \{\boldsymbol{a} \in \mathsf{NFA} : \mathtt{L}(\boldsymbol{a}) = \mathtt{A}_s^*\}$: Deciding whether a given NFA is universal is a PSPACE-complete problem, [9].

$\mathsf{UNIV\_BNFA} = \{\boldsymbol{b} \in \mathsf{BNFA} : \mathtt{L}(\boldsymbol{b}) = \mathtt{A}_s^\ell$, where ℓ is the word length of $\boldsymbol{b}\}$: Deciding whether a given block NFA of some word length ℓ accepts all words of length ℓ is a coNP-complete problem, [12].

$\mathsf{UNIV\_MAXLEN\_NFA} = \{(\boldsymbol{a}, \ell) : \boldsymbol{a} \in \mathsf{NFA}, \ell$ is unary in $\mathbb{N}$, $\mathtt{L}(\mathtt{A}_s^{\leq \ell}) \subseteq \mathtt{L}(\boldsymbol{a})\}$: Deciding whether $\mathtt{L}(\mathtt{A}_s^{\leq \ell}) \subseteq \mathtt{L}(\boldsymbol{a})$, for given $\boldsymbol{a} \in \mathsf{NFA}$ and **unary** $\ell \in \mathbb{N}_0$, is coNP-complete, [5].

$\mathsf{ADFA\_SUBSET\_NFA} = \{(\boldsymbol{a}, \boldsymbol{b}) : \boldsymbol{a} \in \mathsf{NFA}, \boldsymbol{b} \in \mathsf{ADFA}, \mathtt{L}(\boldsymbol{b}) \subseteq \mathtt{L}(\boldsymbol{a})\}$: Deciding whether $\mathtt{L}(\boldsymbol{b}) \subseteq \mathtt{L}(\boldsymbol{a})$, for given $\boldsymbol{a} \in \mathsf{NFA}$ and $\boldsymbol{b} \in \mathsf{ADFA}$ is PSPACE-complete.

$\mathsf{EMPTY\_DFA} = \{(\boldsymbol{a}_1, \ldots, \boldsymbol{a}_n) : n \in \mathbb{N}, \boldsymbol{a}_i \in \mathsf{DFA}, \cap_{i=1}^n \mathtt{L}(\boldsymbol{a}_i) = \emptyset\}$: Deciding whether the intersection of given DFAs is empty is PSPACE-complete, [5]. Note that the problem remains hard even if we know that the languages of the given DFAs belong to low levels of the dot-depth or the Straubing-Thérien hierarchies [2].

Probability Distributions. Let X be a countable set. A probability distribution on X is a function $D : X \to [0, 1]$ such that

$$\sum_{x \in X} D(x) = 1.$$

The domain of D, denoted by $\operatorname{dom} D$, is the subset $\{x \in X \mid D(x) > 0\}$ of X. If $X = \{x_1, \ldots, x_\ell\}$, for some $\ell \in \mathbb{N}$, then we write $D = \big(D(x_1), \ldots, D(x_\ell)\big)$. Following [8], for any subset S of X, we define the quantity

$$D(S) = \sum_{x \in S} D(x)$$

and refer to it as the probability that a randomly selected element from D is in S. The notation $x \xleftarrow{\$} D$, borrowed from cryptography, means that x is randomly selected from D.

The author of [8] considers three families of probability distributions on $\mathbb{N}_0$ that are meaningful in information and/or number theory. These distributions are called uniform, Lambert and Dirichlet, and are defined, respectively, as follows, where $d \in \mathbb{N}_0, M \in \mathbb{N}, z \in (0, 1)$ and $t \in (1, +\infty)$ are related parameters.

Uniform: $\mathsf{U}_M(n) = 1/M$ for $n < M$, and $\mathsf{U}_M(n) = 0$ otherwise.
Lambert: $\mathsf{L}_{1/z,d}(n) = (1-z)z^{n-d}$ for $n \geq d$, and $\mathsf{L}_{1/z,d}(n) = 0$ otherwise.
Dirichlet: $\mathsf{D}_{t,d}(n) = (1/\zeta(t))(n+1-d)^{-t}$ for $n \geq d$, where ζ is the Riemann zeta function, and $\mathsf{D}_{t,d}(n) = 0$ otherwise.

In fact [8] considers distributions on $\mathbb{N}$, but here we use $\mathbb{N}_0$ instead as we intend to apply these distributions to modelling lengths of words, including possibly the empty word ε whose length is 0. We also note that [8] considers $\mathsf{L}_{1/z,d}$ and $\mathsf{D}_{t,d}$ only for the case where the displacement $d = 1$. We also note that in [7] the same author considers the Dirichlet distribution to be the basis where *"many heuristic probability arguments based on the fictitious uniform distribution on the positive integers become rigorous statements"*.
We shall call any probability distribution N on $\mathbb{N}_0$ a length distribution.

3 Randomized Approximation of [0, 1]-Value Problems

We consider problems for which every instance[1] x has a value $v(x) \in [0,1]$ and we are interested in those instances x for which $v(x) = 1$. Our main set of instances is the set of NFAs (or subsets of that) and the main value function v is the universality index of NFAs, which is defined in Sect. 5. However for the purposes of this section, our main set of instances is $\mathsf{BNFA}[2]$ = all block NFAs over the alphabet $\{0,1\}$, and the $[0,1]$-valued function v is such that $v(\boldsymbol{a}) = |\mathsf{L}(\boldsymbol{a})|/2^n$, where n is the word length of the block NFA $\boldsymbol{a}$. In general, for a fixed but arbitrary $[0,1]$-*valued function* v, we define the language (problem)

$$L_v = \{x : v(x) = 1\}.$$

Deciding whether a given instance x is in L_v might be hard, but *we assume that we are happy if we know whether $v(x) \geq 1-\varepsilon$, for some appropriate* tolerance $\varepsilon \in (0,1)$. So we define the following **approximation** language for L_v:

$$L_{v,\varepsilon} = \{x : v(x) \geq 1-\varepsilon\}.$$

One can verify that $L_v = \bigcap_{\varepsilon \in (0,1)} L_{v,\varepsilon}$; hence L_v can be approximated as close as desired via the languages $L_{v,\varepsilon}$. Unfortunately deciding $L_{v,\varepsilon}$ can be harder than deciding L_v:

Theorem 1. *The following problem about block NFAs is coNP-hard, for any (fixed) $\delta \in (0,1)$ that is computable within polynomial time*[2].

$$B_\delta = \{\boldsymbol{a} \in \mathsf{BNFA}[2] : \frac{|\mathsf{L}(\boldsymbol{a})|}{2^n} \geq \delta, \ \textit{where } n = \textit{word length of } \boldsymbol{a}\}.$$

[1] Following the presentation style of [6, pg 193], we refrain from cluttering the notation with the use of a variable for the set of instances.

[2] A real $x \in (0,1)$ is computable if there is an algorithm that takes as input an integer $n > 0$ and computes the n-th bit of x. It is polynomially computable if the algorithm works in time $O(n^k)$, for some fixed $k \in \mathbb{N}_0$, when the input n is given in unary.

Another idea then is to show that L_v is in the class coRP, that is, there is a polynomial **randomized** algorithm $A(x)$ such that (i) if $x \in L_v$ then $A(x) =$ `True` (with probability 1), and (ii) if $x \notin L_v$ then $A(x) =$ `False` with probability[3] at least 3/4. However, as L_v can be hard, it is unlikely that it is in coRP.

The next idea is to devise an approximating algorithm for L_v via $L_{v,\varepsilon}$. As stated in [6, pg 417], *"The answer to [what constitutes a "good" approximation] seems intimately related to the specific computational task at hand... the importance of certain approximation problems is much more subjective...[which] seems to stand in the way of attempts at providing a comprehensive theory of natural approximation problems"*. It seems that the following approximation method is meaningful. Although our domain of interest involves NFAs, the below definition is given for any set of instances and refers to a fixed but arbitrary [0, 1]-valued function v on these instances.

Definition 1. *Let v be [0, 1]-valued function. A polynomial approximation (PAX) algorithm for L_v is an algorithm $A(x, \varepsilon)$ such that*

- *if $x \in L_v$ then $A(x, \varepsilon) =$ `True`;*
- *if $x \notin L_{v,\varepsilon}$ then $A(x, \varepsilon) =$ `False`;*
- *$A(x, \varepsilon)$ works within polynomial time w.r.t. $1/\varepsilon$ and the size of x.*

Explanation. In the above definition, if $A(x, \varepsilon)$ returns `False` then $x \notin L_v$, that is, $v(x) < 1$. If $A(x, \varepsilon)$ returns `True` then $x \in L_{v,\varepsilon}$, that is, $v(x) \geq 1 - \varepsilon$. Thus, whenever the algorithm returns the answer `False`, this answer is correct and exact; when the algorithm returns `True`, the answer is *correct within the tolerance* ε.

It turns out that, in general, there are problems for which no approximation algorithm can do better than the exact algorithms:

Proposition 1. *There is no polynomial approximation algorithm for the problem UNIV_BNFA, unless P=coNP.*

Remark 1. Theorem 1 implies that, unless P=coNP, block NFA universality over the binary alphabet cannot be approximated by some sequence (B_{δ_n}), with $\lim \delta_n = 0$ and each δ_n being polynomially computable. Based on this observation and on Proposition 1, we conclude that, *in general, it is necessary to add a randomized aspect to our approximation methods.* We also note that there are in fact cases where a PAX algorithm for a hard problem exists.

The next definition is inspired from the "approximate" algorithmic solution of [12] for the task of generating an error-detecting code of N codewords, for given N, if possible, or an error-detecting code of less than N codewords which is "close to" maximal.

---

3 Many authors specify this probability to be at least 2/3, but they state that any value $\geq 1/2$ works [1,6].

Definition 2. *Let v be [0, 1]-valued function. A polynomial randomized approximation (PRAX) algorithm for L_v is a randomized algorithm $A(x, \varepsilon)$ such that*

- *if $x \in L_v$ then $A(x, \varepsilon) = \texttt{True}$;*
- *if $x \notin L_{v,\varepsilon}$ then $\mathrm{P}[A(x, \varepsilon) = \texttt{False}] \geq 3/4$;*
- *$A(x, \varepsilon)$ works within polynomial time w.r.t. $1/\varepsilon$ and the size of x.*

Explanation. In the above definition, if $A(x, \varepsilon)$ returns `False` then $x \notin L_v$. If $A(x, \varepsilon)$ returns `True` then probably $x \in L_{v,\varepsilon}$, in the sense that $x \notin L_{v,\varepsilon}$ would imply $\mathrm{P}[A(x, \varepsilon) = \texttt{False}] \geq 3/4$. Thus, whenever the algorithm returns the answer `False`, this answer is correct ($x \notin L_v$); when the algorithm returns `True`, the answer is *correct within the tolerance* ε *($x \in L_{v,\varepsilon}$) with probability* $\geq 3/4$. The algorithm returns the wrong answer exactly when it returns `True` and $x \notin L_{v,\varepsilon}$, but this happens with probability $< 1/4$.

Use of a PRAX Algorithm. The algorithm can be used as follows to determine the approximate membership of a given x in L_v with a probability that can be as high as desired: Run $A(x, \varepsilon)$ k times, for some desired k, or until the output is `False`. If the output is `True` for all k times then $\mathrm{P}[A(x, \varepsilon) = \texttt{True}$ for k times $\mid x \notin L_{v,\varepsilon}] < 1/4^k$, that is, the probability of incorrect answer is $< 1/4^k$.

4 Word Distributions

A word distribution W is a probability distribution on $\mathtt{A}_s^*$, that is, $W : \mathtt{A}_s^* \to [0, 1]$ such that $\sum_{w \in \mathtt{A}_s^*} W(w) = 1$. If $\boldsymbol{a}$ is an NFA then we use the convention that $W(\boldsymbol{a})$ means $W(\mathtt{L}(\boldsymbol{a}))$. The domain of W is $\operatorname{dom} W = \{w \in \mathtt{A}_s^* \mid W(w) > 0\}$.

Example 1. For a finite language F, we write U_F to denote the uniform word distribution on F, that is, $\mathrm{U}_F(w) = 1/|F|$ for $w \in F$, and $\mathrm{U}_F(w) = 0$ for $w \notin F$. Some important examples of uniform word distributions are:

- $\mathrm{U}_{\mathtt{A}_s^\ell}$, where ℓ is any word length. Then, $\mathrm{U}_{\mathtt{A}_s^\ell}(w) = 1/s^\ell$.
- $\mathrm{U}_{\mathtt{A}_s^{\leq \ell}}$, where ℓ is any word length. Then, $\mathrm{U}_{\mathtt{A}_s^{\leq \ell}}(w) = 1/t$, where $t = \sum_{i=0}^{\ell} s^i$.
- $\mathrm{U}_{\mathtt{L}(\boldsymbol{a})}$, where $\boldsymbol{a}$ is an acyclic NFA. We also simply write $\mathrm{U}_{\boldsymbol{a}}$ for $\mathrm{U}_{\mathtt{L}(\boldsymbol{a})}$.

Definition 3. *Let N be a length distribution. Then $\langle N \rangle$ is the word distribution such that $\langle N \rangle(w) = N(|w|)s^{-|w|}$. Any such word distribution is called a length-based distribution.*

Remark 2. For any length distribution N, we have that $\langle N \rangle(\mathtt{A}_s^n) = N(n)$ and $\langle N \rangle(\mathtt{A}_s^{>n}) = N(\mathbb{N}^{>n})$, where $n \in \mathbb{N}_0$.

Example 2. Using the Lambert length distribution $\mathsf{L}_{s,d}(n) = (1 - 1/s)(1/s)^{n-d}$, we define the Lambert, or geometric, word distribution $\langle \mathsf{L}_{s,d} \rangle$ on $\mathtt{A}_s^*$ such that $\langle \mathsf{L}_{s,d} \rangle(w) = 0$ if $|w| < d$ and, for $|w| \geq d$, $\langle \mathsf{L}_{s,d} \rangle(w) = (1 - 1/s)(1/s)^{2|w|-d}$. Then, for all $n, d \in \mathbb{N}_0$ with $n \geq d$, we have

$$\langle \mathsf{L}_{s,d} \rangle(\mathtt{A}_s^n) = (1 - 1/s)(1/s)^{n-d}, \quad \langle \mathsf{L}_{s,d} \rangle(\mathtt{A}_s^{>n}) = (1/s)^{n+1-d}.$$

In particular, for the alphabet $\mathtt{A}_2 = \{0,1\}$, we have that $\langle \mathsf{L}_{2,1}\rangle(\mathtt{A}_2) = 1/2$, $\langle \mathsf{L}_{2,1}\rangle(\mathtt{A}_2^2) = 1/2^2$, etc.

Example 3. Using the Dirichlet length distribution $\mathsf{D}_{t,d}(n) = (1/\zeta(t))(n+1-d)^{-t}$, we define the Dirichlet word distribution $\langle \mathsf{D}_{t,d}\rangle$ on $\mathtt{A}_s^*$ such that $\langle \mathsf{D}_{t,d}\rangle(w) = 0$ if $|w| < d$ and, for $|w| \geq d$, $\langle \mathsf{D}_{t,d}\rangle(w) = (1/\zeta(t))(|w|+1-d)^{-t}s^{-|w|}$. Then, for all $n, d \in \mathbb{N}_0$ with $n \geq d$, we have $\langle \mathsf{D}_{t,d}\rangle(\mathtt{A}_s^n) = (1/\zeta(t))(n+1-d)^{-t}$ and

$$\langle \mathsf{D}_{t,d}\rangle(\mathtt{A}_s^{>n}) = 1 - (1/\zeta(t)) \sum_{i=1}^{n+1-d} i^{-t}.$$

In particular, for $t = 3$, $d = 1$ and alphabet $\mathtt{A}_2 = \{0,1\}$, we have that $\langle \mathsf{D}_{2,1}\rangle(\mathtt{A}_2^n) = (1/\zeta(3))n^{-3}$.

Selecting a Word from a Distribution. We are interested in word distributions W for which there is an efficient (randomized) algorithm that returns a randomly selected element from W. We shall assume available (randomized) algorithms as follows.

- tossCoin(p): returns 0 or 1, with probability p or $1-p$, respectively, where $p \in [0,1]$, and the algorithm works in constant time for most practical purposes—this is a reasonable assumption according to [1, pg 134].
- selectUnif(s, ℓ): returns a uniformly selected word from $\mathtt{A}_s^\ell$, and the algorithm works in time $O(\ell)$.

Remark 3. As in [1, pg 126], we assume that basic arithmetic operations are performed in constant time. Even if we account for a parameter q for arithmetic precision, the arithmetic operations would require a polynomial factor in q.

The next lemma seems to be folklore, but we include it here for the sake of clarity and self-containment.

Lemma 1. *There is a polynomial randomized algorithm* selectFin(D), *where D is a finite distribution $(D(x_1), \ldots, D(x_n))$ on some set $\{x_1, \ldots, x_n\}$, that returns a randomly selected x_i with probability $D(x_i)$. The algorithm is linear time under the assumption of constant cost of* tossCoin *and arithmetic operations.*

Augmented Word Distributions. Selecting a word from a distribution W with infinite domain dom W could return a very long word, which can be intractable. For this reason we would like to define distributions on $\mathtt{A}_s^* \cup \{\perp\}$, *where '$\perp$' is a symbol outside of* $\mathtt{A}_s$, which could select the outcome '$\perp$' (no word). These could be versions of word distributions in which there is a bound on the length of words they can select. Let W be a word distribution and let $M \in \mathbb{N}_0$. We define the augmented distribution W^M on $\mathtt{A}_s^* \cup \{\perp\}$ such that $W^M(w) = W(w)$, if $|w| \leq M$ and $W^M(\perp) = W(\mathtt{A}_s^{>M})$. The probability that W^M selects a word longer than M is zero. We have that dom $W^M = (\mathrm{dom}\, W \cap \mathtt{A}_s^{\leq M}) \cup \{\perp\}$. Moreover, the following facts about W^M and any language L are immediate

$$W(L \cap \mathtt{A}_s^{\leq M}) = W^M(L \cap \mathtt{A}_s^{\leq M}), \quad W(\mathtt{A}_s^{>M}) = W^M(\perp). \tag{1}$$

5 Universality Index of NFAs

Here we intend to define mathematically the informal concept of an "approximately universal NFA" with respect to a certain fixed language $\mathtt{M}$. Our motivation comes from coding theory where the codes of interest are subsets of $\mathtt{M}$, and it is desirable that a code is a maximal subset of $\mathtt{M}$. Two typical cases are (i) $\mathtt{M} = \mathtt{A}_s^*$, when variable-length codes are considered, such as prefix or suffix codes; and (ii) $\mathtt{M} = \mathtt{A}_s^n$ for some $n \in \mathbb{N}$, when error control codes are considered. Testing whether a regular code C is a maximal subset of $\mathtt{M}$ is a hard problem and, in fact, this problem normally reduces to whether a certain NFA that depends on C accepts $\mathtt{M}$—see e.g., [4,12]. In practice, however, it could be acceptable that a code is "close" to being maximal, or an NFA is "close" to being universal.

Our approach here assumes that the maximum language $\mathtt{M}$ *is equal to* $\operatorname{dom} W$, *where* W *is the word distribution of interest. Let* $\boldsymbol{a}$ *be an NFA, and let* $p \in [0,1]$.

- *We say that* $\boldsymbol{a}$ *is* **universal relative** *to* W, *if* $\mathtt{L}(\boldsymbol{a}) = \operatorname{dom} W$.
- *We say that* $\boldsymbol{a}$ *is* **p-universal relative** *to* W, *if* $W(\boldsymbol{a}) \geq p$. *We call the quantity* $W(\boldsymbol{a})$ *the* **universality index** *of* $\boldsymbol{a}$ *(relative to* W*).*

Example 4. Let $\boldsymbol{b}$ be a block NFA. If $|\mathtt{L}(\boldsymbol{b})|/s^\ell \geq p$, where ℓ is the word length of $\boldsymbol{b}$, then $\boldsymbol{b}$ is p-universal relative to the uniform distribution on $\mathtt{A}_s^\ell$ and the quantity $|\mathtt{L}(\boldsymbol{b})|/s^\ell$ is the universality index of $\boldsymbol{b}$.

Remark 4. The universality index $W(\boldsymbol{a})$ represents the probability that a randomly selected word from W is accepted by $\boldsymbol{a}$. When $W(\boldsymbol{a})$ is close to 1 then $\boldsymbol{a}$ is close to being universal, that is, $\mathtt{L}(\boldsymbol{a})$ is close to $\operatorname{dom} W$. The concept of a p-universal NFA formalizes the loose concept of an approximately universal NFA. Thus, for example, we can talk about a 98%-universal block NFA with respect to the uniform distribution on $\mathtt{A}_s^\ell$, where ℓ is the word length of the NFA.

Remark 5. The method of [11] embeds a given $\boldsymbol{t}$-code[4] K into a maximal one by successive applications of an operator μ_t on K which yields supersets K_i of K until these converge to a maximal $\boldsymbol{t}$-code. The operation μ_t on each K_i (represented as an NFA) can be time-expensive and one can simply stop at a step where the current superset K_i is close to maximal, or according to the concepts of this paper, when the NFA for $\big(\boldsymbol{t}(K_i) \cup \boldsymbol{t}^{-1}(K_i) \cup K_i\big)$ is close to universal.

Consider the case where $\boldsymbol{b}$ is a block NFA of length ℓ and W is the uniform word distribution on $\mathtt{A}_s^\ell$. In this work, we view estimating the universality index of $\boldsymbol{b}$ as a *parameter estimation problem* for finite populations [14, pg 72]: let p be an unknown population parameter (ratio of elements having some attribute over the cardinality of the population). Select n elements from the population (here, n words from $\mathtt{A}_s^\ell$) and compute c, the number of these elements having the attribute of interest (here, words that are in $\mathtt{L}(\boldsymbol{b})$). Then, c/n is an estimate for

[4] Depending on $\boldsymbol{t}$, which is a transducer, one can have prefix codes, suffix codes, infix codes, error control codes.

the population parameter p (here, the estimate is for $W(\boldsymbol{b})$) in the sense that the expected value of the random variable c/n is equal to p and $\mathrm{P}[\,|c/n-p|>\varepsilon] < e^{-n\varepsilon^2/2}+e^{-n\varepsilon^2/3}$. Here we extend the idea of parameter estimation to various distributions on languages. Moreover, we use the simpler Chebysev inequality for bounding the error probability, as it gives in practice a smaller bound than the one in the above inequality. Let X be a random variable and let $a>0$. The Chebyshev inequality is $\mathrm{P}[\,|X-\mathcal{E}(X)|\geq a]\leq \sigma^2/a^2$, where σ^2 is the variance of X. When X is the binomial random variable with parameters n = 'number of trials' and p ='probability of success in one trial', then $\mathcal{E}(X)=np$ and $\sigma^2=np(1-p)$. For $p\in[0,1]$, the maximum value of $p(1-p)$ is 1/4; therefore, the above inequality becomes as follows:

$$\mathrm{P}[\,|X-\mathcal{E}(X)|\geq a]\leq n/(4a^2). \tag{2}$$

```
UnivIndex_W(a, n)                 UnivIndexMaxLen_W(a, n, M)
  cnt := 0;                         cnt := 0;
  repeat n times:                   repeat n times:
    w <-$- W;                         w <-$- W^M;
    if (w ∈ L(a))                     if (w = ⊥ or w ∈ A_s^{≤M} ∩ L(a))
          cnt := cnt+1;                     cnt := cnt+1;
  return cnt / n;                   return cnt / n;
```

Fig. 1. These random processes refer to a particular word distribution W. The left one returns an estimate of the universality index $W(\boldsymbol{a})$ of the given NFA $\boldsymbol{a}$. For the right one, when M is chosen such that $W^M(\bot)$ is small enough, then the returned quantity cnt/n can be an acceptable estimate of $W(\boldsymbol{a})$.

Lemma 2. *Let* $\boldsymbol{a}$ *be an NFA, let* W *be a word distribution, and let* $p,g\in[0,1]$ *with* $p>g$. *Consider the random process* $\mathsf{UnivIndex}_W(\boldsymbol{a},n)$ *in Fig. 1, and let* Cnt *be the random variable for the value of* cnt *when the algorithm returns. If* $W(\boldsymbol{a})<g$ *then* $\mathrm{P}[\mathtt{Cnt}/n\geq p]\leq\frac{1}{4n(p-g)^2}$.

In Sect. 6 we give a polynomial randomized approximation algorithm (PRAX) for testing universality of block NFAs, which is based on the left random process in Fig. 1. That process, however, cannot lead to a PRAX for the universality of NFAs accepting infinite languages, as the selection $w \xleftarrow{\$} W$ could produce a word of exponential length. The right process in Fig. 1 makes sure that a selected word cannot be longer than a desired $M\in\mathbb{N}_0$—in Sect. 7 we investigate how this can lead to a PRAX for the universality of any NFA relative to tractable word distributions.

Lemma 3. *Let* $\boldsymbol{a}$ *be an NFA, let* W *be a word distribution, let* $M\in\mathbb{N}_0$, *and let* $p,g\in[0,1]$ *such that* $p>g+W(\mathtt{A}_s^{>M})$. *Consider the random process*

$\mathsf{UnivIndexMaxLen}_W(\boldsymbol{a}, n, M)$ *in Fig. 1, and let* $\mathtt{Cnt}$ *be the random variable whose value is equal to the value of* cnt *when the algorithm returns. If* $W(\boldsymbol{a}) < g$ *then*

$$\mathrm{P}[\mathtt{Cnt}/n \geq p] \leq \frac{1}{x} + \frac{1}{4n\big(p - g - xW(\mathtt{A}_s^{>M})\big)^2}, \quad \text{for all } x \in \Big(1, \frac{p-g}{W(\mathtt{A}_s^{>M})}\Big).$$

6 Randomized Approximation of NFA Problems Relative to Uniform Distributions

In this section we consider polynomial randomized approximation algorithms for the problems ADFA_SUBSET_NFA, UNIV_BNFA, UNIV_MAXLEN_NFA. As discussed below, the latter two problems are essentially special cases of the problem ADFA_SUBSET_NFA, but they can also be answered using a couple of more standard tools leading to more efficient algorithms.

Theorem 2. *Algorithm* $\mathsf{ADFASubsetNFA}(\boldsymbol{a}, \boldsymbol{b}, \varepsilon)$ *in Fig. 2 is a polynomial randomized approximation algorithm for ADFA_SUBSET_NFA.*

```
ADFASubsetNFA(a, b, ε)
    n := ⌈1/ε²⌉;
    repeat n times:
        w := selectUnif(b);
        if (w ∉ L(a)) return False;
    return True;
```

```
ADFASubsetNFA(a, b, ε)
    n := ⌈1/ε²⌉;   cnt := 0;
    repeat n times:
        w := selectUnif(b);
        if (w ∈ L(a)) cnt := cnt + 1;
    if (cnt < n) return False
    else return True;
```

Fig. 2. On the left is the PRAX for ADFA_SUBSET_NFA: whether $\mathtt{L}(\boldsymbol{b}) \subseteq \mathtt{L}(\boldsymbol{a})$ for given NFA $\boldsymbol{a}$ and given acyclic DFA $\boldsymbol{b}$. This is equivalent to whether $\mathtt{L}(\boldsymbol{b}) \subseteq \mathtt{L}(\boldsymbol{a}) \cap \mathtt{L}(\boldsymbol{b})$. The function $\mathsf{selectUnif}(\boldsymbol{b})$ returns a uniformly selected word from $\mathtt{L}(\boldsymbol{b})$. The version on the right is logically equivalent; it mimics the left process in Fig. 1 and is intended to give a more clear exposition of correctness.

The next corollary follows from the above theorem; however, using a more self-contained choice of tools we can get more efficient algorithms with estimates of their time complexity.

```
UnivBlockNFA(a, ε)
    ℓ := the word length of L(a);
    n := ⌈1/ε²⌉;
    repeat n times:
        w := selectUnif(s, ℓ);
        if (w ∉ L(a)) return False;
    return True;
```

```
UnivMaxLenNFA(a, ℓ, ε)
    t := 1 + s + ··· + s^ℓ;
    N := (1/t, s/t, ..., s^ℓ/t);
    n := ⌈1/ε²⌉;
    repeat n times:
        k := selectFin(N);
        w := selectUnif(s, k);
        if (w ∉ L(a)) return False;
    return True;
```

Corollary 1. UnivBlockNFA($\boldsymbol{a}, \varepsilon$) *is a PRAX algorithm for block NFA universality and works in time* $O(\ell\,|\boldsymbol{a}|(1/\varepsilon)^2)$, *where* ℓ *is the word length of* $\boldsymbol{a}$. UnivMaxLenNFA($\boldsymbol{a}, \ell, \varepsilon$) *is a PRAX algorithm for* UNIV_MAXLEN_NFA. *In fact the algorithm works in time* $O(\ell\,|\boldsymbol{a}|(1/\varepsilon)^2)$ *under the assumption of constant cost of* tossCoin *and of arithmetic operations.*

Use of Algorithm UnivBlockNFA($\boldsymbol{a}, \varepsilon$). Suppose that we want to test whether a block NFA $\boldsymbol{a}$ of some word length ℓ is universal relative to the uniform distribution on $\mathtt{A}_s^\ell$, and that we allow a 2% approximation tolerance, that is, we consider it acceptable to say that $\boldsymbol{a}$ is universal when it is in fact 98%-universal. Then we run the algorithm using $\varepsilon = 0.02$. If $\boldsymbol{a}$ is universal, then the algorithm correctly returns `True`. If $\boldsymbol{a}$ is not 98%-universal, then the probability that the algorithm returns `True` is at most 1/4. Note that for this choice of arguments, the loop would iterate at most 2500 times.

7 Randomized Approximation of NFA Universality

Here we present an analogue to the uniform distribution algorithms for the case where NFAs accept infinite languages and universality is relative to some word distribution $\langle T\rangle$. The PRAX algorithm of this section is based on the right process in Fig. 1 and requires that $\langle T\rangle$ be tractable, which loosely speaking means that words longer than a certain length $M = M(\varepsilon)$ have low probability and can be ignored when one wants to approximate the universality index of the given NFA *within a given tolerance* ε—recall, this approach is consistent with our interpretation of languages in the context of coding and information theory.

Definition 4. *A length distribution* T *is called* **tractable**, *if the following conditions hold true.*

1. *For all* $\varepsilon \in (0,1)$, *there is* $M \in \mathbb{N}_0$ *such that* $T(\mathbb{N}^{>M}) \leq \varepsilon$, M *is of polynomially bounded magnitude w.r.t.* $1/\varepsilon$, *that is,* $M = O((1/\varepsilon)^k)$ *for some* $k \in \mathbb{N}_0$, *and there is an algorithm* $\mathsf{maxLen}_T(\varepsilon)$ *that returns such an* M *and works within polynomial time w.r.t.* $1/\varepsilon$.
2. *There is an algorithm* $\mathsf{prob}_T(m)$, *where* $m \in \mathbb{N}_0$, *that returns the value* $T(m)$ *and works within polynomial time w.r.t* m.

Theorem 3. *Let* T *be a tractable length distribution.* $\mathsf{UnivNFA}_T(\boldsymbol{a}, \varepsilon)$ *in Fig. 3 is a PRAX algorithm for NFA universality relative to* $\langle T\rangle$.

Theorem 3 can be applied to the Lambert and Dirichlet Distributions.

Corollary 2. *There is a polynomial randomized approximation algorithm for NFA universality relative to the Lambert distribution. In fact the algorithm works in time* $O(|\boldsymbol{a}|(1/\varepsilon)^2 \log(1/\varepsilon))$ *under the assumption of constant cost of* tossCoin *and of arithmetic operations.*

Corollary 3. *There is a polynomial randomized approximation algorithm for NFA universality relative to the Dirichlet distribution. In fact the algorithm works in time* $O(|\boldsymbol{a}|(1/\varepsilon)^2 \sqrt[t-1]{1/\varepsilon^2})$ *under the assumption of constant cost of* tossCoin *and of arithmetic operations.*

```
UnivNFA_T(a, ε)
    ε := min(ε, 1/6);
    n := ⌈5/(ε − 5ε²)²⌉;
    M := maxLen_T(ε²);
    for each ℓ = 0, ..., M
        t_ℓ := prob_T(ℓ);
    D := (t_0, ..., t_M, 1 − Σ_{ℓ=0}^{M} t_ℓ);
    repeat n times:
        ℓ := selectFin(D);
        if (ℓ ≠ ⊥) w := selectUnif(s, ℓ);
        if (ℓ ≠ ⊥ and w ∉ L(a))
            return False;
    return True;
```

Fig. 3. The PRAX algorithm for NFA universality with respect to a certain tractable word distribution $\langle T\rangle$—see Theorem 3. The algorithm selects repeatedly either a word w of length $\le M$ from $\langle T\rangle$ or the outcome '$\perp$'. The finite probability distribution D refers to the outcomes $\{0, 1, \ldots, M, \perp\}$; that is, a length $\ell \le M$ or '$\perp$'. Statement $w \xleftarrow{\$} W^M$ of the right process in Fig. 1 corresponds, for $W = \langle T\rangle$, to the first two statements of the 'repeat' loop.

8 Concluding Remarks

The concept of approximate maximality of a block code introduced in [12] leads naturally to the concept of approximately universal NFAs. These concepts are meaningful in coding theory where the languages of interest are finite or even regular and can be represented by automata, [3,13,16].

Our approach can be used to define approximate versions of other hard problems such as EMPTY_DFA and the problem of whether two given NFAs accept the same language. Algorithm UnivNFA can be used to decide approximate universality of a context-free language $\mathtt{L}(\boldsymbol{a})$, where now $\boldsymbol{a}$ is a context-free grammar. Of course context-free grammar universality is undecidable! However, extending our approach to grammars is outside our motivation from coding and information theory and we cannot tell whether it could lead to any fruitful results.

It can be shown that every coNP language L is a $[0,1]$-value language L_v; hence, it can be approximated by languages $L_{v,\varepsilon}$. As this generalization is outside the scope of the present paper, we leave it as a topic for future research.

References

1. Arora, S., Barak, B.: Computational Complexity - A Modern Approach. Cambridge University Press, New York (2009)
2. Arrighi, E., et al.: On the complexity of intersection non-emptiness for star-free language classes. CoRR, abs/2110.01279 (2021)
3. Berstel, J., Perrin, D., Reutenauer, C.: Codes and Automata. Cambridge University Press, Cambridge (2009)

4. Dudzinski, K., Konstantinidis, S.: Formal descriptions of code properties: decidability, complexity, implementation. Int. J. Found. Comput. Sci. **23**(1), 67–85 (2012)
5. Fernau, H., Krebs, A.: Problems on finite automata and the exponential time hypothesis. Algorithms **10**(1), 24 (2017)
6. Goldreich, O.: Computational complexity - A Conceptual Perspective. Cambridge University Press, Cambridge (2008)
7. Golomb, S.W.: A class of probability distributions on the integers. J. Number Theory **2**, 189–192 (1970)
8. Golomb, S.W.: Probability, information theory, and prime number theory. Discret. Math. **106**(107), 219–229 (1992)
9. Hopcroft, J.E., Motwani, R., Ullman, J.D.: Introduction to Automata Theory, Languages, and Computation, 2nd edn. Addison-Wesley-Longman (2001)
10. Jürgensen, H.: Complexity, information, energy. Int. J. Found. Comput. Sci. **19**(4), 781–793 (2008)
11. Konstantinidis, S., Mastnak, M.: Embedding rationally independent languages into maximal ones. J. Automata Lang. Comb. **21**(4), 311–338 (2016)
12. Konstantinidis, S., Moreira, N., Reis, R.: Randomized generation of error control codes with automata and transducers. RAIRO - Theo. Inform. Appl. **52**, 169–184 (2018)
13. Marcus, B.H., Siegel, P., Roth, R.: Constrained systems and coding for recording channels. In: Handbook of Coding Theory, pp. 1635–1764. Elsevier (1998). http://www.math.ubc.ca/~marcus/Handbook/
14. Mitzenmacher, M., Upfal, E.: Probability and Computing: Randomization and Probabilistic Techniques in Algorithms and Data Analysis, 2nd edn. Cambridge University Press, Cambridge (2017)
15. Rozenberg, G., Salomaa, A. (eds.): Handbook of Formal Languages. Springer, Heidelberg (1997). https://doi.org/10.1007/978-3-642-59136-5
16. Vardy, A.: Trellis structure of codes. In: Handbook of Coding Theory, pp. 1989–2117. Elsevier, Amsterdam (1998)

Lazy Regular Sensing

Orna Kupferman[1(✉)] and Asaf Petruschka[2]

[1] School of Engineering and Computer Science, The Hebrew University, Jerusalem, Israel
orna@cs.huji.ac.il

[2] Department of Mathematics and Computer Science, The Weizmann Institute of Science, Rehovot, Israel
asaf.petruschka@weizmann.ac.il

Abstract. A complexity measure for regular languages based on the *sensing* required to recognize them was recently introduced by Almagor, Kuperberg, and Kupferman. Intuitively, the sensing cost quantifies the detail in which a random input word has to be read in order to decide its membership in the language, when the input letters composing the word are truth assignments to a finite set of *signals*. We introduce the notion of *lazy sensing*, where the signals are not sensed simultaneously. Rather, the signals are ordered, and a signal is sensed only if the values of the signals sensed so far have not determined the successor state. We study four classes of lazy sensing, induced by distinguishing between the cases where the order of the signals is static or dynamic (that is, fixed in advance or depends on the values of the signals sensed so far), and the cases where the order is global or local (that is, the same for all states of the automaton, or not). We examine the different classes of lazy sensing and the saving they enable, with respect to each other and with respect to (non-lazy) sensing. We also examine the trade offs between sensing cost and size. Our results show that the good properties of sensing are preserved in the lazy setting. In particular, saving sensing does not conflict with saving size: in all four classes, the lazy-sensing cost of a regular language can be attained in the minimal automaton recognizing the language.

1 Introduction

The classical complexity measure for regular languages is the size of a minimal deterministic automaton that recognizes the language. In [1], the authors introduced a new complexity measure, namely the *sensing cost* of the language. Intuitively, the sensing cost of a language measures the detail with which a random input word needs to be read in order to decide membership in the language. The study is motivated by the use of finite-state automata in reasoning about on-going behaviors of reactive systems. In particular, when *monitoring* a computation, we seek a monitor that minimizes the activation of sensors used in the

Work partially supported by the Israel Science Foundation, ISF grant agreement no 2357/19.

Published by Springer Nature Switzerland AG 2022
Y.-S. Han and G. Vaszil (Eds.): DCFS 2022, LNCS 13439, pp. 155–169, 2022.
https://doi.org/10.1007/978-3-031-13257-5_12

monitoring process, and when *synthesizing* a system, we prefer I/O-transducers that satisfy a given specification while minimizing the activation of sensors (of input signals) [1]. Sensing has been studied in several other computer-science contexts. In theoretical computer science, in methodologies such as PCP and property testing, we are allowed to sample or query only part of the input [5]. In more practical applications, mathematical tools in signal processing are used to reconstruct information based on compressed sensing [3], and in the context of data streaming, one cannot store in memory the entire input, and therefore has to approximate its properties according to partial "sketches" [8].

The automata used in formal methods are over alphabets of the form 2^P, for a finite set P of signals. Consider a deterministic automaton (DFA) $\mathcal{A}$ over an alphabet 2^P. For a state q of $\mathcal{A}$, we say that a signal $p \in P$ is *sensed* in q if at least one transition taken from q depends on the truth value of p. The *sensing cost* of q is the number of signals it senses, and the sensing cost of a run is the average sensing cost of states visited along the run. The definition is extended to DFAs by defining the sensing cost of $\mathcal{A}$ as the limit of the expected sensing of runs over words of increasing length, assuming a uniform distribution of the letters in 2^P, thus each signal $p \in P$ holds in each moment in time with probability $\frac{1}{2}$. It is easy to extend the setting to a non-uniform distribution on the letters, given by a Markov chain. The sensing cost of a language $L \subseteq (2^P)^*$ is then the infimum of the sensing costs of DFAs for L.

In this work, we refine the notion of regular sensing from [1], which we call *naive sensing*, to a new notion called *lazy sensing*. Intuitively, in naive sensing, the signals in P are sensed simultaneously. Consequently, if a signal p is defined to be sensed in a state q, then a sensor for p must indeed be activated whenever a run of the DFA is in state q and needs to determine the successor state. In lazy sensing, the signals are not sensed simultaneously. Instead, they can be activated "on demand", one after the other, and we may reach a decision about the successor state before they are all sensed. This is demonstrated in the following simple example.

Example 1. Let $P = \{a, b\}$, and consider a state q_0 with three successor states q_1, q_2, and q_3, and transitions as shown on the right. According to the definition in [1], both a and b are sensed in q_0. Indeed, in naive sensing, when the signals are sensed simultaneously, both a and b must be sensed in order to determine the successor state.

In lazy sensing, we can start by sensing only the signal a. If a is `True`, then we know that the successor state is q_1, and there is no need to sense b. Accordingly, if we assume that a has probability $\frac{1}{2}$ to be `True`, the number of sensors we are expected to activate in state q_0 is only $1\frac{1}{2}$, rather than 2. □

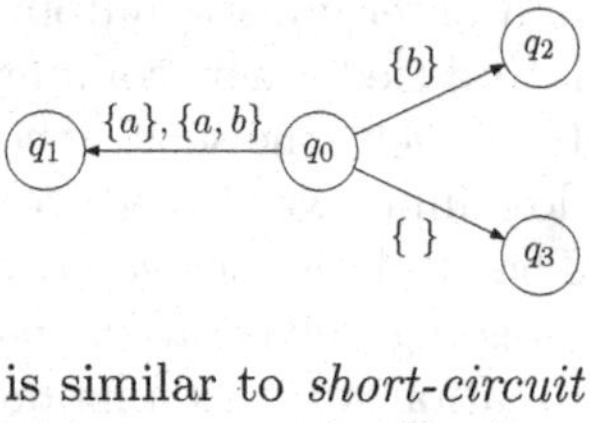

The underlying idea of lazy sensing is simple and is similar to *short-circuit evaluation* in programming languages. There, the second argument of a Boolean operator is executed or evaluated only if the first argument does not suffice to determine the value of the expression [7]. Our study examines such a lazy evaluation in the context of DFAs.

In order to perform lazy sensing, each state of the DFA should be equipped with a data structure that directs it which signal to sense next. We examine four different classes of lazy sensing, induced by the following two parameters: (1) Is ordering of signals sensed *dynamic* or *static*: in the dynamic classes, the order may depend on the truth value of signals sensed earlier. That is, the data structure supports policies like "if a is `True`, then next sense b, and if a is `False`, then next sense c". In the static classes, the data structure is a linear order on the signals – the order in which they are going to be sensed, regardless of the result. (2) Is the sensing policy *local* or *global*: in the local classes, each state may have its own data structure. In the global ones, the same data structure is used for all the states. Note that both parameters are irrelevant in short-circuit evaluation in programming languages. Indeed, lazy evaluation concerns Boolean expressions, each evaluated independently, and the control flow is induced by the structure of the expression.

The difference between the dynamic and static classes can be viewed as follows. Consider a DFA with state space Q, and consider a state $q \in Q$. The data structure maintaining the transitions from q is a *sensing tree*: a decision tree in which each vertex is labeled by a signal in $p \in P$ and has two successors, corresponding to the two truth values that p may have. Each path in the tree corresponds to a set of assignments to the signals in P – assignments that are consistent with the truth values that the path assigns to signals that appear in it. Accordingly, if we label the leaves of the tree by states in Q, then each sensing tree maintains a function $f : 2^P \to Q$. In the static classes, all paths in the sensing tree follow the same fixed order of the signals in P. Thus, the sensing tree is related to a *multiple-valued decision diagram* [2,6]. On the other hand, in the dynamic classes, the order of the signals in each path of the sensing tree may be different.

For all the four classes, the lazy sensing cost of a state $q \in Q$ is the expected number of signals sensed when a transition from q is taken and sensing is performed according to the sensing tree. Then, the lazy sensing cost of a DFA is the limit of expected sensing of runs overs words of increasing length, with the best possible choice of the allowed data structure. For example, in the static-global class, this best possible choice is a single vector of the signals in P, maintaining a linear order that is used by all states of the DFA. Finally, the sensing cost of a regular language L is the infimum of sensing costs of a DFA for L.

We examine the different classes of lazy sensing and the saving they enable, with respect to each other and with respect to naive sensing. We also examine the trade offs between sensing cost and size. Our results show that the good properties of naive sensing are preserved in lazy sensing. In particular, the lazy sensing cost of a DFA can be calculated by using the stationary distribution of its induced Markov chain. Also, saving sensing does not conflict with saving size: in all four classes, the lazy sensing cost of a regular language can be attained in the minimal automaton recognizing the language.

Due to the lack of space, some proofs are omitted and can be found in the full version, in the authors' URLs.

2 Defining Lazy Sensing

2.1 Deterministic Finite Automata

A *deterministic automaton on finite words* (DFA, for short) is $\mathcal{A} = \langle \Sigma, Q, q_0, \delta, \alpha \rangle$, where Σ is a finite alphabet, Q is a finite set of states, $q_0 \in Q$ is an initial state, $\delta : Q \times \Sigma \to Q$ is a transition function, and $\alpha \subseteq Q$ is a set of accepting states. A run of $\mathcal{A}$ on a word $w = \sigma_1 \cdot \sigma_2 \cdots \sigma_m \in \Sigma^*$ is the sequence of states $q_0, q_1, \ldots, q_m$ such that $q_{i+1} = \delta(q_i, \sigma_{i+1})$ for all $i \geq 0$. The run is accepting if $q_m \in \alpha$. A word $w \in \Sigma^*$ is accepted by $\mathcal{A}$ if the run of $\mathcal{A}$ on w is accepting. For $i \geq 0$, we use $w[1,i]$ to denote the prefix $\sigma_1 \cdot \sigma_2 \cdots \sigma_i$ of w, and use $\delta(w[1,i])$ to denote the state q_i that $\mathcal{A}$ visits after reading the prefix $w[1,i]$. Note that $w[1,0] = \epsilon$. The language of $\mathcal{A}$, denoted $L(\mathcal{A})$, is the set of words that $\mathcal{A}$ accepts. For a state $q \in Q$, we use $\mathcal{A}^q$ to denote $\mathcal{A}$ with initial state q.

2.2 Potentially Sensed Signals

We study languages over an alphabet $\Sigma = 2^P$, for a finite set P of signals. A letter $\sigma \in \Sigma$ corresponds to a truth assignment to the signals. When we define languages over Σ, we use predicates on P in order to denote sets of letters. For example, if $P = \{a, b, c\}$, then the expression $(\mathtt{True})^* \cdot a \cdot b \cdot (\mathtt{True})^*$ describes all words over 2^P that contain a subword $\sigma_a \cdot \sigma_b$ with $\sigma_a \in \{\{a\}, \{a,b\}, \{a,c\}, \{a,b,c\}\}$ and $\sigma_b \in \{\{b\}, \{a,b\}, \{b,c\}, \{a,b,c\}\}$.

Consider a DFA $\mathcal{A} = \langle 2^P, Q, q_0, \delta, \alpha \rangle$. For a state $q \in Q$ and a signal $p \in P$, we say that p is *potentially sensed in* q if there exists a set $S \subseteq P$ such that $\delta(q, S \setminus \{p\}) \neq \delta(q, S \cup \{p\})$. Intuitively, a signal is potentially sensed in q if knowing its value may affect the destination of at least one transition from q. We use $psensed(q)$ to denote the set of signals potentially sensed in q.

Recall the situation in Example 1. For $S = \emptyset$, we have $\delta(q_0, S \cup \{a\}) = q_1$ and $\delta(q_0, S \setminus \{a\}) = q_3$, so a is potentially sensed in q_0. Also, $\delta(q_0, S \cup \{b\}) = q_2$ and $\delta(q_0, S \setminus \{b\}) = q_3$, so b is also potentially sensed in q_0.

In the naive sensing setting, studied in [1], sensing of input signals happens simultaneously; that is, we sense together all of the signals whose truth value might affect the decision to which state to proceed. Accordingly, the notions of a sensed signal in [1] and our definition above of a potentially sensed signal coincide. In the following sections, we formalize the notion of *lazy sensing*, where sensing need not be simultaneous.

2.3 Sensing Trees

The main feature of lazy sensing is a data structure termed *sensing tree*, which directs the order in which signals are sensed. A *sensing tree* is a labeled tree $T = \langle V, E, \tau \rangle$, where V is a set of vertices, $E \subseteq V \times \{\mathtt{True}, \mathtt{False}\} \times V$ is a set of directed labeled edges, and $\tau : V \to P \cup Q$ is a labelling function. Each vertex $v \in V$ is either *internal*, in which case it has exactly two children, v_{left} and v_{right}, with $\langle v, \mathtt{False}, v_{left} \rangle$ and $\langle v, \mathtt{True}, v_{right} \rangle$, or is a *leaf*, in which case

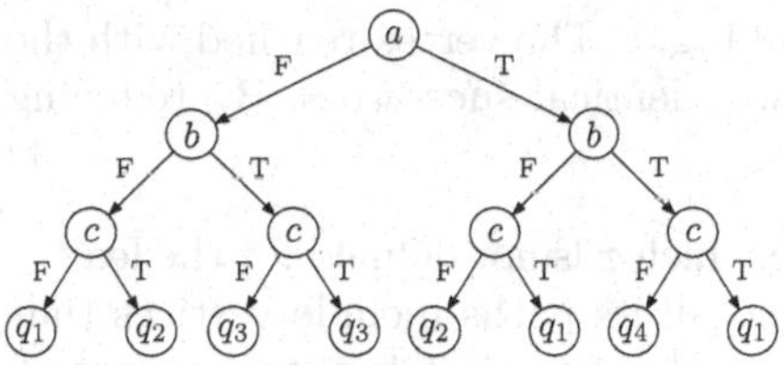

Fig. 1. The sensing tree T.

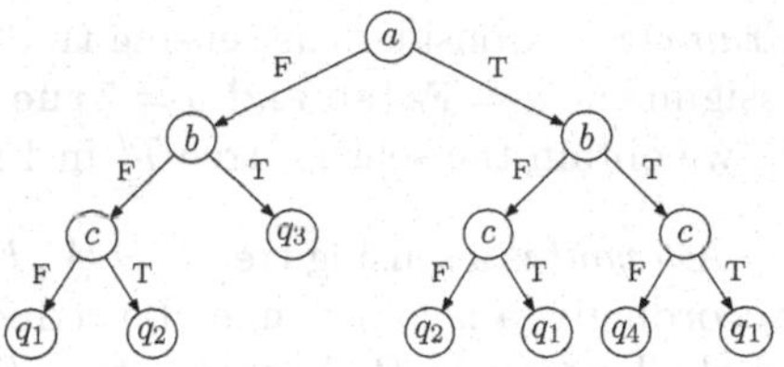

Fig. 2. Reducing the tree T.

it has no children. Let $Int(T)$ and $Leaves(T)$ denote the sets of internal vertices and leaves of T, respectively. We assume that T has a single *root* – a vertex with no incoming edges.

The labelling function τ labels internal vertices by signals in P and labels leaves by states in Q. The function τ is such that for each signal $p \in P$ and leaf $\ell \in V$, the single path from the root to ℓ includes at most one vertex labeled p. Accordingly, each subset $S \in 2^P$ corresponds to a single leaf, namely the leaf reached by following the path that corresponds to the assignment S. Formally, reading an input $S \in 2^P$, we start from the root of the tree, and then in each step, we sense the signal p that labels the current vertex. If it is `True` (i.e., $p \in S$), we proceed to the right child. If it is `False` (i.e., $p \notin S$), we proceed to the left child. By the requirement on τ, we encounter each signal at most once. In particular, as some signals may not appear in the traversed path, the above process may reach a leaf before all signals have been sensed. Let $f_T : 2^P \to Leaves(T)$ map each $S \in 2^P$ to the leaf that corresponds to S. We sometimes refer to a sensing tree also as a function $T : 2^P \to Q$, where for every $S \in 2^P$, we have that $T(S) = \tau(f_T(S))$, thus each assignment is mapped to the label of the leaf that corresponds to S. Also, for $S \in 2^P$, we use $sensed(T, S)$ for the set of signals sensed in the process of finding $T(S)$. Note that $|sensed(T, S)|$ is the length of the path from the root to $f_T(S)$.

Example 2. Let $P = \{a, b, c\}$ and $Q = \{q_1, q_2, q_3, q_4\}$. The tree T appearing in Fig. 1 represents the function f with $f(\emptyset) = f(\{a, c\}) = f(\{a, b, c\}) = q_1$, $f(\{c\}) = f(\{a\}) = q_2$, $f(\{b\}) = f(\{b, c\}) = q_3$, and $f(\{a, b\}) = q_4$. □

We assume that sensing trees are *reduced*: they do not include redundant tests, namely internal vertices whose two children root identical subtrees. A sensing tree may be reduced in polynomial time by repeatedly replacing an internal vertex with two identical children by one of its children. It is not hard to see that the order in which such replacements are applied is not important.[1]

[1] Note that the above definition of a reduced tree is *syntactic*, in the sense it examines whether subtrees are identical. An alternative *semantic* definition removes a vertex if its two children root subtrees that represent the same function. Since the order of the signals along different paths may be different, two subtrees that represent the same function need not be identical, even if both are reduced. Thus, the semantic definition may result in smaller sensing trees. However, reducing trees according to

Example 3. Consider the sensing tree T from Fig. 1. The vertex reached with the assignment $a = \texttt{False}$ and $b = \texttt{True}$ has two identical successors. By reducing T, we obtain the sensing tree T' in Fig. 2. □

A *layout* is a sensing tree $L = \langle V, E, \tau \rangle$ in which τ is not defined for the leaves. Accordingly, a layout cannot be reduced, and all its paths include vertices that label all signals in P. A sensing tree T *follows* a layout L if T is obtained from L by reducing the sensing tree obtained by extending τ to the leaves. Intuitively, L directs the required sensing in T, but some tests that exist in L can be skipped in T.

2.4 The Sensing Cost of a Sensing Tree

Consider a sensing tree $T = \langle V, E, \tau \rangle$. The *sensing cost* of T is the expected number of signals that are sensed when evaluating an assignment $S \in 2^P$. Recall that we assume that each signal is valid with probability $\frac{1}{2}$. Thus, the probability of each assignment is $\frac{1}{2^{|P|}}$. Accordingly, the sensing cost of T, denoted $scost(T)$, is $scost(T) = \frac{1}{2^{|P|}} \sum_{S \in 2^P} |sensed(T, S)|$.

An equivalent definition of $scost(T)$ is based on a discounted sum of the vertices in T. For $v \in V$, let $depth(v)$ denote the length of the path from the root to v. Thus, the depth of the root is 0, the depth of its children is 1, and so on. Since the probability to reach the internal vertex v when reading an assignment $S \in 2^P$ that is chosen uniformly at random, is $2^{-depth(v)}$, we have the following.

Lemma 1. *For every sensing tree T, we have that $scost(T) = \sum_{v \in Int(T)} 2^{-depth(v)}$.*

Example 4. The sensing cost of the tree T' from Fig. 2 is $\frac{1}{8} \cdot (3 + 3 + 2 + 2 + 3 + 3 + 3 + 3) = 2\frac{3}{4}$. Using discounted sum, we get $1 + 2 \cdot \frac{1}{2} + 3 \cdot \frac{1}{4} = 2\frac{3}{4}$. □

2.5 Static vs. Dynamic Sensing Trees

The sensing tree T' from Fig. 2 is such that the labelling function τ follows the same order of the signals in P in all its branches. Indeed, all branches first sense a, then b, and then c, possibly skipping some of the signals (specifically, skipping c after reading $a = \texttt{False}$ and $b = \texttt{True}$). This corresponds to situations where the order of signals sensed is decided in advance and is *static.* In contrast, the order of signals sensed may be *dynamic* and depends on the valuation of signals sensed earlier.

Example 5. Consider the function f represented by the sensing tree T' from Fig. 2. The two sensing trees appearing in Fig. 3 represent f too. Both are reduced. The tree on the left is static, and it follows the order $c < b < a$. It is reduced, and still its sensing cost is 3, as all tree signals are read in all assignments. The tree on the right is dynamic: When $a = \texttt{False}$, the next signal to sense is b. When $a = \texttt{True}$, the next signal to sense is c. Its sensing cost is $2\frac{1}{2}$, which is in fact the minimal sensing cost required for evaluating f. □

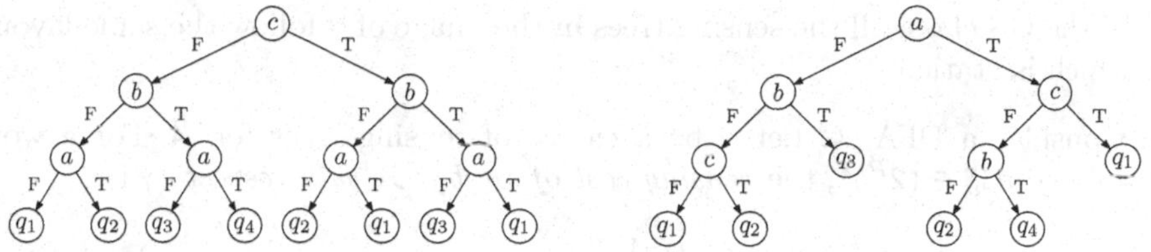

Fig. 3. A static (left) and a dynamic (right) sensing tree for f.

Note that, like a sensing tree, a layout may be static or dynamic. In particular, a static layout corresponds to a permutation on P. Indeed, such a layout is a sensing tree in which the vertices along all paths from the root to a leaf are labeled by all signals in P, with all paths follow the same ordering.

2.6 The Sensing Cost of a DFA and a Regular Language

Consider a DFA $\mathcal{A} = \langle 2^P, Q, q_0, \delta, \alpha \rangle$. Essentially, the sensing cost of $\mathcal{A}$ is the expected number of signals that $\mathcal{A}$ needs to sense in each transition when it runs on a random long word. Defining the sensing cost of $\mathcal{A}$, we first have to define the expected number of signals that $\mathcal{A}$ needs to sense in each state $q \in Q$. In [1], this is the number of potentially sensed signals in q. Defining the lazy sensing cost of $\mathcal{A}$, we allow the states to maintain sensing trees that represent the transition function. Indeed, the function $\delta : Q \times 2^P \to Q$ induces, for each state $q \in Q$, a function $\delta_q : 2^P \to Q$, where for every assignment $S \in 2^P$, we have that $\delta_q(S) = \delta(q, S)$. We distinguish between four classess, induced by the following two parameters.

- *Static vs. Dynamic.* That is, whether the sensing trees for δ_q are static or dynamic.
- *Global vs. Local.* That is, whether the sensing trees of the different states follow the same layout.

We denote the four classes by SG, SL, DG, and DL.

Let $\mathcal{T}$ be the set of all sensing trees (over P and Q, which we omit from the notation). A *legal choice of sensing trees* for the DFA $\mathcal{A}$ is a function $\gamma : Q \to \mathcal{T}$, such that for every state $q \in Q$, the sensing tree $\gamma(q)$ represents the function δ_q, and the following hold. Note that we can view γ as a mapping of states to layouts, which are then reduced to sensing trees. In particular, note that there is a unique way to reduce a layout to a sensing tree for a given function $f : 2^P \to Q$.

- In the LD class, there are no restrictions on γ.
- In the LS class, the image of γ contains only static sensing trees.
- In the GD class, all the sensing trees in the image of γ follow the same layout.

the semantic definition is more complex. All our results apply also to the semantic definition.

- In the GS class, all the sensing trees in the image of γ follow the same layout, which is static.

Consider a DFA $\mathcal{A}$. Let γ be a choice of sensing trees for $\mathcal{A}$. For a word $w = w_1 \cdots w_m \in (2^P)^*$, the *sensing cost of* w *by* $\mathcal{A}$ *with respect* γ is

$$scost_{\mathcal{A},\gamma}(w) = \frac{1}{m}\sum_{i=0}^{m-1} |sensed(\gamma(\delta(w[1,i]), w_{i+1}))|.$$

That is, $scost_{\mathcal{A},\gamma}(w)$ is the average number of signals that a state in the run of $\mathcal{A}$ on w senses when it reads w using the sensing trees chosen by γ. Note that the definition does not take into account the last state in the run, namely $\delta(w[1,m])$, as indeed no letter is read in it.

The *sensing cost of* $\mathcal{A}$ *with respect to* γ is then defined as the expected sensing cost of words of length tending to infinity, when the letters in 2^P are uniformly distributed. Formally,

$$scost(\mathcal{A},\gamma) = \lim_{m\to\infty} |2^P|^{-m} \sum_{w\in(2^P)^m} scost_{\mathcal{A},\gamma}(w).$$

That is, $scost(\mathcal{A},\gamma)$ is the expected sensing cost of words of length tending to infinity, when the letters in 2^P are uniformly distributed.

Now, the *sensing cost of* $\mathcal{A}$ is the sensing cost of $\mathcal{A}$ using an optimal legal choice $\gamma : Q \to \mathcal{T}$ of sensing trees. Formally, for every class $\zeta \in \{LD, LS, GD, GS\}$, we define $\zeta scost(\mathcal{A})$ as $\min\{\zeta scost(\mathcal{A},\gamma) : \gamma \in Q^{\mathcal{T}}$ is legal in $\zeta\}$.

Finally, the *sensing cost of a regular language* $L \subseteq (2^P)^*$ is the infimum of the sensing costs of DFAs that recognize L. That is, for every class $\zeta \in \{LD, LS, GD, GS\}$, we have that $\zeta scost(L) = \inf\{\zeta scost(\mathcal{A}) : L(\mathcal{A}) = L\}$. We use infimum in the definition since the number of DFAs recognizing L is unbounded. In fact, a-priori, there is no guarantee that $\zeta scost(L)$ is attained by a DFA.

3 Probability-Based Definition of Lazy-Sensing Cost

The definition of sensing cost of a DFA in Sect. 2.6 is not effective, in the sense it does not suggest a way to calculate the sensing cost of a DFA. In this section we describe an alternative definition, which does suggest such a way. Essentially, while the definition in Sect. 2.6 refers to the sensing cost of words of increasing length, our definition here refers to the sensing costs of states visited by random walks on the DFA. We first need some definitions and notations about probability.

A *Markov chain* $M = \langle S, P\rangle$ consists of a finite state space S and a stochastic transition matrix $P : S \times S \to [0,1]$. That is, for all $s \in S$, we have $\sum_{s'\in S} P(s,s') = 1$.

Consider a directed graph $G = \langle V, E\rangle$. A *strongly connected component* (SCC) of G is a maximal (with respect to containment) set $C \subseteq V$ such that for all $x, y \in C$, there is a path from x to y. An SCC (or state) is *ergodic* if no other SCC is reachable from it, and is *transient* otherwise.

An automaton $\mathcal{A} = \langle \Sigma, Q, q_0, \delta, \alpha\rangle$ induces a directed graph $G_{\mathcal{A}} = \langle Q, E\rangle$ in which $\langle q, q'\rangle \in E$ iff there is a letter σ such that $q' = \delta(q, \sigma)$. When we talk about the SCCs of $\mathcal{A}$, we refer to those of $G_{\mathcal{A}}$. Recall that we assume that the letters in Σ are uniformly distributed, thus $\mathcal{A}$ also corresponds to a Markov chain $M_{\mathcal{A}}$ in which the probability of a transition from state q to state q' is $p_{q,q'} = \frac{1}{|\Sigma|}|\{\sigma \in \Sigma : \delta(q, \sigma) = q'\}|$. Let $\mathcal{C}$ be the set of $\mathcal{A}$'s SCC, and $\mathcal{C}_e \subseteq \mathcal{C}$ be the set of its ergodic SCC's.

Consider an ergodic SCC $C \in \mathcal{C}_e$. Let P_C be the matrix describing the probability of transitions in C. Thus, the rows and columns of P_C are associated with states, and the value in coordinate q, q' is $p_{q,q'}$. By [4], there is a unique probability vector $\pi_C \in [0, 1]^C$ such that $\pi_C P_C = \pi_C$. This vector describes the *stationary distribution* of C: for all $q \in C$ it holds that $\pi_C(q) = \lim_{m\to\infty} \frac{E_m^C(q)}{m}$, where $E_m^C(q)$ is the average number of occurrences of q in a run of $M_{\mathcal{A}}$ of length m that starts anywhere in C [4]. Thus, intuitively, $\pi_C(q)$ is the probability that a long run that starts in C ends in q. In order to extend the distribution to the entire Markov chain of $\mathcal{A}$, we have to take into account the probability of reaching each of the ergodic components. The *SCC-reachability distribution* of $\mathcal{A}$ is the function $\rho : \mathcal{C}_e \to [0, 1]$ that maps each ergodic SCC C of $\mathcal{A}$ to the probability that $M_{\mathcal{A}}$ eventually reaches C, starting from the initial state. The *limiting distribution* $\pi : Q \to [0, 1]$ is now defined by $\pi(q) = 0$, if q is transient, and $\pi(1) = \pi_C(q) \cdot \rho(C)$, if q is in some $C \in \mathcal{C}_e$. By [4], the limiting distributions can be computed in polynomial time by solving a system of linear equations.

Intuitively, the limiting distribution of state q describes the probability of a run on a random and long input word to end in q. Formally, we have the following lemma.

Lemma 2 [1]. *Let $E_m(q)$ be the expected number of occurrences of a state q in a run of length m of $M_{\mathcal{A}}$ that starts in q_0. Then, $\pi(q) = \lim_{m\to\infty} \frac{E_m(q)}{m}$.*

The alternative definition is based on the following lemma, see proof in the full version.

Lemma 3. *Let $\mathcal{A} = \langle 2^P, Q, q_0, \delta, \alpha\rangle$ be a DFA, and let γ be a choice of sensing trees for $\mathcal{A}$. Then,*

$$scost(\mathcal{A}, \gamma) = \lim_{m\to\infty} |2^P|^{-m} \sum_{w\in(2^P)^m} \frac{1}{m} \sum_{i=0}^{m-1} scost(\gamma(\delta(w[1, i]))).$$

Lemma 3 enables us to follow the exact same considerations in [1], thus computing the lazy-sensing cost of a DFA by examining its induced Markov chain. Formally, we have the following.

Theorem 1. *Let $\mathcal{A}$ be a DFA with alphabet 2^P, state space Q, and limiting distribution $\pi : Q \to [0,1]$. Then, for every choice γ of sensing trees for $\mathcal{A}$, we have that $scost(\mathcal{A}, \gamma) = \sum_{q \in Q} \pi(q) \cdot scost(\gamma(q))$.*

4 Lazy-Sensing Cost vs. Size

In this section we examine the trade-off between the size of a DFA and its sensing cost in the four lazy classes of sensing. It is shown in [1] that in the naive setting of sensing, namely when all signals are read simultaneously, minimizing the size of a DFA goes hand in hand with minimizing its sensing cost. Thus, minimal naive sensing is attained in a minimal-size DFA. In this section, we show that this good news is carried over to lazy sensing.

Consider a language $L \subseteq \Sigma^*$. For two finite words u_1 and u_2, we say that u_1 and u_2 are *right L-indistinguishable*, denoted $u_1 \sim_L u_2$, if for every $z \in \Sigma^*$, we have that $u_1 \cdot z \in L$ iff $u_2 \cdot z \in L$. Thus, $\sim_L$ is the Myhill-Nerode right congruence used for minimizing automata. For $u \in \Sigma^*$, let $[u]$ denote the equivalence class of u in $\sim_L$ and let $\langle L \rangle$ denote the set of all equivalence classes. Each class $[u] \in \langle L \rangle$ is associated with the *residual language* $u^{-1}L = \{w : uw \in L\}$. When L is regular, the set $\langle L \rangle$ is finite, and induces the *residual automaton* of L, defined by $\mathcal{R}_L = \langle \Sigma, \langle L \rangle, \delta^L, [\epsilon], \alpha \rangle$, with $\delta^L([u], a) = [u \cdot a]$, for all $[u] \in \langle L \rangle$ and $a \in \Sigma$. Also, α contains all classes $[u]$ with $u \in L$. The DFA $\mathcal{R}_L$ is well defined and is the unique minimal DFA for L.

Lemma 4. *Consider a regular language $L \subseteq \Sigma^*$. For every DFA $\mathcal{A}$ with $L(\mathcal{A}) = L$ and lazy-sensing class $\zeta \in \{LD, LS, GD, GS\}$, it holds that $\zeta scost(\mathcal{R}_L) \leq \zeta scost(\mathcal{A})$.*

Proof: Let $\mathcal{A} = \langle 2^P, Q, q_0, \delta, \alpha \rangle$ be a DFA such that $L(\mathcal{A}) = L$. Consider a reachable state $q \in Q$. Let $u \in (2^P)^*$ be a word such that $\mathcal{A}$ reaches the q after reading u, thus $q = \delta^*(q_0, u)$. Recall that $\mathcal{R}_L$ reaches the state $[u]$ after reading u. We claim that for every layout T of a sensing tree over P, we have that $scost(T_{[u]}) \leq scost(T_q)$, where $T_{[u]}$ is the sensing tree obtained from T by reducing it according to the transitions of $\mathcal{R}_L$ from $[u]$, and T_q is the sensing tree obtained from T by reducing it according to the transitions of $\mathcal{A}$ from q.

By Lemma 1, for every sensing tree T, we have $scost(T) = \sum_{v \in Int(T)} 2^{-depth(v)}$. Accordingly, it suffices to prove that for all letters $\sigma, \sigma' \in 2^P$ if $\delta(q, \sigma) = \delta(\sigma')$, then $\delta^L([u], \sigma) = \delta^L([u], \sigma')$. Indeed, this would guarantee that every vertex that is deleted from the layout T when it is reduced to T_q is also deleted when T is reduced to $T_{[u]}$. In the full version, we prove this claim. □

Since $L(\mathcal{R}_L) = L$, then for every class $\zeta \in \{LD, LS, GD, GS\}$, we have that $\zeta scost(L) \leq \zeta scost(\mathcal{R}_L)$. Thus, together with Lemma 4, we can conclude with the following.

Theorem 2. *For every regular language $L \subseteq (2^P)^*$ and lazy-sensing class $\zeta \in \{LD, LS, GD, GS\}$, we have that $\zeta scost(L) = \zeta scost(\mathcal{R}_L)$.*

5 Comparing the Different Sensing Classes

In this section we examine the saving of sensing that the lazy classes enable. We start by comparing the lazy classes with the setting in [1], where all signals are sensed simultaneously, and continue to examine the relations among the four lazy classes.

5.1 Lazy vs. Naive Sensing

Recall that in the setting of [1], which we refer to as *naive sensing*, the sensing cost of a DFA $\mathcal{A}$ is defined as follows (we use the prefix N for naive).

$$Nscost(\mathcal{A}) = \lim_{m\to\infty} |2^P|^{-m} \sum_{w\in(2^P)^m} \frac{1}{m}\sum_{i=0}^{m-1} |psensed(\delta(w[1,i]))|,$$

as all the potentially sensed signals must in fact be sensed. The sensing cost of a regular language in the naive sensing setting is then defined as $Nscost(L) = \inf\{Nscost(\mathcal{A}) : L(\mathcal{A}) = L\}$. We first show that, as expected, the sensing cost in all lazy classes is never higher than the naive one.

Theorem 3. *For every DFA $\mathcal{A}$ over an alphabet 2^P and for every lazy-sensing class $\zeta \in \{LD, LS, GD, GS\}$, we have that $\zeta scost(\mathcal{A}) \leq Nscost(\mathcal{A})$.*

Proof: We prove the theorem for the static classes LS and GS. Since every choice function γ that is legal in these classes is legal also in the corresponding dynamic class, the result for LD and GD follows. Let $\mathcal{A} = \langle 2^P, Q, q_0, \delta, \alpha\rangle$, and let γ be a choice of sensing trees for the DFA $\mathcal{A}$ that is legal with respect to $\zeta \in \{LS, GS\}$. We claim that for every state $q \in Q$, if $p \notin psensed(q)$, then there is no internal vertex with the label p in $\gamma(q)$. Since this holds for all choices function γ, in particular these that attain $\zeta scost(\mathcal{A})$, the theorem follows.

In order to prove the claim, consider a state q and let $\gamma(q) = \langle V, E, \tau\rangle$. Consider an internal vertex $v \in V$ such that $\tau(v) = p$. If $p \notin psensed(q)$, then for every $S \in 2^P$, we have that $\delta(q, S\setminus\{p\}) = \delta(q, S \cup \{p\})$. Therefore, regardless of ζ, the subtrees of $\langle V, E, \tau\rangle$ with roots v_{left} and v_{right} calculate the same function. Since ζ is static, this implies that v_{left} and v_{right} root identical subtrees, and so we can reduce $\langle V, E, \tau\rangle$ by redirecting the edge that enters v to v_{left}. □

Corollary 1. *For every regular language $L \subseteq (2^P)^*$ and lazy-sensing class $\zeta \in \{LD, LS, GD, GS\}$, we have that $\zeta scost(L) \leq Nscost(L)$.*

We now show that, on the one hand, there are cases where lazy sensing is not helpful (Theorem 4), and, on the other hand, there are cases where the saving that lazy sensing enables is unbounded (Theorem 5).

Theorem 4. *For every finite set P of signals, there is a regular language $L \subseteq (2^P)^*$ such that for every lazy-sensing class $\zeta \in \{LD, LS, GD, GS\}$, we have that $\zeta scost(L) = Nscost(L)$.*

Proof: Let $L = \{w_1 \cdots w_m \in (2^P)^* : m \geq 1 \text{ and } |w_m| \text{ is even}\}$ be the language of all words in $(2^P)^*$ that end with a letter that consists of an even number of signals. A DFA $\mathcal{A}$ for L must sense all the signals in P in all states. Indeed, the DFA $\mathcal{A}$ has to identify, in all states, whether the current input letter consists of an even number of signals. Thus, for every state of q of $\mathcal{A}$ and choice function γ, we have that $scost(\gamma(q)) = |P|$. By Theorem 1 and the definition of the naive sensing cost of a DFA, we conclude that $\zeta scost(\mathcal{A}) = Nscost(\mathcal{A}) = |P|$. Since the above holds for every DFA $\mathcal{A}$ recognizing L, the result follows. □

Theorem 5. *For every $n \geq 1$, there is a regular language L_n over $2^{\{p_1,\ldots,p_n\}}$ such that $Nscost(L_n) = n$, yet for every lazy-sensing class $\zeta \in \{LD, LS, GD, GS\}$, we have that $\zeta scost(L_n) < 2$.*

Proof: Let $P_n = \{p_1, ..., p_n\}$ be a set of n signals, let $\sigma = P_n$, and let L_n be the language of all words with an even number of occurrences of the letter σ. A minimal DFA $\mathcal{A}_n$ that recognizes L_n consists of two states, keeping track of the parity of occurrences of σ, see Fig. 4 below.

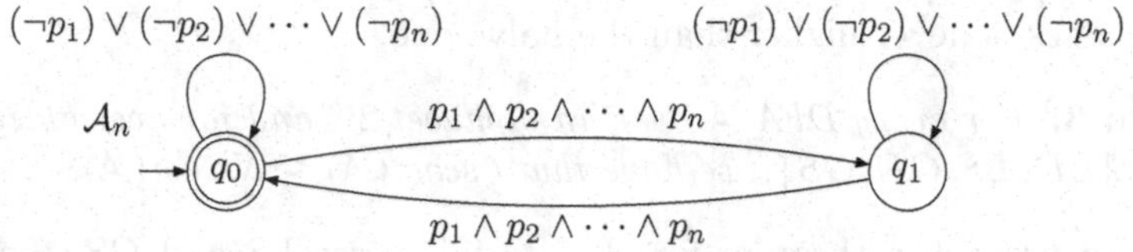

Fig. 4. Lazy sensing is better than naive sensing.

It is easy to see that $psensed(q_0) = psensed(q_1) = P_n$. Indeed, for every $p_i \in P_n$ we have $\delta(q_0, P_n \cup \{p_i\}) = q_1 \neq q_0 = \delta(q_0, P_n \setminus \{p_i\})$ and $\delta(q_1, P_n \cup \{p_i\}) = q_0 \neq q_1 = \delta(q_1, P_n \setminus \{p_i\})$. Since q_0 and q_1 are the only states of $\mathcal{A}_n$, it follows that $Nscost(\mathcal{A}_n) = n$. Also, as the naive sensing cost of a regular language is attained in the minimal DFA recognizing the language [1], it follows that $Nscost(L_n) = n$.

We now consider the lazy sensing cost of L_n. By Theorem 2, here too we can consider the DFA $\mathcal{A}_n$. It is easy to see that a sensing tree T of minimal sensing cost for each of the states q_i, with $i \in \{0, 1\}$, consists of n internal vertices, one in each height from 0 to $n - 1$, labeled by all of the signals in P_n in some arbitrary order.

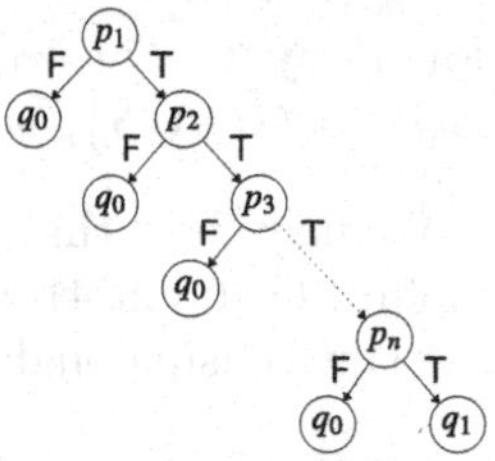

For each such internal vertex, its left child is a leaf labeled q_i. If the vertex is in height different from $n-1$, its right child is another internal vertex. If it is in height $n - 1$, its right child is a leaf labeled with q_{1-i}. The figure on the right shows such a minimal sensing tree for the state q_0.

It is not hard to see that the suggested sensing tree is legal in all classes ζ. Indeed, the same layout is used for q_0 and q_1, and the tree follows an order on

P that is independent of the values read. By Lemma 1, we have that $scost(T) = \sum_{v \in Int(T)} 2^{-depth(v)} = \sum_{i=0}^{n-1} 2^{-i} = 2 - \frac{1}{2^{n-1}}$. Thus, by Theorems 2 and 1, for all classes $\zeta \in \{LD, LS, GD, GS\}$, we have that $\zeta scost(L_n) = scost(\mathcal{A}_n) = 2 - \frac{1}{2^{n-1}} < 2$. □

5.2 Comparison of the Different Lazy-Sensing Classes

In this section, we compare the sensing costs in the different lazy sensing classes. First, since every choice function that is legal in the global classes is legal in the local ones, and every choice function that is legal in the static classes is legal in the dynamic ones, we immediately have the following.

Theorem 6. *For every regular language $L \subseteq (2^P)^*$, the following holds*

$$(i)\ \ LDscost(L) \leq GDscost(L), \qquad (ii)\ \ LSscost(L) \leq GSscost(L),$$
$$(iii)\ \ LDscost(L) \leq LSscost(L), \qquad (iv)\ \ GDscost(L) \leq GSscost(L).$$

Theorem 4 implies that there are languages for which the sensing costs in the four classes coincide. In the following, we describe cases where the inequalities in Theorem 6 are strict. In addition, we show that the local-static class and the global-dynamic class are incomparable: there is a language L with $LSscost(L) < GDscost(L)$ and also a language L with $LSscost(L) > GDscost(L)$.

We start with the advantage of the local classes over the global ones:

Lemma 5. *There exists a regular language $L \subseteq (2^P)^*$ such that $LDscost(L) = LSscost(L) < GDscost(L) = GSscost(L)$.*

Proof: Let $P = \{a, b\}$ and consider the DFA $\mathcal{A}$ with alphabet 2^P shown in Fig. 5.

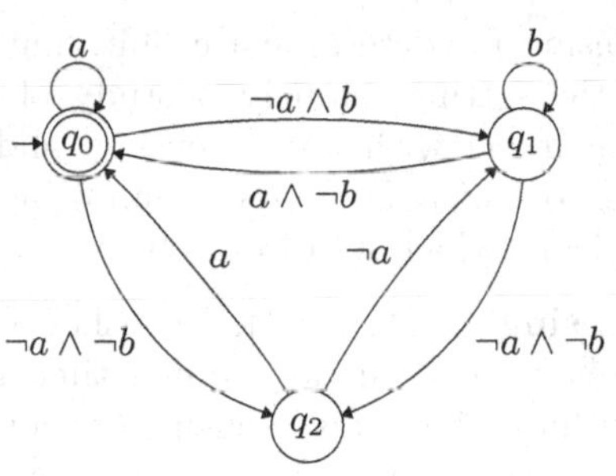

Fig. 5. Local lazy sensing is better than global one.

It can be easily verified that $\mathcal{A}$ is a minimal DFA, for example using the standard DFA minimization algorithm. In the full version, we prove that $LDscost(\mathcal{A}) = LSscost(\mathcal{A}) < GDscost(\mathcal{A}) = GSscost(\mathcal{A})$, which, by Theorem 2, implies that $L(\mathcal{A})$ satisfies the conditions in the lemma. □

We continue with the advantage of the dynamic classes over the static ones:

Lemma 6. *There exists a regular language* $L \subseteq (2^P)^*$ *such that* $LDscost(L) = GDscost(L) < LSscost(L) = GSscost(L)$.

Proof: Let $P = \{a, b, c\}$ and consider the DFA $\mathcal{A}$ with alphabet 2^P shown in Fig. 6.

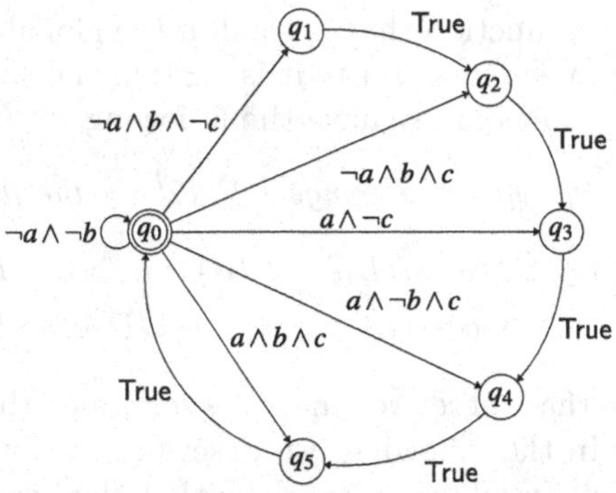

Fig. 6. Dynamic lazy sensing is better than static one.

Again, it can be verified that $\mathcal{A}$ is minimal, thus it is left to prove that $LDscost(\mathcal{A}) = GDscost(\mathcal{A}) < LSscost(\mathcal{A}) = GSscost(\mathcal{A})$, which we do in the full version. □

6 Directions for Future Research

We introduced lazy sensing for deterministic finite automata. We studied the basic problems about the setting, namely a study of four natural classes of lazy sensing, their comparison with naive sensing, and the trade-off between minimizing the sensing cost of a DFA and minimizing its size. We left open several interesting problems, which we discuss below.

Computing Lazy Sensing Cost: In [1], it is shown that the naive sensing cost of a DFA can be calculated in polynomial time using standard Markov chain algorithms. Accordingly, the naive sensing cost of a regular language can also be calculated in polynomial time using the classical minimization algorithm for DFA. In order to compute the sensing cost in lazy-sensing classes, one also needs to find the optimal sensing trees for a given DFA.

The involved questions now depend on the lazy-sensing class. For the SL class, the problem is strongly related to the problem of finding an optimal ordering for the variables in a BDD, and the complexity depends on the way the transition function of the DFA is given. In the GS class, there is the extra requirement that the same order is used in the transition functions of all states. Then, in the dynamic classes, the layouts we may use need not follow an ordering for the variables, and techniques from the theory of BDDs are less relevant.

Random Lazy Sensing: While dynamic and local lazy sensing may save more than static and global lazy sensing, they require the maintenance of more complex data structures. In addition to studying lazy sensing classes with some bounded level of dynamics or locality, it is interesting to examine a stochastic approach, where the signal to be sensed next is chosen randomly. It is not hard to see that our results in Sects. 4 and 5.1 apply also to the random lazy setting, when we examine the expected sensing cost of a DFA, with expectation now referring to both the input words and the order in which signals are sampled.

References

1. Almagor, S., Kuperberg, D., Kupferman, O.: Regular sensing. In: Proceedings of 34th Conference on Foundations of Software Technology and Theoretical Computer Science. LIPIcs, vol. 29, pp. 161–173. Schloss Dagstuhl - Leibniz-Zentrum fuer Informatik, Germany (2014)
2. Burch, J.R., Clarke, E.M., McMillan, K.L., Dill, D.L., Hwang, L.J.: Symbolic model checking: 10^{20} states and beyond. Inf. Comput. **98**(2), 142–170 (1992)
3. Donoho, D.L.: Compressed sensing. IEEE Trans. Inform. Theory **52**, 1289–1306 (2006)
4. Grinstead, C., Laurie Snell, J.: 11: Markov chains. In: Introduction to Probability. American Mathematical Society (1997)
5. Kindler, G.: Property testing, PCP, and Juntas. Ph.D. thesis, Tel Aviv University University (2002)
6. Miller, D.M., Drechsler, R.: On the construction of multiple-valued decision diagrams. In: 32nd IEEE International Symposium on Multiple-Valued Logic, pp. 245–253. IEEE Computer Society (2002)
7. Minker, J., Minker, R.G.: Optimization of Boolean expressions-historical developments. IEEE Ann. Hist. Comput. **2**(3), 227–238 (1980)
8. Muthukrishnan, S.: Theory of data stream computing: where to go. In: Proceedings of 30th Symposium on Principles of Database Systems, pp. 317–319 (2011)

State Complexity of Finite Partial Languages

Martin Kutrib(✉) and Matthias Wendlandt

Institut für Informatik, Universität Giessen, Arndtstr. 2, 35392 Giessen, Germany
{kutrib,matthias.wendlandt}@informatik.uni-giessen.de

Abstract. Partial word finite automata are deterministic finite automata that may have state transitions on a special symbol $\diamond$ which represents an unknown symbol or a hole in the word. Together with a subset of the input alphabet that gives the symbols which may be substituted for the $\diamond$, a partial word finite automaton ($\diamond$-DFA) represents a regular language. However, this substitution implies a certain form of limited nondeterminism in the computations when the $\diamond$-transitions are replaced by ordinary transitions. In this paper we consider the state complexity of partial word finite automata accepting finite languages. We study the state complexity of the NFA to $\diamond$-DFA conversion for finite languages as well as the state complexity of the $\diamond$-DFA to DFA conversion for finite languages. Then we consider the operational state complexity with respect to complementation, union, reversal, and concatenation of finite languages. It turns out that the upper and lower bounds for all these operations are exponential. Moreover, we establish a state complexity hierarchy on the number of productive $\diamond$-transitions that may appear in $\diamond$-DFAs accepting finite languages. The levels of the hierarchy are separated by quadratic state costs.

Keywords: Partial words · finite languages · deterministic finite automata · minimal automata · determinization · operational state complexity · hierarchies on the number of unknown symbol transitions

1 Introduction

Partial words are strings where certain positions are not specified. These positions are often called holes or don't cares and printed by a diamond symbol $\diamond$. Apart from theoretical reasons, the basic motivation for studying this mechanism comes from the study of biological operations in connection with DNA strands. The first time the idea of words with don't cares has been investigated goes back to [12], where they were considered in connection with string matching. The term *partial word* was firstly defined in [2].

Partial words were mainly investigated in connection with combinatorics on words. A survey can be found in [4]. An interesting motivation in theory for this model is that ordinary languages can be compressed by the usage of holes.

Published by Springer Nature Switzerland AG 2022
Y.-S. Han and G. Vaszil (Eds.): DCFS 2022, LNCS 13439, pp. 170–183, 2022.
https://doi.org/10.1007/978-3-031-13257-5_13

Consider for example the language L over the ternary alphabet $\Sigma = \{a, b, c\}$, $L = \{aaa, aba, aca\}$. It can be compressed by using a hole into $L' = \{a \diamond a\}$. Simply by replacing the diamond by a, b, or c the original language L can be achieved. In 2012, partial words were studied in connection with families of formal languages [11]. In particular, a regular language is represented by the image of a partial language under a substitution that only replaces the hole symbols. In connection with DFAs it turned out that the usage of holes can be somehow seen as a limited nondeterminism, since it allows to define DFAs with outgoing edges that are labeled with ordinary symbols and additionally with a diamond. If some of the ordinary symbols may be substituted for the hole symbol as well, the corresponding state allows a nondeterministic choice with respect to the target language (see for example [1,11,16]).

The applications of defining language families by partial words via partial word finite automata have also been investigated from a complexity point of view. Concerning the descriptional complexity, in [1] it has been shown that the state complexity for a DFA that simulates a partial word DFA is exponential in general. Moreover also the state complexity of the simulation of an NFA by a partial word DFA may become exponential. In [19] further basic constructions, the operational state complexity for Boolean operations, and a hierarchy dependent on the number of $\diamond$-transitions in the state graph are addressed. Concerning the computational complexity, different problems as, for example, minimization have been studied for partial word automata [5,16].

The main aim of this paper is to extend the investigations on the descriptional complexity of partial word automata to finite languages.

Finite languages are an important subclass of regular languages. They are accepted by incomplete acyclic DFAs. Acyclic automata are widely used in applications, for example as efficient data structure for dictionary representation. The time needed to access an entry is linear in its word length. Another example is the manipulation of Boolean functions, where minimal acyclic automata are used to obtain fast algorithms for problems as satisfiability test, equivalence test, and function composition [6]. For finite languages, linear time minimization algorithms are known [21] while the minimization of general DFAs takes $O(n \log n)$ time. Another important construction is the determinization of nondeterministic finite automata. The powerset construction requires a tight bound of 2^n for general regular languages. For finite languages a smaller tight bound has been obtained in [22]. It is of order $O(\ell^{\frac{n}{1+\log_2 \ell}})$ and depends on the alphabet size ℓ. Further results for DFAs accepting finite languages include the maximal number of states of the minimal DFA accepting a subset of Σ^k or $\Sigma^{\leq k}$ [8,10]. A different approach to represent finite languages by finite automata has been introduced in [9]. The concept is known as cover automata, where the idea is that a DFA may accept also words not belonging to the finite language as long as these words are longer than the longest word in the finite language. Cover automata have attracted great interest and have since been intensively investigated.

The paper is organized as follows. In the next section we present the underlying definitions and preliminary remarks. Section 3 deals with the state trade-offs for converting the representation of a finite language from an NFA to a partial word finite automaton ($\diamond$-DFA) as well as with the state trade-offs for converting the representation from a $\diamond$-DFA to a DFA. For both conversions an upper bound of order $O(\ell^{\frac{n}{1+\log_2 \ell}})$ follows from the state costs of the determinization. We prove a lower bound of order $O(\ell^{\frac{n}{2\log_2 \ell}})$ for the $\diamond$-DFA to DFA conversion. For the NFA to $\diamond$-DFA conversion we can show the lower bound of $O(\ell^{\frac{n}{1+\log_2 \ell}})$. However, it is not tight since we start with a $(2n+1)$-state NFA and use an alphabet of size 2ℓ. Anyway, the state costs for both conversions are exponential. Section 4 considers the operational state complexity for complementation, union, reversal, and concatenation. It turns out that upper and lower bounds are exponential. In the last section we consider the impact of the number of productive $\diamond$-transitions in a partial word finite automaton, where a transition is called productive, if it does not lead to the rejecting sink state. For $\diamond$-DFAs representing general regular languages, it is known that even the reduction of one of these transitions may lead to an exponential state explosion [19]. In contrast to these results, here it comes out that the state costs for removing one productive $\diamond$-transition is quadratic. Therefore, removing any constant number of $\diamond$-transitions from a $\diamond$-DFA accepting a finite language causes only a polynomial state blow-up.

2 Preliminaries

We denote the non-negative integers $\{0, 1, 2, \dots\}$ by $\mathbb{N}$. Let Σ^* denote the set of all words over the finite alphabet Σ. and $\Sigma^{\leq k}$ denote its restriction to words of length at most k, for any $k \geq 0$. A subset $L \subseteq \Sigma^*$ is said to be a *formal language* over Σ. We write $\overline{L}$ for the *complement* of L with respect to Σ, that is for $\Sigma^* \setminus L$. The *empty word* is denoted by λ and the *reversal* of a word w by w^R. For the *length* of w we write $|w|$. We use $\subseteq$ for *inclusions* and $\subset$ for *strict inclusions*.

Setting $\Sigma_\diamond = \Sigma \cup \{\diamond\}$, where $\diamond \notin \Sigma$ represents *undefined positions* or *holes*, a *partial word* over Σ is a sequence of symbols from $\Sigma_\diamond$. Denoting the set of all partial words over Σ by $\Sigma_\diamond^*$, a *partial language* over Σ is a subset of $\Sigma_\diamond^*$. Partial languages can be transformed to (ordinary) languages by using $\diamond$-substitutions over Σ. A $\diamond$-substitution $\sigma\colon \Sigma_\diamond^* \to 2^{\Sigma^*}$ satisfies $\sigma(a) = \{a\}$, for all $a \in \Sigma$, $\sigma(\diamond) \subseteq \Sigma$, and $\sigma(uv) = \sigma(u)\sigma(v)$, for $u, v \in \Sigma_\diamond^*$. As a result, σ is fully defined by $\sigma(\diamond)$, for example, if $\sigma(\diamond) = \{a, b\}$ and $L = \{\diamond b, \diamond c\}$ then $\sigma(L) = \{ab, bb, ac, bc\}$. So, applying σ to a partial language $L \subseteq \Sigma_\diamond^*$ results in a (ordinary) language $\sigma(L) \subseteq \Sigma^*$.

A *nondeterministic finite automaton* (NFA) is a system $M = \langle Q, \Sigma, \delta, q_0, F\rangle$, where Q is the finite set of *internal states*, Σ is the finite set of *input symbols*, $q_0 \in Q$ is the *initial state*, $F \subseteq Q$ is the set of *accepting states*, and $\delta\colon Q \times \Sigma \to 2^Q$ is the *transition function*. In the forthcoming, we sometimes refer to δ as a subset of $Q \times \Sigma \times Q$. A finite automaton M is *deterministic* (DFA) if and only if $|\delta(q, a)| = 1$, for all $q \in Q$ and $a \in \Sigma$. In this case, we simply write $\delta(q, a) = q'$ for $\delta(q, a) = \{q'\}$ assuming that the transition function is a total mapping $\delta\colon Q \times \Sigma \to Q$. Note that here any DFA is complete, that is, the transition function is total, whereas it may be a partial function for NFAs in the sense that the transition function of nondeterministic machines may map to the empty set. A finite automaton is said to be *minimal* if there is no finite automaton of the same type with fewer states, accepting the same language. Note that a rejecting sink state is counted for DFAs, since they are always complete, whereas it is not counted for NFAs, since their transition function may map to the empty set.

Generally speaking, a language L can be represented by a partial language L' together with a $\diamond$-substitution σ such that $\sigma(L') = L$. In particular, for regular languages, from the descriptional complexity point of view it is an interesting question to what extent there are regular languages L' such that the minimal DFA accepting L' has less states than the minimal DFA accepting L? In order to distinguish between finite automata accepting (ordinary) languages from those accepting partial languages, we refer to the latter as *partial word deterministic finite automata* ($\diamond$-DFA). Thus, $\diamond$-DFAs treat the hole symbol $\diamond$ as an ordinary input letter.

Given some $\diamond$-DFA M with $\diamond$-substitution σ, we construct its *canonical* DFA as follows. First, M is modified to the NFA $\hat{M}$ by resolving the $\diamond$-substitution. That is, any $\diamond$-transition is replaced by transitions on the symbols in $\sigma(\diamond)$. Then, $\hat{M}$ is determinized and the outcome is minimized. This construction is presented as Algorithm 1 in [1].

The intermediate NFA in the construction exhibits the limited nondeterminism provided by $\diamond$-DFAs. In fact, for each state of the NFA, there are at most two outgoing transitions for each input symbol.

The number of states of the (complete) minimal DFA accepting a regular language L is denoted by $\min_{DFA}(L)$. Similarly, $\min_{NFA}(L)$ denotes the minimal number of states necessary for some NFA to accept L. For partial languages, we write $\min_{\diamond\text{-}DFA}(L)$ to denote the minimal number of states of a $\diamond$-DFA accepting a language L' such that there exists a $\diamond$-substitution σ with $\sigma(L') = L$.

In connection with lower bounds on the number of states necessary for an automaton to accept a given language, the problem arises to prove the minimality of a given automaton. While a couple of techniques exist to prove the minimality of DFAs, only a few techniques exist for NFAs. The situation is much worse for $\diamond$-DFAs. Clearly, a $\diamond$-DFA can be seen as a DFA over the alphabet $\Sigma_\diamond$. But, in general, the minimization of a $\diamond$-DFA M changes the language that it represents, that is, $\sigma(L(M))$. The problem to find a minimal $\diamond$-DFA (together with a $\diamond$-substitution) for a given regular language has been studied in detail in [5], where algorithms are given for the construction of minimal partial languages, associated with some $\diamond$-substitution, as well as approximation algorithms for the construction of minimal $\diamond$-DFAs. However, for particular languages that witness certain lower bounds, their minimality has to be proved almost from scratch.

For our purposes the so-called (extended) *fooling set* technique (see, for example, [3,14,18]) is useful. It is a technique to prove lower bounds on the number of states necessary for an NFA to accept a given language.

Theorem 1. *Let $L \subseteq \Sigma^*$ be a regular language and suppose there exists a set of pairs $P = \{\,(x_i, y_i) \mid 1 \leq i \leq n\,\}$ such that (1) $x_i y_i \in L$, for $1 \leq i \leq n$, and (2) $i \neq j$ implies $x_i y_j \notin L$ or $x_j y_i \notin L$, for $1 \leq i, j \leq n$. Then any* *nondeterministic finite automaton accepting L has at least n states. Here P is called an (extended)* fooling set *for L.*

3 State Trade-Offs Between Nondeterminism, Partial Words, and Determinism

Ranges of possible state trade-offs between NFAs and ◇-DFAs as well as between ◇-DFAs and DFAs have been studied in [1] for several types of regular languages, some of them are finite. Here we turn to the worst case scenarios for both trade-offs for general finite languages over fixed alphabets. It turned out that the size of the alphabet plays a crucial role for the state complexity of finite languages. For example, in [20] it is shown that for each n-state NFA accepting a finite language over a binary alphabet, there exists an equivalent DFA which has $O(2^{\frac{n}{2}})$ states, and that this bound is tight in the order of magnitude. However, for larger alphabet sizes this upper bound is no longer true. The general case of an arbitrary ℓ-letter alphabet, $\ell \geq 2$, has been solved in [22]. It is shown that for any n-state NFA accepting a finite language over an ℓ-letter alphabet there is an equivalent DFA with $O(\ell^{\frac{n}{1+\log_2 \ell}})$ states. Moreover, this bound is tight.

3.1 State Complexity of the NFA to ◇-DFA Conversion

An upper bound for the state trade-off between NFAs and ◇-DFAs accepting finite languages is given by the mentioned determinization.

Corollary 2. *Let $n \geq 1$ and $\ell \geq 2$ be integers, Σ be an ℓ-letter alphabet, and $L \subseteq \Sigma^*$ be an arbitrary finite language accepted by an n-state NFA. Then $O(\ell^{\frac{n}{1+\log_2 \ell}})$ states are sufficient for a ◇-DFA that accepts L.*

In order to obtain a lower bound we consider an idea of [11] and show a generalized result. In particular, we can translate the lower bounds of the state trade-offs for the determinization of NFAs to lower bounds of the state trade-offs for the NFA to ◇-DFA conversion. In this way, we derive lower bounds dependent on the sizes of languages that can be plugged in. So, in particular, for our purposes we can use finite languages.

Lemma 3. *Let $n \geq 1$ and $\ell \geq 2$ be integers, Σ be an ℓ-letter alphabet, and M be a minimal n-state NFA accepting a language over Σ that does not contain a word of length one. There exists a regular language L over a 2ℓ-letter alphabet such that there is an NFA accepting L with at most $2n + 1$ states and any ◇-DFA accepting L has at least $\min_{\diamond\text{-}DFA}(L(M)) + \min_{DFA}(L(M)) - 3$ states. Moreover, L is finite if and only if $L(M)$ is finite.*

Lemma 3 can be applied to obtain lower bounds for infinite languages as well. In [11] it has been shown that there exists a regular language such that any minimal NFA accepting it has at most $2n + 1$ states and every ◇-DFA requires at least $2^n - 2^{n-2}$ states for its representation. Before we continue with finite languages, we improve this lower bound in the next proposition.

Proposition 4. *Let $n \geq 3$ be an integer. There exists a $(2n+1)$-state NFA M such that any $\diamond$-DFA representing $L(M)$ has at least 2^n states.*

Proof. In order to apply Lemma 3 we take some minimal n-state NFA M that does not accept any word of length one and that causes the maximal state blow-up for determinization. That is, any equivalent DFA has at least 2^n states.

Now the application of Lemma 3 yields that there is a regular language L such that there is an NFA accepting L with at most $2n+1$ states and any $\diamond$-DFA accepting L has at least 2^n states. □

A lower bound for the NFA to $\diamond$-DFA state trade-off for finite languages is shown in the next theorem. The proof uses the witness languages for the lower bound of the NFA to DFA state trade-offs for finite languages derived in [22].

Theorem 5. *Let $\ell \geq 2$ and $n \geq 2\lceil \log_2 \ell \rceil + 2$ be integers, and Σ be an ℓ-letter alphabet. There exists a $(2n+1)$-state NFA accepting a finite language such that any $\diamond$-DFA representing the same language has at least $\Omega(\ell^{\frac{n}{1+\log_2 \ell}})$ states.*

Proof. First, we define the witness languages for the assertion. To this end, we take the witness languages from [22]. Let $\Sigma = \{a_1, a_2, \ldots, a_\ell\}$ be an ℓ-letter alphabet. Then we set $t = \lceil \log_2 \ell \rceil$ and $m = \lfloor \frac{n}{t+1} \rfloor$. Each letter in Σ is encoded by the t-digit binary sequence that is the binary expansion of its index minus one. For each $1 \leq i \leq t$, we define the set $S_i = \{\, a_j \in \Sigma \mid \text{ the } i\text{th digit of } j-1 \text{ is } 1 \,\}$. Then, language L'_n is defined as

$$\{\, w = v_t x_t v_{t-1} x_{t-1} \cdots v_1 x_1 v_0 \mid v_j \in \Sigma^{m-1}, x_j \in S_j, 1 \leq j \leq t, \text{ and } |w| = n-1 \,\}.$$

Now, let L_n be the set of all suffixes of length at least m of all words in L'_n. In order to obtain an n-state NFA accepting L_n we start with an n-state DFA that accepts L'_n. Basically, the DFA consists of a chain of n-states that allows to check the length $n-1$ of the words and to check that the symbols at the positions $m, 2m, \ldots, t \cdot m$ are from the sets $S_t, S_{t-1}, \ldots, S_1$, respectively. Then, an NFA is obtained from the DFA by first adding λ-transitions from the initial state to all except the last m states. However, it is well known that the λ-transitions can be removed without increasing the number of states and, thus, the NFA has n states. These sophisticated languages have been constructed in [22], where it is shown that any DFA accepting L_n has at least $(\ell^{\lfloor \frac{n}{1+\log_2 \ell} \rfloor + 1} - 1)/\ell - 1) \in \Omega(\ell^{\frac{n}{1+\log_2 \ell}})$ states.

Next, we turn to plug the languages L_n in Lemma 3. Clearly, we have $m \geq 2$, for all $n \geq 2\lceil \log_2 \ell \rceil + 2$, and, thus, the language L_n does not contain any word of length one. Moreover, since the maximal length of the words in L_n is $n-1$, any NFA accepting L_n has at least n states. So, the preconditions of Lemma 3 are met and we derive that there is a regular language L such that there is an NFA accepting L with at most $2n+1$ states and any $\diamond$-DFA accepting L has at least $\Omega(\ell^{\frac{n}{1+\log_2 \ell}})$ states. □

It is worth noticing that the lower bound of Theorem 5 is not tight for finite languages. The reason is that the alphabet size does matter for finite languages and that the finite language L which witnesses the lower bound is over a 2ℓ-letter alphabet. So, a converted lower bound is $\Omega((\frac{\ell}{2})^{\frac{n}{\log_2 \ell}})$.

3.2 State Complexity of the $\diamond$-DFA to DFA Conversion

Here we turn to the question of how many states can we save when we allow wildcard symbols in the sense of $\diamond$-substitutions for DFAs. To this end, we consider the state trade-off between $\diamond$-DFAs and DFAs. For infinite languages it is known that $2^n - 1$ is a tight bound for this trade-off [1].

The situation for finite languages is different. On the one hand, the maximal state blow-up for determinization is different. On the other hand, to our knowledge no NFA being limited nondeterministic in a suitable form is known that witnesses the maximal state blow-up for the determinization in the finite language case. However, we clearly have the upper bound of the general determinization also as upper bound for the $\diamond$-DFA to DFA conversion.

Corollary 6. *Let $n \geq 1$ and $\ell \geq 2$ be integers, Σ be an ℓ-letter alphabet, and $L \subseteq \Sigma^*$ be an arbitrary finite language accepted by an n-state $\diamond$-DFA. Then $O(\ell^{\frac{n}{1+\log_2 \ell}})$ states are sufficient for a DFA that accepts L.*

For a lower bound we proceed as follows.

Theorem 7. *Let $n \geq 3$ and $\ell \geq 2$ be integers. There exists an n-state $\diamond$-DFA representing a finite language over an ℓ-letter alphabet such that any DFA accepting this language has at least $\Omega(\ell^{\frac{n}{2 \cdot \log_2 \ell}})$ states.*

Proof. Let $\Sigma = \{a_1, a_2, \dots, a_\ell\}$ be an ℓ-letter alphabet. We set $k = \lfloor \frac{n-1}{2} \rfloor$ and define the finite language L_k as $\{\, w \mid w = ua_1v, u \in \Sigma^{\leq k-1}, v \in \Sigma^{k-1} \,\}$. The $\diamond$-DFA depicted in Fig. 1 accepts L_k with $2k+1$ states and $\diamond$-substitution $\sigma(\diamond) = \Sigma$.

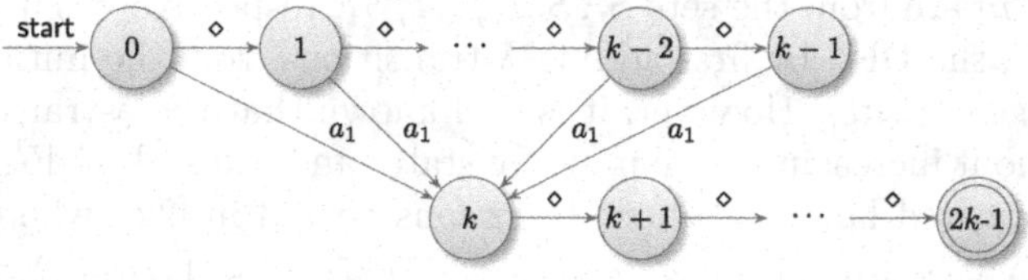

Fig. 1. A $(2k+1)$-state $\diamond$-DFA with $\diamond$-substitution $\sigma(\diamond) = \Sigma$ such that any DFA accepting the language represented has $\Omega(\ell^{\frac{n}{2 \cdot \log_2 \ell}})$ states. The rejecting sink state is not depicted.

It has been proven that any DFA that accepts L_k has at least $2^{k+1} - 1$ states [22]. Transforming $2 = \ell^{\log_\ell 2} = \ell^{\frac{1}{\log_2 \ell}}$, for $n = 2k+2 > 2k+1$ we obtain the lower bound $\ell^{\frac{k+1}{\log_2 \ell}} - 1 \in \Omega(\ell^{\frac{n}{2 \cdot \log_2 \ell}})$. □

4 Operational State Complexity

Let $\circ$ be a fixed operation on languages that preserves regularity. Then the $\circ$-language operation problem for $\diamond$-DFAs is defined as follows:

- Given an n-state $\diamond$-DFA M_1 with $\diamond$-substitution σ_1 and an m-state $\diamond$-DFA M_2 with $\diamond$-substitution σ_2,
- how many states are sufficient and necessary in the worst case (in terms of n and m) for a $\diamond$-DFA M_3 with some $\diamond$-substitution σ_3 such that $\sigma_3(L(M_3)) = \sigma_1(L(M_1)) \circ \sigma_2(L(M_2))$?

Obviously, this problem generalizes to unary language operations like, for example, complementation or reversal.

An upper bound for the operation of complementation follows immediately from the $\diamond$-DFA to DFA conversion. Given M_1 and σ_1, it is sufficient to construct the canonical DFA M' that accepts $\sigma_1(L(M_1))$. Now interchanging accepting and non-accepting states of M' gives a DFA that accepts the complement of $\sigma_1(L(M_1))$. Since, for all regular languages L, $\min\diamond\text{-DFA}(L) \leq \min_{DFA}(L)$ [11], we have the following proposition.

Proposition 8. *Let $n \geq 1$ and $\ell \geq 2$ be integers, and M_1 be an n-state $\diamond$-DFA with $\diamond$-substitution σ_1 accepting a finite language over an ℓ-letter alphabet. Then $O(\ell^{\frac{n}{1+\log_2 \ell}})$ states are sufficient for a $\diamond$-DFA M_2 with some $\diamond$-substitution σ_2 such that $\sigma_2(L(M_2))$ is the complement of $\sigma_1(L(M_1))$.*

The lower bound for the complementation is as follows.

Theorem 9. *Let $n > 3$ and $\ell \geq 2$ be integers. There exists an $(n+1)$-state $\diamond$-DFA M_1 with $\diamond$-substitution σ_1 accepting a finite language over an ℓ-letter alphabet, such that any $\diamond$-DFA M_2 with any $\diamond$-substitution σ_2, where $\sigma_2(L(M_2))$ is the complement of $\sigma_1(L(M_1))$, has at least $\Omega(\ell^{\frac{n}{3\cdot\log_2 \ell}})$ states.*

Proof. Let $\Sigma = \{a_1, a_2, \ldots, a_\ell\}$ be an ℓ-letter alphabet. We set $k = \lceil \frac{n}{3} \rceil$ and define the finite language L_k as

$$\{\, w \mid w = u_1 a_1 v x u_2, u_1, u_2 \in \Sigma^{\leq k-1}, v \in \Sigma^{k-1}, x \in \Sigma \setminus \{a_1\} \,\}.$$

The $\diamond$-DFA depicted in Fig. 2 accepts L_k with $3k+1$ states and $\diamond$-substitution $\sigma(\diamond) = \Sigma$.

In order to show that even any minimal NFA accepting the complement $\overline{L_k}$ has at least 2^k states, we apply Theorem 1 by providing a fooling set P as follows.

Let $h\colon \Sigma^* \to \{0,1\}^*$ be the homomorphism $h(a_1) = a_1$ and $h(x) = a_2$, for $x \in \Sigma \setminus \{a_1\}$. Then we set $P = \{\, (v, v) \mid v \in h(\Sigma^k) \,\}$. To verify the fooling set property of P for $\overline{L_k}$, first we note that vv belongs to $\overline{L_k}$, for every $v \in \{a_1, a_2\}^k$. Next, let (v_1, v_1) and (v_2, v_2) be two different pairs in P. Since v_1 and v_2 are different, there exists a position $1 \leq p \leq k$ at which v_1 has symbol a_1 and v_2 has symbol a_2, or vice versa. Therefore, either $v_1 v_2$ or $v_2 v_1$ is of the form $y_1 y_2 \cdots y_{p-1} a_1 y_{p+1} \cdots y_k z_1 z_2 \cdots z_{p-1} a_2 z_{p+1} \cdots z_k$ and, thus, belongs to L_k.

So, P is the desired fooling set. It includes 2^k pairs which induces that any minimal NFA accepting $\overline{L_k}$ has at least 2^k states. Since, in general, $\min_{NFA}(L) \leq \min_{\diamond\text{-}DFA}(L)$ [11], we derive that any $\diamond$-DFA that accepts $\overline{L_k}$ has at least 2^k states as well.

Transforming $2 = \ell^{\log_\ell 2} = \ell^{\frac{1}{\log_2 \ell}}$, for $n = 3k > 3k-1 > 3k-2$, we obtain the lower bound $\ell^{\frac{k}{\log_2 \ell}} \in \Omega(\ell^{\frac{n}{3 \cdot \log_2 \ell}})$. □

Concerning the two remaining Boolean operations, it is clear that, in general, neither the union nor the intersection of partial languages gives a partial language whose substitution is the union or intersection of the substitutions of the given partial languages. So a simple cross-product construction does not help. In the following, we consider the union. The idea for the union of general regular languages from [19] yields the currently best upper bound. It applies also for finite languages. The construction is to take a $\diamond$-DFA for one of the given partial languages and the canonical DFA for the other one, and build their cross-product automaton which is a $\diamond$-DFA. The proof of the following theorem is almost literally the same as in the case of general regular languages.

Theorem 10. *Let $m \geq n \geq 1$ and $\ell \geq 2$ be integers, M_1 be an m-state $\diamond$-DFA with $\diamond$-substitution σ_1, accepting a finite language and M_2 be an n-state $\diamond$-DFA with $\diamond$-substitution σ_2 accepting a finite language over an ℓ-letter alphabet. Then $O(m \cdot \ell^{\frac{n}{1+\log_2 \ell}})$ states are sufficient for a $\diamond$-DFA M_3 with some $\diamond$-substitution σ_3 such that $\sigma_3(L(M_3)) = \sigma_1(L(M_1)) \cup \sigma_2(L(M_2))$.*

A lower bound for the union can be obtained along the lines of the proof of Lemma 3.

Proposition 11. *Let $m \geq n \geq 3$ and $\ell \geq 2$ be integers. There exist an m-state $\diamond$-DFA M_1 with $\diamond$-substitution σ_1 accepting a finite language over an ℓ-letter alphabet and an n-state $\diamond$-DFA M_2 with $\diamond$-substitution σ_2 accepting a finite language over a disjoint ℓ-letter alphabet such that any $\diamond$-DFA M_3 with any $\diamond$-substitution σ_3 where $\sigma_3(L(M_3)) = \sigma_1(L(M_1)) \cup \sigma_2(L(M_2))$ has at least $m + \Omega(\ell^{\frac{n}{2 \cdot \log_2 \ell}}) - 3$ states.*

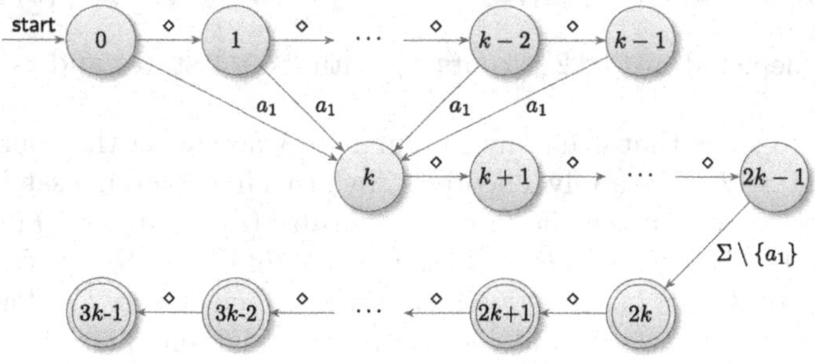

Fig. 2. A $(3k+1)$-state $\diamond$-DFA with $\diamond$-substitution $\sigma(\diamond) = \Sigma$ that witnesses the lower bound for the complementation. The rejecting sink state is not depicted.

Next, we turn to the operation reversal. Since the reversal operation commutes with the $\diamond$-substitution an upper bound follows from the upper bound for the reversal of finite languages.

Proposition 12. *Let $n \geq 3$ and $\ell \geq 2$ be integers, and M_1 be an n-state $\diamond$-DFA with $\diamond$-substitution σ_1 accepting a finite language over an ℓ-letter alphabet. Then $O(\ell^{\frac{n}{1+\log_2 \ell}})$ states are sufficient for a $\diamond$-DFA M_2 with some $\diamond$-substitution σ_2 such that $\sigma_2(L(M_2))$ is the reversal of $\sigma_1(L(M_1))$.*

The lower bound for the reversal is once more derived with the help of the witness languages for the lower bound of the NFA to DFA state trade-offs for finite languages shown in [22].

Theorem 13. *Let $n \geq 2$ and $\ell \geq 2$ be integers. There exists a $2n$-state $\diamond$-DFA M_1 with $\diamond$-substitution σ_1 accepting a finite language over a 2ℓ-letter alphabet, such that any $\diamond$-DFA M_2 with any $\diamond$-substitution σ_2, where $\sigma_2(L(M_2))$ is the reversal of $\sigma_1(L(M_1))$, has at least $\Omega(\ell^{\frac{n}{1+\log_2 \ell}})$ states.*

Proof. In order to define the witness languages for the assertion we start with the witness language L_n for the lower bound of the NFA to DFA state trade-offs for finite languages from [22], that has been defined in the proof of Theorem 5. This language is derived as set of all suffixes of a certain minimal length of all words from language L'_n, where L'_n is accepted by some incomplete DFA consisting of a chain of n-states with one accepting state. Therefore, the reversal of L'_n and, thus, the reversal of L_n is accepted by some incomplete n-state DFA.

Now, we are going to use two copies $N_1 = \langle Q_1, \Sigma_1, \delta_1, q_{0,1}, F_1 \rangle$ and $N_2 = \langle Q_2, \Sigma_2, \delta_2, q_{0,2}, F_2 \rangle$ of this DFA with disjoint state sets and disjoint sets of input symbols. These two copies are assembled to an incomplete DFA $N = \langle (Q_1 \cup Q_2 \cup \{q_0\}) \setminus \{q_{0,1}, q_{0,2}\}, \Sigma_1 \cup \Sigma_2, \delta, q_0, F_1 \cup F_2 \rangle$ by merging the initial states. So, for all but the initial state, the transition function δ contains all transitions of δ_1 and δ_2. For q_0 we set $\delta(q_0, a) = \delta_1(q_{0,1}, a)$, for $a \in \Sigma_1$, and $\delta(q_0, a') = \delta_2(q_{0,2}, a')$, for $a' \in \Sigma_2$. Finally, we add the input symbol $\diamond$ and a rejecting sink state and direct all transitions that are undefined so far to it. In particular, these are all $\diamond$-transitions. The result of this construction is a (complete) $2n$-state $\diamond$-DFA M_1 accepting the language $\hat{L}_n^R \cup \tilde{L}_n^R$, where $\hat{L}_n^R$ and $\tilde{L}_n^R$ are essentially L_n^R but over disjoint alphabets.

Now we turn to some $\diamond$-DFA M_2 with $\diamond$-substitution σ_2 such that $\sigma_2(L(M_2))$ is the reversal of $\sigma_1(L(M_1)) = L(M_1)$. As in the proof of Lemma 3 we can conclude that either $\sigma_2(\diamond) \subseteq \Sigma_1$ or $\sigma_2(\diamond) \subseteq \Sigma_2$ (note that $L(M_1)$ does not contain any word of length one).

Both cases can be treated in the same way. So, let us assume that $\sigma_2(\diamond) \subseteq \Sigma_1$. Then, for any word w from $L(M_2) \cap \Sigma_2^* = (\hat{L}_n^R)^R = \hat{L}_n$ we have $\sigma_2^{-1}(w) = \{w\}$ and, thus, w is accepted by M_2. So, we can delete all transitions on $\diamond$ and on symbols from Σ_1 from the transition function of M_2 and obtain a DFA accepting $\hat{L}_n$. By the result of [22] we conclude that the DFA and, thus, M_2 have at least $\Omega(\ell^{\frac{n}{1+\log_2 \ell}})$ states. □

As a final operation we consider the concatenation. Here we have the following more or less straightforward upper bound.

Proposition 14. *Let* $m, n \geq 1$ *and* $\ell \geq 2$ *be integers,* M_1 *be an* m*-state* $\diamond$*-DFA with* $\diamond$*-substitution* σ_1 *accepting a finite language and* M_2 *be an* n*-state* $\diamond$*-DFA with* $\diamond$*-substitution* σ_2 *accepting a finite language, both over an* ℓ*-letter alphabet. Then* $O(\ell^{\frac{m+n-3}{1+\log_2 \ell}})$ *states are sufficient for a* $\diamond$*-DFA* M_3 *with some* $\diamond$*-substitution* σ_3 *such that* $\sigma_3(L(M_3)) = \sigma_1(L(M_1))\sigma_2(L(M_2))$.

Proof. A first step is to extend the given $\diamond$-DFAs to NFAs by replacing any $\diamond$-transition by corresponding transitions on the symbols that may be substituted for $\diamond$. Additionally, the rejecting sink states are removed. In this way, we obtain an $(m-1)$-state NFA accepting $\sigma_1(L(M_1))$ and an $(n-1)$-state NFA accepting $\sigma_2(L(M_2))$. In [17] the upper bound $m+n-1$ for the nondeterministic concatenation of finite languages has been shown. By applying this construction we obtain an $(m+n-3)$-state NFA accepting $\sigma_1(L(M_1))\sigma_2(L(M_2))$. Finally, this NFA is determinized. The outcome is a DFA with at most $O(\ell^{\frac{m+n-3}{1+\log_2 \ell}})$ states, which is clearly also an upper bound for any $\diamond$-DFA. □

For the lower bound of the concatenation we have the following result.

Theorem 15. *Let* $m, n \geq 3$ *and* $\ell \geq 2$ *be integers. There exist an* m*-state* $\diamond$*-DFA* M_1 *with* $\diamond$*-substitution* σ_1 *accepting a finite language over an* ℓ*-letter alphabet and an* n*-state* $\diamond$*-DFA* M_2 *with* $\diamond$*-substitution* σ_2 *accepting a finite language over a disjoint* ℓ*-letter alphabet such that any* $\diamond$*-DFA* M_3 *with any* $\diamond$*-substitution* σ_3 *where* $\sigma_3(L(M_3)) = \sigma_1(L(M_1))\sigma_2(L(M_2))$ *has at least* $\Omega(\ell^{\frac{\min\{m,n\}}{2 \cdot \log_2 \ell}})$ *states.*

5 Hierarchy of $\diamond$-Transitions

Here we turn to consider the number of productive $\diamond$-transitions in a $\diamond$-DFA, where a transition is called productive, if it does not lead to the rejecting sink state. Corollary 6 and Theorem 7 provide upper and lower bounds for the $\diamond$-DFA to DFA conversion. So, the state costs for removing all $\diamond$-transitions follow. But this raises the question for the state costs when only some of the productive $\diamond$-transitions are removed. Here, we consider the following (k_1, k_2)-$\diamond$-transition problem:

- Let $k_1 > k_2 \geq 0$ be two integers.
- Given an n-state $\diamond$-DFA M_1 with $\diamond$-substitution σ_1 having at most k_1 productive $\diamond$-transitions and accepting a finite language,
- how many states are sufficient and necessary in the worst case (in terms of n) for a $\diamond$-DFA M_2 with some $\diamond$-substitution σ_2 having at most k_2 productive $\diamond$-transitions such that $\sigma_2(L(M_2)) = \sigma_1(L(M_1))$?

For general regular languages exponential lower bounds are known [19]. In particular, the lower bound for the (k_1, k_1-1)-$\diamond$-transition problem turned out to be exponential in the order of magnitude. Moreover, for every further productive $\diamond$-transition that is removed, an exponential number of states is additionally necessary in the worst case.

Again, the situation is different for finite languages. Here we will show that the state costs for removing one productive $\diamond$-transition is quadratic. Therefore, the (k_1, k_2)-$\diamond$-transition problem for finite languages causes only a polynomial state blow-up. We continue with the upper bound.

Proposition 16. *Let $n \geq 3$, $\ell \geq 2$, and $k \geq 1$ be integers, and M_1 be an n-state $\diamond$-DFA with $\diamond$-substitution σ_1 having k productive $\diamond$-transitions that accepts a finite language over an ℓ-letter alphabet. Then $O(n^2)$ states are sufficient for a $\diamond$-DFA M_2 with $\diamond$-substitution σ_2 having at most $k-1$ productive $\diamond$-transitions, such that $\sigma_2(L(M_2)) = \sigma_1(L(M_1))$.*

Proof. Let $\{p_0, p_1, \dots, p_{n-1}\}$ be the state set of M_1, where p_0 is the initial state. We safely may assume that M_1 is minimal. Since M_1 accepts a finite language its state graph does not contain any cycle. Therefore, we can order the states such that if p_j is reachable from p_i then $i < j$. So, we may assume that p_{n-1} is the rejecting sink state. Now we determine the state with a maximal index less or equal to $n-2$ that has an outgoing $\diamond$-transition. Say that it is state p_i.

We construct M_2 from M_1 as follows, where δ_1 and δ_2 denote their transition functions. We start with M_1 and replace the $\diamond$-transition from state p_i by the transitions $\delta_2(p_i, x) = \delta_1(p_i, \diamond)$, for all $x \in \sigma_1(\diamond)$. The results is an NFA. Finally, the NFA is determinized to obtain the $\diamond$-DFA M_2 (where $\sigma_2 = \sigma_1$). Clearly, by the construction M_2 has at most $k-1$ productive $\diamond$-transitions and $\sigma_2(L(M_2)) = \sigma_1(L(M_1))$.

In order to determine the number of states of M_2 we consider the state p_i. Since the state set was ordered and state p_i was the one with the largest index that has an outgoing $\diamond$-transition (except for the sink state p_{n-1}), in particular, all states reachable from p_i (except for the sink state p_{n-1}) do not have an outgoing $\diamond$-transition. Moreover, the determinization of the constructed NFA by the powerset construction reveals only single NFA states or pairs of NFA states as states of the resulting $\diamond$-DFA M_2. We conclude that M_2 has at most $n + \binom{n}{2} \in O(n^2)$ states. □

The next theorem provides a lower bound that is tight in the order of magnitude. Ingredients of the construction are DFAs that have been constructed in [15]. These DFAs witness a lower bound of $\Omega(\min\{m, n\}^2)$ for the deterministic state complexity of union of finite languages.

Theorem 17. *Let $k \geq 1$ be a constant integer. Then, for infinitely many $n \geq 1$, there exists an n-state $\diamond$-DFA M_1 with $\diamond$-substitution σ_1 having k productive $\diamond$-transitions, that accepts a finite language over the alphabet $\{\diamond, a, b, \#, \$\}$, such that any $\diamond$-DFA M_2 with $\diamond$-substitution σ_2 having at most $k-1$ productive $\diamond$-transitions and $\sigma_2(L(M_2)) = \sigma_1(L(M_1))$ has at least $\Omega(n^2)$ states.*

6 Conclusion

In this paper, we have studied some aspects of state complexity of partial word finite automata accepting finite languages. In particular, we considered the 'determinization'. Since the $\diamond$-substitutions imply a certain form of limited nondeterminism we looked at the two problems to convert an NFA to a $\diamond$-DFA as well as to convert a $\diamond$-DFA to a DFA. For both conversions the upper bound is of order $O(\ell^{\frac{n}{1+\log_2 \ell}})$. It turned out that a lower bound for the $\diamond$-DFA to DFA conversion is of order $O(\ell^{\frac{n}{2\log_2 \ell}})$. For the NFA to $\diamond$-DFA conversion we could show the lower bound of $O(\ell^{\frac{n}{1+\log_2 \ell}})$.

However, the lower bound for the NFA to $\diamond$-DFA conversion is not tight for finite languages. The reason is that the alphabet size does matter for finite languages and that the finite language which witnesses the lower bound is over a 2ℓ-letter alphabet. So, a converted lower bound is $\Omega((\frac{\ell}{2})^{\frac{n}{\log_2 \ell}})$. Moreover, the lower bound for the $\diamond$-DFA to DFA conversion, that is $O(\ell^{\frac{n}{2\log_2 \ell}})$, has been presented in a form that incorporates the alphabet size. The reason is that the alphabet size matters for finite languages and we wish to have a better comparison with other bounds. In fact, we have $O(\ell^{\frac{n}{2\log_2 \ell}}) = O(2^{n/2})$. This presentation has been chosen at several places. Anyway, the state costs for both conversions are exponential.

Then we considered the operational state complexity with respect to complementation, union, reversal, and concatenation of finite languages. It turns out that the upper and lower bounds for all these operations are exponential. However, upper and lower bounds do not match. It would be interesting to know whether the upper and/or lower bounds can be improved. Moreover, there are several operations for which the operational state complexity is still untouched, and it would clearly be of interest to determine upper and lower bounds for these operations as well.

Finally, we considered the impact of the number of productive $\diamond$-transitions in a partial word finite automaton. It came out that the state costs for removing one productive $\diamond$-transition is quadratic. This bound is tight in the order of magnitude. So, removing any constant number of $\diamond$-transitions from a $\diamond$-DFA accepting a finite language causes only a polynomial state blow-up.

References

1. Balkanski, E., Blanchet-Sadri, F., Kilgore, M., Wyatt, B.J.: On the state complexity of partial word DFAs. Theory Comput. Sci. **578**, 2–12 (2015)
2. Berstel, J., Boasson, L.: Partial words and a theorem of Fine and Wilf. Theory Comput. Sci. **218**, 135–141 (1999)
3. Birget, J.C.: Intersection and union of regular languages and state complexity. Inform. Process. Lett. **43**, 185–190 (1992)
4. Blanchet-Sadri, F.: Algorithmic Combinatorics on Partial Words. CRC Press, Discrete mathematics and its applications (2008)
5. Blanchet-Sadri, F., Goldner, K., Shackleton, A.: Minimal partial languages and automata. RAIRO Inform. Théor. **51**, 99–119 (2017)

6. Bryant, R.E.: Graph-based algorithms for Boolean function manipulation. IEEE Trans. Comput. **35**, 677–691 (1986)
7. Câmpeanu, C., Culik, K., Salomaa, K., Yu, S.: State complexity of basic operations on finite languages. In: Boldt, O., Jürgensen, H. (eds.) WIA 1999. LNCS, vol. 2214, pp. 60–70. Springer, Heidelberg (2001). https://doi.org/10.1007/3-540-45526-4_6
8. Câmpeanu, C., Ho, W.H.: The maximum state complexity for finite languages. J. Autom. Lang. Comb. **9**, 189–202 (2004)
9. Câmpeanu, C., Santean, N., Yu, S.: Minimal cover-automata for finite languages. Theory Comput. Sci. **267**, 3–16 (2001)
10. Champarnaud, J., Pin, J.: A maxmin problem on finite automata. Discrete Appl. Math. **23**, 91–96 (1989)
11. Dassow, J., Manea, F., Mercaş, R.: Regular languages of partial words. Inf. Sci. **268**, 290–304 (2014)
12. Fischer, M.J., Paterson, M.S.: String-matching and other products. In: Complexity of Computation. SIAM-AMS Proceedings, vol. 7, pp. 113–125. AMS (1974)
13. Gao, Y., Moreira, N., Reis, R., Yu, S.: A survey on operational state complexity. J. Autom. Lang. Comb. **21**, 251–310 (2016)
14. Glaister, I., Shallit, J.: A lower bound technique for the size of nondeterministic finite automata. Inform. Process. Lett. **59**, 75–77 (1996)
15. Han, Y.S., Salomaa, K.: State complexity of union and intersection of finite languages. Int. J. Found. Comput. Sci. **19**, 581–595 (2008)
16. Holzer, M., Jakobi, S., Wendlandt, M.: On the computational complexity of partial word automata problems. Fund. Inform. **148**, 267–289 (2016)
17. Holzer, M., Kutrib, M.: Nondeterministic descriptional complexity of regular languages. Int. J. Found. Comput. Sci. **14**, 1087–1102 (2003)
18. Holzer, M., Kutrib, M.: Nondeterministic finite automata-recent results on the descriptional and computational complexity. Int. J. Found. Comput. Sci. **20**, 563–580 (2009)
19. Kutrib, M., Wendlandt, M.: State complexity of partial word finite automata. In: Han, Y.S., Ko, S.K. (eds) DCFS 2021. LNCS, vol. 13037. pp. 113–124. Springer, Cham (2021). https://doi.org/10.1007/978-3-030-93489-7_10
20. Mandl, R.: Precise bounds associated with the subset construction on various classes of nondeterministic finite automata. In: Princeton Conference on Information Sciences and Systems (CISS 1973), pp. 263–267 (1973)
21. Revuz, D.: Minimisation of acyclic deterministic automata in linear time. Theory Comput. Sci. **92**, 181–189 (1992)
22. Salomaa, K., Yu, S.: NFA to DFA transformation for finite languages over arbitrary alphabets. J. Autom. Lang. Comb. **2**, 177–186 (1997)

Yet Another Canonical Nondeterministic Automaton

Hendrik Maarand(✉) and Hellis Tamm

Department of Software Science, Tallinn University of Technology, Tallinn, Estonia
{hendrik,hellis}@cs.ioc.ee

Abstract. Several canonical forms of finite automata have been introduced over the decades. In particular, if one considers the minimal deterministic finite automaton (DFA), the canonical residual finite state automaton (RFSA), and the átomaton of a language, then the átomaton can be seen as the dual automaton of the minimal DFA, but no such dual has been presented for the canonical RFSA so far. We fill this gap by introducing a new canonical automaton that we call the maximized prime átomaton, and study its properties. We also describe how these four automata can be extracted from suitable observation tables used in the automata learning context.

Keywords: Canonical automaton · regular language · atoms of regular languages · automata learning

1 Introduction

It is well known that every regular language has a unique minimal deterministic finite automaton (DFA) accepting the language. However, this nice property does not hold for the class of nondeterministic finite automata (NFAs), because a language may have several non-isomorphic NFAs with a minimum number of states. Nevertheless, several canonical forms of NFAs have been introduced over the decades: the *universal automaton* [9], the *canonical residual finite state automaton* (*canonical RFSA*) [6] (also known as *jiromaton* [10]), the *átomaton* [5], and the *maximized átomaton* [12] (same as *distromaton* [10]). We note that none of these NFAs are necessarily minimal NFAs.

While the states of the minimal DFA of a language L correspond to the *(left) quotients* of L, the canonical RFSA of L may have less states, since it is based on the *prime quotients* [6] of L, that is, non-empty quotients that are not unions of other quotients. The states of the átomaton of L correspond to the *atoms* [5] of L, which are non-empty intersections of complemented and uncomplemented quotients. Also, the notion of a *prime atom* was defined in [14], however, no automaton based on prime atoms has been presented so far.

This work was supported by the Estonian Research Council grant PRG1210. H. Maarand was also supported by the ERDF funded Estonian CoE project EXCITE (project 2014-2020.4.01.15-0018).

Published by Springer Nature Switzerland AG 2022
Y.-S. Han and G. Vaszil (Eds.): DCFS 2022, LNCS 13439, pp. 184–196, 2022.
https://doi.org/10.1007/978-3-031-13257-5_14

We fill this gap by introducing a new canonical NFA that we call the *maximized prime átomaton*, because it is a subautomaton of the maximized átomaton and its states correspond to the prime atoms of a language. While the átomaton of L is isomorphic to the reverse NFA of the minimal DFA of L^R [5], we show that the maximized prime átomaton of L is the reverse of the canonical RFSA of L^R. An informal description of the relationship between these automata is presented in the picture below. By applying *saturation* and *reduction* operations [6] to the minimal DFA, the canonical RFSA is obtained. By applying corresponding dual operations to the átomaton, we get the maximized prime átomaton.

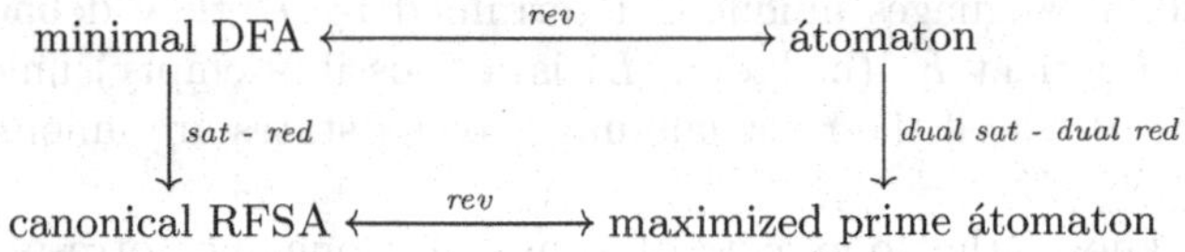

Another way to construct a canonical RFSA is by using a modified subset construction operation C [6,12]. We define a dual operation of C and show how to use this operation to obtain the maximized prime átomaton.

We also describe how the four automata in the above picture can be extracted from suitable observation tables used in the automata learning context [1]. If an observation table is closed and consistent both for rows and columns (Definition 7), then its proper part forms the quotient-atom matrix [8,13] of the language. We believe that it can be helpful to think of these automata in terms of such matrices where the row and column indices are the right and left congruence classes of the language, respectively.

2 Automata, Quotients, and Atoms of Regular Languages

A *nondeterministic finite automaton (NFA)* is a quintuple $\mathcal{N} = (Q, \Sigma, \delta, I, F)$, where Q is a finite, non-empty set of *states*, Σ is a finite non-empty *alphabet*, $\delta : Q \times \Sigma \to 2^Q$ is the *transition function*, $I \subseteq Q$ is the set of *initial states*, and $F \subseteq Q$ is the set of *final states*. We extend the transition function to functions $\delta' : Q \times \Sigma^* \to 2^Q$ and $\delta'' : 2^Q \times \Sigma^* \to 2^Q$, using δ for all these functions. The *left language* of a state q of $\mathcal{N}$ is $L_{I,q}(\mathcal{N}) = \{w \in \Sigma^* \mid q \in \delta(I, w)\}$, and the *right language* of q is $L_{q,F}(\mathcal{N}) = \{w \in \Sigma^* \mid \delta(q, w) \cap F \neq \emptyset\}$. A state q of $\mathcal{N}$ is *reachable* if $L_{I,q}(\mathcal{N}) \neq \emptyset$, and it is *empty* if $L_{q,F}(\mathcal{N}) = \emptyset$. The *language accepted* by an NFA $\mathcal{N}$ is $L(\mathcal{N}) = \{w \in \Sigma^* \mid \delta(I, w) \cap F \neq \emptyset\}$. Two NFAs are *equivalent* if they accept the same language. An NFA is *minimal* if it has a minimum number of states among all equivalent NFAs. The *reverse* of an NFA $\mathcal{N} = (Q, \Sigma, \delta, I, F)$ is the NFA $\mathcal{N}^R = (Q, \Sigma, \delta^R, F, I)$, where $q \in \delta^R(p, a)$ if and only if $p \in \delta(q, a)$ for $p, q \in Q$ and $a \in \Sigma$.

A *deterministic finite automaton (DFA)* is a quintuple $\mathcal{D} = (Q, \Sigma, \delta, q_0, F)$, where Q, Σ, and F are as in an NFA, $\delta : Q \times \Sigma \to Q$ is the transition function, and q_0 is the initial state. The *left quotient*, or simply *quotient*, of a language L by a word $w \in \Sigma^*$ is the language $w^{-1}L = \{x \in \Sigma^* \mid wx \in L\}$. It is well known that the left quotients of L are the right languages of the states of the minimal DFA of L. Any NFA $\mathcal{N}$ can be *determinized* by the well-known subset construction, yielding a DFA $\mathcal{N}^D$ that has only reachable states.

Let L be a non-empty regular language with quotients $K_0, \dots, K_{n-1}$. An *atom* of L is any non-empty language of the form $\widetilde{K_0} \cap \cdots \cap \widetilde{K_{n-1}}$, where $\widetilde{K_i}$ is either K_i or $\overline{K_i}$, and $\overline{K_i}$ is the complement of K_i with respect to Σ^* [5]. An atom is *initial* if it has L (rather than $\overline{L}$) as a term; it is *final* if it contains ε. There is exactly one final atom, the atom $\widehat{K_0} \cap \cdots \cap \widehat{K_{n-1}}$, where $\widehat{K_i} = K_i$ if $\varepsilon \in K_i$, and $\widehat{K_i} = \overline{K_i}$ otherwise. If $\overline{K_0} \cap \cdots \cap \overline{K_{n-1}}$ is an atom, then it is called the *negative* atom, all the other atoms are *positive*. Thus atoms of L are pairwise disjoint languages uniquely determined by L; they define a partition of Σ^*. Every quotient K_i (including L) is a (possibly empty) union of atoms. An NFA $\mathcal{N}$ is *atomic* if the right languages of its states are unions of atoms of $L(\mathcal{N})$.

It is well known that quotients of L are in a one-one correspondence with the equivalence classes of the *Nerode right congruence* $\equiv_L$ of L [11] defined as follows: for $x, y \in \Sigma^*$, $x \equiv_L y$ if for every $v \in \Sigma^*$, $xv \in L$ if and only if $yv \in L$. Atoms of L are the classes of the *left congruence* ${}_L\!\equiv$ of L: for $x, y \in \Sigma^*$, $x \;{}_L\!\equiv y$ if for every $u \in \Sigma^*$, $ux \in L$ if and only if $uy \in L$ [7].

Let $A = \{A_0, A_1, \dots, A_{m-1}\}$ be the set of atoms of L, let A_I be the set of initial atoms, and let A_{m-1} be the final atom.

The *átomaton* of L is the NFA $\mathcal{A} = (S_A, \Sigma, \alpha, I_A, \{s_{m-1}\})$ where $S_A = \{s_0, s_1, \dots, s_{m-1}\}$, $I_A = \{s_i \in S_A \mid A_i \in A_I\}$, and $s_j \in \alpha(s_i, a)$ if and only if $A_j \subseteq a^{-1}A_i$, for all $i, j \in \{0, \dots, m-1\}$ and $a \in \Sigma$. It was shown in [5] that the atoms of L are the right languages of the states of the átomaton, and that the reverse NFA of the átomaton is the minimal DFA of the reverse language L^R.

The next theorem is a slightly modified version of the result by Brzozowski [4]:

Theorem 1. *If an NFA $\mathcal{N}$ has no empty states and $\mathcal{N}^R$ is deterministic, then $\mathcal{N}^D$ is minimal.*

By Theorem 1, for any NFA $\mathcal{N}$, the DFA $\mathcal{N}^{RDRD}$ is the minimal DFA equivalent to $\mathcal{N}$. This result is known as Brzozowski's double-reversal method for DFA minimization. In [5], a generalization of Theorem 1 was presented, providing a characterization of the class of NFAs for which applying determinization procedure produces a minimal DFA:

Theorem 2. *For any NFA $\mathcal{N}$, the DFA $\mathcal{N}^D$ is minimal if and only if $\mathcal{N}^R$ is atomic.*

3 Residual Finite State Automata

Residual finite state automata (RFSAs) were introduced by Denis, Lemay, and Terlutte in [6]. In this section, we state some basic properties of RFSAs. However, we note here that we usually prefer to use the term "quotient" over "residual".

An NFA $\mathcal{N} = (Q, \Sigma, \delta, I, F)$ is a *residual finite state automaton* (RFSA) if for every state $q \in Q$, $L_{q,F}(\mathcal{N})$ is a quotient of $L(\mathcal{N})$. Clearly, any DFA having only reachable states, is an RFSA.

Let L be a regular language over Σ. A non-empty quotient of L is *prime* if it is not a union of other quotients. Let $K' = \{K_0, \ldots, K_{n'-1}\}$ be the set of prime quotients of L.

The *canonical RFSA* of L is the NFA $\mathcal{R} = (Q_{K'}, \Sigma, \delta, I_{K'}, F_{K'})$, where $Q_{K'} = \{q_0, \ldots, q_{n'-1}\}$, $I_{K'} = \{q_i \in Q_{K'} \mid K_i \subseteq L\}$, $F_{K'} = \{q_i \in Q_{K'} \mid \varepsilon \in K_i\}$, and $\delta(q_i, a) = \{q_j \in Q_{K'} \mid K_j \subseteq a^{-1}K_i\}$ for every $q_i \in Q_{K'}$ and $a \in \Sigma$.

The canonical RFSA is a state-minimal RFSA with a maximal number of transitions. One way to build a canonical RFSA is to use the *saturation* and *reduction* operations defined in the following.

Let $\mathcal{N} = (Q, \Sigma, \delta, I, F)$ be an NFA. The *saturation* operation S, applied to $\mathcal{N}$, produces the NFA $\mathcal{N}^S = (Q, \Sigma, \delta_S, I_S, F)$, where $\delta_S(q, a) = \{q' \in Q \mid aL_{q',F}(\mathcal{N}) \subseteq L_{q,F}(\mathcal{N})\}$ for all $q \in Q$ and $a \in \Sigma$, and $I_S = \{q \in Q \mid L_{q,F}(\mathcal{N}) \subseteq L(\mathcal{N})\}$. An NFA $\mathcal{N}$ is saturated if $\mathcal{N}^S = \mathcal{N}$. Saturation may add transitions and initial states to an NFA, without changing its language. If $\mathcal{N}$ is an RFSA, then $\mathcal{N}^S$ is an RFSA.

For any state q of $\mathcal{N}$, let $R(q)$ be the set $\{q' \in Q \backslash \{q\} \mid L_{q',F}(\mathcal{N}) \subseteq L_{q,F}(\mathcal{N})\}$. A state q is *erasable* if $L_{q,F}(\mathcal{N}) = \bigcup_{q' \in R(q)} L_{q',F}(\mathcal{N})$. If q is erasable, a *reduction* operator ϕ is defined as follows: $\phi(\mathcal{N}, q) = (Q', \Sigma, \delta', I', F')$ where $Q' = Q \backslash \{q\}$, $I' = I$ if $q \notin I$, and $I' = (I \backslash \{q\}) \cup R(q)$ otherwise, $F' = F \cap Q'$, $\delta'(q', a) = \delta(q', a)$ if $q \notin \delta(q', a)$, and $\delta'(q', a) = (\delta(q', a) \backslash \{q\}) \cup R(q)$ otherwise, for every $q' \in Q'$ and every $a \in \Sigma$. If q is not erasable, let $\phi(\mathcal{N}, q) = \mathcal{N}$.

If $\mathcal{N}$ is saturated and if q is an erasable state of $\mathcal{N}$, then $\phi(\mathcal{N}, q)$ is obtained by deleting q and its associated transitions from $\mathcal{N}$. An NFA $\mathcal{N}$ is *reduced* if there is no erasable state in $\mathcal{N}$. Applying ϕ to $\mathcal{N}$ does not change its language. If $\mathcal{N}$ is an RFSA, then $\phi(\mathcal{N}, q)$ is an RFSA. The following proposition is from [6]:

Proposition 1. *If an NFA $\mathcal{N}$ is a reduced saturated RFSA of L, then $\mathcal{N}$ is the canonical RFSA for L.*

The canonical RFSA can be obtained from a DFA having only reachable states, by using saturation and reduction operations.

Next we will discuss another method to compute the canonical RFSA, suggested in [6]. In Sect. 2, we recalled the result that for any NFA $\mathcal{N}$, the DFA $\mathcal{N}^{RDRD}$ is the minimal DFA equivalent to $\mathcal{N}$. In [6], a similar double-reversal method is proposed to obtain a canonical RFSA from a given NFA, using a modified subset construction operation C to be applied to an NFA as follows:

Definition 1. *Let $\mathcal{N} = (Q, \Sigma, \delta, I, F)$ be an NFA. Let Q_D be the set of states of the determinized version $\mathcal{N}^D$ of $\mathcal{N}$. A state $s \in Q_D$ is* coverable *if there is a set $Q_s \subseteq Q_D \backslash \{s\}$ such that $s = \bigcup_{s' \in Q_s} s'$. The NFA $\mathcal{N}^C$ is defined as $(Q_C, \Sigma, \delta_C, I_C, F_C)$, where $Q_C = \{s \in Q_D \mid s \text{ is not coverable}\}$, $I_C = \{s \in Q_C \mid s \subseteq I\}$, $F_C = \{s \in Q_C \mid s \cap F \neq \emptyset\}$, and $\delta_C(s, a) = \{s' \in Q_C \mid s' \subseteq \delta(s, a)\}$ for any $s \in Q_C$ and $a \in \Sigma$.*

Applying the operation C to any NFA $\mathcal{N}$ produces an RFSA $\mathcal{N}^C$. Denis et al. [6] have the following result:

Theorem 3. *If an NFA $\mathcal{N}$ has no empty states and $\mathcal{N}^R$ is an RFSA, then $\mathcal{N}^C$ is the canonical RFSA.*

By Theorem 3, for any NFA $\mathcal{N}$, the RFSA $\mathcal{N}^{RCRC}$ is the canonical RFSA equivalent to $\mathcal{N}$. Hence, the operation C has a similar role for RFSAs as determinization has for DFAs.

In Sect. 2, we recalled Theorem 2 from [5], a generalization of Theorem 1, characterizing the class of NFAs to which applying the determinization procedure produces a minimal DFA. Theorem 3 was generalized in [12] in a similar way:

Theorem 4. *For any NFA $\mathcal{N}$ of L, $\mathcal{N}^C$ is a canonical RFSA if and only if the left languages of $\mathcal{N}$ are unions of left languages of the canonical RFSA of L.*

4 Maximized Átomaton

Let L be a non-empty regular language, $K = \{K_0, \ldots, K_{n-1}\}$ be the set of quotients, and $A = \{A_0, \ldots, A_{m-1}\}$ be the set of atoms of L, with the set of initial atoms $A_I \subseteq A$, and the final atom A_{m-1}.

In [12], the notions of a *maximized atom* and the *maximized átomaton* of a regular language L were introduced. For every atom A_i of L, the corresponding *maximized atom* M_i is the union of all the atoms which occur in every quotient containing A_i:

Definition 2. *The* maximized atom M_i *of an atom* A_i *is the union of atoms* $M_i = \bigcup\{A_h \mid A_h \subseteq \bigcap_{A_i \subseteq K_k} K_k\}$.

Clearly, since atoms are pairwise disjoint, and every quotient is a union of atoms, $M_i = \bigcap_{A_i \subseteq K_k} K_k$. In [12], the following properties of maximized atoms were shown:

Proposition 2. *Let A_i and A_j be some atoms of L. The following properties hold:*

1. *$A_i \subseteq M_i$.*
2. *If $A_i \neq A_j$, then $M_i \neq M_j$.*
3. *$A_i \subseteq M_j$ if and only if $M_i \subseteq M_j$.*
4. *$A_j \subseteq a^{-1}M_i$ if and only if $M_j \subseteq a^{-1}M_i$.*

Let $M = \{M_0, \ldots, M_{m-1}\}$ be the set of the maximized atoms of L. The *maximized átomaton* was defined in [12] as follows:

Definition 3. *The* maximized átomaton *of L is the NFA defined as $\mathcal{M} = (Q_M, \Sigma, \mu, I_M, F_M)$, where $Q_M = \{q_0, q_1, \ldots, q_{m-1}\}$, $I_M = \{q_i \in Q_M \mid A_i \in A_I\}$, $F_M = \{q_i \in Q_M \mid A_{m-1} \subseteq M_i\}$, and $q_j \in \mu(q_i, a)$ if and only if $M_j \subseteq a^{-1}M_i$, for all $i, j \in \{0, \ldots, m-1\}$ and $a \in \Sigma$.*

It was shown in [12] that the maximized átomaton $\mathcal{M}$ of L is isomorphic to the reverse NFA of the saturated version of the minimal DFA of L^R.

Using results from [13] and Proposition 2, we can see that the right language of any state of the maximized átomaton is the corresponding maximized atom:

Proposition 3. *For every state $q_i \in Q_M$ of the maximized átomaton $\mathcal{M} = (Q_M, \Sigma, \mu, I_M, F_M)$ of L, the equality $L_{q_i, F_M}(\mathcal{M}) = M_i$ holds.*

5 Maximized Prime Átomaton

We recall that a non-empty quotient is *prime* if it is not a union of other quotients.

The notion of a *prime atom* was defined in [14] as follows: any positive atom $A_i = \bigcap_{j \in S_i} K_j \cap \bigcap_{j \in \overline{S_i}} \overline{K_j}$, where $S_i \subseteq \{0, \ldots, n-1\}$ and $\overline{S_i} = \{0, \ldots, n-1\} \setminus S_i$, is *prime* if the set $\{K_j \mid j \in S_i\}$ of uncomplemented quotients in the intersection of A_i is not a union of such sets of quotients corresponding to other atoms.

By results in [5], it is known that the reverse of the átomaton $\mathcal{A}$ of L is the minimal DFA of L^R. Since the right language of any state of $\mathcal{A}$ is some atom of L, and the right language of any state of $\mathcal{A}^R$ is some quotient of L^R, there is a natural one-one-correspondence between the set of atoms of L and the set of quotients of L^R, based on the state set of $\mathcal{A}$ (and $\mathcal{A}^R$). Also, there is a one-one correspondence between the set of prime atoms of L and the set of prime quotients of L^R:

Proposition 4. *The right language of any state of the átomaton $\mathcal{A}$ of L is a prime atom of L if and only if the right language of the same state of $\mathcal{A}^R$ is a prime quotient of L^R.*

Now, let $A' \subseteq A$ be the set of prime atoms of L, and let $M' \subseteq M$ be the corresponding set of maximized prime atoms. We define the *maximized prime átomaton* of L as follows:

Definition 4. *The* maximized prime átomaton *of L is the NFA defined by $\mathcal{M}' = (Q_{M'}, \Sigma, \mu, I_{M'}, F_{M'})$, where $Q_{M'} = \{q_i \mid M_i$ is prime$\}$, $I_{M'} = Q_{M'} \cap I_M$, $F_{M'} = Q_{M'} \cap F_M$, and $q_j \in \mu(q_i, a)$ if and only if $M_j \subseteq a^{-1}M_i$, for $q_i, q_j \in Q_{M'}$ and $a \in \Sigma$.*

In [12], it was shown that the maximized átomaton $\mathcal{M}$ of L is isomorphic to $\mathcal{E}^{SR}$, where $\mathcal{E}$ is the minimal DFA of L^R. That is, $\mathcal{M}^R$ is isomorphic to $\mathcal{E}^S$. Now, the canonical RFSA of L^R is the reduced version of $\mathcal{E}^S$, where those states of $\mathcal{E}^S$ corresponding to non-prime quotients of L^R, have been removed. Since by Proposition 4, the states of $\mathcal{E}$ corresponding to prime quotients of L^R are exactly those states of $\mathcal{E}^R$ corresponding to prime atoms of L, the canonical RFSA of L^R is isomorphic to the subautomaton of $\mathcal{M}^R$, where the states corresponding to non-prime atoms, together with their in- and out-transitions, have been removed. We have the following result:

Proposition 5. *The maximized prime átomaton $\mathcal{M}'$ of L is isomorphic to the reverse NFA of the canonical RFSA of L^R.*

There is a one-one correspondence between the set M' of maximized prime atoms and the state set $Q_{M'}$ of the maximized prime átomaton of L. However, the right language of a state q_i of $\mathcal{M}'$ is not necessarily equal to the corresponding maximized prime atom M_i. By a result in [12], for the left language L_i of a state q_i of the canonical RFSA of L^R, the inclusions $A_i^R \subseteq L_i \subseteq M_i^R$ hold, where A_i and M_i are respectively the corresponding atom and the maximized atom of L. Since the right language of any state of the maximized prime átomaton of L is the reverse of the left language of the corresponding state of the canonical RFSA of L^R, we can state the following:

Proposition 6. *For any state q_i of the maximized prime átomaton $\mathcal{M}'$ of L, the inclusions $A_i \subseteq L_{q_i,F_{M'}}(\mathcal{M}') \subseteq M_i$ hold.*

By Proposition 5, we are able to obtain the maximized prime átomaton of L by finding the canonical RFSA of L^R, and then reversing it. Since by Theorem 3, for any NFA $\mathcal{N}$, the RFSA $\mathcal{N}^{RCRC}$ is the canonical RFSA equivalent to $\mathcal{N}$, it is clear that $\mathcal{N}^{CRCR}$ is the maximized prime átomaton of L.

We define an operation *coC* to be applied to an NFA as follows:

Definition 5. *Let $\mathcal{N} = (Q, \Sigma, \delta, I, F)$ be an NFA. Let Q_{coD} be the set of states of the determinized version $\mathcal{N}^{RD}$ of $\mathcal{N}^R$. A state $s \in Q_{coD}$ is* coverable *if there is a set $Q_s \subseteq Q_{coD}\backslash\{s\}$ such that $s = \bigcup_{s' \in Q_s} s'$. The NFA $\mathcal{N}^{coC} = (Q_{coC}, \Sigma, \delta_{coC}, I_{coC}, F_{coC})$ is defined as follows: $Q_{coC} = \{s \in Q_{coD} \mid s$ is not coverable$\}$, $I_{coC} = \{s \in Q_{coC} \mid s \cap I \neq \emptyset\}$, $F_{coC} = \{s \in Q_{coC} \mid s \subseteq F\}$, and for any $s, s' \in Q_C$ and $a \in \Sigma$, $s' \in \delta_{coC}(s, a)$ if and only if for every $q \in s$ there is some $q' \in s'$ such that $q' \in \delta(q, a)$.*

Clearly, $\mathcal{N}^{coC}$ is isomorphic to $\mathcal{N}^{RCR}$. Hence, given any NFA $\mathcal{N}$ of L, the maximized prime átomaton of L can be obtained by applying first the operation C to $\mathcal{N}$, yielding $\mathcal{N}^C$, and then applying *coC* to $\mathcal{N}^C$, resulting in the automaton $\mathcal{N}^{C(coC)}$. Also, the NFA $\mathcal{N}^{(coC)C}$ is the canonical RFSA of L. The following theorem holds:

Theorem 5. *For any NFA $\mathcal{N}$ of L, the NFA $\mathcal{N}^{coC}$ is the maximized prime átomaton of L if and only if the right language of every state of $\mathcal{N}$ is a union of right languages of the maximized prime átomaton of L.*

Example 1. We consider a modification of an example from [6], and define a family of NFAs $\mathcal{B}_n = (Q, \Sigma, \delta, I, F)$, $n \geqslant 1$, where $Q = \{q_0, \ldots, q_{n-1}\}$, $\Sigma = \{a, b\}$, $I = \{q_i \mid 0 \leqslant i < n/2\}$, $F = \{q_0\}$, and $\delta(q_i, a) = \{q_{(i+1) \bmod n}\}$ for $i = 0, \ldots, n-1$, and $\delta(q_0, b) = \{q_0, q_1\}$, $\delta(q_1, b) = \{q_{n-1}\}$, and $\delta(q_i, b) = \{q_{i-1}\}$ for $1 < i < n$. The NFA $\mathcal{B}_4$ is shown in Fig. 1 and its reverse $\mathcal{B}_4^R$ is in Fig. 2.

We claim that the NFA $\mathcal{B}_n^R$ is a canonical RFSA of $L(\mathcal{B}_n)^R$. Indeed, $\mathcal{B}_n^R$ is an RFSA, because the right languages of $\mathcal{B}_n^R$ are quotients of $L(\mathcal{B}_n^R)$: $L_{q_0,F}(\mathcal{B}_n^R) = \varepsilon^{-1}L(\mathcal{B}_n^R)$ and $L_{q_i,F}(\mathcal{B}_n^R) = (a^{n-i})^{-1}L(\mathcal{B}_n^R)$, for $i = 1, \ldots, n-1$. Denoting $K_i = (a^{(n-i) \bmod n})^{-1}L(\mathcal{B}_n^R)$ and noticing that $a^{(i-\lceil n/2 \rceil+1) \bmod n}, \ldots, a^{i \bmod n} \in K_i$, and $a^{(i+1) \bmod n}, \ldots, a^{(i+\lfloor n/2 \rfloor) \bmod n} \notin K_i$, for $i = 0, \ldots, n-1$, it is easy to see that K_i's are pairwise incomparable. Therefore, $\mathcal{B}_n^{RC}$ is isomorphic to $\mathcal{B}_n^R$, and it is clear that $\mathcal{B}_n^R$ is a canonical RFSA of $L(\mathcal{B}_n)^R$.

Hence, by Proposition 5, $\mathcal{B}_n$ is the maximized prime átomaton of $L(\mathcal{B}_n)$. Also, by Theorem 3, $\mathcal{B}_n^C$ is the canonical RFSA of $L(\mathcal{B}_n)$. The automaton $\mathcal{B}_n^C$ has $\binom{n}{\lceil n/2 \rceil}$ states, because any candidate state of $\mathcal{B}_n^C$ with more than $\lceil n/2 \rceil$ elements can be covered by those with exactly $\lceil n/2 \rceil$ elements. Thus, for $n \geqslant 4$, $\mathcal{B}_n$ is smaller than the canonical RFSA for $L(\mathcal{B}_n)$, and the difference between the sizes of these two NFAs grows with n. Moreover, $\mathcal{B}_n$ is a minimal NFA for $L(\mathcal{B}_n)$, as can be seen by the *fooling set method* [2] using the fooling set $\{(\varepsilon, a^n), (a, a^{n-1}), \ldots, (a^{n-1}, a)\}$ of size n.

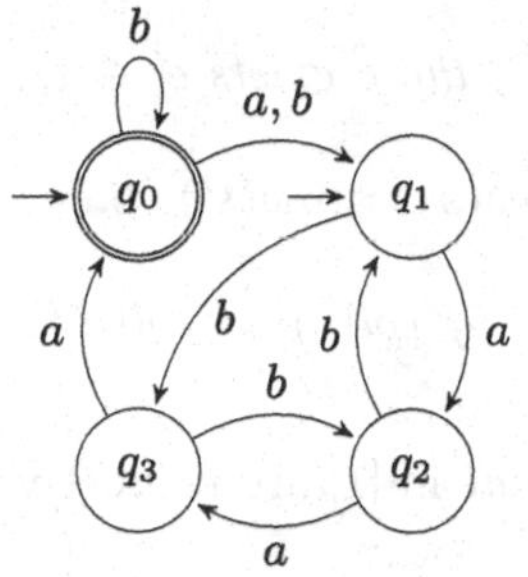

Fig. 1. The automaton $\mathcal{B}_4$.

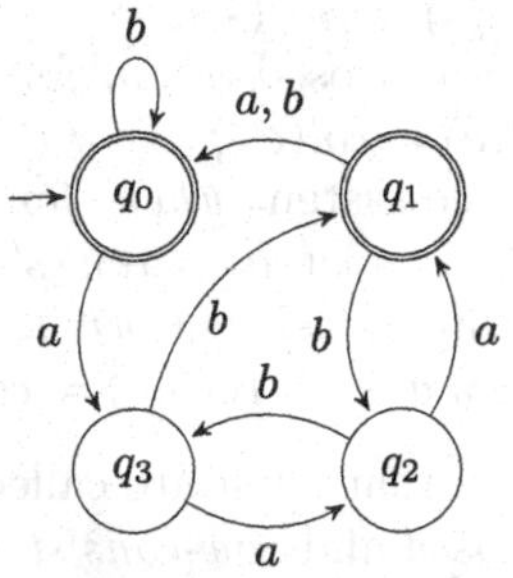

Fig. 2. The automaton $\mathcal{B}_4^R$.

6 Observation Tables

We now turn to observation tables known from the L^* learning algorithm [1] and how to read out various canonical automata from suitable observation tables. These tables can be seen as submatrices of the quotient-atom matrix [13] of a language, which is used, for example, in finding a minimal NFA of the language [8,13].

The L^* algorithm works by performing *membership* (whether a word belongs to the unknown language) and *equivalence* (whether a hypothesis is equivalent to the unknown language) queries. Informally, an observation table is used in the L^* algorithm to collect the observations that have been made so far and also to organize the observations in such a manner that it can be determined which observations need to be performed next. The membership queries are always performed for words composed from a prefix s and a suffix e. If the result of the membership query for the word se is positive, then the entry in the table at row s and column e is set to 1, otherwise it is set to 0.

Definition 6. *An* observation table *is a triple* $\mathcal{T} = (S, E, T)$ *where* $S \subseteq \Sigma^*$ *is a prefix-closed set of words,* $E \subseteq \Sigma^*$ *is a suffix-closed set of words and* $T : \Sigma^* \to 2$ *is a finite function. The* proper *part of the table consists of* S *rows and*

E columns. The row extensions *of the table consist of the rows* $S \cdot \Sigma \backslash S$. *The* column extensions *of the table consist of the columns* $\Sigma \cdot E \backslash E$. *The entry in the table at row s and column e is* $T(se)$.

A *row* of $\mathcal{T} = (S, E, T)$ is an E-indexed vector consisting of the corresponding entries of the table. That is, for $s \in S$ and $e \in E$, $row(s)(e) = T(se)$. A *column* of $\mathcal{T}$ is an S-indexed vector. That is, for $e \in E$ and $s \in S$, $col(e)(s) = T(se)$. Note that $row(sa)(e) = row(s)(ae) = col(ae)(s) = col(e)(sa)$.

Definition 7. *An observation table* $\mathcal{T} = (S, E, T)$ *is called*

- row-closed *when, for every* $s \in (S \cdot \Sigma) \backslash S$, *there exists* $s' \in S$ *such that* $row(s) = row(s')$;
- column-closed *when, for every* $e \in (\Sigma \cdot E) \backslash E$, *there exists* $e' \in E$ *such that* $col(e) = col(e')$;
- row-consistent *when, for every* $s, s' \in S$, *if* $row(s) = row(s')$, *then, for every* $a \in \Sigma$, $row(sa) = row(s'a)$.
- column-consistent *when, for every* $e, e' \in E$, *if* $col(e) = col(e')$, *then, for every* $a \in \Sigma$, $col(ae) = col(ae')$.

Note that what are called *closed* and *consistent* in [1] are respectively called *row-closed* and *row-consistent* in our setting.

We also use $row(S)$ to denote the set $\{row(s) \mid s \in S\}$ and $col(E)$ for $\{col(e) \mid e \in E\}$. Two indices s_1 and s_2 are equivalent when $row(s_1) = row(s_2)$. This partitions S and we write $[s]$ for the equivalence class of s as well as its representative. Similarly, we have an equivalence relation on E and we write $[e]$ for the equivalence class of e and its representative. We can use the lexicographically minimal element as the representative.

6.1 Row Automaton

Let $\mathcal{T} = (S, E, T)$ be a row-closed and row-consistent observation table. Define a function $suc : row(S) \times \Sigma \to row(S)$ as $suc(r, a) = row([r]a)$. The co-domain is $row(S)$ as for any $r \in row(S)$, we have $[r] \in S$ and by being row-closed, there is an $s \in S$ such that $row([r]a) = row(s)$. Since the table is consistent, this function respects the equivalence classes.

Definition 8. *The* row automaton *of* $\mathcal{T}$, *denoted by* $A_{row}(\mathcal{T})$, *is the automaton* $(Q, \Sigma, \delta, q_0, F)$ *where* $Q = row(S)$, $\delta(q, a) = suc(q, a)$, $q_0 = row(\varepsilon)$ *and* $F = \{q \in Q \mid q(\varepsilon) = 1\}$. *The transition function* δ *extends to words by* $\delta(q, \varepsilon) = q$ *and* $\delta(q, ua) = \delta(\delta(q, u), a)$. *The language of the automaton is* $L(A_{row}(\mathcal{T})) = \{u \in \Sigma^* \mid \delta(q_0, u) \in F\}$.

Proposition 7. *If* $\mathcal{T}$ *is row-closed and row-consistent, then* $A_{row}(\mathcal{T})$ *is the minimal DFA accepting* $L(A_{row}(\mathcal{T}))$.

Since $A_{row}(\mathcal{T})$ is minimal, the left language of a state $row(s)$ is a right congruence class of $L(A_{row}(\mathcal{T}))$ and we denote it by $[s]_{row}$. Furthermore, this congruence class contains the equivalence class $[s]$ of S. This is the automaton constructed by the L^* algorithm.

6.2 Column Automaton

Let $\mathcal{T} = (S, E, T)$ be a column-closed and column-consistent observation table. Define a function $pre : \Sigma \times col(E) \longrightarrow col(E)$ as $pre(a, c) = col(a[c])$. The co-domain is $col(E)$ as for any $c \in col(E)$, we have $[c] \in E$ and by being column-closed, there is an $e \in E$ such that $col(a[c]) = col(e)$. Since the table is consistent, this function respects the equivalence classes.

Definition 9. *The* column automaton *of* $\mathcal{T}$, *denoted by* $A_{col}(\mathcal{T})$, *is the automaton* $(Q, \Sigma, \delta, I, f)$ *where* $Q = col(E)$, $\delta(q, a) = \{q' \in Q \mid q = pre(a, q')\}$, $I = \{q \in Q \mid q(\varepsilon) = 1\}$ *and* $f = col(\varepsilon)$. *The transition function extends to sets of states and words in the usual way:* $\delta(K, a) = \bigcup\{\delta(k, a) \mid k \in K\}$ *and* $\delta(K, \varepsilon) = K$ *and* $\delta(K, ua) = \delta(\delta(K, u), a)$. *The language of the automaton is* $L(A_{col}(\mathcal{T})) = \{u \in \Sigma^* \mid f \in \delta(I, u)\}$.

Proposition 8. *If* $\mathcal{T}$ *is column-closed and column-consistent, then* $A_{col}(\mathcal{T})$ *is the átomaton of* $L(A_{col}(\mathcal{T}))$.

Since $A_{col}(\mathcal{T})$ is the átomaton, the right language of a state $col(e)$ is an atom and thus a left congruence class of $L(A_{col}(\mathcal{T}))$ which we denote by $[e]_{col}$. Furthermore, this congruence class contains the equivalence class $[e]$ of E. This automaton can be learned by a column-oriented variant of L^*. Recall that the reverse of the átomaton is the minimal DFA of the reverse language.

6.3 Rows and Columns

Let $\mathcal{T} = (S, E, T)$ be an observation table that is closed and consistent both for rows and columns. We have $A_{row}(\mathcal{T})$ and $A_{col}(\mathcal{T})$ associated with $\mathcal{T}$.

Proposition 9. *For any* $u, v \in \Sigma^*$, *we have* $uv \in L(A_{row}(\mathcal{T}))$ *if and only if* $row([u]_{row})([v]_{col}) = 1$.

We thus see that the right language of the state of the row automaton corresponding to u (that is $row([u]_{row})$) consists of those words v for which the entry at row $[u]_{row}$ and column $[v]_{col}$ is 1.

Proposition 10. *For any* $u, v \in \Sigma^*$, *we have* $uv \in L(A_{col}(\mathcal{T}))$ *if and only if* $col([v]_{col})([u]_{row}) = 1$.

Similarly, we see that the left language of the state of the column automaton corresponding to v (that is $col([v]_{col})$) consists of those words u for which the entry at column $[v]_{col}$ and row $[u]_{row}$ is 1. Since $row(s)(e) = col(e)(s)$, we can state the following:

Proposition 11. *For any observation table* $\mathcal{T}$ *that is closed and consistent both for rows and columns, the equality* $L(A_{row}(\mathcal{T})) = L(A_{col}(\mathcal{T}))$ *holds.*

6.4 Primes

Rows and columns are vectors of Booleans. We partially order such vectors by extending the order $0 \leqslant 1$ to vectors as the product order. For any $s, s' \in S$, we say $row(s) \leqslant row(s')$ when, for every $e \in E$, $row(s)(e) \leqslant row(s')(e)$. The *join* of two rows is given pointwise: $(row(s) \vee row(s'))(e) = row(s)(e) \vee row(s')(e)$. Column vectors are treated similarly.

We say that a vector v is covered by $\{v_1, \ldots, v_n\}$ when $v = v_1 \vee \ldots \vee v_n$. We say that a vector v is *prime* wrt. a set of vectors $V = \{v_1, \ldots, v_n\}$ if v is not zero and no subset $V' \subseteq V$ covers v. The set of prime vectors of a set V, denoted by $primes(V)$, consists of those $v \in V$ that are prime wrt. $V \backslash v$. Every $v \in V$ is covered by the vectors below it in $primes(V)$. The primes are also referred to as the *join-irreducible* elements [10].

6.5 Prime Row Automaton

From the prime rows of an observation table we can construct an NFA that accepts the same language as the row automaton.

Definition 10. *Let $\mathcal{T} = (S, E, T)$ be closed and consistent for rows and columns. The* prime row automaton *of $\mathcal{T}$, denoted by $A_{row'}(\mathcal{T})$, is the automaton given by $(Q, \Sigma, \Delta, I, F)$ where $Q = primes(row(S))$, $I = \{q \in Q \mid q \leqslant row(\varepsilon)\}$, $F = \{q \in Q \mid q(\varepsilon) = 1\}$, $\Delta(q, a) = \{q' \in Q \mid q' \leqslant \delta(q, a)\}$ and δ is the transition function of $A_{row}(\mathcal{T})$.*

Recall that the right language of a state $row(s)$ in the $A_{row}(\mathcal{T})$ consists of those left congruence classes (atoms) for which the corresponding entry in the vector $row(s)$ is 1. Thus a prime row corresponds to a state whose right language is prime, i.e., it is not a union of right languages of other states. Furthermore, the right language of a state $row(s)$ in $A_{row'}(\mathcal{T})$ is the same as in $A_{row}(\mathcal{T})$.

Proposition 12. *If $\mathcal{T}$ is closed and consistent for rows and columns, then $A_{row'}(\mathcal{T})$ is the canonical RFSA of $L(A_{row}(\mathcal{T}))$.*

The canonical RFSA can be learned with the NL^* algorithm [3] which, however, has different conditions on consistency and closedness of the table than the construction given here.

6.6 Prime Column Automaton

From the prime columns of an observation table we can construct an NFA that accepts the same language as the column automaton.

Definition 11. *Let $\mathcal{T} = (S, E, T)$ be closed and consistent for rows and columns. The* prime column automaton *of $\mathcal{T}$, denoted by $A_{col'}(\mathcal{T})$, is the automaton given by $(Q, \Sigma, \Delta, I, F)$ where $Q = primes(col(E))$, $I = \{q \in Q \mid q(\varepsilon) = 1\}$, $F = \{q \in Q \mid q \leqslant col(\varepsilon)\}$, $\Delta(q, a) = \{q' \mid \exists q''. q' \in \delta(q'', a) \wedge q \leqslant q''\}$ and δ is the transition function of $A_{col}(\mathcal{T})$.*

Recall that the left language of a state $col(e)$ in the column automaton consists of those right congruence classes for which the corresponding entry in the vector $col(e)$ is 1. Thus, a prime column corresponds to a state whose left language is prime, i.e., it is not a union of left languages of other states. Furthermore, the left language of a state $col(e)$ in $A_{col'}(\mathcal{T})$ is the same as in $A_{col}(\mathcal{T})$.

Proposition 13. *If $\mathcal{T}$ is closed and consistent for rows and columns, then $A_{col'}(\mathcal{T})$ is the maximized prime átomaton of $L(A_{col}(\mathcal{T}))$.*

The maximized prime átomaton can be learned with a column-oriented variant of NL^*, but, again, the conditions on consistency and closedness of the table would be different than the construction given here.

6.7 Learning NFAs

An observation table that is closed and consistent for rows and columns can be obtained from a table that is closed and consistent only for rows or only for columns. For example, when L^* terminates, then we have a minimal DFA and an observation table that is row-closed and -consistent. We can then use the learned automaton to fill in the missing parts of the table to make it closed and consistent also for columns. From such a table we can construct the átomaton and also calculate the prime elements to construct the canonical RFSA and the maximized prime átomaton.

7 Conclusions

We introduced a new canonical NFA for regular languages, the maximized prime átomaton, and studied its properties. Being the dual automaton of the canonical RFSA, the maximized prime átomaton can be considered as a candidate for a small NFA representation of a language.

We described how four canonical automata – the minimal DFA, the canonical RFSA, the átomaton, and the maximized prime átomaton – can be obtained from suitable observation tables used in automata learning algorithms. We also believe that interpreting these observation tables in terms of quotients and atoms of a language can provide new insights on automata learning problems.

References

1. Angluin, D.: Learning regular sets from queries and counterexamples. Inf. Comput. **75**(2), 87–106 (1987). https://doi.org/10.1016/0890-5401(87)90052-6
2. Birget, J.: Intersection and union of regular languages and state complexity. Inf. Process. Lett. **43**(4), 185–190 (1992). https://doi.org/10.1016/0020-0190(92)90198-5
3. Bollig, B., Habermehl, P., Kern, C., Leucker, M.: Angluin-style learning of NFA. In: Boutilier, C. (ed.) IJCAI 2009, Proceedings of the 21st International Joint Conference on Artificial Intelligence, Pasadena, California, USA, 11–17 July 2009, pp. 1004–1009 (2009). http://ijcai.org/Proceedings/09/Papers/170.pdf

4. Brzozowski, J.A.: Canonical regular expressions and minimal state graphs for definite events. In: Proceedings of Symposium on Mathematical Theory of Automata. MRI Symposia Series, vol. 12, pp. 529–561. Polytechnic Press, Polytechnic Institute of Brooklyn, N.Y. (1963)
5. Brzozowski, J.A., Tamm, H.: Theory of átomata. Theor. Comput. Sci. **539**, 13–27 (2014)
6. Denis, F., Lemay, A., Terlutte, A.: Residual finite state automata. Fund. Inform. **51**, 339–368 (2002)
7. Iván, S.: Complexity of atoms, combinatorially. Inf. Process. Lett. **116**(5), 356–360 (2016)
8. Kameda, T., Weiner, P.: On the state minimization of nondeterministic finite automata. IEEE Trans. Comput. **19**(7), 617–627 (1970)
9. Lombardy, S., Sakarovitch, J.: The universal automaton. In: Flum, J., Grädel, E., Wilke, T. (eds.) Logic and Automata: History and Perspectives [in Honor of Wolfgang Thomas]. Texts in Logic and Games, vol. 2, pp. 457–504. Amsterdam University Press (2008)
10. Myers, R.S.R., Adámek, J., Milius, S., Urbat, H.: Coalgebraic constructions of canonical nondeterministic automata. Theor. Comput. Sci. **604**, 81–101 (2015)
11. Nerode, A.: Linear automaton transformations. Proc. Amer. Math. Soc. **9**, 541–544 (1958)
12. Tamm, H.: Generalization of the double-reversal method of finding a canonical residual finite state automaton. In: Shallit, J., Okhotin, A. (eds.) DCFS 2015. LNCS, vol. 9118, pp. 268–279. Springer, Cham (2015). https://doi.org/10.1007/978-3-319-19225-3_23
13. Tamm, H.: New interpretation and generalization of the Kameda-Weiner method. In: 43rd International Colloquium on Automata, Languages, and Programming (ICALP 2016). Leibniz International Proceedings in Informatics (LIPIcs), vol. 55, pp. 116:1–116:12. Schloss Dagstuhl-Leibniz-Zentrum für Informatik, Dagstuhl (2016)
14. Tamm, H., van der Merwe, B.: Lower bound methods for the size of nondeterministic finite automata revisited. In: Drewes, F., Martín-Vide, C., Truthe, B. (eds.) LATA 2017. LNCS, vol. 10168, pp. 261–272. Springer, Cham (2017). https://doi.org/10.1007/978-3-319-53733-7_19

Union-Complexities of Kleene Plus Operation

Benedek Nagy(✉)

Department of Mathematics, Faculty of Arts and Sciences,
Eastern Mediterranean University, Famagusta, North Cyprus, Mersin-10, Turkey
nbenedek.inf@gmail.com

Abstract. Union-free expressions are used in union normal form to decompose any regular language to a finite union of union-free languages. Based on the automata characterisation of the union-free languages, by restricting the 1CFPAs not to have transitions by the empty word, or to be deterministic, the n-union-free and the deterministic union-free languages are defined. Union-complexity as a measure of descriptional complexity of regular languages was introduced recently. By the minimum number of union-free/n-union-free/deterministic union-free languages needed to get a regular language as their union, its union-complexity/n-union-complexity/d-union-complexity is defined. It is already known that union-complexity and n-union-complexity are finite for every regular language, however there are regular languages with infinite d-union-complexity. Operational union-complexity, that is, to predict the union-complexity of a language obtained by a language operation from languages with known union-complexity is an important and interesting question belonging to the field of descriptional complexity of formal systems. In the present paper, the Kleene plus, the positive Kleene closure operator is studied. As the Kleene star and plus operations have very different effects on the union-free languages, it is an interesting problem to investigate how the union-complexities may change under this operation. In particular, we show that the union-complexity of a regular language is not growing when this operation is being applied on it. On the other hand, the n-union-complexity of the Kleene plus of an n-union-free language remains 1, but the n-union-complexity of the Kleene plus of other regular languages may grow. Further, the deterministic union-complexity may jump to an infinite value even if the original language had a relatively small deterministic union-complexity, e.g., 4.

Keywords: union-complexity · union-free languages · regular expressions · Kleene closure

1 Introduction

Various classes of subregular languages are important from various points of view, see, e.g., [5,9]. The union-free languages are defined by regular expressions without the union, they are the star-dot regular languages [2]. Automata

Y.-S. Han and G. Vaszil (Eds.): DCFS 2022, LNCS 13439, pp. 197–211, 2022.
https://doi.org/10.1007/978-3-031-13257-5_15

theoretical characterisation [11] allowed to define the deterministic counterpart: the deterministic union-free languages [3,7,8] and by the nondeterministic λ-transition-free automata, the n-union-free languages. The classes of the union-free, n-union-free and d-union-free languages form a proper hierarchy [14] and they were studied in [2,4,7,11], [14] and [3,8], respectively. Based on possible decomposition of regular languages to finite unions of those languages, the union-complexity, n-union-complexity and d-union-complexity are defined [1,10,12,13,15] (note that this latter could be infinite according to [8] even if the language is regular). The operational union-complexity is studied in details under various operations in [15], except, e.g. Kleene plus. On the other hand, the class of union-free languages is closed under concatenation, Kleene plus and also under Kleene star. Moreover, for any regular language, its Kleene star is union-free, but a similar statement does not hold for Kleene plus. Further, this class is not closed under union and this gives the possibility to define the union normal form and union-complexity of regular languages. Since Kleene plus and Kleene star behave in different ways from our point of view, it is worth to study Kleene plus and we concentrate on this issue in this paper. Closure, or indeed, more precisely, anti-closure properties of n-union-free and d-union-free languages were studied in [8,14], respectively. The non trivial closure properties of the classes of n-union-free and d-union-free languages also give the challenge to analyse the analogous union-complexity measures under various operations. Here as we already mentioned, the Kleene plus is in our focus.

While another usual measure of descriptional complexity of regular languages is connected to the minimal number of states of the accepting finite automata, the union-complexity is closely connected to the union normal form and thus to the regular expressions describing the language [10,12,13].

2 Preliminaries

In this section, first we recall the definition of the union-free languages and the corresponding class of finite automata. We assume that the reader is familiar with the basic concepts of formal languages and automata, thus for each unexplained concepts she/he is referred to any standard textbook on the topic, e.g., to [6] or to the Handbook chapter [17]. Here we show only specific notions closely related to the topic of this paper. The empty word is denoted by λ; Σ is a finite alphabet, while $\cup, \cdot, ^*, ^+$ denote the usual operations on languages, i.e., the union, the concatenation, the Kleene star and the Kleene plus. Now we recall some (formal) concepts, definitions and notions from earlier mentioned studies.

A regular expression is a *union-free expression* if only the operators concatenation and Kleene star are used in its description. A regular language is a *union-free language* if there is a union-free expression that defines it.

We note here that in the literature sometimes a wider class of languages are called union-free, those which have a description by operations concatenation, Kleene star and complement [9], somewhat similarly as the description of star-free languages goes by concatenation, union and complement [17].

Now we briefly recall the concept of finite automata and fix some notations.

A 5-tuple $\mathbf{A} = (Q, S, \Sigma, \delta, F)$ is a *non-deterministic finite automaton*, with the finite set of states Q. Further, $S \in Q$ is the initial state, Σ is the (input) alphabet and $F \subset Q$ is the set of final (or accepting) states. The function $\delta : Q \times (\Sigma \cup \{\lambda\}) \to 2^Q$ is the transition function.

A *path* $Q_0 a_1 Q_1 a_2 Q_2 \dots a_{n-1} Q_{n-1} a_n Q_n$ where $Q_{i+1} \in \delta(Q_i, a_{i+1})$ for every $0 \le i < n$ (with $n > 0$) is called a *cycle* if $Q_0 = Q_n$. A path without any repeated state is called a *cycle-free path.*

A path is called an *accepting path,* if it ends in a final state. Further, it is an accepting path of a word w if it is written as $(S = Q_0) a_1 Q_1 a_2 Q_2 ... a_{n-1} Q_{n-1} a_n Q_n$ with $Q_n \in F$ and $w = a_1 a_2 ... a_n$ $(a_i \in \Sigma \cup \{\lambda\})$, i.e., it is an accepting path starting at the initial state. A word is accepted by the finite automata if it has an accepting path.

Definition 1 (1CFPA, n-1CFPA, d-1CFPA). *A nondeterministic finite automaton* $\mathbf{A}$ *is a* **1** ***cycle-free path automaton****, a* 1CFPA, *for short, if there is a unique cycle-free accepting path from each of its states. Moreover, if the automaton* $\mathbf{A}$ *does not have any* λ*-transitions, then it is an* n-1CFPA, *and if* $\mathbf{A}$ *is deterministic, then it is a* d-1CFPA.

In this paper, we use only automata with the following property: for each state Q_i of the automaton there is a word such that it has an accepting path that contains Q_i. Consequently, there is no useless or sink state and the automaton may not be fully determined, i.e., it may happen that for a state Q_i and an input letter a the transition function assigns the empty set.

As a consequence of the definition above, a 1CFPA has exactly one final state. From now on F will refer not only to the set of final states, but to its unique element, as well, in case of a 1CFPA. One of the main results of [11] states that the family of languages which are described by union-free expressions and the family of languages recognized by 1CFPAs are exactly the same. Based on this relation, two further classes of union-free languages are defined as follows:

Definition 2 (d-union-free and n-union-free languages). *A language is* deterministic union-free *if there is a deterministic 1CFPA which accepts it [8, 13]. The short form* d-union-free *will also be used for these languages. Further, the* n-union-free *languages are exactly those union-free languages that can be accepted by n-1CFPA [14].*

Observe that by definition, in a 1CFPA, a transition between two distinct states cannot be part of the unique cycle-free path from any state to the final state, if there is a parallel transition between the same two states. The issue with parallel transitions can be resolved by a construction duplicating some parts of the automaton. Based on this, every x-union-free language ($x \in \{\lambda$, n, d$\}$) is accepted by an x-1CFPA such that for any two distinct states P, R there is at most one letter such that there is a transition from P to R with that letter.Therefore, in various constructions and proofs, w.l.o.g., we may assume that there is no transition with two different letters between two distinct states of the automaton.

Since in a 1CFPA, from every state R, there is exactly one transition that goes to the direction of F (without cycle), the word which transfers the state R to F in a cycle-free path is unique for each state. We recall that the *backbone* of the automaton is the cycle-free path from the initial state (S) to the final state (F). The word accepted by the backbone is called the *backbone word.*

The following facts are known about union-free languages [11]:

- An x-union-free ($x \in \{\lambda, \text{n}, \text{d}\}$) language is either infinite or contains at most one word.
- The shortest word of a union-free language L is unique and it is the backbone word. In a union-free language each word contains the backbone word (maybe in a scattered way).

The usual expression tree concept can be used to represent regular expressions. To each leaf of the tree a letter of the alphabet or the empty word is assigned. To each other vertex the sign of a regular operation is assigned such that a vertex with assigned $\cup$ or $\cdot$ has exactly two children in tree, while a vertex with assigned * or $^+$ has exactly one child. Let L be a union-free language. Note that $\lambda \in L$ if and only if the backbone word is the empty word. This implies that every letter is under a Kleene star in the tree of the regular expression. Under these circumstances the language can be accepted by a 1CFPA with backbone word λ. If L is n-union-free and $\lambda \in L$, then $S = F$ in the corresponding n-1CFPA. Since every 1CFPA (and thus d-1CFPA) has exactly one accepting state, languages which cannot be accepted by deterministic finite automata with only one final state are not d-union-free languages.

It is known (see, [8,11]) that the family of union-free languages is closed under the operations concatenation, Kleene star and Kleene plus. The family of n-union-free languages is not closed under union and concatenation, but it is closed under Kleene plus [14]. Furthermore, the class of unary n-union-free languages is closed under concatenation, Kleene star, Kleene plus. On the other hand, we have only anti-closure properties for the d-union-free languages: e.g., their class is not closed under union, concatenation, Kleene star, [8] and Kleene plus [14].

In fact, all d-union-free languages are n-union-free languages and all n-union-free languages are union-free. The language a^*b^* is union-free. However, it is not n-union-free [14]. The language $a(b \cup ba)^*$ is n-union-free, but not d-union-free [8]. Thus, there is a proper hierarchy among the three mentioned union-free classes.

By the decomposition result mentioned in [2,10,16], the union-complexity of regular languages is defined in [10,12]. As one of the main results of [14] states, every regular language is a union of finitely many n-union-free languages. Based on these analogies, we present the definition in a general way (based also on [15]). However, it should be noted that while every regular language can be expressed as a union of a finite number of union-free and also as a union of a finite number of n-union-free languages, similar statement does not hold in general for the d-union-free languages (as proven in [8]), therefore, the d-union-complexity may be infinite although the studied language is regular. The following definition gives back the original definition by the choice $x = \lambda$; gives the n-union-complexity with $x =$ n; moreover it also gives the d-union-complexity with $x =$ d.

Definition 3 (Union-complexity, n-union-complexity and d-union-complexity). *Let $x \in \{\lambda, n, d\}$. The form $L = \bigcup_{i=1}^{k} L_i$ is a minimal x-decomposition of the language L if each L_i is an x-union-free language and there is no $m < k$ such that $L = \bigcup_{i=1}^{m} K_i$, where each K_i is x-union-free. Then, k is called the* x-union-complexity *of the language L. However, in the case that L cannot be written in the form $\bigcup_{i=1}^{k} L_i$ with any natural number k for deterministic union-free languages L_i $(1 \leq i \leq k)$, then L has an infinite deterministic union-complexity.*

The class of union-free languages is an interesting class including several languages since for each regular language L, the language L^* is union-free regular. We can summarise some others of the simplest known results about the union-complexities (see, e.g., [14]):

- The x-union-complexity of an x-union-free languages is at most 1 ($x \in \{\lambda$, n, d$\}$); it is 0 for the empty language and 1 for every nonempty x-union-free language.
- For every finite language, its x-union-complexity is exactly the cardinality of the language.
- A language is regular if and only if its union-complexity is finite.
- A language is regular if and only if its n-union-complexity is finite.

As we already mentioned, the d-union-complexity could be infinite, as, e.g., one of the main results of [8] states:

Proposition 1. *The language defined by the regular expression $((a \cup b)(a \cup b))^*$ cannot be expressed as a union of a finitely many deterministic union-free languages.*

In [1] it has been proven that the union-complexity of regular languages is computable. However, the method is very complex and cannot be used in practical applications. Some bounds may be computed much faster, e.g., an x-decomposition (may also be called *x-union normal form*) of a regular language defines an upper bound for its x-union-complexity.

Before continuing with further more technical concepts, we are already at the stage that all the necessary concepts are shown to understand an example that could highlight the non-trivial nature of the problem we investigate here.

Example 1. Let us consider the language L defined by $(a^*b \cup dc^*)$. On the one hand, the language has 2 shortest words, b and d, and thus it is not union-free. On the other hand, Fig. 1 shows the two d-1CFPAs that accept a^*b and dc^*, respectively proving that L has union-complexity, n-union-complexity and d-union-complexity 2.

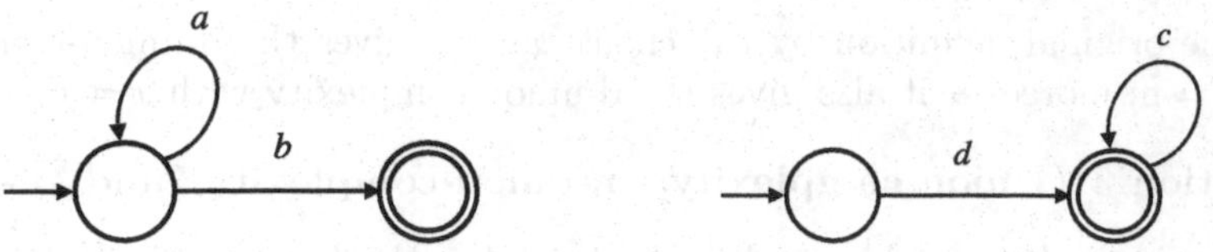

Fig. 1. Two deterministic 1-cycle-free-path-automata: the accepted languages, a^*b (left) and dc^* (right) are d-union-free.

Let us consider now L^+, i.e., $(a^*b \cup dc^*)^+$. As it has again 2 shortest words, b and d, this is neither union-free. On the one hand, one can easily check that L^+ is the union of the two languages accepted by 1CFPAs of Fig. 2, as the 1CFPA on the left accepts exactly those words of L^+ which start with a^*b and the 1CFPA on the right accepts exactly those which start with d. On the other hand, both of the 1CFPAs use λ-transitions, i.e., they are not n-1CFPAs and not d-1CFPAs.

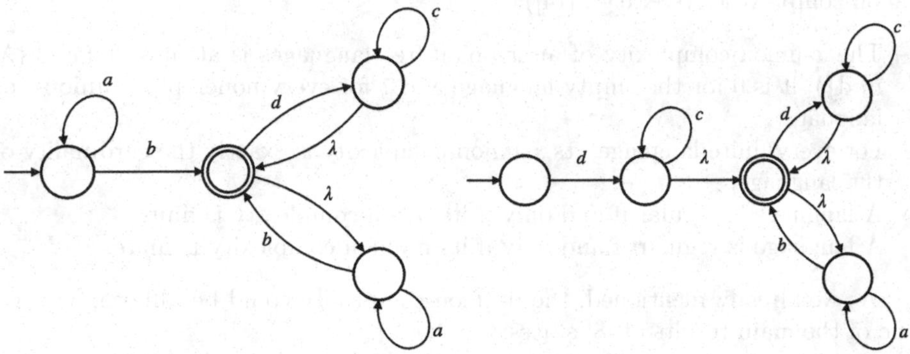

Fig. 2. Two nondeterministic 1-cycle-free-path-automata with λ-transitions such that the union of their accepted languages is exactly $(a^*b \cup dc^*)^+$.

Furthermore, we show that the n-union-complexity of L^+ is greater than 2. The proof is by contradiction, thus assume that there are 2 n-1CFPAs such that the union of their accepted languages is exactly L^+. As there are two shortest words in L^+, the backbone of one of the n-1CFPAs, let us say, **A**, must be S_AbF_A and the backbone of the other, let us say, **B**, must be S_BdF_B. The word db is also in L^+, thus one of the 1CFPAs **A** or **B** must accept it. The n-1CFPA accepts db, must use the above described backbone transition, and another transition to process the other letter, thus this other transition must be a self-loop transition. Thus, in the former case, there is a cycle in **A** as S_AdS_A, while in the latter case there is a cycle in **B** as F_BbF_B. Now, on the one hand, $ab \in L^+$, and this must be accepted by **A** which implies the cycle S_AaS_A in **A**. However, if **A** has also the cycle with letter d on its initial state (as we assumed in the first case), then **A** would also accept the word adb which is clearly not in L^+. Thus the first case cannot hold, db cannot be accepted by **A**. Now, on the other hand, we have that $dc \in L^+$, and this word must be accepted by **B**. However, it implies the cycle F_BcF_B in **B**. But, now, **B** would also accept $dbc \notin L^+$, which provides the contradiction and the proof that L^+ has a larger n-union-complexity than 2.

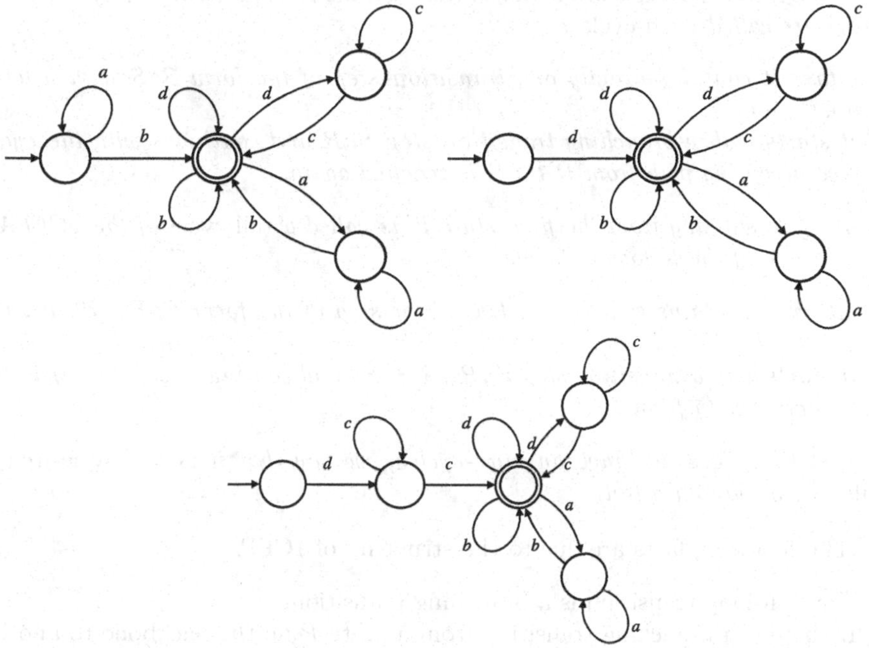

Fig. 3. Three n-1CPAs such that the union of their accepted languages is exactly $(a^*b \cup dc^*)^+$.

Now, to prove that L^+ has n-union-complexity 3, consider the union of the languages accepted by n-1CFPAs shown in Fig. 3. In fact the automaton on the left accepts the words of L^+ that start with a^*b, the n-1CFPA in the middle accepts those which start with d, but not with dc^+, while the n-1CFPA on the right is accepting the words that start with a word of dc^+.

Observing that the 1CFPAs we used in the previous descriptions are highly not deterministic, i.e., in many of them there are more than one transition from some states by the same letter, the d-union-complexity of the language L^+ could be even much higher than 3. We may conjecture it here, without any other explanations, that it is infinite.

Now, we also give new concepts, the tail (and tail-cycles) of the 1CFPAs and another technical concept, the branching (states and transitions).

Definition 4 (branching, head, tail). *A state $P \neq F$ of a 1CFPA is called a* branching state *if there are at least two different transitions from this state, i.e.,* *there is a transition which does not follow the only cycle-free accepting path from P, these transitions are called* branching transitions. *The final state F is called a branching state if there is a transition from it, moreover, all of the transitions from F are branching transitions (as none of them is part of the empty path F, i.e., the shortest cycle-free path from F to F).*

If the initial state is a branching state, then the cycle(s) in one of the following forms are called head-cycles*:*

- *either it contains exactly one transition step of the form SaS with a letter $a \in \Sigma$; or*
- *it starts with a branching transition step SaR and continues with the cycle-free accepting path from R till S is reached again.*

A cycle starting from the final state F is called a tail-cycle *of the 1CFPA if it is in one of the following forms:*

- *either it contains exactly one transition step of the form FaF with a letter $a \in \Sigma$; or*
- *it starts with a transition step FaR ($R \neq F$) and continues with the cycle-free accepting path from R.*

If a 1CFPA does not have any tail-cycles, we say that it is tail-cycle-free *or* tailless *(or without a tail).*

The following facts are due to the structure of 1CFPAs.

- Any self-loop transition is a branching transition.
- If there is a branching transition from a state P on the backbone to another state R in the backbone, then R has a longer cycle-free accepting path than P has.
- If there is a branching transition from a state P on the backbone and its transition goes to the state R that is not on the backbone, then the cycle-free accepting path from R reaches the backbone before or on P, i.e., maybe some of the last steps of the cycle starting from P with the branching transition is already on the backbone to reach P again.
- If there is a branching transition from a state $P \neq F$ in a tail-cycle to another state R, then R has a longer cycle-free accepting path than P has, moreover, this cycle-free path arrives back to the tail-cycle before or in P (i.e., on one of the states that the cycle already touched after F by reaching P).
- A tail-cycle may reach the backbone in any of its states P and then, it must follow the backbone till reaching F. (In a special case, it may contain only F from the backbone.)
- A branching transition from a state P going to R always implies that all accepting paths from R will reach P again.
- The number of tail-cycles of a 1CFPA is the number of the (branching) transitions from F.

Now we also define another new concept, the set of substates:

Definition 5. *A state $R \neq P$ is a substate of P if there is a branching transition from P to R. Moreover, the states which are not in the shortest (i.e., cycle-free) path from S to P, but are in the cycle-free accepting path from R are also substates of P, the set of these states is denoted as $sub(P_R)$. Further, the set of states of the cycle starting with the branching transition from P to R and then following the cycle-free accepting path till P is reached again is denoted by $sub^\circ(P_R)$.*

We have the following:

- The states on the backbone are not substates of any state of the 1CFPA.
- Each state of an 1CFPA is either on the backbone or it is a substate of another state.
- A tail-cycle contains F, some of the substates of F (if there are more tail-cycles) and maybe some other states of the backbone.

The language $\emptyset$ is a very special language, its union-complexity is 0, as well as its n-union-complexity and d-union-complexity are also 0, since we need 0 languages to unite them to obtain it. On the other hand, the Kleene plus of $\emptyset$ is itself, that is, $\emptyset^+ = \emptyset$. There is not so much about to say this special languages, and thus, in the rest of the paper we may assume that the language we consider is not the empty one.

We recall some of the main results of [15], the operational union-complexity of the three regular operations, union, concatenation and Kleene star.

Proposition 2. *Let L_1 and L_2 be two regular languages with union-complexities n and m, respectively. Then the union of them, i.e., $L = L_1 \cup L_2$ could have the union-complexity at most $n + m$. Moreover, this bound is tight, i.e., for any two positive integers n, m, there are languages L_1 and L_2 with union-complexities n and m, such that their union has union-complexity exactly $n + m$.*

Proposition 3. *Let L_1 and L_2 be two regular languages with union-complexities n and m, respectively. Then the concatenation of them, i.e., $L = L_1 \cdot L_2$, could have the union-complexity at most $n \cdot m$, and this bound is tight.*

Proposition 4. *Let L be a regular language with union-complexity n. Then the language L^* has the union-complexity exactly* 1 *independently of the value of n.*

Now, we are ready to present our main results concerning the union-complexity of languages created by Kleene plus operation.

3 Operational Union-Complexity of the Kleene Plus Operation

First, we present the case of the general union-complexity, and then in subsections we show the cases of the n-union-complexity and the d-union-complexity. One of our main result, complementing the results shown in [15] is as follows.

Theorem 1. *Let L be a regular language with union-complexity n. Then the language L^+, the Kleene plus of L has a union-complexity of at most n.*

Proof. Obviously $L^+ = L \cdot L^*$. From Propositions 3 and 4 and one may establish the upper bound as $n \cdot 1 = n$.

To prove that this bound is tight, let us start with a language over an n-ary alphabet Σ_n. Let $L_n = \Sigma_n = \{a_1, \ldots, a_n\}$. Then, $L_n^+ = \Sigma_n^+$ has clearly n shortest words, i.e., the letters of the alphabet as words showing that its union-complexity cannot be less than n.

However, this construction uses a larger and larger alphabet with growing value of n. After this initial result on the tightness, let us consider the binary alphabet $\Sigma_2 = \{0, 1\}$. Let us encode n different letters with a binary block code. More precisely, let $L_2 = \{10^k, 10^{k-1}1, \ldots, 1w_i, \ldots, 1w_{n-1}\}$, where w_i is the binary representation of number i with k digits. (The value of k should be at least $\lceil \log_2(n) \rceil$ to make this possible.)

Clearly, L_2 is a finite language with n words, thus its union-complexity is n. Now, the union-complexity of L_2^+ can be estimated from below by the number of its shortest words which is n and gives the proof of the tightness already for the case of a binary alphabet. □

The unary alphabet plays some special importance and it is also interesting since already some of the closure properties of the union-free languages works in a different manner for this special case, consider, e.g., the closure under concatenation [14].

Although over the unary alphabet, the properties of the Kleene star and the Kleene plus are usually very similar, we intend to show that they work in a different way when the union-complexity is studied. It is well-known, and we have already mentioned, that L^* of any regular language has the union-complexity 1. Now we show that this is not the case with L^+ even if the regular language is over a unary alphabet.

Theorem 2. *The regular language L described by $a^4(a^9)^* \cup a^7(a^5)^*$ has the union-complexity 2. Further its Kleene plus, L^+ has also union-complexity 2.*

Proof. As 4 and 9 are co-primes, the language L_1 defined by $(a^4(a^9)^*)^+$ is co-finite, i.e., there are only finitely many natural numbers ℓ such that a^ℓ is not in the language L_1, and thus, the difference of a^* and L_1 is a finite language. A similar statement is true for $(a^7(a^5)^*)^+$. In the former, the following positive lengths are missing: 1, 2, 3, 5, 6, 7, 9, 10, 11, 14, 15, 18, 19, 23, 27. As usual over the unary alphabet, the words can be identified by their lengths. By a theorem of Frobenius (actually, Sylvester has published in the 1880's its solution for the case we need), the longest word that cannot be given in the form $4k_1 + 9k_2$ by nonnegative integer values of k_1 and k_2 is $4 \times 9 - (4 + 9) = 36 - 13 = 23$, however, we have the condition $k_1 \geq 1$ which shifts this limit a little bit. In fact, $(a^4(a^9)^*)^+$ has all the words of length $4k_1$ with $k_1 \geq 1$, all the words of length $4k_1 + 9$, $4k_1 + 18$ and $4k_1 + 27$. These for sets of integers contain all the integers $\ell > 27$.

For the following lengths of the above list, a word with length exists in the language L^+:

$7 : 7,$	$11 : 4 + 7,$
$14 : 7 + 7,$	$15 : 4 + 4 + 7,$
$18 : 4 + 7 + 7,$	$19 : 7 + 7 + 5,$
$23 : 4 + 7 + 7 + 5,$	$27 : 4 + 4 + 7 + 7 + 5.$

The co-finite language L^+ does not have the lengths 1, 2, 3, 5, 6, 9 and 10, i.e., $L^+ = \{a^4, a^7, a^8\} \cup \{a^k \mid k > 10\}$. Now, we show that L^+ is not union-free. If it would be, then the backbone word must be $aaaa$, as it is the shortest word of L^+. Further the 1CFPA must also accept a^7 meaning that there is a cycle accessible from the backbone by pumping 3 as into the word. However, then by doing this pumping cycle again, the word a^{10} would be obtained and accepted. This is contradicting to the fact that a^{10} is not in L^+. Thus, this language is not union-free, it has a union-complexity of at least 2. By applying Theorem 1, since L has union-complexity 2, it cannot be more than 2. Therefore, it has been proven that L^+ has union-complexity 2. □

The precise investigation of the unary case is left for the future:

Open Problem 1. Whether the result stated in Theorem 1 is also tight in the case of the unary alphabet for larger union-complexities, is left open.

3.1 On n-Union-Complexity

In this subsection, the n-union-complexity is studied. As we already mentioned, for each regular language, its n-union-complexity is a finite number. On the one hand, the closure of the class of the n-union-free languages under Kleene plus ([14]) gives the immediate corollary:

Corollary 1. *Let L be a language with n-union-complexity 1. Then, the n-union-complexity of the language L^+ is also 1.*

On the other hand, as we have seen in Example 1, the union-complexity and the n-union-complexity may behave in a different manner. Moreover, the constructions in the proofs of Propositions 3 and 4 were based on language operations (like regular expressions) [15], which can be translated to automata only with intensive usage of λ-transitions: remember that the class of n-union-free languages is not closed under concatenation. Thus, we may need to find new constructions to estimate the n-union-complexity.

Theorem 3. *Let a regular language L be given with an n-union-complexity k. Further, let $L_1, \ldots, L_k$ be some n-union-free languages such that $L = \bigcup_{i=1}^{k} L_i$. Let $\mathbf{A}_i$ be an n-1CFPA accepting L_i for each $1 \leq i \leq k$. Let the number of tail-cycles of $\mathbf{A}_i$ be t_i. Then, the n-union-complexity of L^+ is at most $m = k + \sum_{i=1}^{k} t_i$.*

Proof. The proof is a construction to show that L^+ is the union of m n-union-free languages. Based on the condition given in the theorem, let $\mathbf{A}_1, \ldots, \mathbf{A}_k$, be k n-1CFPAs that accept the languages $L_1, \ldots, L_k$ such that $L = \bigcup_{i=1}^{k} L_i$.

Let the structure of each $\mathbf{A}_i$ be given with its backbone states and the sets of the substates including the substates of the tail-cycles (if any). See Fig. 4, top left.

Now, let us have $t_i + 1$ copies of each $\mathbf{A}_i$, a copy $\mathbf{B}_i$ that is similar to the original, but does not include any of the tail-cycles of $\mathbf{A}_i$ (see Fig. 4, top right); and a copy $\mathbf{C}_i^\ell$ for each tail-cycle which are expanded variants of $\mathbf{A}_i$ as it is explained below (ℓ is the numbering of the tail-cycles of the automaton, $1 \le \ell \le t_i$). Let the backbone of $\mathbf{C}_i^\ell$ be $S_i^\ell a_i^\ell \ldots F_i^\ell b_i^\ell \overline{R}_i^\ell \ldots \overline{F}_i^\ell$ where $S_i^\ell a_i^\ell \ldots F_i^\ell$ is a copy of the backbone of $\mathbf{A}_i$ and $F_i^\ell b_i^\ell \ldots \overline{F}_i^\ell$ is a copy of the ℓ-th tail-cycle, that is starting with the copy of the branching transition $F_i^\ell b_i^\ell R_i^\ell$. Thus, the backbone of $\mathbf{C}_i^\ell$ contains a copy of each backbone state of $\mathbf{A}_i$ and also an (additional) overlined copy of the states of $sub^\circ(F_i^\ell{}_{R_i^\ell})$. Let now all the cycles of $\mathbf{A}_i$ be added by adding the substates of each not overlined state, and their substates iteratively by their transitions including all tail-cycles from the state F_i^ℓ. The substates and the cycles of each overlined state should also be added, but the copy $\overline{F}_i^\ell$ of the final state (that actually is the final state of $\mathbf{C}_i^\ell$, but in this way, it will not be part of any cycles in $\mathbf{C}_i^\ell$. (See the second line of Fig. 4.)

So far, by our constructions, each 1CFPA $\mathbf{B}_i$ accepts exactly those words of the language L_i that are accepted without using any transitions of the final state (i.e., without using any of the tail-cycles); and each 1CFPA $\mathbf{C}_i^\ell$ accepts exactly those words of L_i which are accepted in such a way that from the final state the last used branching transition defines the tail-cycle ℓ in $\mathbf{A}_i$. Now let us take copies of each of these automata, from each one more as the number of its head-cycles (i.e., the number of branching transitions of the initial state), let these copies be $\underline{\mathbf{B}}_i^j$ and $\underline{\mathbf{C}}_i^{\ell,j}$, where j is a nonnegative integer not more than h_i, the number of head-cycles of $\mathbf{A}_i$. Let all $\underline{\mathbf{B}}_i^0$ and $\underline{\mathbf{C}}_i^{\ell,0}$ be identical to $\mathbf{B}_i$ and $\mathbf{C}_i^\ell$, respectively, but without any head-cycles (the transitions and the states of the head-cycles and their substates are simply removed, see the third line of Fig. 4). Further, let $\underline{\mathbf{B}}_i^j$ and $\underline{\mathbf{C}}_i^{\ell,j}$ with $j > 0$ be defined as follows. (In the next part we use $\ell = 0$ to index the states of $\underline{\mathbf{B}}_i^j$, while $\ell > 0$ for the states of $\underline{\mathbf{C}}_i^{\ell,j}$.) Let the backbone of these automata be $\tilde{S}_i^{\ell,j} b_{i,1}^{\ell,j} \ldots S_i^{\ell,j} a_{i,1}^\ell \ldots F_i^{\ell,j}$ where the part $\tilde{S}_i^{\ell,j} b_{i,1}^{\ell,j} \ldots S_i^{\ell,j}$ is a copy of the j-th head-cycle that starts with branching transition from $S_i^{\ell,j}$ in $\mathbf{A}_i$ and in this way it is becoming not a cycle, but part of the backbone in the new 1CFPA from $\tilde{S}_i^{\ell,j}$ with letter $b_{i,1}^{\ell,j}$; and the rest of the backbone, $S_i^{\ell,j} a_{i,1}^\ell \ldots F_i^{\ell,j}$, is the original backbone of $\underline{\mathbf{B}}_i$ or $\underline{\mathbf{C}}_i^\ell$. Further, all states of the 1CFPA $\underline{\mathbf{B}}_i$ or $\underline{\mathbf{C}}_i^\ell$ are kept, respectively, with their transitions. Also all the substates of the states of the j-th head-cycle (but the initial state) are copied and reached from the states of the first part $\tilde{S}_i^{\ell,j} b_{i,1}^{\ell,j} \ldots S_i^{\ell,j}$ of the backbone, with their transitions (between pairs of copied states). Moreover, all head-cycles and their substates

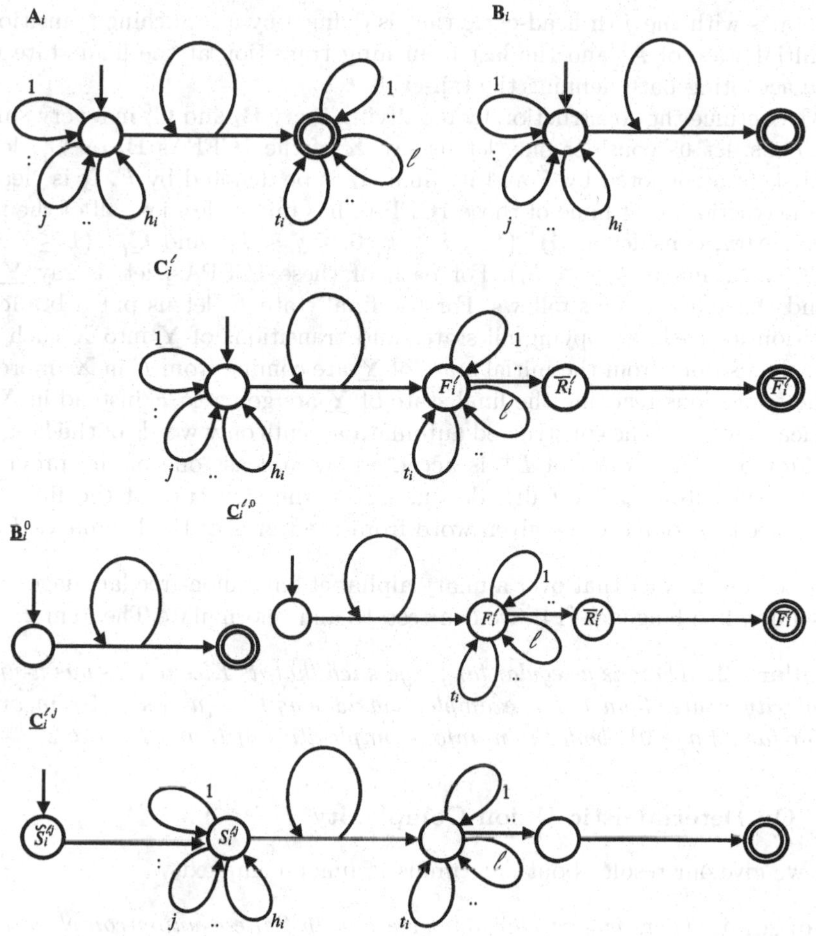

Fig. 4. Some parts of the construction in the proof of Theorem 3.

with their transitions are also copied with a branching transition from $S_i^{\ell,j}$. (See the bottom of Fig. 4.)

In this way, each 1CFPA $\underline{\mathbf{B}}_i^0$ accepts all words of L_i that can be accepted by a path neither containing any branching transition from the initial state of $\mathbf{A}_i$, nor from its final state. Further, each 1CFPA $\underline{\mathbf{B}}_i^j$ accepts exactly those words of L_i that are accepted by a path starting by the j-th branching transition (identifying the j-th head-cycle) from the initial state of $\mathbf{A}_i$ and do not use any branching transitions from the final state of $\mathbf{A}_i$. Also, each $\underline{\mathbf{C}}_i^{\ell,0}$ accepts those words of L_i that are accepted by using none of the head-cycles of $\mathbf{A}_i$, but the ℓ-th tail-cycle was used in the end of the word (the last used branching transition from the final state of $\mathbf{A}_i$ used the branching transition defining the tail-cycle ℓ). Finally, each $\underline{\mathbf{C}}_i^{\ell,j}$ accepts exactly those words of L_i that have an accepting path in $\mathbf{A}_i$

that starts with the j-th head-cycle that is defined by a branching transition at the initial state of $\mathbf{A}_i$ and the last branching transition at the final state used in the accepting path defining the tail-cycle ℓ.

We continue the construction by modifying every $\mathbf{B}_i$ and $\mathbf{C}_i^\ell$ in a very similar way. Thus, let us consider one, let us say $\mathbf{X}$ of the 1CFPAs $\mathbf{B}_i$ or $\mathbf{C}_i^\ell$, let its initial state be denoted by S and its final state be denoted by F. It is clear by the construction, that none of those 1CFPAs has tail-cycles, i.e., all of them are tailless. Now, consider all $\underline{\mathbf{B}}_i^j$ $(1 \le i \le k,\ 0 \le j \le h_i)$ and $\underline{\mathbf{C}}_i^{\ell,j}$ $(1 \le i \le k,\ 1 \le \ell \le t_i$, and $0 \le j \le h_i)$. For each of these 1CFPAs, let us say $\underline{\mathbf{Y}}$, we expand the 1CFPA $\mathbf{X}$ as follows. For the final state F, let us put a branching transition for each $\underline{\mathbf{Y}}$ copying all states and transitions of $\underline{\mathbf{Y}}$ into $\mathbf{X}$ such that all the transitions from the initial state of $\underline{\mathbf{Y}}$ are coming from F in $\mathbf{X}$, moreover all the transitions reaching the final state of $\underline{\mathbf{Y}}$ are going to F instead in $\mathbf{X}$.

Clearly, each of the constructed automata accepts only words of the language L^+. Moreover, any word of L^+ is accepted by at least one of the previously constructed automata, actually, depending on the structure of the first word that is used to compose the given word from the words of the languages L_i. □

Based on the fact that over a unary alphabet any union-free language is also an n-union-free language [14], we can restate and reformulate Theorem 2.

Corollary 2. *There is a regular language such that its Kleene plus has n-union-complexity greater than 1. For example, considering* $L = \{a^k \mid k = 4+9n$ *or* $k = 7+5n$ *for all* $n \ge 0\}$, *both the n-union-complexities of* L *and* L^+ *are* 2.

3.2 On Deterministic Union-Complexity

Now we give our result about deterministic union-complexity.

Theorem 4. *There is a regular language* L *with finite d-union-complexity such that* L^+ *has infinite d-union-complexity.*

Proof. Consider the language $L = \{aa, ab, ba, bb\}$, clearly its d-union-complexity is a 4. Now, let us consider $L^+ = (aa \cup ab \cup ba \cup bb)^+$, which actually contains all nonempty words over $\Sigma = \{a, b\}$ with even lengths. Moreover, every word of Σ^* is a prefix of some words of L^+, thus based on an analogous proof of Proposition 1, L^+ cannot be written as a finite union of deterministic union-free languages [8].

Open Problem 2. Is there any language L with smaller d-union-complexity than 4 such that its Kleene plus, L^+ has already infinite d-union-complexity? May, e.g., the language of Example 1 have this property?

Since the class of deterministic union-free languages is not closed under any of the usual language operations (union, complement, concatenation, Kleene star etc., see [8,13]), it seems to be a non-trivial task, to find operational d-union-complexity of languages.

References

1. Afonin, S., Golomazov, D.: Minimal union-free decompositions of regular languages. In: Dediu, A.H., Ionescu, A.M., Martín-Vide, C. (eds.) LATA 2009. LNCS, vol. 5457, pp. 83–92. Springer, Heidelberg (2009). https://doi.org/10.1007/978-3-642-00982-2_7
2. Brzozwski, J.A.: Regular expression techniques for sequential circuits. Ph.D Dissertation, Department of Electrical Engineering, Princeton University, Princeton, NJ, June 1962
3. Brzozowski, J.A., Davies, S.: Most complex deterministic union-free regular languages. In: Konstantinidis, S., Pighizzini, G. (eds.) DCFS 2018. LNCS, vol. 10952, pp. 37–48. Springer, Cham (2018). https://doi.org/10.1007/978-3-319-94631-3_4
4. Crvenković, S., Dolinka, I., Ésik, Z.: On equations for union-free regular languages. Inform. Comput. **164**(1), 152–172 (2001)
5. Holzer, M., Kutrib, M.: Structure and complexity of some subregular language families. In: The Role of Theory in Computer Science, pp. 59–82 (2017)
6. Hopcroft, J.E., Ullman, J.D.: Introduction to Automata Theory, Languages and Computation. Addison-Wesley Publishing Company, Reading MA (1979)
7. Jirásková, G., Masopust, T.: Complexity in union-free regular languages. Int. J. Found. Comput. Sci. **22**, 1639–1653 (2011)
8. Jirásková, G., Nagy, B.: On union-free and deterministic union-free languages. In: Baeten, J.C.M., Ball, T., de Boer, F.S. (eds.) TCS 2012. LNCS, vol. 7604, pp. 179–192. Springer, Heidelberg (2012). https://doi.org/10.1007/978-3-642-33475-7_13
9. Kutrib, M., Wendlandt, M.: Expressive capacity of subregular expressions. RAIRO ITA: Theory Inf. Appl. **52**(2–3–4), 201–218 (2018)
10. Nagy, B.: A normal form for regular expressions. In: Calude, C.S., Calude, E., Dinnen M.J. (eds.) Supplemental Papers for DLT 2004 (8th International Conference Developments in Language Theory), CDMTCS Report 252, Auckland, pp. 51–60 (2004)
11. Nagy, B.: Union-free regular languages and 1-cycle-free-path-automata. Publ. Math. Debrecen **68**, 183–197 (2006)
12. Nagy, B.: On union-complexity of regular languages, CINTI. In: 11th IEEE International Symposium on Computational Intelligence and Informatics **2010**, pp. 177–182 (2010)
13. Nagy, B.: Union-freeness, deterministic union-freeness and union-complexity. In: Hospodár, M., Jirásková, G., Konstantinidis, S. (eds.) DCFS 2019. LNCS, vol. 11612, pp. 46–56. Springer, Cham (2019). https://doi.org/10.1007/978-3-030-23247-4_3
14. Nagy, B.: Union-freeness revisited – between deterministic and non-deterministic union-free languages. Int. J. Found. Comput. Sci. **32**, 551–573 (2021)
15. Nagy, B.: Operational union-complexity. Inform. Comput. **284**, 104692 (2022)
16. Shallit, J.: A Second Course in Formal Languages and Automata Theory. Cambridge University Press, Cambridge (2008)
17. Yu, S.: Regular languages. In: Rozenberg, G., Salomaa, A. (eds.) Handbook of Formal Languages, pp. 41–110. Springer, Heidelberg (1997). https://doi.org/10.1007/978-3-642-59136-5_2

Author Index

Printed in the United States
by Baker & Taylor Publisher Services